THE FUTURE IS NOW

This is a book of fantasy. A journey into the fascinating future of freedom by our greatest science fiction writers, who dare to imagine an age when revolutionary utopias bring incredible horrors greater than ever experienced before; an epoch when shattering extraterrestrial encounters put all our notions of human liberty to the ultimate test; and so much more . . .

THE FUTURE IS HERE

It is also a book of fact. Where many of today's boldest thinkers challenge us with exciting speculations on the prospects for complete liberation—or totalitarianism—tomorrow, the seeds of which lie with us today. If only we come to see freedom not merely as a gift, but as a precious principle to be defended.

THE FUTURE IS US . . .

A Fawcett Crest Novel
by Larry Niven and Jerry Pournelle:

☐ LUCIFER'S HAMMER   23599 $2.95

THE SURVIVAL
OF FREEDOM

edited by
JERRY POURNELLE

and John F. Carr as Associate Editor

FAWCETT CREST • NEW YORK

This book is dedicated to James and Salle Vaughn, two stead-
fast friends of liberty in days when liberty needs allies.

THE SURVIVAL OF FREEDOM

Published by Fawcett Crest Books, a unit of CBS Publications,
the Consumer Publishing Division of CBS Inc.

ISBN:0-449-24435-0

Printed in the United States of America

First Fawcett Crest Printing: August 1981

10   9   8   7   6   5   4   3   2   1

The editors and publisher are grateful for permission to reprint the
following:
ENTER A PILGRIM by Gordon R. Dickson first appeared in *Analog
Science Fiction*, May 1978. Copyright © 1978 by Condé Nast Publications, Inc. Reprinted by permission of the author and the author's
agent, Blassingame, MacCauley, and Wood.
THE MEASURE OF A MAN by Randall Garrett first appeared in
Astounding Science Fiction, June 1960. Copyright © 1960 by Street
and Smith Publications, Inc. Reprinted by special arrangement
with the author and the author's agent, Tracy Blackstone.
DEFINITIONS by Jerry Pournelle has not been previously published. Copyright © 1981 by Jerry Pournelle. Printed by arrangement
with the author and the author's agent, Blassingame, MacCauley,
and Wood.
CONDITIONS OF FREEDOM by Russell Kirk previously appeared
in *Beyond The Dreams of Avarice*, Regnery, 1956. Copyright © 1956,
1981 by Russell Kirk.
ESCAPE TO THE SUBURBS by Rachel Cosgrove Payes previously

CONTENTS

ENTER A PILGRIM   Gordon R. Dickson   9

THE MEASURE OF A MAN   Randall Garrett   30

DEFINITIONS   Jerry Pournelle   42

CONDITIONS OF FREEDOM   Russell Kirk   47

ESCAPE TO THE SUBURBS   Rachel Cosgrove Payes   55

THE LIBERATION OF EARTH   William Tenn   66

SIERRA MAESTRA   Norman Spinrad   86

LOVE IS NOT ENOUGH   David Friedman   97

AMONG THIEVES   Poul Anderson   107

THE STARS GO OVER THE LONELY OCEAN
    Robinson Jeffers   136

THE TRUE HORROR OF SOVIET INTERNAL EXILE FROM
    DISSENT TO DOCILITY   Victor Herman and
    Fred E. Dohrs   138

SWISS MOVEMENT   Eric Vinicoff and Marcia Martin   148

THE JIGSAW MAN   Larry Niven   174

"REPENT, HARLEQUIN!" SAID THE TICKTOCKMAN
    Harlan Ellison   187

KISS THEM GOODBYE   C. Bruce Hunter   201

MACDONOUGH'S SONG   Rudyard Kipling   210

LIPIDLEGGIN'   F. Paul Wilson   212

GIVE ME LIBERTY   Robert A. Heinlein   222

SQ   Ursula K. Le Guin   230

THE RIGHT TO PUNISHMENT   Jerry Pournelle   242

THE LOOKING GLASS OF THE LAW
    Kevin O'Donnell, Jr.   248

NO MORE PENCILS, NO MORE BOOKS
    John Morressy   257

THE CIVIL RIGHTS DILEMMA   JERRY POURNELLE   269

RAID   TED D. BUTLER   273

FREEDOM IN THE WAKE OF HEGEL AND MARX
  STEFAN T. POSSONY   277

THE HORRIBLE HISTORY OF JONES
  GILBERT KEITH CHESTERTON   295

IDENTITY   A. E. VAN VOGT   298

**DEFENDING AND EXTENDING THE FREEDOM TO
  INNOVATE**   JOHN MCCARTHY   301

THE L-5 SOCIETY   ROBERT A. HEINLEIN   315

FULL FREEDOM   THOMAS WYLDE   318

DODKIN'S JOB   JACK VANCE   334

THE FUTURE OF LIBERTY   JERRY POURNELLE   376

ACKNOWLEDGMENTS   JERRY POURNELLE   382

Editor's Introduction To:

ENTER A PILGRIM

> "The only man who makes slavery possible is the
> slave."—John W. Campbell, Jr.

What is the most important question ever asked?

In 1939, Enrico Fermi, with Leo Szilard and Eugene Wigner, saw freedom endangered by science. Fermi had only the year before been awarded the Nobel Prize in physics for his "identification of new radioactive elements produced by neutron bombardment and for his discovery of nuclear reaction effected by slow neutrons." When he went to Stockholm to receive his prize, Fermi and his family continued to the United States, and he did not return to Mussolini's Italy. The following year, Fermi, Szilard, and Wigner composed their famous letter to President Roosevelt pointing out the danger to peace and freedom if the Nazi regime should be the first to develop weapons based on nuclear energy. The letter was signed by Albert Einstein and on October 11, 1939, delivered to FDR.

The Manhattan Project was the result, and on December 2, 1942, in the squash court at the University of Chicago, Fermi's team achieved mankind's first self-sustained nuclear chain reaction. "The Italian Navigator has landed in the New World," cabled Szilard in a coded announcement; and the world would never again be the same.

Fermi was more than a great research scientist. He was also a highly popular teacher, famous for his "Fermi Questions." He was a master at computing numerical answers with what seemed like no data at all, as for example, "How many golf balls will fit in a suitcase?"

Note that one does not know the size of the suitcase, and few would know the size of a golf ball. But—well, a golf ball is about an inch in diameter (certainly closer to one inch than it is to two inches); a suitcase is perhaps three feet long by two wide by eight inches thick. That would be some 6,912 cubic inches. Since a golf ball is one cubic inch, somewhere between 1,000 and 10,000 fit in a suitcase.

This is a Fermi answer: an answer within one order of magnitude. Note that the answer above is not sensitive to the assumptions. If the suitcase is two and a half feet long instead of three, then there are 5,760 cubic inches. Obviously we can't *fill* the suitcase with balls; the "packing fraction" must be greater than one, and therefore there will be empty space, perhaps as much empty space as there are golf balls. That is still within the 1,000 to 10,000 limit. And so forth.

Other examples of Fermi questions are: How many hairs are there in a rabbit's coat? How many piano tuners are there in Chicago? How many molecules of air in a classroom?

Fermi was fond of asking seemingly impossible questions. Some, as the above, were merely amusing.

One, however, may be the most important question ever asked. There are 100 billion stars in our galaxy. Of those, about a quarter are the right size and brightness for life-as-we-know-it. Half of those remaining will be binaries, unlikely to have planets. Some percentage of planets will be too hot, some too cold; some too new, some too old; some too small, some too large, some improperly inclined, etc.; but if we assume life arises given proper conditions for it, there must still be a very great number of planets with living creatures. Fermi guessed about a billion in our galaxy. Stephen Dole (*Habitable Planets for Man*; New York: American Elsevier Publishing Co., 1970), working for several years with much more sophisticated data, arrived at a figure of 645 million inhabitable planets; and his definition of "inhabitable" requires native life.

Life, we think, tends to evolve intelligence.

Some alien species will not live long enough to become intelligent, some will become intelligent but be uninterested in space and space travel, etc.; but when we discard all those, we still find a vast number (between a few thousand and a few million) planets that ought, by pure random chance, to have space-traveling intelligent life; and of *those*, a respectable number must be millions of years old, meaning that they have long been accustomed to travel between the stars.

Furthermore, there must be a *lot* of them. Start with a population of only a billion. Assume a tiny growth rate, a fraction of 1 percent per (Earth) *century*; and allow compound interest to work for 100 million years.

The answer is larger than most calculators can handle. Thus: if only a tiny fraction of "them" travel between the stars, there will still be millions upon millions of space travelers, and each inhabitable system must on average be visited scores of times. . . .

Thus Fermi's question: "Where are they?"

It is a question that grows in importance as you contemplate it. Fermi knew in 1943 that the human race would soon have the means to send messages to the stars; that within a century we could make our existence unambiguously clear across interstellar distances; yet there ought to be literally thousands of races as intelligent as we, and some will be a very great deal older, and thus more powerful.

This reasoning was the inspiration for PROJECT OZMA and its successors—projects using sophisticated radioastronomical equipment to listen for intelligible signals from the stars. The Search for Extraterrestrial Intelligence (SETI) continues to this day. It has little funding, because it is difficult to explain to Congress why anyone would expect to get results—and even more difficult to explain why the lack of SETI results can be disturbing.

Yet consider: If, in the very near future, we can and indeed (like it or not) must make our presence known across interstellar distances, that will be true of "others" when their civilizations reach roughly the same age as ours. So why haven't they done so? Could it be because intelligence is counterproductive? That "civilization" is a snare, a trap for the unwary leading to species suicide? Is this our eventual fate?

Or could something even uglier be happening. . . .

SETI generally assumes benevolence. We want to find intelligent aliens, because we want to learn from them, and we think they will help us.

They don't have to be benevolent. They may be interested in us in the same way that we might be interested in a planet populated by a new and useful species of cow.

Gordon Dickson writes of such aliens, and of the humans who live under their rule.

Sages tell us that a free man remains free on the rack, while a slave remains a slave though his master removes his chains. Epictetus, the Stoic slave, felt freer than his master.

"He is truly free who desires what he can perform, and does what he desires," Rousseau tells us; but under this definition even the powerless are "free" if they desire nothing.

The Book of Common Prayer tells us that the Service of God is "perfect freedom." Obedience to the Creator is not servility, and theologians tell us we have freedom in order that we may submit, a theme present in most religions. Indeed, "Islam" means "submission." The concept of freedom through service and submission is ancient and honorable.

Submission to tyrants enjoys no such reputation.

ENTER A PILGRIM

by Gordon R. Dickson

In the square around the bronze statue of the Cymbrian bull, the crowd was silent. The spring sky over Aalborg, Denmark, was high and blue; and on the weather-grayed red brick wall of the building before them a man was dying upon the triple blades, according to an alien law. The two invokers, judges and executioners of that law, sat their riding beasts, watching, less than two long paces from where Shane Evert stood among the crowd of humans on foot.

"My son," the older and bulkier of the two was saying to the younger in the heavy Aalaag tongue, plainly unaware that there was a human nearby who could understand him, "as I've told you repeatedly, no creature tames overnight. You've been warned that when they travel in a family the male will defend his mate, the female and male defend their young."

"But, my father," said the younger, "there was no reason. I only struck the female aside with my power-lance to keep her from being ridden down. It was a consideration I intended, not a discipline or an attack . . ."

Their words rumbled in Shane's ears and printed themselves in his mind. Like giants in human form, medieval and out of place, the two massive Aalaag loomed beside him, the clear sunlight shining on the green and silver metal of their armor and on the red, camel-like creatures that served them as riding animals. Their concern was with their conversation and the crowd of humans they supervised in this legal death-watch. Only slightly did they pay attention to the man they had hung on the blades.

Mercifully, for himself as well as for the humans forced to witness his death, it happened that the Dane undergoing execution had been paralyzed by the Aalaag power-lance before he had been thrown upon the three sharp lengths of metal protruding from the wall twelve feet above the ground. The blades had pierced him while he was still unconscious; and he had passed immediately into shock. So that he was not now aware of his own dying; or of his wife, the woman for whom he had incurred the death penalty, who lay dead at the foot of the wall below him. Now he himself was almost dead. But while he was still alive all those in the square were required by Aalaag law to observe.

". . . Nonetheless," the alien father was replying, "the male misunderstood. And when cattle make errors, the master is responsible. You are responsible for the death of this one and his female—which had to be, to show that we are never in error, never to be attacked by those we have conquered. But the responsibility is yours."

Under the bright sun the metal on the alien pair glittered as ancient and primitive as the bronze statue of the bull or the blades projecting from the homely brick wall. But the watching humans would have learned long since not to be misled by appearances.

Tradition, and something like susperstition among the religionless Aalaag, preserved the weapons and armor of a time already more than fifty thousand Earth years lost and gone in their history, on whatever world had given birth to these seven-foot conquerors of humanity. But their archaic dress and weaponry were only for show.

The real power of the two watching did not lie in their swords and power-lances; but in the little black-and-gold rods at their belts, in the jewels of the rings on their massive forefingers, and in the tiny, continually moving orifice in the pommel of each saddle, looking eternally and restlessly left and right among the crowd.

". . . Then it is true. The fault is mine," said the Aalaag son submissively. "I have wasted good cattle."

"It is true good cattle have been wasted," answered his father, "innocent cattle who originally had no intent to challenge our law. And for that I will pay a fine, because I am your father and it is to my blame that you made an error. But you will pay me back five times over because your error goes deeper than mere waste of good cattle, alone."

"Deeper, my father?"

Shane kept his head utterly still within the concealing shadow of the hood to his pilgrim's cloak. The two could have no suspicion that one of the cattle of Lyt Ahn, Aalaag Governor of All Earth, stood less than a lance-length from them, able to comprehend each word they spoke. But it would be wise not to attract their attention. An Aalaag father did not ordinarily reprimand his son in public, or in the hearing of any cattle not of his own household. The heavy voices rumbled on and the blood sang in Shane's ears.

"Much deeper, my son . . ."

The sight of the figure on the blades before him sickened Shane. He had tried to screen it from him with one of his own private imaginings—the image he had dreamed up of a human outlaw whom no Aalaag could catch or conquer. A human who went about the world anonymously, like Shane, in pilgrim robes; but, unlike Shane, exacting vengeance from the aliens for each wrong they did to a man, woman, or child. However, in the face of the bloody reality before Shane on the wall, fantasy had failed. Now, though, out of the corner of his right eye, he caught sight of something that momentarily blocked that reality from his mind, and sent a thrill of unreasonable triumph running through him.

Barely four meters or so beyond and above both him and the riders on the two massive beasts, the sagging branch of an oak tree pushed its tip almost into the line of vision between Shane's eyes and the bladed man; and on the end of the branch, among the new green leaves of the year, was a small, cocoonlike shape, already broken. From it had just recently struggled the still-crumpled shape of a butterfly that did not yet know what its wings were for.

How it had managed to survive through the winter here was beyond guessing. Theoretically, the Aalaag had exterminated all insects in the towns and cities. But here it was; a butterfly of Earth being born even as a man of Earth was dying—a small life for a large. The utterly disproportionate feeling of triumph sang in Shane. Here was a life that had escaped the death sentence of the alien and would live in spite of the Aalaag—that is, if the two now watching on their great red mounts did not notice it as it waved its wings, drying them for flight.

They must not notice. Unobtrusively, lost in the crowd with his rough gray pilgrim's cloak and staff, undistinguished among the other drab humans, Shane drifted right, toward the aliens, until the branch-tip with its emerging butterfly stood squarely between him and the man on the wall.

It was superstition, magic . . . call it what you liked, it was the only help he could give the butterfly. The danger to the small life now beginning on the branch-tip should, under any cosmic justice, be insured by the larger life now ending for the man on the wall. The one should balance out the other. Shane fixed the nearer shape of the butterfly in his gaze so that it hid the further figure of the man on the blades. He bargained with fate. I will not blink, he told himself; and the butterfly will stay invisible to the Aalaag. They will see only the man. . . .

Beside him, neither of the massive, metal-clad figures had noticed his moving. They were still talking.

". . . in battle," the father was saying, "each of us is equal to more than a thousand of such as these. We would be nothing if not that. But though one be superior to a thousand, it does not follow that the thousand is without force against the one. Expect nothing, therefore, and do not be disappointed. Though they are now ours, inside themselves the cattle remain what they were when we conquered them. Beasts, as yet untamed to proper love of us. Do you understand me now?"

"No, my father."

There was a burning in Shane's throat; and his eyes blurred, so that he could hardly see the butterfly, clinging tightly to its branch and yielding at last to the instinctive urge to dry its folded, damp wings at their full expanse. The wings spread, orange, brown and black—like an omen, it was that species of sub-Arctic butterfly called a "Pilgrim"—just as Shane himself was called a "Pilgrim" because of the hooded robe he wore. The day three years gone by at the University of Kansas rose in his mind. He remembered standing in the student union, among the mass of other students and faculty, listening to the broadcast that announced the Earth had been conquered, even before any of them had fully bee.. able to grasp that beings from a further world had landed amongst them. He had not felt anything then except excitement, mixed perhaps with a not unpleasant apprehension.

"Someone's going to have to interpret for us to those aliens," he had told his friends, cheerfully. "Language specialists like me—we'll be busy."

But it had not been *to* the aliens; it had been *for* the aliens, for the Aalaag themselves, that interpreting had needed to be done—and he was not, Shane told himself, the stuff of which underground resistance fighters were made. Only . . . in the last two years . . . Almost directly over him, the voice of the elder Aalaag rumbled on.

". . . To conquer is nothing," the older Aalaag was saying. "Anyone with power can conquer. We rule—which is a greater art. We rule because eventually we change the very nature of our cattle."

"Change?" echoed the younger.

"Alter," said the older. "Over their generations we teach them to love us. We tame them into good kine. Beasts still, but broken to obedience. To this end we leave them their own laws, their religions, their customs. Only one thing we do not tolerate—the concept of defiance against our will. And in time they tame to this."

"But—always, my father?"

"Always, I say!" Restlessly, the father's huge riding animal shifted its weight on its hooves, crowding Shane a few inches sideways. He moved. But he kept his eyes on the butterfly. "When we first arrive, some fight us—and die. Later, some like this one on the wall here, rebel—and likewise die. Only *we* know that it is the heart of the beast that must at last be broken. So we teach them first the superiority of our weapons, then of our bodies and minds; finally, that of our law. At last, with nothing of their own left to cling to, their beast-hearts crack; and they follow us unthinkingly, blindly loving and trusting like newborn pups behind their dam, no longer able to dream of opposition to our will."

"And all is well?"

"All is well for my son, his son, and his son's son," said the father. "But until that good moment when the hearts of the cattle break, each small flicker of the flame of rebellion that erupts delays the coming of their final and utter love for us. Inadvertently here, you allowed that flame to flicker to life once more."

"I was in error. In the future I will avoid such mistakes."

"I shall expect no less," said the father. "And now, the man is dead. Let us go on."

They set their riding beasts in motion and moved off. Around them, the crowd of humans sighed with the release of tension. Up on the triple blades, the victim now hung motionless. His eyes stared, as he hung there without twitch or sound. The butterfly's drying wings waved slowly between the dead face and Shane's. Without warning, the insect lifted like a colorful shadow and fluttered away, rising into the dazzle of the sunlight above the square until it was lost to the sight of Shane. A feeling of victory exploded in him. Subtract one man, he thought, half-crazily. Add one butterfly—one small Pilgrim to defy the Aalaag.

About him, the crowd was dispersing. The butterfly was gone. His feverish elation over its escape cooled and he looked about the square. The Aalaag father and son were more than halfway across it, heading toward a further exiting street. One of the few clouds in the sky moved across the face of the sun, graying and dimming the light in the square. Shane felt the coolness of a little breeze on his hands and face. Around him now, the square was almost empty. In a few seconds he would be alone with the dead man and the empty, cocoon that had given up the butterfly.

He looked once more at the dead man. The face was still, but the light breeze stirred some ends of long blond hair that were hanging down.

Shane shivered in the abrupt chill from the breeze and the withdrawn sun-warmth. His spirits plunged, on a sickening elevator drop into self-doubt and fear. Now that it was all over, there was a shakiness inside him, and a nausea . . . he had seen too many of the aliens' executions these last two years. He dared not go back to Aalaag Headquarters feeling as he did now.

He would have to inform Lyt Ahn of the incident which had delayed him in his courier duties; and in no way while telling it must he betray his natural feelings at what he had seen. The Aalaag expected their personal cattle to be like themselves—Spartan, unyielding, above taking notice of pain in themselves or others. Any one of the human cattle who allowed his emotions to become visible would be "sick," in Aalaag terms. It would reflect on the character of an Aalaag master—even if he was Governor of All Earth—if he permitted his household to contain unhealthy cattle.

Shane could end up on the blades himself, for all that Lyt Ahn had always seemed to like him, personally. He would have to get his feelings under control, and time for that was short. At best, he could steal perhaps half an hour more from his schedule in addition to what had already been spent watching the execution—and in those thirty minutes he must manage to pull himself together. He turned away, down a street behind him leading from the square, following the last of the dispersing crowd.

The street had been an avenue of small shops once, interspersed with an occasional larger store or business establishment. Physically, it had not changed. The sidewalks and the street pavement were free of cracks and litter. The windows of the stores were whole, even if the display areas behind the glass were mainly empty of goods. The Aalaag did not tolerate dirt or rubble. They had wiped out with equal efficiency and impartiality the tenement areas of large cities, and the ruins of the Parthenon and Athens; but the level of living permitted to most of their human cattle was bone-bare minimal, even for those who were able to work long hours.

A block and a half from the square, Shane found and turned in at a doorway under the now-dark shape of what had once been the lighted neon sign of a bar. He entered a large gloomy room hardly changed from the past, except that the back shelf behind the bar itself was bare of the multitude of liquor bottles which it had been designed to hold. Only small amounts of distilled liquors were allowed to be made, nowadays. People drank the local wine, or beer.

Just now the place was crowded, with men for the most part. All of them silent after the episode in the square; and all of them drinking draft ale with swift, heavy gulps from the tall, thick-walled glasses they held in their hands. Shane worked his way down to the service area in the far corner where the bartender stood, loading trays with filled glasses for a single waitress to take to the tables and booths beyond the bar.

"One," he said.

A moment later, a full glass was place in front of him. He paid, and leaned with his elbows on the bar, his head in his hands, staring into the depths of the brown liquid.

The memory of the dead man on the blades, with his hair stirring in the wind, came back to Shane. Surely, he thought, there must be some portent in the butterfly also being called a Pilgrim? He tried to put the image of the insect between himself and the memory of the dead man, but here, away from the blue sky and sunlight, the small shape would not take form in his mind's eye. In desperation, Shane reached again for his private mental comforter—the fantasy of the man in a hooded robe who could defy all Aalaag and pay them back for what they had done. Almost he managed to evoke it. But the Avenger image would not hold in his head. It kept being pushed aside by the memory of the man on the blades . . .

"Undskylde!" said a voice in his ear. *"Herre . . . Herre!"*

For a fraction of a second he heard the words only as

foreign noises. In the emotion of the moment, he had slipped into thinking in English. Then the sounds translated. He looked up, into the face of the bartender. Beyond, the bar was already half empty once more. Few people nowadays could spare more than a few minutes from the constant work required to keep themselves from going hungry—or, worse yet, keep themselves from being forced out of their jobs and into becoming legally exterminable vagabonds.

"Excuse me," said the bartender again; and this time Shane's mind was back in Denmark with the language. "Sir. But you're not drinking."

It was true. Before Shane the glass was still full. Beyond it, the bartender's face was thin and curious, watching him with the amoral curiosity of a ferret.

"I . . ." Shane checked himself. Almost he had started explaining who he was—which would not be safe. Few ordinary humans loved those of their own kind who had become servants in some Aalaag household.

"Disturbed by what you saw in the square, sir? It's understandable," said the bartender. His green eyes narrowed. He leaned closer and whispered. "Perhaps something stronger than beer? How long since you've had some *schnapps?*"

The sense of danger snapped awake in Shane's mind. Aalborg had once been famous for its aquavit, but that was before the Aalaag came. The bartender must have spotted him as a stranger—someone possibly with money. Then suddenly he realized he did not care what the bartender had spotted, or where he had gotten a distilled liquor. It was what Shane needed right now—something explosive to counter the violence he had just witnessed.

"It'll cost you ten," murmured the bartender.

Ten monetary units was a day's wage for a skilled carpenter—though only a small fraction of Shane's pay for the same hours. The Aalaag rewarded their household cattle well. Too well, in the minds of most other humans. That was one of the reasons Shane moved around the world on his master's errands wearing the cheap and unremarkable robe of a Pilgrim.

"Yes," he said. He reached into the pouch at the cord about

his waist and brought forth his money clip. The bartender drew in his breath with a little hiss.

"Sir," he said, "you don't want to flash a roll, even a roll like that, in here nowadays."

"Thanks. I ..." Shane lowered the money clip below bartop level as he peeled off a bill. "Have one with me."

"Why, yes, sir," said the bartender. His eyes glinted, like the metal of the Cymbrian bull in the sunlight. "Since you can afford it ..."

His thin hand reached across and swallowed the bill Shane offered him. He ducked below the counter level and came up holding two of the tall glasses, each roughly one-fifth full with a colorless liquid. Holding glasses between his body and Shane's so that they were shielded from the view of others in the bar, he passed one to Shane.

"Happier days," he said, tilted up his glass to empty it at a swallow. Shane imitated him; and the harsh oiliness of the liquor flamed in his throat, taking his breath away. As he had suspected, it was a raw, illegally distilled, high-proof liquid with nothing in common with the earlier aquavit but the name it shared. Even after he had downed it, it continued to cling to and sear the lining of his throat, like sooty fire.

Shane reached automatically for his untouched glass of beer to lave the internal burning. The bartender had already taken back their two liquor glasses and moved away down the bar to serve another customer. Shane swallowed gratefully. The thick-bodied ale was gentle as water after the rough-edged moonshine. A warmth began slowly to spread through his body. The hard corners of his mind rounded; and on the heels of that soothing, without effort this time, came his comforting, familiar daydream of the Avenger. The Avenger, he told himself, had been there unnoticed in the square during the executions, and by now he was lying in wait in a spot from which he could ambush the Aalaag father and son, and still escape before police could be called. A small black and golden rod, stolen from an Aalaag arsenal, was in his hand as he stood to one side of an open window, looking down a street up which two figures in green and silver armor were riding toward him ...

"Another, sir?"

It was the bartender back again. Startled, Shane glanced at his ale glass and saw that it, too, was now empty. But another shot of that liquid dynamite? Or even another glass of the ale? He could risk neither. Just as in facing Lyt Ahn an hour or so from now he must be sure not to show any sign of emotion while reporting what he had been forced to witness in the square, so neither must he show the slightest sign of any drunkenness or dissipation. These, too, were weaknesses not permitted servants of the alien, as the alien did not permit them in himself.

"No," he said, "I've got to go."

"One drink did it for you?" the bartender inclined his head. "You're lucky, sir. Some of us don't forget that easily."

The touch of a sneer in the bitterness of the other's voice flicked at Shane's already overtight nerves. A sudden sour fury boiled up in him. What did this man know of what it was like to *live* with the Aalaag, to be treated always with that indifferent affection that was below contempt—the same sort of affection a human might give a clever pet animal—and all the while to witness scenes like those in the square, not once or twice a year but weekly, perhaps daily?

"Listen—" he snapped; and checked himself. Almost, once more, he had nearly given away what he was and what he did.

"Yes, sir?" said the bartender, after a moment of watching him. "I'm listening."

Shane thought he read suspicion in the other's voice. That reading might only be the echo of his own inner upset, but he could not take a chance.

"Listen," he said again, dropping his voice, "why do you think I wear this outfit?"

He indicated his Pilgrim robe.

"You took a vow." The bartender's voice was dry now, remote.

"No. You don't understand . . ." The unaccustomed warmth of the drink in him triggered an inspiration. The image of the butterfly slid into—and blended with—his image of the Avenger. "You think it was just a bad accident, out there in the square just now? Well, it wasn't. Not just accidental, I mean—I shouldn't say anything."

"Not an accident?" The bartender frowned; but when he spoke again, his voice, like Shane's, was lowered to a more cautious note.

"Of course, the man ending on the blades—it wasn't planned to finish that way," muttered Shane, leaning toward him. "The Pilgrim—" Shane broke off. "You don't know about the Pilgrim?"

"The Pilgrim? What Pilgrim?" The bartender's face came close. Now they were both almost whispering.

"If you don't know I shouldn't say—"

"You've said quite a lot already—"

Shane reached out and touched his six-foot staff of polished oak, leaning against the bar beside him.

"This is one of the symbols of the Pilgrim," he said. "There're others. You'll see his mark one of these days and you'll know that attack on the Aalaag in the square didn't just happen by accident. That's all I can tell you."

It was a good note to leave on. Shane picked up the staff, turned quickly and went out. It was not until the door to the bar closed behind him that he relaxed. For a moment he stood breathing the cooler air of the street, letting his head clear. His hands, he saw, were trembling.

As his head cleared, sanity returned. A cold dampness began to make itself felt on his forehead in the outside air. What had gotten into him? Risking everything just to show off to some unknown bartender? Fairy tales like the one he had just hinted at could find their way back to Aalaag ears—specifically to the ears of Lyt Ahn. If the aliens suspected he knew something about a human resistance movement, they would want to know a great deal more from him; in which case death on the triple blades might turn out to be something he would long for, not dread.

And yet, there had been a great feeling during the few seconds he had shared his fantasy with the bartender, almost as if it were something real. Almost as great a feeling as the triumph he had felt on seeing the butterfly survive. For a couple of moments he had come alive, almost, as part of a world holding a Pilgrim-Avenger who could defy the Aalaag. A Pilgrim who left his mark at the scene of each Aalaag crime as a promise of retribution to come. *The* Pilgrim, who in the end would rouse the world to overthrow its tyrant, alien murderers.

He turned about and began to walk hurriedly toward the square again, and to the street beyond it that would take him to the airport where the Aalaag courier ship would pick him up. There was an empty feeling in his stomach at the prospect of facing Lyt Ahn, but at the same time his mind was seething. If only he had been born with a more athletic body and the insensitivity to danger that made a real resistance fighter. The Aalaag thought they had exterminated all cells of human resistance two years since. The Pilgrim *could* be real. His role was a role any man really knowledgeable about the aliens could play—if he had absolutely no fear, no imagination to make him dream nights of what the Aalaag would do to him when, as they eventually must, they caught and unmasked him. Unhappily, Shane was not such a man. Even now, he woke sweating from nightmares in which the Aalaag had caught him in some small sin, and he was about to be punished. Some men and women, Shane among them, had a horror of deliberately inflicted pain. . . . He shuddered, grimly, fear and fury making an acid mix in his belly that shut out awareness of his surroundings.

Almost, this cauldron of inner feelings brewed an indifference to things around him that cost him his life. That and the fact that he had, on leaving the bar, instinctively pulled the hood of his robe up over his head to hide his features; particularly from anyone who might later identify him as having been in a place where a bartender had been told about someone called "the Pilgrim." He woke from his thoughts only at the faint rasp of dirt-stiff rags scuffing on cement pavement, behind him.

He checked and turned quickly. Not two meters behind, a man carrying a wooden knife and a wooden club studded with glass chips, his thin body wound thick with rags for armor, was creeping up on him.

Shane turned again, to run. But now, in the suddenly tomblike silence and emptiness of the street, two more such men, armed with clubs and stones, were coming out from between buildings on either side to block his way. He was caught between the one behind and the two ahead.

His mind was suddenly icy and brilliant. He had moved in one jump through a flash of fear into something beyond fright, into a feeling tight as a strung wire, like the reaction on nerves of a massive dose of stimulant. Automatically, the last two years of training took over. He flipped back his hood so that it could not block his peripheral vision, and grasped his staff with both hands a foot and a half apart in its middle, holding it up at the slant before him, and turning so as to try to keep them all in sight at once.

The three paused.

Clearly, they were feeling they had made a mistake. Seeing him with the hood over his head, and his head down, they must have taken him for a so-called praying pilgrim; one of those who bore staff and cloak as a token of nonviolent acceptance of the sinful state of the world which had brought all people under the alien yoke. They hesitated.

"All right, Pilgrim," said a tall man with reddish hair, one of the two who had come out in front of him, "throw us your pouch and you can go."

For a second, irony was like a bright metallic taste in Shane's mouth. The pouch at the cord around a pilgrim's waist contained most of what worldly goods he might own; but the three surrounding him now were "vagabonds"—*Nonservs*—individuals who either could not or would not hold the job assigned them by the aliens. Under the Aalaag rule, such outcasts had nothing to lose. Faced by three like this, almost any pilgrim, praying or not, would have given up his pouch. But Shane could not. In his pouch, besides his own possessions, were official papers of the Aalaag government that he was carrying to Lyt Ahn; and Lyt Ahn, warrior from birth and by tradition, would neither understand nor show mercy to a servant who failed to defend property he carried. Better the clubs and stones Shane faced now than the disappointment of Lyt Ahn.

"Come and get it," he said.

His voice sounded strange in his own ears. The staff he held seemed light as a bamboo pole in his grasp. Now the vagabonds were moving in on him. It was necessary to break out of the ring they were forming around him and get his back to something so that he could face them all at the same time . . . There was a storefront to his left just beyond the short, gray-haired vagabond moving in on him from that direction.

Shane feinted at the tall, reddish-haired man to his right, then leaped left. The short-bodied vagabond struck at him with a club as Shane came close, but the staff in Shane's hand brushed it aside and the staff's lower end slammed home, low down on the body of the vagabond. He went down without a sound and lay huddled up. Shane hurdled him, reached the storefront and turned about to face the other two.

As he turned, he saw something in the air, and ducked automatically. A rock rang against the masonry at the edge of the glass store window, and glanced off. Shane took a step sideways to put the glass behind him on both sides.

The remaining two were by the curb, now, facing him, still spread out enough so that they blocked his escape. The reddish-haired man was scowling a little, tossing another rock in his hand. But the expanse of breakable glass behind Shane deterred him. A dead or battered human was nothing; but broken store windows meant an immediate automatic alarm to the Aalaag police; and the Aalaag were not merciful in their elimination of Nonservs.

"Last chance," said the reddish-haired man. "Give us the pouch—"

As he spoke, he and his companion launched a simultaneous rush at Shane. Shane leaped to his left to take the man on that side first, and get out away from the window far enough to swing his stave freely. He brought its top end down in an overhand blow that parried the club-blow of the vagabond and struck the man himself to the ground, where he sat, clutching at an arm smashed between elbow and shoulder.

Shane pivoted to face the reddish-haired man, who was now on tiptoes, stretched up with his own heavy club swung back in both hands over his head for a crushing down-blow.

Reflexively, Shane whirled up the bottom end of his staff; and the tough, fire-hardened tip, traveling at eye-blurring speed, smashed into the angle where the other man's lower jaw and neck met.

The vagabond tumbled; and lay still in the street, his head unnaturally sideways on his neck.

Shane whirled around, panting, staff ready. But the man whose arm he had smashed was already running off down the street in the direction from which Shane had just come. The other two were still down and showed no intention of getting up.

The street was still.

Shane stood, snorting in great gasps of air, leaning on his staff. It was incredible. He had faced three armed men— armed at least in the same sense that he himself was armed— and he had defeated them all. He looked at the fallen bodies and could hardly believe it. All his practice with the quarter-staff . . . it had been for defense; and he had hoped never to have to use it against even one opponent. Now, here had been three . . . and he had won.

He felt strangely warm, large and sure. Perhaps, it came to him suddenly, this was the way the Aalaag felt. If so, there could be worse feelings. It was something lung-filling and spine-straightening to know yourself a fighter and a conqueror. Perhaps it was just this feeling he had needed to have, to understand the Aalaag—he had needed to conquer, powerfully, against great odds as they did. . . .

He felt close to rejecting all the bitterness and hate that had been building in him the past two years. Perhaps *might* actually could make *right*. He went forward to examine the men he had downed.

They were both dead. Shane stood looking down at them. They had appeared thin enough, bundled in their rags, but it was not until he stood directly over them that he saw how bony and narrow they actually were. They were like claw-handed skeletons.

He stood, gazing down at the last one he had killed; and slowly the fresh warmth and pride within him began to leak out. He saw the stubbled sunken cheeks, the stringy neck, and the sharp angle of the jawbone jutting through the skin of the dead face against the concrete. These features jumped at his mind. The man must have been starving—literally starving. He looked at the other dead man and thought of the one who had run away. All of them must have been starving, for some days now.

With a rush, his sense of victory went out of him; and the sickening bile of bitterness rose once more in his throat. Here, he had been dreaming of himself as a warrior. A great hero—the slayer of two armed enemies. Only the weapons carried by those enemies had been sticks and stones, and the enemies themselves were half-dead men with barely the strength to use what they carried. Not Aalaag, not the powerfully armed world conquerors challenged by his imaginary Pilgrim, but humans like himself reduced to near-animals by those who thought of these and Shane, in common, as "cattle."

The sickness flooded all through Shane. Something like a ticking time bomb in him exploded. He turned and ran for the square.

When he got there, it was still deserted. Breathing deeply, he slowed to a walk and went across it, toward the now still body on the triple blades, and the other body at the foot of the wall. The fury was gone out of him now, and also the sickness. He felt empty, empty of everything—even of fear. It was a strange sensation to have fear missing—to have it all over with; all the sweats and nightmares of two years, all the trembling on the brink of the precipice of action.

He could not say exactly, even now, how he had finally come to step off that precipice at last. But it did not matter. Just as he knew that the fear was not gone for good. It would return. But that did not matter, either. Nothing mattered, even the end he must almost certainly come to, now. The only thing that was important was that he had finally begun to act, to do something about a world he could no longer endure as it was.

Quite calmly he walked up to the wall below the blades holding the dead man. He glanced around to see if he was observed; but there was no sign of anyone either in the square or watching from the windows that overlooked it.

He reached into his pocket for the one piece of metal he was allowed to carry. It was the key to his personal living quarters in Lyt Ahn's residence, at Denver—"warded" as all such keys had to be, so that they would not set off an alarm by disturbing the field which the Aalaag had set up over every city and hamlet, to warn of unauthorized metal in the possession of humans. With the tip of the key, Shane scratched a rough figure on the wall below the body: the Pilgrim and his staff.

The hard tip of the metal key bit easily through the weathered surface of the brick to the original light red color underneath. Shane turned away, putting the key back into his pouch. The shadows of late afternoon had already begun to fall from the buildings to hide what he had done. And the bodies would not be removed until sunrise—this by Aalaag law. By the time the figure scratched on the brick was first seen by one of the aliens he would be back among the "cattle" of Lyt Ahn's household, indistinguishable among them.

Indistinguishable, but different, from now on—in a way the Aalaag had yet to discover. He turned and walked swiftly away down the street that would bring him to the alien courier ship that was waiting for him. The colorful flicker of a butterfly's wings—or perhaps it was just the glint of a reflection off some high window that seemed momentarily to wink with color—caught the edge of his vision. Perhaps, the thought came suddenly and warmly, it actually was the butterfly he had seen emerge from its cocoon in the square. It was good to feel that it might be the same, small, free creature.

"Enter a Pilgrim," he whispered to it triumphantly. "Fly, little brother. Fly!"

THE MEASURE OF A MAN

Randall Garrett has had a long and varied—not to say checkered—career in science fiction. As a youth he once caused an early SF convention to be thrown out of its hotel. He later developed a means of introducing himself to ingenues that to this day furnishes an endless source of amusement to those in the know.

Randall was one of the most prolific writers of the '50s. He employed half a dozen pseudonyms and as many collaborators. It is said that at least one issue of the old *Analog Science Fiction* was completely written by Randall Garrett and Poul Anderson.

One of his favorite themes was heroism. Without it, Randall said, freedom cannot survive; and indeed, a society which cannot inspire courage and loyalty does not deserve survival.

Civilizations sometimes fall to the fierceness of their enemies, but far more often they collapse because no one will defend them. "In order for evil to triumph," said Edmund Burke, "it is only necessary that good men do nothing."

THE MEASURE OF A MAN

by Randall Garrett

Alfred Pendray pushed himself along the corridor of the battleship *Shane*, holding the flashlight in one hand and using the other hand and his good leg to guide and propel himself by. The beam of the torch reflected queerly from the pastel green walls of the corridor, giving him the uneasy sensation that he was swimming underwater instead of moving through the blasted hulk of a battleship, a thousand light-years from home.

He came to the turn in the corridor, and tried to move to

the right, but his momentum was greater than he had thought, and he had to grab the corner of the wall to keep from going on by. That swung him around, and his sprained ankle slammed agonizingly against the other side of the passageway.

Pendray clenched his teeth and kept going. But as he moved down the side passage, he went more slowly, so that the friction of his palm against the wall could be used as a brake.

He wasn't used to maneuvering without gravity; he'd been taught it in Cadets, of course, but that was years ago and parsecs away. When the pseudograv generators had gone out, he'd retched all over the place, but now his stomach was empty, and the nausea had gone.

He had automatically oriented himself in the corridors so that the doors of the various compartments were to his left and right, with the ceiling "above" and the deck "below." Otherwise, he might have lost his sense of direction completely in the complex maze of the interstellar battleship.

Or, he corrected himself, *what's left of a battleship.*

And what *was* left? Just Al Pendray and less than half of the once-mighty *Shane.*

The door to the lifeboat hold loomed ahead in the beam of the flashlight, and Pendray braked himself to a stop. He just looked at the dogged port for a few seconds.

Let there be a boat in there, he thought. *Just a boat, that's all I ask. And air,* he added as an afterthought. Then his hand went out to the dog handle and turned.

The door cracked easily. There was air on the other side. Pendray breathed a sigh of relief, braced his good foot against the wall, and pulled the door open.

The little lifeboat was there, nestled tightly in her cradle. For the first time since the *Shane* had been hit, Pendray's face broke into a broad smile. The fear that had been within him faded a little, and the darkness of the crippled ship seemed to be lessened.

Then the beam of his torch caught the little red tag on the air lock of the lifeboat. *Repair Work Under Way—Do Not Remove This Tag Without Proper Authority.*

That explained why the lifeboat hadn't been used by the other crewmen.

Pendray's mind was numb as he opened the air lock of the small craft. He didn't even attempt to think. All he wanted was to see exactly how the vessel had been disabled by the repair crew. He went inside.

The lights were working in the lifeboat. That showed that its power was still functioning. He glanced over the instrument-and-control panels. No red tags on them, at least. Just to make sure, he opened them up, one by one, and looked inside. Nothing wrong, apparently.

Maybe it had just been some minor repair—a broken lighting switch or something. But he didn't dare hope yet.

He went through the door in the tiny cabin that led to the engine compartment, and he saw what the trouble was.

The shielding had been removed from the atomic motors.

He just hung there in the air, not moving. His lean, dark face remained expressionless, but tears welled up in his eyes and spilled over, spreading their dampness over his lids.

The motors would run, all right. The ship could take him to Earth. But the radiation leakage from those motors would kill him long before he made it home. It would take ten days to make it back to base, and twenty-four hours of exposure to the deadly radiation from those engines would be enough to insure his death from radiation sickness.

His eyes were blurring from the film of tears that covered them; without gravity to move the liquid, it just pooled there, distorting his vision. He blinked the tears away, then wiped his face with his free hand.

Now what?

He was the only man left alive on the *Shane*, and none of the lifeboats had escaped. The Rat cruisers had seen to that.

They weren't really rats, those people. Not literally. They looked humanoid enough to enable plastic surgeons to disguise a human being as one of them, although it meant sacrificing the little fingers and little toes to imitate the four-digited Rats. The Rats were at a disadvantage there; they couldn't add any fingers. But the Rats had other advantages—they bred and fought like, well, like rats.

Not that human beings couldn't equal them or even surpass them in ferocity, if necessary. But the Rats had nearly a thousand years of progress over Earth. Their Industrial Revolution had occurred while the Angles and the Saxons and the Jutes were pushing the Britons into Wales. They had put their first artificial satellites into orbit while King Alfred the Great was fighting off the Danes.

They hadn't developed as rapidly as Man had. It took them roughly twice as long to go from one step to the next, so that their actual superiority was only a matter of five hundred years, and Man was catching up rapidly. Unfortunately, Man hadn't caught up yet.

The first meeting of the two races had taken place in interstellar space, and had seemed friendly enough. Two ships had come within detector distance of each other, and had circled warily. It was almost a perfect example of the Leinster Hypothesis; neither knew where the other's home world was located, and neither could go back home for fear that the other would be able to follow. But the Leinster Hypothesis couldn't be followed to the end. Leinster's solution had been to have the parties trade ships and go home, but that only works when the two civilizations are fairly close in technological development. The Rats certainly weren't going to trade their ship for the inferior craft of the Earthmen.

The Rats, conscious of their superiority, had a simpler solution. They were certain, after a while, that Earth posed no threat to them, so they invited the Earth ship to follow them home.

The Earthmen had been taken on a carefully conducted tour of the Rats' home planet, and the captain of the Earth ship—who had gone down in history as "Sucker" Johnston— was convinced that the Rats meant no harm, and agreed to lead a Rat ship back to Earth. If the Rats had struck then, there would never have been a Rat-Human War. It would have been over before it started.

But the Rats were too proud of their superiority. Earth was too far away to bother them for the moment; it wasn't in their line of conquest just yet. In another fifty years, the planet would be ready for picking off.

Earth had no idea that the Rats were so widespread. They

had taken and colonized over thirty planets, completely destroying the indigenous intelligent races that had existed on five of them.

It wasn't just pride that had made the Rats decide to wait before hitting Earth; there was a certain amount of prudence, too. None of the other races they had met had developed space travel; the Earthmen might be a little tougher to beat. Not that there was any doubt of the outcome, as far as they were concerned—but why take chances?

But, while the Rats had fooled "Sucker" Johnston and some of his officers, the majority of the crew knew better. Rat crewmen were little short of slaves, and the Rats made the mistake of assuming that the Earth crewmen were the same. They hadn't tried to impress the crewmen as they had the officers. When the interrogation officers on Earth questioned the crew of the Earth ship, they, too, became suspicious. Johnston's optimistic attitude just didn't jibe with the facts.

So, while the Rat officers were having the red carpet rolled out for them, Earth Intelligence went to work. Several presumably awe-stricken men were allowed to take a conducted tour of the Rat ship. After all, why not? The Twentieth Century Russians probably wouldn't have minded showing their rocket plants to an American of Captain John Smith's time, either.

But there's a difference. Earth's government knew Earth was being threatened, and they knew they had to get as many facts as they could. They were also aware of the fact that if you know a thing *can* be done, then you will eventually find a way to do it.

During the next fifty years, Earth learned more than it had during the previous hundred. The race expanded, secretly, moving out to other planets in that sector of the galaxy. And they worked to catch up with the Rats.

They didn't make it, of course. When, after fifty years of presumably peaceful—but highly limited—contact, the Rats hit Earth, they found out one thing. That the mass and energy of a planet armed with the proper weapons cannot be outclassed by any conceivable concentration of spaceships.

Throwing rocks at an army armed with machine guns may

seem futile, but if you hit them with an avalanche, they'll go under. The Rats lost three-quarters of their fleet to planet-based guns and had to go home to bandage their wounds.

The only trouble was that Earth couldn't counterattack. Their ships were still outclassed by those of the Rats. And the Rats, their racial pride badly stung, were determined to wipe out Man, to erase the stain on their honor wherever Man could be found. Somehow, some way, they must destroy Earth.

And now, Al Pendray thought bitterly, they would do it.

The *Shane* had sneaked in past Rat patrols to pick up a spy on one of the outlying Rat planets, a man who'd spent five years playing the part of a Rat slave, trying to get information on their activities there. And he had had one vital bit of knowledge. He'd found it and held on to it for over three years, until the time came for the rendezvous.

The rendezvous had almost come too late. The Rats had developed a device that could make a star temporarily unstable, and they were ready to use it on Sol.

The *Shane* had managed to get off-planet with the spy, but they'd been spotted in spite of the detector nullifiers that Earth had developed. They'd been jumped by Rat cruisers and blasted by the superior Rat weapons. The lifeboats had been picked out of space, one by one, as the crew tried to get away.

In a way, Alfred Pendray was lucky. He'd been in the sick bay with a sprained ankle when the Rats hit, sitting in the X-ray room. The shot that had knocked out the port engine had knocked him unconscious, but the shielded walls of the X-ray room had saved him from the blast of radiation that had cut down the crew in the rear of the ship. He'd come to in time to see the Rat cruisers cut up the lifeboats before they could get well away from the ship. They'd taken a couple of parting shots at the dead hulk, and then left it to drift in space—and leaving one man alive.

In the small section near the rear of the ship, there were still compartments that were airtight. At least, Pendray decided, there was enough air to keep him alive for a while. If only he could get a little power into the ship, he could get the rear air purifiers to working.

He left the lifeboat and closed the door behind him. There was no point in worrying about a boat he couldn't use.

He made his way back toward the engine room. Maybe there was something salvageable there. Swimming through the corridors was becoming easier with practice; his Cadet training was coming back to him.

Then he got a shock that almost made him faint. The beam of his light had fallen full on the face of a Rat. It took him several seconds to realize that the Rat was dead, and several more to realize that it wasn't a Rat at all. It was the spy they had been sent to pick up. He'd been in the sick bay for treatments of the ulcers on his back gained from five years of frequent lashings as a Rat slave.

Pendray went closer and looked him over. He was still wearing the clothing he'd had on when the *Shane* picked him up.

Poor guy, Pendray thought. *All that hell—for nothing.*

Then he went around the corpse and continued toward the engine room.

The place was still hot, but it was thermal heat, not radioactivity. A dead atomic engine doesn't leave any residual effects.

Five out of the six engines were utterly ruined, but the sixth seemed to be in working condition. Even the shielding was intact. Again, hope rose in Alfred Pendray's mind. If only there were tools!

A half hour's search killed that idea. There were no tools aboard capable of cutting through the hard shielding. He couldn't use it to shield the engine on the lifeboat. And the shielding that been on the other five engines had melted and run; it was worthless.

Then another idea hit him. Would the remaining engine work at all? Could it be fixed? It was the only hope he had left.

Apparently, the only thing wrong with it was the exciter circuit leads, which had been sheared off by a bit of flying metal. The engine had simply stopped instead of exploding.

That ought to be fixable. He could try; it was something to do, anyway.

It took him the better part of two days, according to his watch. There were plenty of smaller tools around for the job, although many of them were scattered and some had been ruined by the explosions. Replacement parts were harder to find, but he managed to pirate some of them from the ruined engines.

He ate and slept as he felt the need. There was plenty of food in the sick bay kitchen, and there is no need for a bed under gravity-less conditions.

After the engine was repaired, he set about getting the rest of the ship ready to move—if it *would* move. The hull was still solid, so the infraspace field should function. The air purifiers had to be reconnected and repaired in a couple of places. The lights ditto. The biggest job was checking all the broken leads to make sure there weren't any short circuits anywhere.

The pseudogravity circuits were hopeless. He'd have to do without gravity.

On the third day, he decided he'd better clean the place up. There were several corpses floating around, and they were beginning to be noticeable. He had to tow them, one by one, to the rear starboard air lock and seal them between the inner and outer doors. He couldn't dump them, since the outer door was partially melted and welded shut.

He took the personal effects from the men. If he ever got back to Earth, their next-of-kin might want the stuff. On the body of the imitation Rat, he found a belt-pouch full of microfilm. The report of the Rats' new weapon? Possibly. He'd have to look it over later.

On the "morning" of the fourth day, he started the single remaining engine. The infraspace field came on, and the ship began moving at multiples of the speed of light. Pendray grinned, *Half gone, will travel,* he thought gleefully.

If Pendray had had any liquor aboard, he would have gotten mildly drunk. Instead, he sat down and read the spools of microfilm, using the projector in the sick bay.

He was not a scientist in the strict sense of the word. He was a navigator and a fairly good engineer. So it didn't surprise him any that he couldn't understand a lot of the report. The mechanics of making a semi-nova out of a normal star were more than a little bit over his head. He'd read a little and then go out and take a look at the stars, checking their movement so that he could make an estimate of his speed. He'd jury-rigged a kind of control on the hull field, so he could aim the hulk easily enough. He'd only have to get within signaling range, anyway. An Earth ship would pick him up.

If there was any Earth left by the time he got there.

He forced his mind away from thinking about that.

It was not until he reached the last spool of microfilm that his situation was forcibly brought to focus in his mind. Thus far, he had thought only about saving himself. But the note at the end of the spool made him realize that there were others to save.

The note said: *These reports* must *reach Earth before 22 June 2287. After that, it will be too late.*

22 June!

That was—let's see . . .

This is the eighteenth of September, he thought. *June of next year is—nine months away. Surely I can make it in that time. I've got to.*

The only question was, how fast was the hulk of the *Shane* moving?

It took him three days to get the answer accurately. He knew the strength of the field around the ship, and he knew the approximate thrust of the single engine by that time. He had also measured the motions of some of the nearer stars. Thank heaven he was a navigator and not a mechanic or something! At least he knew the direction and distance to Earth, and he knew the distance of the brighter stars from where the ship was.

He had two checks to use, then. Star motion against engine thrust and field strength. He checked them. And rechecked them. And hated the answer.

He would arrive in the vicinity of Sol some time in late July—a full month too late.

What could he do? Increase the output of the engine? No. It was doing the best it could now. Even shutting off the lights wouldn't help anything; they were a microscopic drain on that engine.

He tried to think, tried to reason out a solution, but nothing would come. He found time to curse the fool who had decided the shielding on the lifeboat would have to be removed and repaired. That little craft, with its lighter mass and more powerful field concentration, could make the trip in ten days.

The only trouble was that ten days in that radiation hell would be impossible. He'd be a very well-preserved corpse in half that time, and there'd be no one aboard to guide her.

Maybe he could get one of the other engines going! Sure. He *must* be able to get one more going, somehow. Anything to cut down on that time!

He went back to the engines again, looking them over carefully. He went over them again. Not a single one could be repaired at all.

Then he rechecked his velocity figures, hoping against hope that he'd made a mistake somewhere, dropped a decimal point or forgotten to divide by two. Anything. Anything!

But there was nothing. His figures had been accurate the first time.

For a while, he just gave up. All he could think of was the terrible blaze of heat that would wipe out Earth when the Rats set off the sun. Man might survive. There were colonies that the Rats didn't know about. But they'd find them eventually. Without Earth, the race would be set back five hundred—maybe five thousand—years. The Rats would have plenty of time to hunt them out and destroy them.

And then he forced his mind away from that train of thought. There had to be a way to get there on time. Something in the back of his mind told him that there *was* a way.

He had to think. Really think.

On 7 June 2287, a signal officer on the Earth destroyer *Muldoon* picked up a faint signal coming from the general direction of the constellation of Sagittarius. It was the standard emergency signal for distress. The broadcaster only had a very short range, so the source couldn't be too far away.

He made his report to the ship's captain. "We're within easy range of her, sir," he finished. "Shall we pick her up?"

"Might be a Rat trick," said the captain. "But we'll have to take the chance. Beam a call to Earth, and let's go out there dead slow. If the detectors show anything funny, we turn tail and run. We're in no position to fight a Rat ship."

"You think this might be a Rat trap, sir?"

The captain grinned. "If you are referring to the *Muldoon* as a rat trap, Mr. Blake, you're both disrespectful and correct. That's why we're going to run if we see anything funny. This ship is already obsolete by our standards; you can imagine what it is by theirs." He paused. "Get that call in to Earth. Tell 'em this ship is using a distress signal that was obsolete six months ago. And tell 'em we're going out."

"Yes, sir," said the signal officer.

It wasn't a trap. As the *Muldoon* approached the source of the signal, their detectors picked up the ship itself. It was a standard lifeboat from a battleship of the *Shannon* class.

"You don't suppose that's from the *Shane*, do you?" the captain said softly as he looked at the plate. "She's the only ship of that class that's missing. But if that's a *Shane* lifeboat, what took her so long to get here?"

"She's cut her engines, sir!" said the observer. "She evidently knows we're coming."

"All right. Pull her in as soon as we're close enough. Put her in Number Two lifeboat rack; it's empty."

When the door of the lifeboat opened, the captain of the *Muldoon* was waiting outside the lifeboat rack. He didn't know exactly what he had expected to see, but it somehow seemed fitting that a lean, bearded man in a badly worn uniform and a haggard look about him should step out.

The specter saluted. "Lieutenant Alfred Pendray, of the *Shane*," he said, in a voice that had almost no strength. He held up a pouch. "Microfilm," he said. "Must get to Earth immediately. No delay. Hurry."

"Catch him!" the captain shouted. "He's falling!" But one of the men nearby had already caught him.

In the sick bay, Pendray came to again. The captain's questioning gradually got the story out of Pendray.

". . . So I didn't know what to do then," he said, his voice a breath whisper. "I knew I had to get that stuff home. Somehow."

"Go on," said the captain, frowning.

"Simple matter," said Pendray. "Nothing to it. Two equations. Little ship goes thirty times as fast as big ship—big *hulk*. Had to get here before 22 June. *Had* to. Only way out, y'unnerstand.

"Anyway. Two equations. Simple. Work 'em in your head. Big ship takes months, little one takes ten days. But can't stay in a little ship ten days. No shielding. Be dead before you get here. See?"

"I see," said the captain patiently.

"*But*—and here's a 'mportant point: If you stay on the big ship for eight an' a half months, then y' only got to be in the little ship for a day an' a half to get here. Man can live that long, even under that radiation. See?" And with that, he closed his eyes.

"Do you mean you exposed yourself to the full leakage radiation from a lifeboat engine for thirty-six hours?"

But there was no answer.

"Let him sleep," said the ship's doctor. "If he wakes up again, I'll let you know. But he might not be very lucid from here on in."

"Is there anything you can do?" the captain asked.

"No. Not after a radiation dosage like that." He looked down at Pendray. "His problem was easy, mathematically. But not psychologically. That took real guts to solve."

"Yeah," said the captain gently. "All he had to do was *get* here alive. The problem said nothing about his staying that way."

DEFINITIONS
by Jerry Pournelle

More people have died for freedom than could define it; probably more people would be willing to die for liberty than could tell you what it is. There have been and remain many views of liberty, some mutually supporting, some contradictory.

Conservatives value liberty; but they value society more. They may find censorship distasteful, but they have often been willing to employ it. Motion pictures, magazines, books, sex shops, and radical newspapers have been among their victims. If asked to defend their actions, they will cite Oliver Wendell Holmes. No man has a right falsely to cry "Fire!" in a crowded theater; society has a duty to protect itself when it spies a clear and present danger, whether from conspiracy or speech.

The conservative is apt to quote Cicero: "In the end, we are all slaves to the law, for that is the condition of our freedom." Without law there are no rights; and without rights there are no liberties. Society and the law must be protected, for if they fall, so does everything else.

The liberal disagrees; at least until recently, the modern liberal view has been that there is never any grounds for censorship; that free speech is an absolute right. Even in time of war the enemy's views should be heard; perhaps especially in time of war, for what else are we fighting for but liberty? And freedom is indivisible. . . .

Unfortunately one can no longer so simply divide liberal and conservative thoughts on suppression and censorship. Modern liberals may pay lip service to their champion, John Stuart Mill, but they do not in fact follow his advice: as witness that San Francisco, a community which prides itself on its liberal school board and politicians, recently removed all copies of *Mary Poppins* from library bookshelves on the grounds that the book is racist and ought to be suppressed.

In the famous essay *On Liberty*, Mill says:

one very simple principle, as entitled to cover absolutely the dealings of society with the individual in
the way of compulsion and control. . . . That principle is, that the sole end for which mankind are
warranted, individually or collectively, in interfering
with the liberty of action of any of their number, is
self-protection. That the only purpose for which power
can rightfully be exercised over any member of a
civilized community, against his will, is to prevent
harm to others. His own good, either physical or
moral, is not a sufficient warrant. He cannot rightfully be compelled to do or forbear because it will be
better for him to do so, because it will make him
happier, because, in the opinion of others, to do so
would be wise, or even right.

Those are noble words, and liberal successors to Mill are
fond of repeating them; yet we live in a time when Steve
McQueen fled to Mexico in order to receive the cancer treatment of his choice; when my fans must smuggle cyclamates
to me from Canada; when the drug DMSO, not known to have
harmful side effects, cannot be sold as a drug, and the FDA,
discovering that it is sold as a paint thinner, moves to
suppress its sale entirely lest some use it in unauthorized
treatment of arthritis.

We live in a time of persecutions. Consider: Leading researchers believe thymosin (the secretions of the thymus
gland) has a major role in self-immunization against cancer.
There are those with a right to an opinion who say we "catch"
cancer every day of our lives, but the immune system destroys the defective cells. In humans, though, the thymus
gland self-destructs at about age forty. It no longer secretes
thymosin; and without thymosin the immune system cannot
properly operate. After age forty, the chances of contracting
cancer (and other disabling or fatal diseases) go up enormously. There is evidence—admittedly inconclusive—that
regular doses of thymosin for those over forty would have a
highly beneficial effect; may indeed prevent many if not most

cancers. This is not quackery, but theory held by highly respected medical researchers.

Note that in young normal humans thymosin is daily secreted; that this is as natural a substance as one may imagine, so that there is no question of harmful side effects.

It matters not at all. Our government "protects" us from those who might sell us thymosin. (Our government also "protects" us by requiring that we pay tribute to an M.D. for permission to buy any one of literally thousands of drugs; but we cannot *legally* buy thymosin in the United States no matter how much tribute we pay.)

Several years ago, medical researchers at the Medical Branch of the University of Texas wanted to test the efficacy of thymosin in treatment of cancer in children born with defective thymus glands. Five children were selected for treatment. By the time Washington's minions—those nobles whose task it is to protect us from quackery—issued permits for experimental use of the drug, two of the children were dead. The other three, I am happy to report, are alive—as might be the dead children had the FDA not "protected" them. One wonders if their parents feel well served.

So far have we come from Mill's ideas on liberty. Today's "freedoms" include the right not to be exploited by a drug company; which means in effect that if we wish products not approved by the government, we must either flee the country or pay a premium to smugglers and black marketeers. We are well protected by a highly paid bureaucracy which seems strangely reluctant ever to consider that we might be better served were they less zealous for our welfare.

There is more. Professor James A. Dinnan, fifty, of the Department of Education, University of Georgia, is as I write this languishing in a federal prison for the heinous crime of refusing to disclose his vote in a faculty tenure hearing; and this in the name of freedom.

It seems that a woman assistant professor, Maija Blaubergs, filed suit claiming that she was not promoted to a tenured position because of her sex; and the courts, in order to protect her rights, saw fit to inquire into the secret ballots of the faculty committee whose task it is to recommend academic promotion in that department. Professor Dinnan refused to disclose his vote. For this he remains jailed; ironically at Eglin Air Force Base, surrounded by young men and women sworn to uphold and defend, with their lives if need be, the Constitution of the United States.

One despairs at finding a "modern liberal" definition of liberty and freedom; a definition which includes the Miranda Decision protecting known criminals, yet sanctions the jailing of Professor Dinnan. One suspects John Stuart Mill, the champion of tolerance, would not totally be pleased with his intellectual descendants.

For Mill, free speech was indeed an absolute; there was never justification for persecution of ideas, for how, in the absence of firm and vigorous debate, could we know which ideas are true? Nor did he have any illusions that truth would always win against fire and sword and the rack. Mill lived far too early to have heard Goering say, "The noblest of sentiments and most honorable of spirits are easily suppressed if their bearer is beaten to death with a rubber truncheon"; but he would probably have agreed. Thoughts may remain free, but "It is a piece of idle sentimentality that truth, merely as truth, has any inherent power denied to error, of prevailing against the dungeon and the stake."

But if Mill stood for tolerance, that did not mean he held no opinions with passion. His views have been summarized by Isaiah Berlin:

> Toleration implies a certain disrespect. I tolerate your absurd beliefs and your foolish acts, though I know them to be absurd and foolish. Mill would, I think, have agreed. He believed that to hold an opinion deeply is to throw our feelings into it. He once declared that when we deeply care, we must dislike those who hold the opposite views.
>
> He asked us not necessarily to respect the views of others—far from it—only to try to understand and tolerate them; only tolerate; disapprove, think ill of,

if need be mock and despise, but tolerate; for without some anti-pathetic feeling, there was, he thought, no deep conviction; and without deep conviction there were no ends of life, and then the awful abyss on the edge of which he had himself once stood would yawn before us.

But without tolerance the conditions for rational criticism, rational condemnation, are destroyed. He therefore pleads for reason and toleration at all costs. To understand is not necessarily to forgive. We may argue, attack, reject, condemn with passion and hatred. But we may not suppress or stifle: for that is to destroy the bad and the good, and is tantamount to collective moral and intellectual suicide.

This is Mill's faith.

(Isaiah Berlin, *Four Essays on Liberty*, Oxford, 1969)

Editor's Note

When we conceived this anthology, we had intended to include Eric Frank Russell's classic anarchist tale, *And Then There Were None*. Alas, the story is over 25,000 words in length, and would have taken a quarter of the book.

Thus it is not here; but we recommend it to your attention.

CONDITIONS OF FREEDOM

Every now and again one meets people who can only be described as *good*. Such are Russell and Annette Kirk, two distinct individuals—yet it is nearly impossible to think of one without the other.

I first met Russell Kirk more years ago than I care to remember. I was then in graduate school, and he was world-famous, having with his *The Conservative Mind* almost singlehandedly brought the case for American intellectual conservatism to academic attention—and respectability.

Over the years we became good friends, though I have not often been able to enjoy his company; but when I have seen him, the occasion is likely to be memorable. I distinctly recall as one of the most pleasant events of my life the night I drove him from San Diego to my home in Buena Park, stopping en route for a late session with Msgr. Lloyd-Russell, formerly Professor of English at Loyola and then in semiretirement (if so powerful an intellect could ever have been said to retire) as Rector of Mission San Juan Capistrano.

Kirk's influence on American letters has been profound. Most of those who today think of themselves as philosophical conservatives have been his students—whether in person, or through his books and columns and articles. This short essay on liberty may show why.

CONDITIONS OF FREEDOM
by Russell Kirk

"Orders and degrees," Milton says, "jar not with liberty, but well consist." My thesis here is that freedom, in the modern world, is increasingly endangered: the freedom of the few, and also, in the long run, the freedom of the many. And I believe that we shall be unable to maintain any successful defense of our freedoms until we recognize once more those principles of order under which freedom in our tradition—the body of rights and privileges acquired gradually through many centuries of English and American social experience—acquired real meaning. Every right is married to a duty; every freedom owns a corresponding responsibility; and there cannot be genuine freedom unless there is also genuine order in the moral realm and the social realm.

Order, in the moral realm, is the realization of a body of transcendent values—indeed, a hierarchy of values—which give purpose to existence and motive to conduct. Order, in society, is the harmonious arrangement of classes and functions which guards justice and gives willing consent to law and ensures that we all shall be safe together. Although there cannot be freedom without order, in some sense there is always a conflict between the claims of order and the claims of freedom. We often express this conflict as the competition between the desire for liberty and the desire for security.

Although modern technological revolution and modern mass-democracy have made this struggle more intense, there is nothing new about it in essence. President Washington, remarked that "individuals entering into a society must give up a share of their liberty to preserve the rest." But doctrinaires of one ideology or another, in our time, continue to cry out for absolute security, absolute order, or for absolute freedom, power to assert the ego in defiance of all convention. At the moment, this fanatic debate may be particularly well discerned in the intemperate argument over academic freedom. I feel that in asserting freedom as an absolute, somehow divorced from order, we are repudiating our historic legacy of freedom and exposing ourselves to the danger of absolutism, whether that absolutism be what Tocqueville calls "democratic despotism" or what recently existed in Germany and now exists in Russia. "To begin with unlimited freedom," Dostoevski writes in *The Devils*, "is to end with unlimited despotism."

A wide and witty editor, Mr. Malcolm Muggeridge, in a talk called "Farewell to Freedom?" (*Queen's Quarterly*, winter, 1954–55) expressed the peril more eloquently than I can. He spoke with immediate reference to British society, but added that the same influences are at work throughout our world:

> A recurrent nightmare, with me, is that in our inimitable English way we are allowing a servile State to come to pass of itself without our noticing it; that one morning I shall wake up and find that, with the Monarchy still extant, Honourable and Right Honourable Members still meeting in Westminster, the *Times* and the *Manchester Guardian*, the *New Statesman* and the *Spectator* and *Punch* still regularly appearing, the cricket still being played at Lords, and the B.B.C. still providing its daily offering from "Bright and Early" to "Good-night, everyone, good-night," we have nevertheless become a totalitarian society. In this nightmare it seems clear that all the faceless men, the men without opinions, have been posted in key positions for a bloodless take-over, and that no one is prepared to join a Resistance Movement in defense of freedom because no one remembers what freedom means. The walls of Jericho fell down, not because the trumpet blast was strong, but because the walls themselves were crumbling. People, that is to say, are never enslaved unless they have become slaves already. They swim into the Great Leviathan's mouth. He does not need to chase them.

Mr. E. H. Carr, in his *New Society*, argues that although "freedom for the few" is diminishing in our world, nevertheless "freedom for the many" is increasing. But he is unable to define "freedom for the many"; he seems to mean, really, "material prosperity for the many." Now material prosperity, pure economic "security," is not the same thing as either freedom or order. Nor is it the same thing as happiness. An

Athenian slave might be more comfortable than many free-men, but he was not free, nor did he truly participate in the Athenian order.

It is quite possible that the man who desires freedom and the rights of order must be prepared to sacrifice certain security. A slave, in Aristotle's definition, is a being who allows others to make his choices for him. It is quite possible for a man, in ancient or modern times, to be materially prosperous, and freed from the necessity of choice, and yet servile. It is also possible that he may suffer no outrageous oppression. But he must always lack one thing, this servile man, and that is true manhood, the dignity of man. He remains a child; he never comes into man's birthright, which is the pleasure and the pain of making one's own choices.

Some of these problems of freedom upon which I have touched are examined by John Stuart Mill in his *On Liberty*. There is value in that essay; but I think that there is also weakness in it, and danger; and the current revival of the doctrines of Mill in some quarters, amounting almost to adulation, tends to confuse the whole discussion of this problem. We are living in the twentieth century, not in the nineteenth, and we now perceive vast difficulties which Mill ignored. Yet Professor Commager informs us that "we cannot too often repair to John Stuart Mill's *On Liberty*," and implies that this essay is, like the laws of the Medes and the Persians, immutable. A far more perceptive thinker than Mr. Commager—Mr. David Riesman—shares in this adulation of Mill, and is almost John Stuart Mill *redivivus*. Yet, as M. Bertrand de Jouvenel observes ("A Discussion of Freedom," *Cambridge Journal*, September, 1953), Mill was unaware of any real difficulty in defining "liberty," though Cicero saw the necessity for distinguishing between *libido* and *voluntas*. To Mill, "liberty" might mean "doing as we like," or "pursuing our own good in our own way," or acting "according to [our] own inclination and judgment."

Nevertheless, Mill's *On Liberty* at present is being employed very interestingly by persons who pretend to believe in an absolute freedom which no society ever has been able to tolerate—and that in an age which requires the highest

degree of order and cooperation, when "the great wheel of
circulation" upon which our economy and our physical security depend necessarily is more to us than ever before. Some
of these persons—curiously archaic in their opinions, although
they pride themselves upon their modernity—are old-fangled
Benthamite liberals, dedicated to "rugged individualism" in
the era of the atomic pile; others (and these more grimly
ominous, probably) are the new-fangled collectivistic liberals, desirous of receiving everything from the state, but
insistent that they owe the state nothing in return—not even
loyalty. John Milton knew such gentlemen three centuries
ago:

> This is got by casting pearls to hogs,
> That bawl for *freedom* in their senseless mood,
> And still revolt when truth would set them free.
> License they mean when they cry *liberty;*
> For who loves that, must first be wise and good.

My general argument is this: liberty, prescriptive freedom
as we Americans know it, cannot endure without order. Our
constitutions were established that order might make true
freedom possible. For all our American talk of private judgment, dissent, and individualism, still our national character
has the stamp of a respect for order almost superstitious in its
power: respect for the moral traditions inculcated by our
religion, and for the prescriptive political forms which we,
more than any other people in the world, have maintained
little altered in this time when Whirl is king of most of the
universe. I think that we would do a most terrible mischief to
our freedoms if we ceased to respect our established order and
began, instead, to run after an abstract, Jacobin *liberté*—in
this age of the triumph of technology, of all times.

What is lacking in the thought of Mill and his modern
disciples, it seems to me, is any real understanding of the
principle of order. First, any coherent and beneficial freedom
must have the sanction of moral order: it must accord with
principles, religious in origin, that establish a hierarchy of
values and set bounds to the ego. Second, any coherent and

beneficial freedom must have the check of social order: it must accord with a rule of law, regular in its operation, that recognizes and enforces prescriptive rights, protects minorities against majorities and majorities against minorities, and gives some meaning to the idea of human dignity. *Freedom* as an abstraction is the liberty in whose name crimes are committed. Freedom, as realized in the prescriptive, separate, limited, balanced, well-defined rights of persons and groups, operating within a state governed by moral principle, is the quality which makes it possible for men to become truly human.

I am rather embarrassed at saying these things, for they have been said often before, and a great mass of historical evidence supports them. But every great question has to be argued afresh in every generation, and first principles have to be declared over and over again. Truly, we learn from history that we learn nothing from history.

When most people use the word "freedom" nowadays, they use it in the sense of the French Revolutionaries; freedom from tradition, from established social institutions, from religious doctrines, from prescriptive duties. I think that this employment of the word does much mischief. For we do not live in an age—and there are such ages—which is oppressed by the dead weight of archaic establishments and obsolete custom. The danger in our era, rather, is that the fountains of the great deep will be broken up and that the pace of alteration will be so rapid that generation cannot link with generation. Our era, necessarily, is what Matthew Arnold called an epoch of concentration. Or, at least, the thinking American needs to turn his talents to concentration, the buttressing and reconstruction of our moral and social heritage. This is a time not for anarchic freedom, but for ordered freedom.

There are much older and stronger concepts of freedom than that espoused by the French Revolutionaries. In the Christian tradition, freedom is submission to the will of God. This is no paradox. As he that would save his life must lose it, so the man who desires true freedom must recognize a Providential order which gives all freedoms their sanction. The theory of "natural rights" depends upon the premise of an unalterable human nature bestowed upon man by God. Only acceptance of a divine order can give enduring freedom to a society; for this lacking, there is no reason why the strong and the clever, the dominant majority or the successful oligarch, should respect the liberties of anyone else. Freedom without the theory of natural rights becomes simply the freedom of those who hold power to do as they like with the lives of those whose interests conflict with theirs.

And in the Christian tradition, as in the Judaic tradition and the Stoic philosophy and the religions of India, there subsists also the belief that freedom is the absence of worldly desire. Not to lust after the things of the flesh, or after power, or after fame: this is true freedom, the freedom of Stilbo confronting the Macedonian tyrant, or of Socrates before the Athenian assembly. This is the freedom of Diogenes asking Alexander to stand out of the sun. The man who has made his peace with the universe is free, however poor he may be; the man who seeks always to gratify his appetites is servile, however rich he may be.

We live in an age which, for good or ill, has come to depend upon the highest degree of cooperation and discipline ever known to civilization. Our economy, our political structure, our very physical existence could not abide for twenty-four hours the triumph of the "absolute liberty" which Lamartine and other enthusiasts of the nineteenth century preached. Our problem is how to reconcile respect for true human dignity, personality, with the demands of social cooperation. And that is a most difficult problem.

Very few people really are interested in true freedom, in any era; most folk always go for security, secular conformity, and enforced routine, at the price of independence. But the freedom of the few who really deserve freedom—and they are fewer in our time than ever they were before, I am inclined to believe—is infinitely precious; and in the long run, the security and contentment of the whole of humanity depend upon the survival of that freedom for a few.

The great danger just now is that, in the name of general

security, we shall neglect altogether the claims of the minority who need and deserve freedom. We seem bent upon establishing a universal equalitarian domination which will call itself free and democratic, but which will have made existence almost impossible for those natures that seek to obey the will of God and to abjure unhallowed desire.

ESCAPE TO THE SUBURBS

I have never met Rachel Payes, prolific (thirty books) writer though she is; but when I was President of SFWA, she was one of the very few members not personal friends to send me encouraging letters.

The Payes family includes at least two members of SFWA: Rachel and her son Rob. Her daughter Ruth is a talented artist. And she somehow finds the time to read nearly every science fiction book and story published.

Russell Kirk tells us that freedom without order is meaningless. In today's paper I find the following story:

A three-judge panel of the California Court of Appeals has unanimously reversed the conviction of Deborah C. for shoplifting. In October 1979, Deborah entered the dressing room of a department store, where she stuffed several items of clothing into her bag. She then left the store without offering to pay. These facts are not in dispute.

Unknown to Deborah C. a store security officer was peeking under the door—having seen her remove several items of clothing from the store racks and take them to the dressing room. He saw her put the clothing in her bag; and when she left the store, he arrested her. She admitted the theft and told the store officer her brother and sister had told her to take those clothes. . . .

She was duly convicted in Juvenile Court.

"When store officers are merely recovering stolen goods for their employers," the appeals court held, "they are not subject to the same search and seizure standards as police officers." But the standards *do* apply to security officers "where the employees act with intent to institute prosecutions."

Moreover, "since her confession was an obvious result of the illegal search, all of the evidence against this minor is inadmissable; and therefore the adjudication of the court below must be reversed."

The court also held that Deborah's rights were violated when she was earlier arrested at another department store; a security officer had seen her take jewelry, and when she left the store detained her outside. He had not advised her of her right to remain silent, and she confessed volubly. . . .

The accounts do not say whether the jewelry and clothing in these cases were returned to the store or given back to Deborah.

A common complaint of those who live in minority communities —ghettoes, if you will—is that prices are higher there than in the suburbs. Store owners reply that their prices *must* be higher, to reflect the very high cost of doing business. "When I managed a store in the Valley," a food chain executive said, "I didn't have to post guards to keep people from running off with whole carts full of meat."

It is not contended that most ghetto inhabitants are thieves; and it is not just that the honest must suffer for all.

But query: Although the American Civil Liberties Union exults over the decision in the case of Deborah C., has that decision brought nearer the day when Rachel's story is not science fiction at all?

ESCAPE TO THE SUBURBS

by Rachel Cosgrove Payes

"We'll never get away with it, Juan."

"Come on, Willie. Ain't you and me soul brothers?"

The youth nodded solemnly, his Masai braids swinging over a black forehead. He was taller than Juan, heavier muscled, stronger; but his wiry soul brother had the brains. Willie acknowledged Juan's superiority, bowed to his judgment.

"We can make it, Willie, we can escape."

Willie rolled fearful eyes until only the whites showed. "Man, doan let no one hear you say them words." His voice dropped to a whisper. "Escape to the suburbs? How?"

They were plowing through the fetid masses downtown. It was nearing noon, and there was a surge of humanity, hot and malodorous, toward the feeding stations.

Willie tugged at Juan's arm. "Man, you're headed wrong. The algae cake station's over that way."

"Come on, Willie. We gotta talk—private."

Talk private—what a laugh. Where on the whole island fortress of Manhattan was there privacy, except in the towers? The teeming millions bred and lived and died in each others' pockets. After the final pull-out, when city government gave up and fled to Jersey, the masses who were left quit taking the pills and produced bumper crops of babies. They talked of increasing their power by increasing their numbers—they'd take over whitey—make the suburbs their own—live high. But all they did was make the island a hell of population density.

Juan maneuvered his way into a doorway, ousting the couple there with a show of his flick knife. "Come on, Willie. We gotta talk. We're gonna get off this island."

"Man, you can't do it. It's guarded all the way. Look what happened to Lil and Sammy just last week. Tried to swim it, and those whitey guards on the Jersey shore spitted 'em like fish."

"Not gonna swim it, Willie. I know the patrols ain't blind. And I doan wanna be speared—nor shredded with a grenade. What's the point of escapin' if we get killed? Use your head for somethin' more'n a holder for those pigtails, man," and he reached up and gave a tug on one of Willie's braids, making his soul brother yelp in anguish.

"Ouch, that hurts. Anybody but you, Juan—"

"Peace, brother. About our escape."

Willie shuddered. Just talking about escape brought goose bumps out on him, even though it was August, and the heat and humidity bore down on him like a collapsed wall. Tempers were short, fights common. There were many who didn't make it through a Manhattan August—a lot of flesh around. Rumor had it that not all bodies got dropped into the rivers. Some went into soup pots instead of rat meat. And escape was dangerous. The Bronx patrolled—New Jersey killed without challenging—Brooklyn guarded its borders jealously. The tunnels and bridges had been blown when the last city government forces fled secretly in the night, leaving the masses trapped and embittered. It wasn't safe to mention escape to the suburbs. If the word got around that you had a sure-fire method, every gang on every block tried to torture your secret from you.

"Willie, we fly out of this hellhole."

"Man, you've flipped. Whatta we do—sprout wings like the pigeons? Soar like the gulls?"

"Naw. We use hang gliders."

Willie made a deep, disgusted sound, a growl, at the back of his throat. "Glide. Come on, Juan. They tried it just last week. I seen 'em, and so did you. Potted 'em in the air, busted up them gliders with machine guns. They fell like stones into the East River."

"True, man true. They was dummies. Do they think they can fly low over the water and not get caught?"

It had been the Forked Devils who'd tried it. They'd made gliders—worked on them for weeks, guarding their enclave, a rotting pier, with the ferocity of ancient robber barons. Willie and Juan had spied on them from a vantage spot in one of the crumbling towers. Juan even had a little telescope he'd rigged himself. He was clever at making things, and scrounging the stuff to make them. The Forked Devils had built their gliders from bamboo struts—electrical conduit they'd pulled from the walls of decaying buildings—wood they'd pried from door facings—driftwood—sheets of plastic they'd stolen from the tenters, who would wake to find their homes gone from over their heads. Then they made huge wings—deltas, mostly. And practiced flying by taking off along the crumbling remains of the East River Drive. When the wind was right, some of them lifted as much as twenty feet. One stayed aloft five minutes, dangling from straps under his armpits. They practiced takeoffs, they soared, they turned and glided and landed. And all the time, the spies on the other bank watched and waited.

"Juan, I doan wanna fly."

"Willie, we're soul brothers. I wouldn't be happy living in the suburbs without you."

"This is all in your head, escape to the suburbs. I'd never manage there—I'm too black. You—" He reached out a big black hand and touched Juan's cheek with the gentleness of a mother. "You could pass, there."

"Willie, I'll kick in your fool head. There's plenty of blacks escaped, before the tunnels blew."

"I doan believe it."

"True. I talked with an old man, must be nearly sixty, miracle he's still alive, he's so ancient. He tole me about it—he was alive when the tunnels blew."

"Nobody's that old, Juan."

"Willie I doan lie to my soul brother. This old man, hair white, can't hardly move, his little grandson gets the algae cakes for him at the feeding station, this old man says lot of blacks in the suburbs."

Willie shrugged. "Still doan make no diff. We can't fly and you know it, Juan."

"Can, too. Gotta start out high, thas all. Fly way over their heads, so high they won't even see us."

Juan's voice was low and persuasive. Willie protested; but all the time he was saying "no," he knew in his heart that he'd do whatever Juan wanted. They'd been together all their lives. If Juan escaped, Willie knew he'd have to go, too. He couldn't live without Juan. If Juan were gone, he'd just lie down in the street and die.

"Okay, Juan, I'll listen. But I ain't promisin'."

Willie saw that smile on Juan's face, a kind of sly twisting of full lips. Anybody else would worry to see Juan smile that way. It'd spell trouble; but not for Willie. Juan loved him like a brother. Together, with Juan's wits and Willie's brawn, they made a team. Nothin' could stop 'em. Juan kept after Willie all the time—"Think of number one, Willie. Doan worry about the others—just about yourself." It was Juan's philosophy. And Willie agreed out loud; but always added, inside his head, "Think of you, too, Juan. Before me, think of you."

Juan produced two algae cakes he'd acquired somehow,

gave one to a hungry Willie, munched the other himself.

"We leave high, Willie. From way up on top of a tower."

Again Willie rolled fearful eyes. He didn't like heights. Some lived fairly high in the old towers; but with power cut off, elevators sat useless except as a family home. Most didn't want to climb too many steps. It ate up energy. And with the meager rations the helos ferried in each day, dropping them at the stations so there'd be no danger of groups overpowering the crews and escaping in the whirlies, you didn't have much energy to waste. Just keeping alive in the city was a full-time job. So most of the tall towers were deserted, falling into disrepair through the years.

"I doan like high places, Juan. You know that."

"Takes both of us to lug the supplies, man. You want me to leave you behind, alone?" There was a hardness in Juan's voice that Willie knew too well. Even with him, the soul brother, Juan could be harsh.

"You know I go with you, Juan." Willie's voice was resigned. For Juan, he'd scale Empire, if Juan said climb.

"First we gotta scrounge." Juan was good at that, better than Willie. But Willie went along, the strong back to carry the supplies. "I watched the Forked Devils, know which gliders work best. Gotta keep 'em light but strong, make a big delta wing. And I doan fancy hangin' high up there in the wind by my arms. Pull 'em outta the sockets. We'll rig us little seats hangin' down from the wing—sit there and fly over the East River in comfort."

Thinking about all that height, dangling beneath a fragile wing of plastic, made Willie feel like vomiting.

"No other way, Juan?"

"No other way."

They spent days assembling materials for two gliders. Toward the end, Juan went scrounging alone, leaving Willie in their hiding place in an odorous sewer to guard what they had already acquired.

"Guard it with your life, man. This stuff gets stolen, I swear I'll cut you up."

"Juan, I'm your soul brother."

"Yeah—so guard with your life."

Sometimes even Willie was afraid of Juan. When he used that low, cold tone it froze Willie's gizzard to a lump of ice inside of him.

The day came when Juan brought back only food.

"Man, we feed good! Where'd you get all them algae cakes?" Willie reached a hungry hand, only to feel a sharp thrill of pain. "Hey, man, you nicked my hand."

"Keep hands off, Willie. We gotta make them cakes last. No more goin' to the feedin' stations. Tonight we climb the tower—and we doan come down, except on wings."

Almost afraid to ask, Willie said, "Which tower?"

"Empire. Wind's off the Hudson, blow us to Long Island."

It was too much for Willie. "You're crazy, Juan. Empire—it goes to the sky. And what happens if the wind blows us out into the ocean? I heard it goes forever, water and water and nothin' else. Fall in there, we're dead."

"You call livin' here alive? I'd rather fall from on top of Empire and squash on the street than live here any longer. You go with me, Willie, or I go alone."

Even as he protested, Willie knew he'd go. He'd probably die—but he'd go whever Juan led.

Once he made up his mind, Willie turned practical. Juan had the brains, sure; but sometimes he was a dreamer, thinking up schemes that wouldn't work.

"Look, how we get up Empire? They live on the stairs. It's too high to climb the sides."

"And you get sick lookin' down." Again the hard tone that Willie hated and feared. "We fight our way up—one at a time, Willie."

"You're crazy."

"Gotta do it. One stays below to guard the stuff. That's you, man, you're bigger. I work my way above where they live, send down a rope, haul up the stuff."

"And then?"

"You come up alone."

"Man, they doan like strangers, the stair livers."

Juan shrugged. "So cut 'em a little. You're big, Willie. Lean on 'em. If I can make it, so can you."

Willie'd done his share of cutting, but he never liked it. But if Juan said cut, he'd kill a dozen or more.

After dark, they moved, keeping to the sewers until they reached a manhole near Empire. Juan, in the lead, eased the cover and looked cautiously about.

"Come on, Willie. We can make it."

Adept at fading into the shadows, they reached the side of the tower, burdened with their glider materials. Juan paced from the corner, said, "This is where you wait," and was gone.

Willie, back to the wall, one foot on the bundles, knife ready, waited with growing apprehension. It was a mad scheme, doomed to fail. Juan would die on the stairs. There'd be too little air at the top of the tower—he'd heard tales—he fought off one thief, cut a second, and was losing faith when something touched his head. With a gargle of fear, Willie crouched and swung above him, only to find that the attacker was the rope Juan had carried wound about his slender body like a snake.

Nerves jittering, Willie fastened the first bundle and gave three tugs to the rope, their signal. Juan had made it. Once he'd hauled up both bundles, Willie would fight his way through to his soul brother. Then they'd ascend the awesome heights of Empire to the very top.

Willie saw the signs that Juan had passed this way. One dead, at least a dozen bleeding. With his size, with knife on the ready, Willie met little resistance. "Jes' goin' through, doan wann camp on you," he called at each landing. Ten stories, twenty stories, he toiled. The ranks thinned. Finally a landing with no one living on it—and a whisper from the darkness.

"Willie? Is that you?"

The climb was endless. The bundles were heavy, and even Willie's sturdy legs began to ache.

"Must be in the clouds." He was glad it was dark outside, so that he couldn't see how high they were.

Finally, with dawn just blurring the stars, they reached the top. Juan let Willie rest briefly, they ate a cake, and drank from the plastic jug of water.

"Now we build the gliders."

"Good we can work indoors." Willie refused to go out on the platform to look at the city. He'd watched Juan's long hair blow in the wind. "Come back, Juan. You'll blow away."

"That's what I want to do, man." His eyes gleamed and he exuded an air of recklessness that worried Willie.

Once they set to work on the gliders, though, Juan was all business. He'd even sketched out rough plans, and his skilled fingers assembled the struts of electrical conduit, lashed them together, stretched the plastic taut.

"How we get 'em out the door, Juan?"

Juan gave him one of those "you dummy" looks. "It folds, Willie. Think I'd boxed myself in?"

It was evening when the gliders were finished.

"First thing in the morning, before whitey is awake, we fly."

Juan doled out more cakes and water. They ate in silence, both of them awed by being alone. It made Willie uneasy; for though he hated the horrid crowding down below, this silence, this being able to move without bumping into someone, was unnatural. And the flight tomorrow—he couldn't even think about it. That night Willie's dreams were frightening.

An urgent hand shook him awake. "Time, man. There's a stiff breeze, the sun is up—we fly!"

They soon found the breeze to be a hazard. Willie's folded glider, once he'd maneuvered it outside, was caught by a gust, snapped open, and almost got away from him. Only Juan's quick reflexes saved it.

"Better lash 'em to one of them posts, Willie. Then, when we're ready, in the seats and hanging on, we slash the ropes with our knives and off we go."

Willie stayed near the door, afraid to step far out onto the platform. Looking straight ahead, he saw only the tips of one or two other towers. Beneath his feet he felt the tower sway slightly in the wind, and a rush of nausea almost overwhelmed him.

"Come on, help me with my glider."

Gritting his teeth, Willie angled Juan's folded glider outside, holding it carefully so the wind couldn't fill it too quickly. Juan tethered it, then spread it on the platform and stretched it taut, making the final fastening that kept the frame rigid, made it into a huge delta wing.

"We have to leave from over there, where the parapet has crumbled. Easier than balancing up on that railing."

Willie took one look where Juan was pointing, and his gut knotted with terror. A great gap in the wall left them without any protection. If they fell—

"Juan, I can't—"

"Willie, I'm gonna fly now. If you doan come, you stay here alone."

Juan fitted his arms through the straps and braced himself so that the wind didn't carry him away too soon. Willie followed suit, his knees trembling, swallowing hard to keep down his meager breakfast. Then he followed Juan, shuffling his feet for traction, to the edge of the platform. Willie planned not to look down, knowing it would be disastrous; but some horrid fascination drew his eyes to the panorama stretched out far below him. There lay the city, its towers in ruins, its streets already dotted with the ants he knew had to be people. Vertigo swept over him, and he collapsed to his knees, cowering under the canopy of his hang glider, which filled and tugged in the morning breeze, threatening to sweep him over the edge into that ghastly void.

From above him, Willie heard Juan's voice. "Come on, man, I'm aloft. I'm cuttin' the rope now."

Forcing his eyes open, Willie looked up, not down. There, dangling from the giant kite, hung Juan, his face jubilant, knife in hand ready to slash the tether and free himself for his impossible journey.

"No, doan go, man. You'll die!"

In an agony of fear, Willie slipped out of his glider harness and caught at the taut rope linking Juan to the tower. With powerful hands, he hauled in the glider.

"Leggo!" Juan's voice was cold with anger; but for once, Willie ignored his friend's displeasure.

"Not gonna let you chance it, Juan. I can't fly—and you can't leave me here alone. We're soul brothers."

He reached up one massive arm and caught Juan's foot, tugging at his friend to bring him back, ignoring the drop at his feet, intent only on keeping Juan here with him.

Then there was a glint in the morning sun, and pain seared Willie's hand. Snatching it back, he saw blood drip from a long gash across the black flesh.

"You cut me!" His cry was anguished disbelief.

"Nobody holds me here." Juan's face was contorted, vicious. "I'm flyin' now, Willie. Ain't gonna stay for you—for no one. Gotta look out for number one."

Again the knife flashed, and the breeze caught the glider, lifted it, and swept it away to the west.

The backflash of the tether caught Willie across the face, almost blinding him. He fell to the platform, one arm dangling into the abyss. When his terror abated, he looked into the sky. Far away the black dot soared, as Juan made his escape to the suburbs.

Crying, the tears running down his cheeks unwiped, Willie inched away from the broken parapet to the relative safety of the central platform. The enormity of his solitude crushed him, and he couldn't get to the stairway fast enough. He had to get down from the tower, back into the crush of crowds, back to the security of the masses in the city.

Editor's Introduction To:

THE LIBERATION OF EARTH

"If I knew," wrote Thoreau, "that a man was coming to my house with the fixed intention of doing me good, I would run for my life." What might he have thought of those who promise peace, and freedom, and liberation?

I suppose I have been told, but I cannot remember why Professor Phillip Klass of Penn State uses the pseudonym William Tenn (or indeed any pseudonym at all). Despite the comparatively small number of stories he has published, Klass has become an authority in the science fiction field.

He does have his quirks. It has long been his lament that he never received research grants. "God doesn't want me to have a grant," he bemoaned.

So of course this year he got one, which took him from State College, Pennsylvania, to Berkeley, California—where, incidentally, he played house-sitter to Poul Anderson's place for a good part of the summer. It wasn't an enormous grant; one does hope it was large enough to compensate for robbing him of a favorite lament. One also expects this is not the last.

When I first met Phil Klass, I was President of SFWA; which probably explains why he wanted me to lecture to his classes. I arrived early, and sat in on his creative writing seminar; and I can testify that, unlike most professors of English, Dr. Klass keeps the bull puckey to a minimum. His students are fortunate; there are not many teachers so universally respected for their writing abilities.

This story is a classic. Of course, almost *all* of William Tenn's stories are classics.

THE LIBERATION OF EARTH

by William Tenn

This, then, is the story of our liberation. Suck air and grab clusters. Heigh-ho, here is the tale.

August was the month, a Tuesday in August. These words are meaningless now, so far have we progressed; but many things known and discussed by our primitive ancestors, our unliberated, unreconstructed forefathers, are devoid of sense to our free minds. Still the tale must be told, with all of its incredible place names and vanished points of reference.

Why must it be told? Have any of you a *better* thing to do? We have had water and weeds and lie in a valley of gusts. So rest, relax and listen. And suck air, suck air.

On a Tuesday in August, the ship appeared in the sky over France in a part of the world then known as Europe. Five miles long the ship was, and word has come down to us that it looked like an enormous silver cigar.

The tale goes on to tell of the panic and consternation among our forefathers when the ship abruptly materialized in the summer-blue sky. How they ran, how they shouted, how they pointed!

How they excitedly notified the United Nations, one of their chiefest institutions, that a strange metal craft of incredible size had materialized over their land. How they sent an order *here* to cause military aircraft to surround it with loaded weapons, gave instructions *there* for hastily grouped scientists, with signaling apparatus, to approach it with friendly gestures. How, under the great ship, men with cameras took pictures of it; men with typewriters wrote stories about it; and men with concessions sold models of it.

All these things did our ancestors, enslaved and unknowing, do.

Then a tremendous slab snapped up in the middle of the ship and the first of the aliens stepped out in the complex tripodal gait that all humans were shortly to know and love so well. He wore a metallic garment to protect him from the effects of our atmospheric peculiarities, a garment of the opaque, loosely folded type that these, the first of our liberators, wore throughout their stay on Earth.

Speaking in a language none could understand, but booming deafeningly through a huge mouth about halfway up his twenty-five feet of height, the alien discoursed for exactly one hour, waited politely for a response when he had finished, and, receiving none, retired into the ship.

That night, the first of our liberation! Or the first of our first liberation, should I say? *That* night, anyhow! Visualize our ancestors scurrying about their primitive intricacies: playing ice hockey, televising, smashing atoms, red-baiting, conducting giveaway shows and signing affidavits—all the incredible minutiae that made the olden times such a frightful mass of cumulative detail in which to live—as compared with the breathless and majestic simplicity of the present.

The big question, of course, was—what had the alien said? Had he called on the human race to surrender? Had he announced that he was on a mission of peaceful trade and, having made what he considered a reasonable offer—for, let us say, the north polar ice cap—politely withdrawn so that we could discuss his terms among ourselves in relative privacy? Or, possibly, had he merely announced that he was the newly appointed ambassador to Earth from a friendly and intelligent race—and would we please direct him to the proper authority so that he might submit his credentials?

Not to know was quite maddening.

Since decision rested with the diplomats, it was the last possibility which was held, very late that night, to be most likely; and early the next morning, accordingly, a delegation from the United Nations waited under the belly of the motionless starship. The delegation had been instructed to welcome the aliens to the outermost limits of its collective linguistic ability. As an additional earnest of mankind's friendly intentions, all military craft patrolling the air about the great ship were ordered to carry no more than one atom bomb in their racks, and to fly a small white flag—along with the U.N. banner and their own national emblem. Thus did our ancestors face this, the ultimate challenge of history.

When the alien came forth a few hours later, the delegation stepped up to him, bowed, and, in the three official languages of the United Nations—English, French and Russian—asked him to consider this planet his home. He listened to them gravely, and then launched into his talk of the day before—which was evidently as highly charged with emotion and significance to him as it was completely incomprehensible to the representatives of world government.

Fortunately, a cultivated young Indian member of the secretariat detected a suspicious similarity between the speech of the alien and an obscure Bengali dialect whose anomalies he had once puzzled over. The reason, as we all know now, was that the last time Earth had been visited by aliens of this particular type, humanity's most advanced civilization lay in a moist valley in Bengal; extensive dictionaries of that language had been written, so that speech with the natives of Earth would present no problem to any subsequent exploring party.

However, I move ahead of my tale, as one who would munch on the succulent roots before the dryer stem. Let me rest and suck air for a moment. Heigh-ho, truly those were tremendous experiences for our kind.

You, sir, now you sit back and listen. You are not yet of an age to Tell the Tale. I remember, *well enough do I remember* how my father told it, and his father before him. You will wait your turn as I did; you will listen until too much high land between water holes blocks me off from life.

Then *you* may take your place in the juiciest weed patch and, reclining gracefully between sprints, recite the great epic of our liberation to the carelessly exercising young.

Pursuant to the young Hindu's suggestions, the one professor of comparative linguistics in the world capable of understanding and conversing in this peculiar version of the dead dialect was summoned from an academic convention in New York where he was reading a paper he had been working on for eighteen years: *An Initial Study of Apparent Relationship Between Several Past Participles in Ancient Sanscrit and an Equal Number of Noun Substantives in Modern Szechuanese.*

Yea, verily, all these things—and more, many more—did

our ancestors in their besotted ignorance contrive to do. May we not count our freedoms indeed?

The disgruntled scholar, minus—as he kept insisting bitterly—some of his most essential word lists, was flown by fastest jet to the area south of Nancy which, in those long-ago days, lay in the enormous black shadow of the alien spaceship.

Here he was acquainted with his task by the United Nations delegation, whose nervousness had not been allayed by a new and disconcerting development. Several more aliens had emerged from the ship carrying great quantities of immense, shimmering metal which they proceeded to assemble into something that was obviously a machine—though it was taller than any skyscraper man had ever built, and seemed to make noises to itself like a talkative and sentient creature. The first alien still stood courteously in the neighborhood of the profusely perspiring diplomats; ever and anon he would go through his little speech again, in a language that had been almost forgotten when the cornerstone of the library of Alexandria was laid. The men from the U.N. would reply, each one hoping desperately to make up for the alien's lack of familiarity with his own tongue by such devices as hand gestures and facial expressions. Much later, a commission of anthropologists and psychologists brilliantly pointed out the difficulties of such physical, gestural communication with creatures possessing—as these aliens did—five manual appendages and a single, unwinking compound eye of the type the insects rejoice in.

The problems and agonies of the professor as he was trundled about the world in the wake of the aliens, trying to amass a usable vocabulary in a language whose peculiarities he could only extrapolate from the limited samples supplied him by one who must inevitably speak it with the most outlandish of foreign accents—these vexations were minor indeed compared to the disquiet felt by the representatives of world government. They beheld the extraterrestrial visitors move every day to a new site on their planet and proceed to assemble there a titanic structure of flickering metal which muttered nostalgically to itself, as if to keep alive the memory of those faraway factories which had given it birth.

True, there was always the alien who would pause in his evidently supervisory labors to release the set little speech; but not even the excellent manners he displayed, in listening to upward of fifty-six replies in as many languages, helped dispel the panic caused whenever a human scientist, investigating the shimmering machines, touched a projecting edge and promptly shrank into a disappearing pinpoint. This, while not a frequent occurrence, happened often enough to cause chronic indigestion and insomnia among human administrators.

Finally, having used up most of his nervous system as fuel, the professor collated enough of the language to make conversation possible. He—and, through him, the world—was thereupon told the following:

The aliens were members of a highly advanced civilization which had spread its culture throughout the entire galaxy. Cognizant of the limitations of the as yet underdeveloped animals who had latterly become dominant upon Earth, they had placed us in a sort of benevolent ostracism. Until either we or our institutions had evolved to a level permitting, say, at least *associate* membership in the galactic federation (under the sponsoring tutelage, for the first few millennia, of one of the older, more widespread and more important species in that federation)—until that time, all invasions of our privacy and ignorance—except for a few scientific expeditions conducted under conditions of great secrecy—had been strictly forbidden by universal agreement.

Several individuals who had violated this ruling—at great cost to our racial sanity, and enormous profit to our reigning religions—had been so promptly and severely punished that no known infringements had occurred for some time. Our recent growth curve had been satisfactory enough to cause hopes that a bare thirty or forty centuries more would suffice to place us on applicant status with the federation.

Unfortunately, the peoples of this stellar community were many, and varied as greatly in their ethical outlook as their biological composition. Quite a few species lagged a considerable social distance behind the Dendi, as our visitors called themselves. One of these, a race of horrible, wormlike organisms known as the Troxxt—almost as advanced technologically as they were retarded in moral development—had suddenly volunteered for the position of sole and absolute ruler of the galaxy. They had seized control of several key suns, with their attendant planetary systems, and, after a calculated decimation of the races thus captured, had announced their intention of punishing with a merciless extinction all species unable to appreciate from these object lessons the value of unconditional surrender.

In despair, the galactic federation had turned to the Dendi, one of the oldest, most selfless, and yet most powerful of races in civilized space, and commissioned them, as the military arm of the federation, to hunt down the Troxxt, defeat them wherever they had gained illegal suzerainty, and destroy forever their power to wage war.

This order had come almost too late. Everywhere the Troxxt had gained so much the advantage of attack, that the Dendi were able to contain them only by enormous sacrifice. For centuries now, the conflict had careened across our vast island universe. In the course of it, densely populated planets had been disintegrated; suns had been blasted into novae; and whole groups of stars ground into swirling cosmic dust.

A temporary stalemate had been reached a short while ago, and, reeling and breathless, both sides were using the lull to strengthen weak spots in their perimeter.

Thus, the Troxxt had finally moved into the till-then peaceful section of space that contained our solar system—among others. They were thoroughly uninterested in our tiny planet with its meager resources; nor did they care much for such celestial neighbors as Mars or Jupiter. They established their headquarters on a planet of Proxima Centauri, the star nearest our own sun, and proceeded to consolidate their offensive-defensive network between Rigel and Aldebaran. At this point in their explanation, the Dendi pointed out, the exigencies of interstellar strategy tended to become too complicated for anything but three-dimensional maps; let us here accept the simple statement, they suggested, that it became immediately vital for them to strike rapidly, and make the Troxxt position on Proxima Centauri untenable—

to establish a base inside their lines of communication.

The most likely spot for such a base was Earth.

The Dendi apologized profusely for intruding on our development, an intrusion which might cost us dear in our delicate developmental state. But, as they explained—in impeccable pre-Bengali—before their arrival we had, in effect, become (all unknowingly) a satrapy of the awful Troxxt. We could now consider ourselves liberated.

We thanked them much for that.

Besides, their leader pointed out proudly, the Dendi were engaged in a war for the sake of civilization itself, against an enemy so horrible, so obscene in its nature, and so utterly filthy in its practices, that it was unworthy of the label of intelligent life. They were fighting, not only for themselves, but for every loyal member of the galactic federation; for every small and helpless species; for every obscure race too weak to defend itself against a ravaging conqueror. Would humanity stand aloof from such a conflict?

There was just a slight bit of hesitation as the information was digested. Then: *"No!"* humanity roared back through such mass-communication media as television, newspapers, reverberating jungle drums, and mule-mounted backwoods messenger. *"We will not stand aloof! We will help you destroy this menace to the very fabric of civilization! Just tell us what you want us to do!"*

Well, nothing in particular, the aliens replied with some embarrassment. Possibly in a little while there might *be* something—*several* little things, in fact—which could be *quite* useful; but, for the moment, if we would concentrate on not getting in their way when they serviced their gunmounts, they would be very grateful, really. . . .

This reply tended to create a large amount of uncertainty among the two billion of Earth's human population. For several days afterward, there was a planetwide tendency— the legend has come down to us—of people failing to meet each other's eyes.

But then man rallied from this substantial blow to his pride. He would be useful, be it ever so humbly, to the race which had liberated him from potential subjugation by the

ineffably ugly Troxxt. For this, let us remember well our
ancestors! Let us hymn their sincere efforts amid their
ignorance!

All standing armies, all air and sea fleets, were reorgan-
ized into guard patrols around the Dendi weapons: no human
might approach within two miles of the murmuring machinery,
without a pass countersigned by the Dendi. Since they were
never known to sign such a pass during the entire period of
their stay on this planet, however, this loophole provision
was never exercised as far as is known; and the immediate neighborhood of the extraterrestrial weapons became
and remained henceforth wholesomely free of two-legged
creatures.

Cooperation with our liberators took precedence over all
other human activities. The order of the day was a slogan
first given voice by a Harvard professor of government in a
querulous radio round table on "Man's Place in a Somewhat
Overcivilized Universe."

"Let us forget our individual egos and collective conceits,"
the professor cried at one point. "Let us subordinate everything—to the end that the freedom of the solar system in
general, and Earth in particular, must and shall be preserved!"

Despite its mouth-filling qualities, this slogan was repeated
everywhere. Still, it was difficult sometimes to know exactly
what the Dendi wanted—partly because of the limited number of interpreters available to the heads of the various
sovereign states, and partly because of their leader's tendency to vanish into his ship after ambiguous and equivocal
statements, such as the curt admonition to "Evacuate
Washington!"

On that occasion, both the Secretary of State and the
American President perspired fearfully through five hours of
a July day in all the silk-hatted, stiff-collared, dark-suited
diplomatic regalia that the barbaric past demanded of political leaders who would deal with the representatives of another people. They waited and wilted beneath the enormous
ship—which no human had ever been invited to enter, despite the wistful hints constantly thrown out by university
professors and aeronautical designers—they waited patiently

and wetly for the Dendi leader to emerge and let them know whether he had meant the State of Washington or Washington, D.C.

The tale comes down to us at this point as a tale of glory. The capitol building taken apart in a few days, and set up almost intact in the foothills of the Rocky Mountains; the missing Archives, that were later to turn up in the children's room of a public library in Duluth, Iowa; the bottles of Potomac River water carefully borne westward and ceremoniously poured into the circular concrete ditch built around the President's mansion (from which unfortunately it was to evaporate within a week because of the relatively low humidity of the region)—all these are proud moments in the galactic history of our species, from which not even the later knowledge that the Dendi wished to build no gun site on the spot, nor even an ammunition dump, but merely a recreation hall for their troops, could remove any of the grandeur of our determined cooperation and most willing sacrifice.

There is no denying, however, that the ego of our race was greatly damaged by the discovery, in the course of a routine journalistic interview, that the aliens totaled no more powerful a group than a squad; and that their leader, instead of the great scientist and key military strategist that we might justifiably have expected the Galactic Federation to furnish for the protection of Terra, ranked as the interstellar equivalent of a buck sergeant.

That the President of the United States, the Commander-in-Chief of the Army and the Navy, had waited in such obeisant fashion upon a mere noncommissioned officer was hard for us to swallow; but that the impending Battle of Earth was to have a historical dignity only slightly higher than that of a patrol action was impossibly humiliating.

And then there was the matter of "lendi".

The aliens, while installing or servicing their planet-wide weapon system, would occasionally fling aside an evidently unusable fragment of the talking metal. Separated from the machine of which it had been a component, the substance seemed to lose all those qualities which were deleterious to mankind and retain several which were quite useful indeed.

For example, if a portion of the strange material was attached to any terrestial metal and insulated carefully from contact with other substances it would, in a few hours, itself become exactly the metal that it touched, whether that happened to be zinc, gold, or pure uranium.

This stuff—"lendi," men have heard the aliens call it—was shortly in frantic demand in an economy ruptured by constant and unexpected emptyings of its most important industrial centers.

Everywhere the aliens went, to and from their weapon sites, hordes of ragged humans stood chanting—well outside the two-mile limit—"Any lendi, Dendi?" All attempts by law enforcement agencies of the planet to put a stop to this shameless, wholesale begging were useless, especially since the Dendi themselves seemed to get some unexplainable pleasure out of scattering tiny pieces of lendi to the scrabbling multitude. When policemen and soldiery began to join the trampling, murderous dash to the corner of the meadows wherein had fallen the highly versatile and garrulous metal, governments gave up.

Mankind almost began to hope for the attack to come, so that it would be relieved of the festering consideration of its own patent inferiorities. A few of the more fanatically conservative among our ancestors probably even began to regret liberation.

They did, children; they did! Let us hope that these would-be troglodytes were among the very first to be dissolved and melted down by the red flameballs. One cannot, after all, turn one's back on progress!

Two days before the month of September was over, the aliens announced that they had detected activity upon one of the moons of Saturn. The Troxxt were evidently threading their treacherous way inward through the solar system. Considering their vicious and deceitful propensities, the Dendi warned, an attack from these wormlike monstrosities might be expected at any moment.

Few humans went to sleep as the night rolled up to and past the meridian on which they dwelt. Almost all eyes were lifted to a sky carefully denuded of clouds by watchful Dendi. There was a brisk trade in cheap telescopes and bits of smoked glass in some sections of the planet; while other portions experienced a substantial boom in spells and charms of the all-inclusive, or omnibus, variety.

The Troxxt attacked in three cylindrical black ships simultaneously; one in the southern hemisphere, and two in the northern. Great gouts of green flame roared out of their tiny craft; and everything touched by this imploded into a translucent, glasslike sand. No Dendi was hurt by these, however, and from each of the now-writhing gunmounts there bubbled forth a series of scarlet clouds which pursued the Troxxt hungrily, until forced by a dwindling velocity to fall back upon Earth.

Here they had an unhappy aftereffect. Any populated area into which these pale pink cloudlets chanced to fall was rapidly transformed into a cemetery—a cemetery, if the truth be told as it has been handed down to us, that had more the odor of the kitchen than the grave. The inhabitants of these unfortunate localities were subjected to enormous increases of temperature. Their skin reddened, then blackened; their hair and nails shriveled; their very flesh turned into liquid and boiled off their bones. Altogether a disagreeable way for one-tenth of the human race to die.

The only consolation was the capture of a black cylinder by one of the red clouds. When, as a result of this, it had turned white-hot and poured its substance down in the form of a metallic rainstorm, the two ships assaulting the northern hemisphere abruptly retreated to the asteroids into which the Dendi, because of severely limited numbers, steadfastly refused to pursue them.

In the next twenty-four hours the aliens—*resident* aliens, let us say—held conferences, made repairs to their weapons and commiserated with us. Humanity buried its dead. This last was a custom of our forefathers that was most worthy of note; and one that has not, of course, survived into modern times.

By the time the Troxxt returned, man was ready for them. He could not, unfortunately, stand to arms as he most ardently desired to do; but he could and did stand to optical instrument and conjurer's oration.

Once more the little red clouds burst joyfully into the upper reaches of the stratosphere; once more the green flames wailed and tore at the chattering spires of lendi; once more men died by the thousands in the boiling backwash of war. But this time, there was a slight difference: the green flames of the Troxxt abruptly changed color after the engagement had lasted three hours; they became darker, more bluish. And, as they did so, Dendi after Dendi collapsed at his station and died in convulsions.

The call for retreat was evidently sounded. The survivors fought their way to the tremendous ship in which they had come. With an explosion from her stern jets that blasted a red-hot furrow southward through France, and kicked Marseilles into the Mediterranean, the ship roared into space and fled home ignominiously.

Humanity steeled itself for the coming ordeal of horror under the Troxxt.

They were truly wormlike in form. As soon as the two night-black cylinders had landed, they strode from their ships, their tiny segmented bodies held off the ground by a complex harness supported by long and slender metal crutches. They erected a domelike fort around each ship—one in Australia and one in the Ukraine—captured the few courageous individuals who had ventured close to their landing sites, and disappeared back into the dark craft with their squirming prizes.

While some men drilled about nervously in the ancient military patterns, others pored anxiously over scientific texts and records pertaining to the visit of the Dendi, in the desperate hope of finding a way of preserving terrestrial independence against this ravening conqueror of the star-spattered galaxy.

And yet all this time, the human captives inside the artifically darkened spaceships (the Troxxt, having no eyes, not only had little use for light but the more sedentary individuals among them actually found such radiation disagreeable to their sensitive, unpigmented skins) were not being tortured for information—nor vivisected in the earnest quest of knowledge on a slightly higher level—but educated.

Educated in the Troxxtian language, that is.

True it was that a large number found themselves utterly inadequate for the task which the Troxxt had set them, and temporarily became servants to the more successful students. And another, albeit smaller, group developed various forms of frustration hysteria—ranging from mild unhappiness to complete catatonic depression—over the difficulties presented by a language whose every verb was irregular, and whose myriads of prepositions were formed by noun-adjective combinations derived from the subject of the previous sentence. But, eventually, eleven human beings were released, to blink madly in the sunlight as certified interpreters of Troxxt.

These liberators, it seemed, had never visited Bengal in the heyday of its millennia-past civilization.

Yes, these *liberators*. For the Troxxt had landed on the sixth day of the ancient, almost mythical month of October. And October the Sixth is, of course, the Holy Day of the Second Liberation. Let us remember, let us revere. (If only we could figure out which day it is on our calendar!)

The tale the interpreters told caused men to hang their heads in shame and gnash their teeth at the deception they had allowed the Dendi to practice upon them.

True, the Dendi had been commissioned by the Galactic Federation to hunt the Troxxt down and destroy them. This was largely because the Dendi *were* the Galactic Federation. One of the first intelligent arrivals on the interstellar scene, the huge creatures had organized a vast police force to protect them and their power against any contingency of revolt that might arise in the future. This police force was ostensibly a congress of all thinking life forms throughout the galaxy; actually, it was an efficient means of keeping them under rigid control.

Most species thus far discovered were docile and tractable, however; the Dendi had been ruling from time immemorial, said they—very well, then, let the Dendi continue to rule. Did it make that much difference?

But, throughout the centuries, opposition to the Dendi grew; and the nuclei of the opposition were the protoplasm-based creatures. What, in fact, had come to be known as the Protoplasmic League.

Though small in number, the creatures whose life cycles were derived from the chemical and physical properties of protoplasm varied greatly in size, structure, and specialization. A galactic community deriving the main wells of its power from them would be a dynamic instead of a static place, where extragalactic travel would be encouraged, instead of being inhibited, as it was at present because of Dendi fears of meeting a superior civilization. It would be a true democracy of species—a real biological republic—where all creatures of adequate intelligence and cultural development would enjoy a control of their destinies at present experienced by the silicon-based Dendi alone.

To this end, the Troxxt, the only important race which had steadfastly refused the complete surrender of armaments demanded of all members of the Federation, had been implored by a minor member of the Protoplasmic League to rescue it from the devastation which the Dendi intended to visit upon it, as punishment for an unlawful exploratory excursion outside the boundaries of the galaxy.

Faced with the determination of the Troxxt to defend their cousins in organic chemistry, and the suddenly aroused hostility of at least two-thirds of the interstellar peoples, the Dendi had summoned a rump meeting of the Galactic Council; declared a state of revolt in being; and proceeded to cement their disintegrating rule with the blasted life forces of a hundred worlds. The Troxxt, hopelessly outnumbered and outequipped, had been able to continue to struggle only because of the great ingenuity and selflessness of other members of the Protoplasmic League, who had risked extinction to supply them with newly developed secret weapons.

Hadn't we guessed the nature of the beast from the enormous precautions it had taken to prevent the exposure of any part of its body to the intensely corrosive atmosphere of Earth? Surely the seamless, barely translucent suits which our recent visitors had worn for every moment of their stay on our world should have made us suspect a body chemistry developed from complex silicon compounds rather than those of carbon?

Humanity hung its collective head and admitted that the suspicion had never occurred to it.

Well, the Troxxt admitted generously, we were extremely inexperienced and possibly a little too trusting. Put it down to that. Our naiveté, however costly to them, our liberators, would not be allowed to deprive us of that complete citizenship which the Troxxt were claiming as the birthright of all.

But as for our leaders, our probably corrupted, certainly irresponsible leaders. . . .

The first executions of U.N. officials, heads of states, and pre-Bengali interpreters as "Traitors to Protoplasm"—after some of the lengthiest and most nearly perfectly fair trials in the history of Earth—were held a week after G-J Day, the inspiring occasion on which, amidst gorgeous ceremonies, humanity was invited to join, first the Protoplasmic League and thence the New and Democratic Galactic Federation of All Species, All Races.

Nor was that all. Whereas the Dendi had contemptuously shoved us to one side as they went about their business of making our planet safe for tyranny, and had, in all probability, built special devices which made the very touch of their weapons fatal for us, the Troxxt—with the sincere friendliness which had made their name a byword for democracy and decency wherever living creatures came together among the stars—our Second Liberators, as we lovingly called them, actually *preferred* to have us help them with the intensive, accelerating labor of planetary defense.

So men's intestines dissolved under the invisible glare of the forces used to assemble the new, incredibly complex weapons; men sickened and died, in scrabbling hordes, inside the mines which the Troxxt had made deeper than any we had dug hitherto; men's bodies broke open and exploded in the undersea oil-drilling sites which the Troxxt had declared were essential.

Children's schooldays were requested, too, in such collecting drives as "Platinum Scrap for Procyon" and "Radioactive Debris for Deneb." Housewives also were implored to save on salt whenever possible—this substance being useful to the Troxxt in literally dozens of incomprehensible ways—

and colorful posters reminded: *"Don't salinate—sugarfy!"*

And over all, courteously caring for us like an intelligent parent, were our mentors, taking their giant supervisory strides on metallic crutches, while their pale little bodies lay curled in the hammocks that swung from each paired length of shining leg.

Truly, even in the midst of a complete economic paralysis caused by the concentration of all major productive facilities on otherworldly armaments, and despite the anguished cries of those suffering from peculiar industrial injuries which our medical men were totally unequipped to handle, in the midst of all this mind-wracking disorganization, it was yet very exhilarating to realize that we had taken our lawful place in the future government of the galaxy and were even now helping to make the universe safe for democracy.

But the Dendi returned to smash this idyll. They came in their huge, silvery spaceships and the Troxxt, barely warned in time, just managed to rally under the blow and fight back in kind. Even so, the Troxxt ship in the Ukraine was almost immediately forced to flee to its base in the depths of space. After three days, the only Troxxt on Earth were the devoted members of a little band guarding the ship in Australia. They proved, in three or more months, to be as difficult to remove from the face of our planet as the continent itself; and since there was now a state of close and hostile siege, with the Dendi on one side of the globe, and the Troxxt on the other, the battle assumed frightful proportions.

Seas boiled; whole steppes burned away; the climate itself shifted and changed under the gruelling pressure of the cataclysm. By the time the Dendi solved the problem, the planet Venus had been blasted from the skies in the course of a complicated battle maneuver, and Earth had wobbled over as orbital substitute.

The solution was simple: since the Troxxt were too firmly based on the small continent to be driven away, the numerically superior Dendi brought up enough firepower to disintegrate all Australia into an ash that muddied the Pacific. This occurred on the twenty-fourth of June, the Holy Day of First

Reliberation. A day of reckoning for what remained of the human race, however.

How could we have been so naive, the Dendi wanted to know, as to be taken in by the chauvinistic pro-protoplasm propaganda? Surely, if physical characteristics were to be the criteria for our racial empathy, we would not orient ourselves on a narrow chemical basis! The Dendi life plasma was based on silicon instead of carbon, true, but did not vertebrates— *appendaged* vertebrates, at that, such as we and the Dendi— have infinitely more in common, in spite of a *minor* biochemical difference or two, than vertebrates and legless, armless, slime-crawling creatures who happened, quite accidentally, to possess an identical organic substance?

As for this fantastic picture of life in the galaxy . . . *well!* The Dendi shrugged their quintuple shoulders as they went about the intricate business of erecting their noisy weapons all over the rubble of our planet. Had we ever seen a representative of these protoplasmic races the Troxxt were supposedly protecting? No, nor would we. For as soon as a race—animal, vegetable or mineral—developed enough to constitute even a *potential* danger to the sinuous aggressors, its civilization was systematically dismantled by the watchful Troxxt. We were in so primitive a state that they had not considered it at all risky to allow us the outward seeming of full participation.

Could we say we had learned a single useful piece of information about Troxxt technology, for all of the work we had done on their machines, for all of the lives we had lost in the process? No, of course not! We had merely contributed our mite to the enslavement of far-off races who had done us no harm.

There was much that we had cause to feel guilty about, the Dendi told us gravely—once the few surviving interpreters of the pre-Bengali dialect had crawled out of hiding. But our collective onus was as nothing compared to that borne by "vermicular collaborationists"—those traitors who had supplanted our martyred former leaders. And then there were the unspeakable human interpreters who had had linguistic traffic with creatures destroying a two-million-year-old galactic peace! Why, killing was almost too good for them, the Dendi murmured as they killed them.

When the Troxxt ripped their way back into possession of Earth some eighteen months later, bringing us the sweet fruits of the Second Reliberation—as well as a complete and most convincing rebuttal of the Dendi—there were few humans found who were willing to accept with any real enthusiasm the responsibilities of newly opened and highly paid positions in language, science, and government.

Of course, since the Troxxt, in order to reliberate Earth, had found it necessary to blast a tremendous chunk out of the northern hemisphere, there were very few humans to be found in the first place. . . .

Even so, many of these committed suicide rather than assume the title of Secretary General of the United Nations when the Dendi came back for the glorious Re-Reliberation, a short time after that. This was the liberation, by the way, which swept the deep collar of matter off our planet, and gave it what our forefathers came to call a pear-shaped look.

Possibly it was at this time—possibly a liberation or so later—that the Troxxt and the Dendi discovered the Earth had become far too eccentric in its orbit to possess the minimum safety conditions demanded of a combat zone. The battle, therefore, zigzagged coruscatingly and murderously away in the direction of Aldebaran.

That was nine generations ago, but the tale that has been handed down from parent to child, to child's child, has lost little in the telling. You hear it now from me almost exactly as *I* heard it. From my father I heard it as I ran with him from water puddle to distant water puddle, across the searing heat of yellow sand. From my mother I heard it as we sucked air and frantically grabbed at clusters of thick green weed, whenever the planet beneath us quivered in omen of a geological spasm that might bury us in its burned-out body, or a cosmic gyration threatened to fling us into empty space.

Yes, even as we do now did we do then, telling the same tale, running the same frantic race across miles of unendurable heat for food and water; fighting the same savage battles with the giant rabbits for each other's carrion—and always, ever and always, sucking desperately at the precious air, which leaves our world in greater quantities with every mad twist of its orbit.

Naked, hungry, and thirsty came we into the world, and naked, hungry, and thirsty do we scamper our lives out upon it, under the huge and never-changing sun.

The same tale it is, and the same traditional ending it has as that I had from my father and his father before him. Suck air, grab clusters, and hear the last holy observation of our history:

"Looking about us, we can say with pardonable pride that we have been about as thoroughly liberated as it is possible for a race and planet to be!"

SIERRA MAESTRA

As I write this, Norman Spinrad is President of Science Fiction Writers of America, usually called SFWA and pronounced Sef-Wah. Years ago, when I was SFWA President, Norman was my Vice President. He lived about a mile up the hill from me, and we often discussed writers' business over breakfast.

Norman has been called a "radical," "a typical product of the '60s Revolution"; and certainly he has often enough been accepted by those who obviously deserve the labels. Yet Norman doesn't really belong to the radicals any more than I truly belong to the conservatives. We both have the same problem: "Our" groups do not feel entirely comfortable with us, nor we with them.

"Sierra Maestra" is a story of revolutionaries.

Revolution is generally put forward as freedom's servant; it is in the name of freedom that most revolutions are launched. The historical evidence is that liberty is seldom well served by that dangerous ally. It would be difficult to imagine a czarist regime with fewer liberties than are today enjoyed by subjects of the Soviet Union. Castro's socialist Cuba has all the corruption of the Batista regime, plus the dubious pleasures of a resident foreign army and an efficient secret police. One doubts that the Iraqis are objectively better off with the Baathists than with their tribal kings, or that caliphs masquerading as ayatollahs have increased the sum of liberty in Iran.

Yet revolution attracts those who think they love liberty. The evidence may be that revolutions more often devour their makers than reward them; that when they do not, it is only because the revolutionaries have—for the noblest of motives, of course—become worse tyrants than the regime they replaced. But hope springs eternal; and besides, revolution is the policy of despair, the desperate measure undertaken because nothing else will work. How many Americans, faced with taxes and laws and endless delays in court, building permits and drug laws, currency restrictions and banking regulations and all the endless machinery of the modern state have never—if only for a moment—wished to see even this benign regime fall in blood?

"Sierra Maestra" tells of a different sort of revolutionary; about Flower People only a few hours from seizing power, not by bloody revolution, but by careful manipulation of The System.

But at what price? What are the costs of thirty years of political evolution, of wearing a public mask that every day becomes more and more a part of you; of decades of deception? Can one hold one's idealism in the face of the utter pain of Society's rejection?

The Bourbons, restored to the throne of France after Napoleon, are said "to have learned nothing and forgotten nothing." Spinrad's revolutionaries, after forty and more years of plotting, have power within their grasp; and they have learned much.

Unfortunately, they remember things best forgotten. Freedom will not prosper under their regime, though they seize power in the name of liberty. . . .

SIERRA MAESTRA

by Norman Spinrad

Sitting here on my mountaintop watching their world crumble, I feel, at this advanced age, neither elation nor remorse, only the entropic force of history following its inexorable course. Did Fidel Castro feel thus watching the Batista regime sagging into decay from its own weight from his remote stronghold in the Sierra Maestra? I doubt it, for Fidel was a much younger man and those were much younger days, when revolution was a word we all took seriously and literally. But de Gaulle, waiting in haughty isolation as the Fourth Republic slowly collapsed toward his inevitability, and Juan Peron, watching Argentina flounder in the vacuum of his long, long exile, I think, would both have appreciated the irony of what I feel as this night slowly falls.

Far below me, Central Park is an oblong island of darkness in the pattern of lights that still covers most of Manhattan, a foreflash of what is soon to come. Even now, I can see the blackout rolling up the West Side from 34th Street to 59th, and the searchlight beam of a police helicopter probing the dark and empty streets for the creatures of night. It is all too easy to fantasize guerrilla armies marshaling in the secret shrubbery of permanently blacked-out Central Park, battalions of legendary muggers imbued with revolutionary consciousness at last.

But such fantasies are for the police, peering down from their helicopters into the shadows. In truth, the muggers are long since gone from the Park for lack of victims mad enough to brave the blackout, deprived of prey by the power of their own mystique. It is even possible to sympathize with them; in the early days of the blackout there must have been a time when they lurked behind their bushes fondling their saps forlornly like Indians hopelessly awaiting the return of the buffalo.

Automatic weapons fire crackles and sparkles for a few moments over the mid-40s and helicopters begin to converge. Watching the beams of their searchlights and listening to the ominous whunk-whunk of their rotors from my penthouse balcony, I feel a surge of adrenaline course through my old arteries, and it is easy to imagine this as the opening rounds of long-awaited Armageddon. But the firing is over before this fantasy can even take shape—just a routine patrol taking pot-shots at suspected looters in the free-fire zone.

I take a last private toke from my joint, fling the still burning butt over the parapet, and watch the glowing ember fall thirty stories into the darkness. "Roaches," we used to call them in the old days when pot was illegal and the smoking of it therefore a sacrament, a tiny act of revolution. In that sense, perhaps, the legalization of marijuana may be seen as the last act of true political cunning of which our enemies were capable, the final co-option. Now, of course, they are no longer capable of even being our enemies—we all become allies of necessity against entropy in the end. How

foolish it seems, to have waged such a protracted and debilitating struggle over the THC molecule. But then, haven't
men fought longer and deadlier wars over pure symbols like
the cross, or even the interpretation of random snatches of
scripture, while the true enemy of us all cackles up there in
the vacuum?

The burning ember, like its half-forgotten symbolic import,
disappears into the arms of darkness, and I finally turn and
walk back into my chambers to confront those who have
gathered at my bidding. How spiderlike that thought seems
as I think it. How spiderlike we have become in our long
secret sojourn in the Sierra Maestra of the soul. Have we
finally made ourselves unfit to wield power by the very
process we have put ourselves through in order to ensnare it?
I smile ruefully and feel more at peace as I encompass the
reality of this moral doubt, for only when those who wield
power maintain a healthy fear of being wielded by it may
justice yet live.

As I walk into the plushness of my huge living room and
see those who have gathered there, I am suddenly struck by
the unpleasant realization that we all have become old and
we all have become rich. In the old days, we feared the one
and at least professed to eschew the other. But we chose long
ago not merely to survive but to attempt to prevail. To
accumulate power without spending it is to accumulate money,
and to acquire wisdom and patience means accumulating
years. So here we are, heirs and paladins of what began
decades ago as a "youthful rebellion" about to come into our
own as graybeards and elder statesmen. We believed in those
days that no one our present age was to be trusted; hopefully
this lesson has been deepened and enriched by irony, rather
than unlearned. If we can be rulers who do not trust ourselves, America may yet be salvaged.

"Heavy thoughts?" Sandra says. Once, in Berkeley, in the
flush of the '60s, we were lovers, and once again, longer
and deeper, in the '80s. In the wrinkled parchment of her
face, I can see the young girl inside her, and the full blossom
of her beauty in middle years. I have loved them both and
some part of me loves them still.

"We've become the people we warned ourselves about," I say, blunting the edge with slyness. "Old fogies conspiring to rule the world from a penthouse. Senators, Congresspeople, capitalists and media barons."

She laughs her bright changeless laugh as we walk across the room to the square of sofas where the others are waiting, and it drives the shadows from my mind. Long ago, she was with me when we so solemnly dedicated our lives to changing the world by next week, and later we were together once more when the Compact was made and we all went our long-term temporary ways to infiltrate by osmosis. Always that laughter made me sing inside, and now I suddenly decide that when the inevitable occurs, Sandra will be with me again, as my Vice-President. Thus do we decide high policy, and why not, it is part of what makes us who we are. We shall be a government not of laws but of living, feeling men and women, a government not of structures but of souls. Still, I cannot help but feel the shade of Juan Peron smirking knowingly over my shoulder in this moment.

As Sandra and I seat ourselves together, I feel the eyes of the others following my movements with a new and disquieting expectancy, as if I am already a figure in some historical diorama, and it seems as if I can already feel the leaden mantle of state falling upon me. Fear comes over me, a ghastly sort of loneliness, a pall of isolation descending. And I resolve that as President I will walk the streets and eat in the restaurants like an ordinary citizen. Better to risk assassins' bullets than this terrifying and certain distancing, this death-in-life. It will be called bravado. Only I will know that it is fear.

"*Mr. President,*" Bart Lorenzi says with gentle sarcasm, and the rest smile. This is as close to a vote as we are prone to come. We have known each other, our destinies and our trajectories, for so long that nothing beyond this is necessary. We are like a family, each with his role, each with his place.

"Aren't you being a bit premature?" I say archly, and at this we all laugh together, for the pattern that has brought us to this moment is decades old, built slowly and carefully like a stone cathedral, no hot-blooded coup d'etat.

As medieval architects drew up plans for cathedrals whose completion they would never live to see, so did we draw up the Compact and assign ourselves our eventual positions in the completed structure according to our inclinations and opportunities. Bart Lorenzi to become our banking baron, financier of industries and minor governments, intimate of the Gnomes of Zurich. Eric Winshell to move slowly up in the hierarchy of the State Department into his present position. Warren Hinckly to build Ecomotors General. Ted Davies to ascend to the Joint Chiefs of Staff. Sandra, Lillian Margulies, Julian Clay, Fred Banyan, Roger Pulaski to cautiously, quietly, and carefully move upward through the conventional political processes until now we have a Chairman of the House Ways and Means Committee, Senators and Representatives of high seniority and Sandra as Speaker of the House.

All of us accumulating subordinates and allies personally loyal to us on our way up, secreting them into the interstices of government, finance, industry, and the military, furthering their careers discreetly as best we could, until now the score of people in this room represent the tip of an enormous iceberg. Not a conspiracy, but an infinitely subtle web of personal loyalties, shared consciousness, common goals, and yes, love.

And I too was chosen for my distant destiny long decades ago. In a sense, I have been running unsuccessfully for the Presidency for a quarter of a century—first almost as a national joke; then as a visionary from my secure Senate seat, accumulating weight and solidity; now, finally, as a remote elder statesman whose old prophecies have long since come to pass, whose far-out and impractical proposals are now seen by the millions as the right roads not taken in the easy clarity of failure's hindsight.

No, there is nothing like prematurity here.

Roger swirls his glass of bourbon, cubes of ice tinkling against the glass, talisman of long years cultivating friendships with southern Senators. "Just got the word from the White House. The Vice-President's letter of resignation has arrived. Your appointment to succeed him will be announced tomorrow morning."

I nod. Even this endgame strategy has been planned for decades. The Agnew resignation and the Nixon resignation pointed the way back in the '70s. The Vice-President resigns or is removed, the choice of a new Vice-President is forced upon the President, he is confirmed by Congress, then the President resigns. Technically, all that is required is Congressional acquiescence to the choice of an incumbent President and the necessary leverage on two men. And Constitutionality is scrupulously maintained. In the beginning this did not seem important to us, but now the decades have taught us the wisdom of remaining within the Constitutional framework. Once the Constitution is successfully breached, the entire document is destroyed and we become a nation of tooth and claw. I shall not play Ceasar to our republic.

"Do you expect any trouble in the Senate?" Sandra asks.

Roger shakes his head. "We've had the votes for a long time. Sanderman may try a filibuster, but I think we have the votes for a quick cloture too."

"Sanderman won't try it," Bart says authoritatively. "I've bought up his notes on that Coastal Island development and he's been made to understand his position."

"It's all in place," Julian says.

The words are like the final stone placed at the top of the last cathedral arch. The coup—and I might as well admit to myself that it *is* a coup d'etat, albeit a Constitutional coup—is but the mechanism for bringing about the technical transfer of power, for midwiving the inevitability we have engineered. For catching the ripe fruit dropping from the tree of history, if one prefers a more dialectical viewpoint.

I turn to Katherine Broxon, publisher of *Time* since Bart acquired it for us seven years ago, and cock an inquisitive eyebrow. "We're printing already. The cover story on the President hinting at his failing health. He'll be able to step aside gracefully."

"No problems with recognition," Eric says. "Even the Japanese will be relieved to have you in office. At least for the time being."

"The polls?"

"It'll be one big sigh of national relief," Katherine says. "The people don't want to wait till the next election. The mood is that they've waited too long already."

I relax against the plush piling of the couch. In addition to a Constitutional coup, we are going to have a democratically approved coup like the return of de Gaulle in '58 or that of Peron in '74. The people are bone-weary of economic depression, fading electrical power, unemployment, permanent inflation, protein starvation, and a government that can only throw up its hands and admit its helplessness. Like a hard granite boulder buried under geological layers of soft sandstone, we bided our time, content to merely endure until the inevitable forces of erosion ate away the strata around us. Until now we stand alone on the desolate plain, the only rock to cleave to. Until even our former enemies turn to us in despair.

I look slowly around the room, each face in turn, confronting each pair of eyes like tunnels through time, seeing beyond the gray hair, the tapestries of wrinkles, the succession of personas we have assumed down the decades, to the changeless essences within. Or changeless they seem from this strange perspective crosswise in time. Are we not the same beings whose eyes met in this same soul-to-soul contact so many years ago when the communal organism that we have become was given birth? In the long-gone terminology of the '60s, have we not remained forever young?

But why do I feel this blossoming of dread, this void unfolding the cold petals of its flower within me? Why do their eyes seem to recede down long stone corridors of perspective, why does my own living room seem like an immense cavern of millennial gloom rimed with the mineral accretions of ages?

I rise from the couch and I can feel the creakiness of my knees, the softness of my internal organs, and my head is like some great hollow globe tottering atop a fleshy structure grown too frail to support it.

"I think I'd like to be alone for a bit," I say, and the simple sentence sounds ridiculously theatrical as my mouth moves around the words; my movements seem exaggeratedly slow and fluid, pregnant with meaning, as I walk across the soft carpet toward the balcony. Images out of films and history books pile up in my mind as I walk—Mussolini stepping out on his balcony to bask in the cheering of the masses. Imperial Ceasars accepting homage. John Kennedy walking down a lonely beach with head bowed, white smoke rising over the Vatican and a sepulchral voice intoning, *"Habemus Papum."*

But when I emerge onto my balcony, there is no sudden ovation, no waiting crowd; nothing greets me but the night. The blackout has spread itself over Manhattan now, only rectilinear islands of light remain in a sparse checkerboard pattern, and to the south the giant buildings of midtown are a cruel and jagged cordillera of dark mountains against a sky in which faint stars shine like the dying lights of America's faded glory far below. Police helicopters whunk-whunk over the somnolent city like carrion flies buzzing around a bonepile, their white searchlight beams moving like ghostly fingers over the empty streets. It is a scene, a moment, of utter loneliness, unfit for the eye of man.

I light another joint, take a tiny puff, and let it glow between my fingers as a candle against the darkness. I force myself to think of the future, of the weeks and months to come, of the "steps that must be taken," as the news magazines will phrase it. Bart will announce the forgiveness of the government notes he has bought up by stealth, nearly a quarter of the National Debt, and that will give the dollar a stability it has not had in decades. But banks will fall like Southeast Asian dominoes and the financial community will scream in rage. The hundred percent tax on profits in excess of ten percent will move the GNP toward full employment stasis, but industrialists and stockholders will fly into a fury as the stock market plummets, perhaps into oblivion. The ban on even private electric cars will hit the ordinary citizen in his pocketbook and his psyche, even though their largest manufacturer, Ecomotors General, will patriotically urge support of the move in the national interest. The food export quotas will make America an object of loathing in Asia and

Africa. It is going to get so much darker before the dawn.
I am going to be a hated man.

This first cold realization squeezes my heart like a fist. No
souls will sing at the sound of my name, no voices will cheer
my motorcade. The transformation will be a decade in the
making; I have always known it, but now I feel it in the
hollow places of my brittle bones. I will not see the lights
come on again, I will not taste the freshened air. I will not see
the food factories churning out their endless bounty. I will
never bask in the love of the people. I will be cursed and
reviled and assassins will mutter my name as they oil their
guns in secret cellars. One day a bullet will burst in my
brain, *sic semper tyrannis.*

I look out over the spectral city and doubt creeps into my
soul. What if we were wrong? What if we have let too much
history slip by as we waited in our Sierra Maestra for the day
of vindication to arrive? What if it is too late; perhaps
entropy has already won its final victory while we husbanded
and conserved our lives and substances to no avail. Perhaps
we should have risked all in hot-blooded revolution and died
in fire rather than ice. We chose and we became that which
we had chosen. Now as we come into our own, we have no
choices left. I am one with the inevitability of history and I
will never know whether for good or ill.

Nor will I be granted even the luxury of sharing my doubts,
for now I must become a man of iron, a monument of stone,
an icon of the certainty I can no longer feel. A current of wind
whistles around my parapet. It is so cold and lonely up here
on the mountaintop.

"Why is this night different from all other nights?" Sandra
has come out onto the balcony beside me. I do not look at her.
I do not have to, I can feel her presence with me; with me yet
apart, for now even she will forever be distanced from me by
the geometries of state. This is what we must share in this
final phase, this is the dowry of our last affair.

I force a laugh, and an advertising jingle from the long-
gone '60s. "We've come a long way, baby, to get where we're
going today."

"A little afraid?" she says softly.

I nod. "And lonely." I suck on the joint and hand it to her. Let this cup pass from me, I think, knowing all too well that it will not. "This is as good a time as any to tell you," I say, grateful to move on to matters of state, already hiding myself in the machineries of power. "You're going to be my Vice-President." I allow her no choice, no pro forma gesture of refusal, as none has been allowed to me.

We turn to each other. She merely nods. There is no surprise, no false disclaimers, thank God. Our eyes meet over a distance that suddenly has widened. We take each other's hands and squeeze old warm flesh.

"It's getting chilly out here," she says, turning to face the lights of the living room where the others wait with questions of cabinet posts and policy, with the eagerness of history waiting to be born.

I nod. "We've got to watch our health now," I say. "We're not as young as we used to be."

Hand in hand, our old bones creaking, we begin the march down from the Sierra Maestra, we descend from our mountain fastness to parade into the cities below.

Editor's Introduction To:

LOVE IS NOT ENOUGH and WHY ANARCHY?

Most radicals want revolution; and revolutionaries want to rule. However, there is an exception; a most profoundly radical group which wants neither revolution nor power.

Any book on freedom must include the views of the anarchists. "But where," one may ask, "are we to find articulate anarchists?" The very word conjures up images of small dark-bearded men carrying round bombs complete with sputtering fuses.

Several years ago I was asked to make a speech about the space program. I'm often asked to give lectures, so there was nothing unusual about this occasion except that the sponsors seemed more than usually inclined to haggle about the fee. It turned out to be a Libertarian gathering.

After my lecture I fell into conversation with an annoyingly argumentative young man. He was clean-shaven and well dressed, and almost frighteningly competent. An audience gathered, and I found myself in the debate of my life.

A few years later it happened again. Following a meeting of the Los Angeles Science Fantasy Society I sat in the Club Room and fell into a conversation which soon became a debate; it was the same opponent as before, and once again an audience gathered. This time, at least, I knew who I was facing. The argument continued until we were both exhausted, about 3:00 A.M.

In both cases I argued the case for the space program. My opponent conceded the value of space, but argued that if we did not go to space under private financing, we ought not go at all.

Thus did I meet Dr. David Friedman, who speaks—and speaks persuasively—for anarcho-capitalism.

The views of the modern anarchist are easy to parody. "They want to sell the army," someone says; and everyone laughs. "No, that can't be right," another says. Then it transpires that they *do* want to sell the army, or at least hire private groups to perform its functions; and the laughter begins again.

Yet whatever their position may be, it is not absurd. We live in a world made by ideas. We live in a world half enslaved by a utopian dream described by Marx and Engels, a dream proved over and over again to be impossible of realization—and we call the anarchists impractical? Certainly their utopia seems more attractive than the reality of the Gulag.

The libertarian and anarchist views of freedom are easy to state: they truly believe that the only reason one man ever has a moral right to interfere with another is as an act of defense. Moreover, they find property rights to be as fundamental as any other human rights; if one cannot enjoy one's property in whatever way one wishes (subject to the restriction that I do not interfere with *your* liberties) then how can one be said to be free?

I recently had occasion to reflect on this. My office is simply too small. My books have done well lately, well enough that I have sufficient money to build an addition; and since I spend a good part of my life in this room, what better way to spend my money? So I engaged an architect.

Three months and one thousand dollars later, I have no addition to my office; but I do have a small piece of paper from the City of Los Angeles granting me permission to build a 12-by-12-foot addition onto my own house. Query: What business is it of theirs? (I long ago presented the city with a petition signed by every one of my neighbors stating that *they* didn't care if I used up part of my front yard.)

The city granted me the permit with one condition: that in *every* hallway and bedroom of my house I install smoke detectors.

Sometimes the anarchist position seems eminently reasonable.

LOVE IS NOT ENOUGH

by David Friedman

In more and more cases . . . politics and politicians not
only contribute to the problem. They are the problem.
—John Shuttleworth, *The Mother Earth News*

One common objection to private property is that it is an
immoral system because it relies on selfishness. This is
wrong. Most people define *selfishness* as an attitude of caring
only for oneself and considering other people's welfare of no
importance. The argument for private property does not
depend on people having such an attitude; it depends only on
different people having different ends and pursuing them.
Each person is selfish only in the sense of accepting and
following his own perception of reality, his own vision of the
good.

This objection is also wrong because it poses false alternatives. Under any institutions, there are essentially only three
ways that I can get another person to help me achieve my
ends: love, trade, and force.

By love I mean making my end your end. Those who love
me wish me to get what I want (except for those who think I
am very stupid about what is good for me). So they voluntari-
ly, "unselfishly" help me. Love is too narrow a word. You
might also share my end, not because it is my end, but
because in a particular respect we perceive the good in the
same way. You might volunteer to work on my political
campaign, not because you love me, but because you think
that it would be good if I were elected. Of course, we might
share the common ends for entirely different reasons, I might
think I was just what the country needed, and you, that I was
just what the country deserved.

The second method of cooperation is trade. I agree to help
you achieve your end if you help me achieve mine.

The third method is force. You do what I want or I shoot
you.

Love—more generally, the sharing of a common end—works
well, but only for a limited range of problems. It is difficult to

99

know very many people well enough to love them. Love can provide cooperation on complicated things among very small groups of people, such as families. It also works among large numbers of people for very simple ends—ends so simple that many different people can completely agree on them. But for a complicated end involving a large number of people—producing this book, for instance—love will not work. I cannot expect all the people whose cooperation I need—typesetters, editors, bookstore owners, loggers, pulpmill workers, and a thousand more—to know and love me well enough to want to publish this book for my sake. Nor can I expect them all to agree with my political views closely enough to view the publication of this book as an end in itself. Nor can I expect them all to be people who want to read the book and who therefore are willing to help produce it. I fall back on the second method: trade.

I contribute the time and effort to produce the manuscript. I get, in exchange, a chance to spread my views, a satisfying boost to my ego, and a little money. The people who want to read the book get the book. In exchange, they give money. The publishing firm and its employees, the editors, give the time, effort, and skill necessary to coordinate the rest of us; they get money and reputation. Loggers, printers, and the like give their effort and skill and get money in return. Thousands of people, perhaps millions, cooperate in a single task, each seeking his own ends.

So, under private property the first method, love, is used where it is workable. Where it is not, trade is used instead.

The attack on private property as selfish contrasts the second method with the first. It implies that the alternative to "selfish" trade is "unselfish" love. But, under private property, love already functions where it can. Nobody is prevented from doing something for free if he wants to. Many people—parents helping their children, volunteer workers in hospitals, scoutmasters—do just that. If, for those things that people are not willing to do for free, trade is replaced by anything, it must be by force. Instead of people being selfish and doing things because they want to, they will be unselfish and do them at the point of a gun.

Is this accusation unfair? The alternative offered by those who deplore selfishness is always government. It is selfish to do something for money, so the slums should be cleaned up by a "youth corps" staffed via "universal service." Translated, that means the job should be done by people who will be put in jail if they do not do it.

A second objection often made to a system of private property is that resources may be misallocated. One man may starve while another has more food than he can eat. This is true, but it is true of any system of allocating resources. Whoever makes the decision may make a decision I consider wrong. We can, of course, set up a government bureau and instruct it to feed the hungry and clothe the naked. That does not mean they will be fed and clothed. At some point, some person or persons must decide who gets what. Political mechanisms, bureaus and bureaucrats, follow their own ends just as surely as individual entrepreneurs follow theirs.

If almost everyone is in favor of feeding the hungry, the politician may find it in his interest to do so. But, under those circumstances, the politician is unnecessary: some kind soul will give the hungry man a meal anyway. If the great majority is against the hungry man, some kind soul among the minority still may feed him—the politician will not.

There is no way to give a politician power that can only be used to do good. If he gives food to someone, he must take it from someone else; food does not appear from thin air. I know of only one occasion in modern peacetime history when large numbers of people starved, although food was available. It occurred under an economic system in which the decision of who "needed" food was made by the government. Joseph Stalin decided how much food was needed by the inhabitants of the Ukraine. What they did not "need" was seized by the Soviet government and shipped elsewhere. During the years 1932 and 1933, some millions of Ukrainians died of starvation. During each of those years, according to Soviet figures, the Soviet Union *exported* about 1.8 million tons of grain. If we accept a high figure for the number who starved—say, eight million—that grain would have provided about two thousand calories a day to each of them.

Yet there *is* something in the socialist's objection to capitalism's "misallocation," something with which I sympathize esthetically, if not economically.

Most of us believe in our hearts that there is only one good and that ideally everyone should pursue it. In a perfect centrally planned socialist state everyone is part of a hierarchy pursuing the same end. If that end is the one true good, that society will be perfect in a sense in which a capitalist society, where everyone pursues his own differing and imperfect perception of the good, cannot be. Since most socialists imagine a socialist government to be controlled by people very like themselves, they imagine that it will pursue the true good—the one that they, imperfectly, perceive. That is surely better than a chaotic system in which all sorts of people other than the socialists perceive all sorts of other goods and waste valuable resources chasing them. People who dream about a socialist society rarely consider the possibility that all those other people may succeed in imposing their ends on the dreamer, instead of the other way around. George Orwell is the only exception who comes to mind.

A third objection made to private property is that men are not really free as long as they need the use of other men's property to print their opinions and even to eat and drink. If I must either do what you tell me or starve, the sense in which I am free may be useful to a political philosopher, but it is not very useful to me.

That is true enough, but it is equally true of any system of public property—and much more important. It is far more likely that there will be one owner of all food if things are owned by governments than if they are owned by private individuals; there are so many fewer governments. Power is diminished when it is divided. If one man owns all the food, he can make me do almost anything. If it is divided among a hundred men, no one can make me do very much for it; if one tries, I can get a better deal from another.

WHY ANARCHY?

by David Friedman

No man's life, liberty or property are safe while the legisla-
ture is in session.   —quoted by Judge Gideon J. Tucker
of New York, c. 1866.

Many libertarians advocate not anarchy, but limited constitutional government. In my discussion of the public good
problem in national defense, I accepted their arguments to
the extent of conceding that there might be circumstances in
which voluntary institutions could not defend themselves
against a foreign state. Under such circumstances a limited
government might perform a useful function. The same public good argument applies, in varying degrees, to things other
than defense. Why, then, do I take as my objective a society of
completely voluntary institutions, of total private property?
Would it not be better to have a severely limited government
doing those few things which it could do better?

Perhaps it would be—if the government stayed that way.
One cannot simply build any imaginable characteristics into
a government; governments have their own internal dynamic.
And the internal dynamic of limited governments is something with which we, to our sorrow, have a good deal of
practical experience. It took about 150 years, starting with a
Bill of Rights that reserved to the states and the people all
powers not explicitly delegated to the federal government, to
produce a Supreme Court willing to rule that growing corn to
feed to your own hogs is interstate commerce and can therefore be regulated by Congress.

Suppose that a government is given the job of doing only
those things that cannot be done well privately because of the
public good problem. Someone, almost certainly the government, must decide what things those are. Practically every
economic activity has some element of public good. Writing
this book will not only benefit those who are entertained by
reading it; it will also, I hope, increase at least infinitesi-
mally the chance that I, and you, will live in an increasingly
free society. That is a public good; I cannot make America

free for me without making it free for you and even free for
people so benighted as not to have bought this book. Does
that mean that our ideal limited government should control
the publishing industry? My judgment is no; the element of
public good is small, and the costs of public control enormous.
The judgment of a government official, with his eye on power
and patronage, might be different.

The logic of limited governments is to grow. There are
obvious reasons for that in the nature of government, and
plenty of evidence. Constitutions provide, at the most, a
modest and temporary restraint. As Murray Rothbard is
supposed to have said, the idea of a limited government that
stays limited is truly utopian. Anarchy at least might work;
limited government has been tried.

Of course, one should ask the same questions about anarchist institutions. What is their internal dynamic? Will private protection agencies, once established, continue as private
profit-making concerns, or will they conclude that theft is
more profitable and become governments? Will the laws of
private arbitration agencies be just laws, allowing individuals to pursue their own affairs without interference, or will
they allow self-righteous majorities to impose their will on
the rest of us, as do many present laws? There is, after all, no
absolute guarantee that the laws of an anarchist society will
themselves be libertarian laws.

I remain a guarded optimist. Anarchist institutions cannot
prevent the members of a sufficiently large and impassioned
majority from forcing their prejudices into private law codes
and so imposing them on the rest of us. But they make it far
more difficult and expensive, and therefore more unlikely,
than under governmental institutions. Anarchist institutions
cannot guarantee that protectors will never become rulers,
but they decrease the power that protectors have separately
or together, and they put at the head of protection agencies
men who are less likely than politicians to regard theft as a
congenial profession.

For all these reasons I believe that anarchist institutions
if they can be estabished and maintained, will be better than
any government, even one initially limited and constitution-

al. I am perfectly willing to accept a slightly less than optimal production of a few public goods in exchange for the security of there being no government to expand into the 95 percent of human affairs where it can do nothing but damage. The ultimate objective of my political actions is not limited government: It is anarchy.

At this point another question is sometimes raised. We are a long way from the objective of a severely limited government and a longer way still from anarchy. Even if anarcho-capitalism is ideally a better system, is it not wise to focus on the more immediate goal of reducing the government and put off to the future any discussion of abolishing it?

I think not. It is important to know what road we must take, but it is also important to know where we want to go. If we are to understand our position ourselves and explain it to others, we must know what ultimately we want, not just what compromises we may be forced to accept.

I suspect that one reason for the enormous success of the socialist ideas of fifty and a hundred years ago—ideas which in many cases are the orthodoxy of today—was the willingness of socialists to be utopian. Their politics were Fabian, but their polemic was not. Their vision of an ultimate perfection was one of the most effective weapons in the practical struggle.

There are utopias and utopias. A utopia that will work only if populated by saints is a perilous vision; there are not enough saints. Such a vision—liberalism, socialism, call it what you will—we have followed; it has led us to where we now are.

I have not tried to construct a utopia in that sense. I have tried, to the best of my ability, to describe plausible institutions under which human beings not very different from ourselves could live. Those institutions must evolve over a period of time, as did the institutions under which we presently live; they cannot be instantly conjured up from the dreams of an enthusiastic young writer. The objective is distant but not necessarily unreachable; it is well to know where one is going before taking even the first step.

Editor's afterword to Friedman essays

It is sometimes said that anarchists are more concerned with property than with people. Not being an anarcho-capitalist, I am perhaps not qualified to respond; but I do have a story.

One evening not long ago I was showing Dr. Friedman my friend Ezekial, who happens to be a Cromemco Z-80 computer. As a part of the demonstration I caused Zeke to be linked with a major eastern university where I have an electronic mailbox. Some of my "mail" consisted of general announcements broadcast to everyone with accounts at that institution.

One group of announcements was particularly interesting: In the past few days there had been several burglaries of automobiles belonging to graduate students who worked late in the computer center. They would leave their cars in a lighted parking lot, only to return to find windows smashed and their stereos, CBs, and other valuta missing. A number of messages speculated on ways to deal with the situation; these included booby traps.

David Friedman instantly asked the following:

A man was sitting at home waiting to hear who had stolen his firewood. Weary of thefts of his wood, he had hollowed out one stick of wood and inserted dynamite. Now he waited to hear who had stolen his wood.

Question: Is this a legitimate use of his property?
Question: Does petty theft deserve death?
Question: Are these equivalent questions?

AMONG THIEVES

Poul Anderson is as good a friend as liberty ever had. Were he or his ilk kings of Earth, we were safe enough. Yet here he writes of heroes who do not live in freedom; indeed do not love liberty. He writes of the hard men and women who stand at the marches of civilization; of the "uniforms that guard you while you sleep."

Neither freedom nor civilization lives long without defenders. Throughout history the barbarians have waited, if not just outside the walls, then just beyond the horizon; and they wait for news that the Citizens cannot—or *will not*—defend themselves. Let that happen, and the walls will be taken in days.

And it happens. Lord knows it happens. Freedom is a fragile thing. History shows us no case of a wealthy republic which long endured. Wealth and freedom destroyed them all. The Citizens were not willing to turn out for their republic. Some disarmed. Others thought to hire mercenaries. Yet others put their trust in alliances and bribes. All fell, or became enslaved by their own armies; sometimes both happened.

We are a wealthy republic. As I write this, we cannot find sufficient sailors to man our fleets; and our fleets are as small as they have ever been since before World War II. We cannot find soldiers to maintain our complex electronic equipment; and we have little enough of the equipment anyway. The abortive raid into the Iranian desert destroyed over half our long-range heavy-lift helicopters. . . .

Meanwhile, the Secretary of Defense acknowledges that we are inferior in strategic weapons. Our land-based missile system is obsolete, and every B-52 pilot is younger than the airplane he flies. We have canceled the B-1 program, and as I write this, the best Washington can propose is the insane M-X system that will lay thousands of miles of road to be covered with trucks carrying missiles. Each missile is itself about a kiloton of chemical explosive—in addition to any nuclear warheads it may carry.

And we are to drive these about the countryside, playing a shell game and keeping secret from Soviet agents which sites have birds and which are empty.

(I recall in 1964 my unit was asked to evaluate the M-X shell-game concept; it took two days for the Pentagon to convince us we were not the victims of an elaborate joke designed to waste our time.)

Meanwhile, the total public debt of the United States is in excess of $6 trillion, with $650 billion of that being funded debt on which we must annually pay interest. The balance represents pensions, veteran's benefits, insurances, social security payments, and other obligations which cannot ethically be evaded even if tomorrow we abolish those programs. Our indebtedness is some twenty times the money supply; indeed, greater than the value of all public and private wealth combined.

Small wonder, then, that late at night Poul Anderson weeps for the next generation. "We have had it good, you and I," he says. "But I cry for our children."

For we have not been frugal. Whatever our proud history, our current generations have no great record of sacrifice for the republic; we have no great reason to believe this will change.

Republics which find no defenders do not survive.

AMONG THIEVES
by Poul Anderson

His Excellency M'Katze Unduma, Ambassador of the Terrestrial Federation to the Double Kingdom, was not accustomed to being kept waiting. But as the minutes dragged into an hour, anger faded before a chill deduction.

In this bleakly clock-bound society a short delay was bad manners, even if it were unintentional. But if you kept a man of rank cooling his heels for an entire sixty minutes, you offered him an unforgivable insult. Rusch was a barbarian, but he was too canny to humiliate Earth's representative without reason.

Which bore out everything that Terrestrial Intelligence

had discovered. From a drunken junior officer, weeping in his cups because Old Earth, Civilization, was going to be attacked and the campus where he had once learned and loved would be scorched to ruin by *his* fire guns—to the battle plans and annotations thereon, which six men had died to smuggle out of the Royal War College—and now, this degradation of the ambassador himself—everything fitted.

The Margrave of Drakenstane had sold out Civilization.

Unduma shuddered, beneath the iridescent cloak, embroidered robe, and ostrich-plume headdress of his rank. He swept the antechamber with the eyes of a trapped animal.

This castle was ancient, dating back some eight hundred years to the first settlement of Norstad. The grim square massiveness of it, fused stone piled into a turreted mountain, was not much relieved by modern fittings. Tableservs, loungers, drapes, jewel mosaics, and biomurals only clashed with those fortress walls and ringing flagstones; fluorosheets did not light up all the dark corners, there was perpetual dusk up among the rafters where the old battle banners hung.

A dozen guards were posted around the room, in breastplate and plumed helmet but with very modern blast rifles. They were identical seven-foot blonds, and none of them moved at all, you couldn't even see them breathe. It was an unnerving sight for a Civilized man.

Unduma snubbed out his cigar, swore miserably to himself, and wished he had at least brought along a book.

The inner door opened on noiseless hinges and a shavepate officer emerged. He clicked his heels and bowed at Unduma. "His Lordship will be honored to receive you now, excellency."

The ambassador throttled his anger, nodded, and stood up. He was a tall thin man, the relatively light skin and sharp features of Bantu stock predominant in him. Earth's emissaries were normally chosen to approximate a local ideal of beauty—hard to do for some of those weird little cultures scattered through the galaxy—and Norstad-Ostarik had been settled by a rather extreme Caucasoid type which had almost entirely emigrated from the home planet.

The aide showed him through the door and disappeared. Hans von Thoma Rusch, Margrave of Drakenstane, Lawman

of the Western Folkmote, Hereditary Guardian of the White
River Gates, et cetera, et cetera, et cetera, sat waiting behind
a desk at the end of an enormous black-and-red tile floor. He
had a book in his hands, and didn't close it till Unduma,
sandals whispering on the great chessboard squares, had
come near. Then he stood up and made a short ironic bow.

"How do you do, your excellency," he said. "I am sorry to be
so late. Please sit." Such curtness was no apology at all, and
both of them knew it.

Unduma lowered himself to a chair in front of the desk. He
would *not* show temper, he thought, he was here for a greater
purpose. His teeth clamped together.

"Thank you, your lordship," he said tonelessly. "I hope you
will have time to talk with me in some detail. I have come on
a matter of grave importance."

Rusch's right eyebrow tilted up, so that the archaic monocle he affected beneath it seemed in danger of falling out. He
was a big man, stiffly and solidly built, yellow hair cropped to
a wiry brush around the long skull, a scar puckering his left
cheek. He wore Army uniform, the gray high-collared tunic
and old-fashioned breeches and shiny boots of his planet; the
trident and suns of a primary general; a sidearm, its handle
worn smooth from much use. If ever the iron barbarian with
the iron brain had an epitome, thought Unduma, here he sat!

"Well, your excellency," murmured Rusch—though the
harsh Norron language did not lend itself to murmurs—"of
course I'll be glad to hear you out. But after all, I've no
standing in the Ministry, except as unofficial advisor, and—"

"Please." Unduma lifted a hand. "Must we keep up the
fable? You not only speak for all the landed warloads—and
the Nor-Samurai are still the most powerful single class in
the Double Kingdom—but you have the General Staff in your
pouch and, ah, you are well thought of by the royal family. I
think I can talk directly to you."

Rusch did not smile, but neither did he trouble to deny
what everyone knew, that he was the leader of the fighting
aristocracy, friend of the widowed Queen Regent, virtual
step-father of her eight-year-old son King Hjalmar—in a
word, that he was the dictator. If he preferred to keep a small

title and not have his name unnecessarily before the public, what difference did that make?

"I'll be glad to pass on whatever you wish to say to the proper authorities," he answered slowly. "Pipe." That was an order to his chair, which produced a lit briar for him.

Unduma felt appalled. This series of—informalities—was like one savage blow after another. Till now, in the three-hundred-year history of relations between Earth and the Double Kingdom, the Terrestrial ambassador had ranked everyone but God and the royal family.

No human planet, no matter how long sundered from the main stream, no matter what strange ways it had wandered, failed to remember that Earth was Earth, the home of man and the heart of Civilization. No *human* planet—had Norstad-Ostarik, then, gone the way of Kolresh?

Biologically, no, thought Unduma with an inward shudder. Nor culturally—yet. But it shrieked at him, from every insolent movement and twist of words, that Rusch had made a political deal.

"Well?" said the Margrave.

Unduma cleared his throat, desperately, and leaned forward. "Your lordship," he said, "my embassy cannot help taking notice of certain public statements, as well as certain military preparations and other matters of common knowledge—"

"And items your spies have dug up," drawled Rusch.

Unduma started. "My lord!"

"My good ambassador," grinned Rusch, "it was you who suggested a straightforward talk. I know Earth has spies here. In any event, it's impossible to hide so large a business as the mobilization of two planets for war."

Unduma felt sweat trickle down his ribs.

"There is . . . you . . . your Ministry has only announced it is a . . . a defense measure," he stammered. "I had hoped . . . frankly, yes, till the last minute I hoped you . . . your people might see fit to join us against Kolresh."

There was a moment's quiet. *So* quiet, thought Unduma. A redness crept up Rusch's cheeks, the scar stood livid and his pale eyes were the coldest thing Unduma had ever seen.

Then, slowly, the Margrave got it out through his teeth:

"For a number of centuries, your excellency, our people hoped Earth might join them."

"What do you mean?" Unduma forgot all polished inanities. Rusch didn't seem to notice. He stood up and went to the window.

"Come here," he said. "Let me show you something."

The window was a modern inset of clear, invisible plastic, a broad sheet high in the castle's infamous Witch Tower. It looked out on a black sky, the sun was down and the glacial forty-hour darkness of northern Norstad was crawling toward midnight.

Stars glittered mercilessly keen in an emptiness which seemed like crystal, which seemed about to ring thinly in contracting anguish under the cold. Ostarik, the companion planet, stood low to the south, a gibbous moon of steely blue; it never moved in that sky, the two worlds forever faced each other, the windy white peaks of one glaring at the warm lazy seas of the other. Northward, a great curtain of aurora flapped halfway around the cragged horizon.

From this dizzy height, Unduma could see little of the town Drakenstane: a few high-peaked roofs and small glowing windows, lamps lonesome above frozen streets. There wasn't much to see anyhow—no big cities on either planet, only the small towns which had grown from scattered thorps, each clustered humbly about the manor of its lord. Beyond lay winter fields, climbing up the valley walls to the hard green blink of glaciers. It must be blowing out there, he saw snowdevils chase ghostly across the blue-tinged desolation.

Rusch spoke roughly: "Not much of a planet we've got here, is it? Out on the far end of nowhere, a thousand light-years from your precious Earth, and right in the middle of a glacial epoch. Have you ever wondered why we don't set up weather-control stations and give this world a decent climate?"

"Well," began Unduma, "of course, the exigencies of—"

"Of war." Rusch sent his hand upward in a chopping motion, to sweep around the alien constellations. Among them burned Polaris, less than thirty parsecs away, huge and cruelly bright. "We never had a chance. Every time we thought we could begin, there would be war, usually with Kolresh, and the labor and materials would have to go for that. Once, about two centuries back, we did actually get stations established, it was even beginning to warm up a little. Kolresh blasted them off the map.

"Norstad was settled eight hundred years ago. For seven of those centuries, we've had Kolresh at our throats. Do you wonder if we've grown tired?"

"My lord, I . . . I can sympathize," said Unduma awkwardly. "I am not ignorant of your heroic history. But it would seem to me . . . after all, Earth has also fought—"

"At a range of a thousand light-years!" jeered Rusch. "The forgotten war. A few underpaid patrolmen in obsolete rustbucket ships to defend unimportant outposts from sporadic Kolreshite raids. We live on their borders!"

"It would certainly appear, your lordship, that Kolresh is your natural enemy," said Unduma. "As indeed it is of all Civilization. of Homo sapiens himself. What I cannot credit are the, ah, the rumors of an, er, alliance—"

"And why shouldn't we?" snarled Rusch. "For seven hundred years we've held them at bay, while your precious so-called Civilization grew fat behind a wall of our dead young men. The temptation to recoup some of our losses by helping Kolresh conquer Earth is very strong!"

"You don't mean it!" The breath rushed from Unduma's lungs.

The other man's face was like carved bone. "Don't jump to conclusions," he answered. "I merely point out that from our side there's a good deal to be said for such a policy. Now if Earth is prepared to make a different policy worth our while—do you understand? Nothing is going to happen in the immediate future. You have time to think about it."

"I would have to . . . communicate with my government," whispered Unduma.

"Of course," said Rusch. His bootheels clacked on the floor as he went back to his desk. "I've had a memorandum prepared for you, an unofficial informal sort of protocol, points which his majesty's government would like to make the basis of negotiations with the Terrestrial Federation. Ah, here!" He picked up a bulky folio. "I suggest you take a leave of absence, your excellency, go home and show your superiors this, ah—"

"Ultimatum," said Unduma in a sick voice.

Rusch shrugged. "Call it what you will." His tone was empty and remote, as if he had already cut himself and his people out of Civilization.

As he accepted the folio, Unduma noticed the book beside it, the one Rusch had been reading: a local edition of Schakspier, badly printed on sleazy paper, but in the original Old Anglic. Odd thing for a barbarian dictator to read. But then, Rusch was a bit of an historical scholar, as well as an enthusiastic kayak racer, meteor polo player, chess champion, mountain climber, and . . . and all-around scoundrel!

Norstad lay in the grip of a ten-thousand-year winter, while Ostarik was a heaven of blue seas breaking on warm island sands. Nevertheless, because Ostarik harbored a peculiarly nasty plague virus, it remained an unattainable paradise in the sky till a bare two hundred fifty years ago. Then a research team from Earth got to work, found an effective vaccine, and saw a mountain carved into their likeness by the Norron folk.

It was through such means—and the sheer weight of example, the liberty and wealth and happiness of its people—that the Civilization centered on Earth had been propagating itself among colonies isolated for centuries. There were none which lacked reverence for Earth the Mother, Earth the Wise, Earth the Kindly: none but Kolresh, which had long ceased to be human.

Rusch's private speedster whipped him· from the icicle walls of Festning Drakenstane to the rose gardens of Sorgenlos in an hour of hell-bat haste across vacuum. But it was several hours more until he and the queen could get away from their courtiers and be alone.

They walked through geometric beds of smoldering blooms, under songbirds and fronded trees, while the copper spires of the little palace reached up to the evening star and the hours-long sunset of Ostarik blazed gold across great quiet waters. The island was no more than a royal retreat, but lately it had known agonies.

Queen Ingra stooped over a mutant rose, tiger striped and a foot across; she plucked the petals from it and said close to weeping: "But I liked Unduma. I don't want him to hate us."

"He's not a bad sort," agreed Rusch. He stood behind her in a black dress uniform with silver insignia, like a formal version of death.

"He's more than that, Hans. He stands for decency—Norstad froze our souls, and Ostarik hasn't thawed them. I thought Earth might—" Her voice trailed off. She was slender and dark, still young, and her folk came from the rainy dales of Norstad's equator, a farm race with gentler ways than the miners and fishermen and hunters of the red-haired ice ape who had bred Rusch. In her throat, the Norron language softened to a burring music; the Drakenstane men spat their words out rough-edged.

"Earth might what?" Rusch turned a moody gaze to the west. "Lavish more gifts on us? We were always proud of paying our own way."

"Oh, no," said Ingra wearily. "After all, we could trade with them, furs and minerals and so on, if ninety per cent of our production didn't have to go into defense. I only thought they might teach us how to be human."

"I had assumed we were still classified Homo sapiens," said Rusch in a parched tone.

"Oh, you know what I mean!" She turned on him, violet eyes suddenly aflare. "Sometimes I wonder if *you're* human, Margrave Hans von Thoma Rusch. I mean free, free to be something more than a robot, free to raise children knowing they won't have their lungs shoved out their mouths when a Kolreshite cruiser hulls one of our spaceships. What is our whole culture, Hans? A layer of brutalized farmhands and factory workers—serfs! A top crust of heel-clattering aristocrats who live for nothing but war. A little folk art, folk music, folk saga, full of blood and treachery. Where are our symphonies, novels, cathedrals, research laboratories . . .

where are people who can say what they wish and make what they will of their lives and be happy?"

Rusch didn't answer for a moment. He looked at her, unblinking behind his monocle, till she dropped her gaze and twisted her hands together. Then he said only: "You exaggerate."

"Perhaps. It's still the basic truth." Rebellion rode in her voice. "It's what all the other worlds think of us."

"Even if the democratic assumption—that the eternal verities can be discovered by counting enough noses—were true," said Rusch, "you cannot repeal eight hundred years of history by decree."

"No. But you could work toward it," she said. "I think you're wrong in despising the common man, Hans . . . when was he ever given a chance, in this kingdom? We could make a beginning now, and Earth could send psychotechnic advisors, and in two or three generations—"

"What would Kolresh be doing while we experimented with forms of government?" he laughed.

"Always Kolresh." Her shoulders, slim behind the burning-red cloak, slumped. "Kolresh turned a hundred hopeful towns into radioactive craters and left the gnawed bones of children in the fields. Kolresh killed my husband, like a score of kings before him. Kolresh blasted your family to ash, Hans, and scarred your face and your soul—" She whirled back on him, fists aloft, and almost screamed: "Do you want to make an ally of Kolresh?"

The Margrave took out his pipe and began filling it. The saffron sundown, reflected off the ocean to his face, gave him a metal look.

"Well," he said, "we've been at peace with them for all of ten years now. Almost a record."

"Can't we find allies? Real ones? I'm sick of being a figurehead! I'd befriend Ahuramazda, New Mars, Lagrange—We could raise a crusade against Kolresh, wipe every last filthy one of them out of the universe!"

"Now who's a heel-clattering aristocrat?" grinned Rusch.

He lit his pipe and strolled toward the beach. She stood for an angry moment, then sighed and followed him.

"Do you think it hasn't been tried?" he said patiently. "For generations we've tried to build up a permanent alliance directed at Kolresh. What temporary ones we achieved have always fallen apart. Nobody loves us enough—and, since we've always taken the heaviest blows, nobody hates Kolresh enough."

He found a bench on the glistening edge of the strand, and sat down and looked across a steady march of surf, turned to molten gold by the low sun and the incandescent western clouds. Ingra joined him.

"I can't really blame the others for not liking us," she said in a small voice. "We are overmechanized and undercultured, arrogant, tactless, undemocratic, hard-boiled . . . oh, yes. But their own self-interest—"

"They don't imagine it can happen to them," replied Rusch contemptuously. "And there are even pro-Kolresh elements, here and there." He raised his voice an octave: "Oh, my dear sir, my dear Margrave, what are you *saying*? Why, of *course* Kolresh would never attack us! They made a *treaty* never to attack us!"

Ingra sighed, forlornly. Rusch laid an arm across her shoulders. They sat for a while without speaking.

"Anyway," said the man finally, "Kolresh is too strong for any combination of powers in this part of the galaxy. We and they are the only ones with a military strength worth mentioning. Even Earth would have a hard time defeating them, and Earth, of course, will lean backward before undertaking a major war. She has too much to lose; it's so much more comfortable to regard the Kolreshite raids as mere piracies, the skirmishes as 'police actions.' She just plain will not pay the stiff price of an army and a navy able to whip Kolresh and occupy the Kolreshite planets."

"And so it is to be war again." Ingra looked out in desolation across the sea.

"Maybe not," said Rusch. "Maybe a different kind of war, at least—no more black ships coming out of *our* sky."

He blew smoke for a while, as if gathering courage, then spoke in a quick, impersonal manner: "Look here. We Norrons are not a naval power. It's not in our tradition. Our navy has always been inadequate and always will be. But we can breed the toughest soldiers in the known galaxy, in unlimited numbers; we can condition them into fighting machines, and equip them with the most lethal weapons living flesh can wield.

"Kolresh, of course, is just the opposite. Space nomads, small population, able to destroy anything their guns can reach but not able to dig in and hold it against us. For seven hundred years, we and they have been the elephant and the whale. Neither could ever win a real victory over the other; war became the normal state of affairs, peace a breathing spell. Because of the mutation, there will always be war, as long as one single Kolreshite lives. We can't kill them, we can't befriend them—all we can do is to be bled white to stop them."

A wind sighed over the slow thunder on the beach. A line of sea birds crossed the sky, thin and black against glowing bronze.

"I know," said Ingra. "I know the history, and I know what you're leading up to. Kolresh will furnish transportation and naval escort; Norstad-Ostarik will furnish men. Between us, we may be able to take Earth."

"We will," said Rusch flatly. "Earth has grown plump and lazy. She can't possibly rearm enough in a few months to stop such a combination."

"And all the galaxy will spit on our name."

"All the galaxy will lie open to conquest, once Earth has fallen."

"How long do you think we would last, riding the Kolresh tiger?"

"I have no illusions about them, my dear. But neither can I see any way to break this eternal deadlock. In a fluid situation, such as the collapse of Earth would produce, we might be able to create a navy as good as theirs. They've never yet given us a chance to build one, but perhaps—"

"Perhaps not! I doubt very much it was a meteor which

wrecked my husband's ship, five years ago. I think Kolresh knew of his hopes, of the shipyard he wanted to start, and murdered him."

"It's probable," said Rusch.

"And you would league us with them." Ingra turned a colorless face on him. "I'm still the queen. I forbid any further consideration of this . . . this obscene alliance!"

Rusch sighed. "I was afraid of that, your highness." For a moment he looked gray, tired. "You have a veto power, of course. But I don't think the Ministry would continue in office a regent who used it against the best interests of—"

She leaped to her feet. "You wouldn't!"

"Oh, you'd not be harmed," said Rusch with a crooked smile. "Not even deposed. You'd be in a protective custody, shall we say. Of course, his majesty, your son, would have to be educated elsewhere, but if you wish—"

Her palm cracked on his face. He made no motion.

"I . . . won't veto—" Ingra shook her head. Then her back grew stiff. "Your ship will be ready to take you home, my lord. I do not think we shall require your presence here again."

"As you will, your highness," mumbled the dictator of the Double Kingdom.

Though he returned with a bitter word in his mouth, Unduma felt the joy, the biological rightness of being home, rise warm within him. He sat on a terrace under the mild sky of Earth, with the dear bright flow of the Zambezi River at his feet and the slim towers of Capital City rearing as far as he could see, each gracious, in its own green park. The people on the clean quiet streets wore airy blouses and colorful kilts—not the trousers for men, ankle-length skirts for women, which muffled the sad folk of Norstad. And there was educated conversation in the gentle Tierrans language, music from an open window, laughter on the verandas and children playing in the parks: freedom, law, and leisure.

The thought that this might be rubbed out of history, that the robots of Norstad and the snake-souled monsters of

Kolresh might tramp between broken spires where starved Earthmen hid, was a tearing in Unduma.

He managed to lift his drink and lean back with the proper casual elegance. "No, sir," he said, "they are not bluffing."

Ngu Chilongo, Premier of the Federation Parliament, blinked unhappy eyes. He was a small grizzled man, and a wise man, but this lay beyond everything he had known in a long lifetime and he was slow to grasp it.

"But surely—" he began. "Surely this ... this Rusch person is not insane. He cannot think that his two planets, with a population of, what is it, perhaps one billion, can overcome four billion Terrestrials!"

"There would also be several million Kolreshites to help," reminded Unduma. "However, they would handle the naval end of it entirely—and their navy *is* considerably stronger than ours. The Norron forces would be the ones which actually landed, to fight the air and ground battles. And out of those paltry one billion, Rusch can raise approximately one hundred million soldiers."

Chilongo's glass crashed to the terrace. "What!"

"It's true, sir." The third man present, Mustafa Lefarge, Minister of Defense, spoke in a miserable tone. "It's a question of every able-bodied citizen, male and female, being a trained member of the armed forces. In time of war, virtually everyone not in actual combat is directly contributing to some phase of the effort—a civilian economy virtually ceases to exist. They're used to getting along for years at a stretch with no comforts and a bare minimum of necessities." His voice grew sardonic. "By necessities, they mean things like food and ammunition—not, say, entertainment or cultural activity, as we assume."

"A hundred million," whispered Chilongo. He stared at his hands. "Why, that's ten times our *total* forces!"

"Which are ill-trained, ill-equipped, and ill-regarded by our own civilians," pointed out Lefarge bitterly.

"In short, sir," said Unduma, "while we could defeat either Kolresh or Norstad-Ostarik in an all-out war—though with considerable difficulty—between them they can defeat us."

Chilongo shivered. Unduma felt a certain pity for him. You

had to get used to it in small doses, this fact which Civilization screened from Earth: that the depths of hell are found in the human soul. That no law of nature guards the upright innocent from malice.

"But they wouldn't dare!" protested the Premier. "Our friends . . . everywhere—"

"All the human-colonized galaxy will wring its hands and send stiff notes of protest," said Lefarge. "Then they'll pull the blankets back over their heads and assure themselves that now the big bad aggressor has been sated."

"This note—of Rusch's." Chilongo seemed to be grabbing out after support while the world dropped from beneath his feet. Sweat glistened on his wrinkled brown forehead. "Their terms . . . surely we can make some agreement?"

"Their terms are impossible, as you'll see for yourself when you read," said Unduma flatly. "They want us to declare war on Kolresh, accept a joint command under Norron leadership, foot the bill and—No!"

"But if we have to fight anyway," began Chilongo, "it would seem better to have at least one ally—"

"Has Earth changed that much since I was gone?" asked Unduma in astonishment. "Would our people really consent to this . . . this extortion . . . letting those hairy barbarians write our foreign policy for us— Why, jumping into war, making the first declaration ourselves, it's unconstitutional! It's *un-Civilized!*"

Chilongo seemed to shrink a little. "No," he said. "No, I don't mean that. Of course it's impossible; better to be honestly defeated in battle. I only thought, perhaps we could bargain—"

"We can try," said Unduma skeptically, "but I never heard of Hans Rusch yielding an angstrom without a pistol at his head."

Lefarge struck a cigar, inhaled deeply, and took another sip from his glass. "I hardly imagine an alliance with Kolresh would please his own people," he mused.

"Scarcely!" said Unduma. "But they'll accept it if they must."

"Oh? No chance for us to get him overthrown—assassinated, even?"

"Not to speak of. Let me explain. He's only a petty aristocrat by birth, but during the last war with Kolresh he gained high rank and a personal following of fanatically loyal young officers. For the past few years, since the king died, he's been the dictator. He's filled the key posts with his men: hard, able, and unquestioning. Everyone else is either admiring or cowed. Give him credit, he's no megalomaniac—he shuns publicity—but that simply divorces his power all the more from responsibility. You can measure it by pointing out that everyone knows he will probably ally with Kolresh, and eveyone has a nearly physical loathing of the idea—but there is not a word of criticism for Rusch himself, and when he orders it they will embark on Kolreshite ships to ruin the Earth they love."

"It could almost make you believe in the old myths," whispered Chilongo. "About the Devil incarnate."

"Well," said Unduma. "this sort of thing has happened before, you know."

"Hm-m-m?" Lefarge sat up.

Unduma smiled sadly. "Historical examples," he said. "They're of no practical value today, except for giving the cold consolation that we're not uniquely betrayed."

"What do you mean?" asked Chilongo.

"Well," said Unduma, "consider the astropolitics of the situation. Around Polaris and beyond lies Kolresh territory, where for a long time they sharpened their teeth preying on backward autochthones. At last they started expanding toward the richer human- settled planets. Norstad happened to lie directly on their path, so Norstad took the first blow—and stopped them.

"Since then, it's been seven hundred years of stalemated war. Oh, naturally Kolresh outflanks Norstad from time to time, seizes this planet in the galactic west and raids that one to the north, fights a war with one to the south and makes an alliance with one to the east. But it has never amounted to anything important. It can't, with Norstad astride the most direct line between the heart of Kolresh and the heart of

Civilization. If Kolresh made a serious effort to by-pass Norstad, the Norrons could—and would—disrupt everything with an attack in the rear.

"In short, despite the fact that interstellar space is three-dimensional and enormous, Norstad guards the northern marches of Civilization."

He paused for another sip. It was cool and subtle on his tongue, a benediction after the outworld rotgut.

"Hm-m-m, I never thought of it just that way," said Lefarge. "I assumed it was just a matter of barbarians fighting each other for the usual barbarian reasons."

"Oh, it is, I imagine," said Unduma, "but the result is that Norstad acts as the shield of Earth.

"Now if you examine early Terrestrial history—and Rusch, who has a remarkable knowledge of it, stimulated me to do so—you'll find that this is a common thing. A small semicivilized state, out on the marches, holds off the enemy while the true civilization prospers behind it. Assyria warded Mesopotamia, Rome defended Greece, the Welsh border lords kept England safe, the Transoxanian Tartars were the shield of Persia, Prussia blocked the approaches to western Europe . . . oh, I could add a good many examples. In every instance, a somewhat backward people on the distant frontier of a civilization, receive the worst hammer-blows of the really alien races beyond, the wild men who would leave nothing standing if they could get at the protected cities of the inner society."

He paused for breath. "And so?" asked Chilongo.

"Well, of course, suffering isn't good for people," shrugged Unduma. "It tends to make them rather nasty. The marchmen react to incessant war by becoming a warrior race, uncouth peasants with an absolute government of ruthless militarists. Nobody loves them, neither the outer savages nor the inner polite nations.

"And in the end, they're all too apt to turn inward. Their military skill and vigor need a more promising outlet than this grim business of always fighting off an enemy who always comes back and who has even less to steal than the sentry culture.

"So Assyria sacks Babylon; Rome conquers Greece; Percy rises against King Henry; Tamerlane overthrows Bajazet; Prussia clanks into France—"

"And Norstad-Ostarik falls on Earth," finished Lefarge.

"Exactly," said Unduma. "It's not even unprecedented for the border state to join hands with the very tribes it fought so long. Percy and Owen Glendower, for instance . . . though in that case, I imagine both parties were considerably more attractive than Hans Rusch or Klerak Belug."

"What are we going to do?" Chilongo whispered it toward the blue sky of Earth, from which no bombs had fallen for a thousand years.

Then he shook himself, jumped to his feet, and faced the other two. "I'm sorry, gentlemen. This has taken me rather by surprise, and I'll naturally require time to look at this Norron protocol and evaluate the other data. But if it turns out you're right"—he bowed urbanely—"as I'm sure it will—"

"Yes?" said Unduma in a tautening voice.

"Why, then, we appear to have some months, at least, before anything drastic happens. We can try to gain more time by negotiation. We do have the largest industrial complex in the known universe, and four billion people who have surely not had courage bred out of them. We'll build up our armed forces, and if those barbarians attack we'll whip them back into their own kennels and kick them through the rear walls thereof!"

"I hoped you'd say that," breathed Unduma.

"*I* hope we'll be granted time," Lefarge scowled. "I assume Rusch is not a fool. We cannot rearm in anything less than a glare of publicity. When he learns of it, what's to prevent him from cementing the Kolresh alliance and attacking at once, before we're ready?"

"Their mutual suspiciousness ought to help," said Unduma. "I'll go back there, of course, and do what I can to stir up trouble between them."

He sat still for a moment, then added as if to himself: "Till we do finish preparing, we have no resources but hope."

The Kolreshite mutation was a subtle thing. It did not

show on the surface: physically, they were a handsome people, running to white skin and orange hair. Over the centuries, thousands of Norron spies had infiltrated them, and
frequently gotten back alive; what made such work unusu-
ally difficult was not the normal hazards of impersonation,
but an ingrained reluctance to practice cannibalism and worse.

The mutation was a psychic twist, probably originating in
some obscure gene related to the endocrine system. It was
extraordinarily hard to describe—every categorical statement
about it had the usual quota of exceptions and qualifications.
But one might, to a first approximation, call it extreme
xenophobia. It is normal for Homo sapiens to be somewhat
wary of outsiders till he has established their bona fides; it
was normal for Homo Kolreshi to *hate* all outsiders, from first
glimpse to final destruction.

Naturally, such an instinct produced a tendency to in-
breeding, which lowered fertility, but systematic execution of
the unfit had so far kept the stock vigorous. The instinct also
led to strongarm rule within the nation; to nomadism, where a
planet was only a base like the oasis of the ancient Bedouin,
essential to life but rarely seen; to a cult of secrecy and
cruelty, a religion of abominations; to an ultimate goal of
conquering the accessible universe and wiping out all other
races.

Of course, it was not so simple, nor so blatant. Among
themselves, the Kolreshites doubtless found a degree of ten-
derness and fidelity. Visiting on neutral planets—i.e., planets which it was not yet expedient to attack—they were very
courteous and had an account of defending themselves against
one unprovoked aggression after another, which some found
plausible. Even their enemies stood in awe of their personal
heroism.

Nevertheless, few in the galaxy would have wept if the
Kolreshites all died one rainy night.

Hans von Thomas Rusch brought his speedster to the great
whaleback of the battleship. It lay a light-year from his sun,
hidden by cold emptiness; the co-ordinates had been given
him secretly, together with an invitation which was more
like a summons.

He glided into the landing cradle, under the turrets of guns that could pound a moon apart, and let the mechanism suck him down below decks. When he stepped out into the high, coldly lit debarkation chamber, an honor guard in red presented arms and pipes twittered for him.

He walked slowly forward, a big man in black and silver, to meet his counterpart, Klerak Belug, the Overman of Kolresh, who waited rigid in a blood-colored tunic. The cabin bristled around him with secret police and guns.

Rusch clicked heels. "Good day, your dominance," he said. A faint echo followed his voice. For some unknown reason, this folk liked echoes and always built walls to resonate.

Belug, an aging giant who topped him by a head, raised shaggy brows. "Are you alone, your lordship?" he asked in atrociously accented Norron. "It was understood that you could bring a personal bodyguard."

Rusch shrugged. "I would have needed a personal dreadnought to be quite safe," he replied in fluent Kolra, "so I decided to trust your safe conduct. I assume you realize that any harm done to me means instant war with my kingdom."

The broad, wrinkled lion-face before him split into a grin. "My representatives did not misjudge you, your lordship. I think we can indeed do business. Come."

The Overman turned and led the way down a ramp toward the guts of the ship. Rusch followed, enclosed by guards and bayonets. He kept a hand on his own sidearm—not that it would do him much good, if matters came to that.

Events were approaching their climax, he thought in a cold layer of his brain. For more than a year now, negotiations had dragged on, hemmed in by the requirement of secrecy, weighted down by mutual suspicion. There were only two points of disagreement remaining, but discussion had been so thoroughly snagged on those that the two absolute rulers must meet to settle it personally. It was Belug who had issued the contemptuous invitation.

And he, Rusch, had come. Tonight the old kings of Norstad wept worms in their graves.

The party entered a small, luxuriously chaired room. There were the usual robots, for transcription and reference purposes, and there were guards, but Overman and Margrave were essentially alone.

Belug wheezed his bulk into a seat. "Smoke? Drink?"

"I have my own, thank you." Rusch took out his pipe and a hip flask.

"That is scarcely diplomatic," rumbled Belug.

Rusch laughed. "I'd always understood that your dominance had no use for the mannerisms of Civilization. I daresay we'd both like to finish our business as quickly as possible."

The Overman snapped his fingers. Someone glided up with wine in a glass. He sipped for a while before answering: "Yes. By all means. Let us reach an executive agreement now and wait for our hirelings to draw up a formal treaty. But it seems odd, sir, that after all these months of delay, you are suddenly so eager to complete the work."

"Not odd," said Rusch. "Earth is rearming at a considerable rate. She's had almost a year now. We can still whip her, but in another six months we'll no longer be able to; give her automated factories half a year beyond *that*, and she'll destroy us!"

"It must have been clear to you, sir, that after the Earth Ambassador—what's his name, Unduma—after he returned to your planets last year, he was doing all he could to gain time."

"Oh, yes," said Rusch. "Making offers to me, and then haggling over them—brewing trouble elsewhere to divert our attention—a gallant effort. But it didn't work. Frankly, your dominance, you've only yourself to blame for the delays. For example, your insisting that Earth be administered as Kolreshite territory—"

"My dear sir!" exploded Belug. "It was a talking point. Only a talking point. Any diplomatist would have understood. But you took six weeks to study it, then offered that preposterous counter-proposal that everything should revert to *you*, loot and territory both— Why, if you had been truly willing to co-operate, we could have settled the terms in a month!"

"As you like, your dominance," said Rusch carelessly. "It's

all past now. There are only these questions of troop transport and prisoners, then we're in total agreement."

Klerak Belug narrowed his eyes and rubbed his chin with one outsize hand. "I do not comprehend," he said, "and neither do my naval officers. We have regular transports for your men, nothing extraordinary in the way of comfort, to be sure, but inifintely more suitable for so long a voyage than ... than the naval units you insist we use. Don't you understand? A transport is for carrying men or cargo; a ship of the line is to fight or convoy. You do *not* mix the functions!"

"I do, your dominance," said Rusch. "As many of my soldiers as possible are going to travel on regular warships furnished by Kolresh, and there are going to be Double Kingdom naval personnel with them for liaison."

"But—" Belug's fist closed on his wineglass as if to splinter it. "Why?" he roared.

"My representatives have explained it a hundred times," said Rusch wearily. "In blunt language, I don't trust you. If ... oh, let us say there should be disagreement between us while the armada is en route ... well, a transport ship is easily replaced, after its convoy vessels have blown it up. The fighting craft of Kolresh are a better hostage for your good behavior." He struck a light to his pipe. "Naturally, you can't take our whole fifty-million-man expeditionary force on your battle wagons; but I want soldiers on every warship as well as in the transports."

Belug shook his ginger head. "No."

"Come now," said Rusch. "Your spies have been active enough on Norstad and Ostarik. Have you found any reason to doubt my intentions? Bearing in mind that an army the size of ours cannot be alerted for a given operation without a great many people knowing the fact—"

"Yes, yes," grumbled Belug. "Granted." He smiled, a sharp flash of teeth. "But the upper hand is mine, your lordship. I can wait indefinitely to attack Earth. You can't."

"Eh?" Rusch drew hard on his pipe.

"In the last analysis, even dictators rely on popular support. My Intelligence tells me you are rapidly losing yours. The queen has not spoken to you for a year, has she? And there are many Norrons whose first loyalty is to the Crown. As the thought of war with Earth seeps in, as men have time to comprehend how little they like the idea, time to see through your present anti-Terrestrial propaganda—they grow angry. Already they mutter about you in the beer halls and the officers' clubs, they whisper in ministry cloakrooms. My agents have heard.

"Your personal cadre of young key officers are the only ones left with unquestioning loyalty to you. Let discontent grow just a little more, let open revolt break out, and your followers will be hanged from the lamp posts.

"You can't delay much longer."

Rusch made no reply for a while. Then he sat up, his monocle glittering like a cold round window on winter.

"I can always call off this plan and resume the normal state of affairs," he snapped.

Belug flushed red. "War with Kolresh again? It would take you too long to shift gears—to reorganize."

"It would not. Our war college, like any other, has prepared military plans for all foreseeable combinations of circumstances. If I cannot come to terms with you, Plan No. So-and-So goes into effect. And obviously *it* will have popular enthusiasm behind it!"

He nailed the Overman with a fish-pale eye and continued in frozen tones: "After all, your dominance, I would prefer to fight you. The only thing I would enjoy more would be to hunt you with hounds. Seven hundred years have shown this to be impossible. I opened negotiations to make the best of an evil bargain—since you cannot be conquered, it will pay better to join with you on a course of mutually profitable imperialism.

"But if your stubborness prevents an agreement, I can declare war on you in the usual manner and be no worse off than I was. The choice is, therefore, yours."

Belug swallowed. Even his guards lost some of their blankness. One does not speak in that fashion across the negotiators' table.

Finally, only his lips stirring, he said: "Your frankness is appreciated, my lord. Some day I would like to discuss that aspect further. As for now, though . . . yes, I can see your point. I am prepared to admit some of your troops to our ships of the line." After another moment, still sitting like a stone idol: "But this question of returning prisoners of war. We have never done it. I do not propose to begin."

"*I* do not propose to let poor devils of Norrons rot any longer in your camps," said Rusch. "I have a pretty good idea of what goes on there. If we're to be allies, I'll want back such of my countrymen as are still alive."

"Not many are still sane," Belug told him deliberately.

Rusch puffed smoke and made no reply.

"If I give in on the one item," said Belug, "I have a right to test your sincerity by the other. We keep our prisoners."

Rusch's own face had gone quite pale and still. It grew altogether silent in the room.

"Very well," he said after a long time. "Let it be so."

Without a word, Major Othkar Graaborg led his company into the black cruiser. The words came from the spaceport, where police held off a hooting, hissing, rock-throwing mob. It was the first time in history that Norron folk had stoned their own soldiers.

His men tramped stolidly behind him, up the gangway and through the corridors. Among the helmets and packs and weapons, racketing boots and clashing body armor, their faces were lost, they were an army without faces.

Graaborg followed a Kolreshite ensign, who kept looking back nervously at these hereditary foes, till they reached the bunkroom. It had been hastily converted from a storage hold, and was scant cramped comfort for a thousand men.

"All right, boys," he said when the door had closed on his guide. "Make yourselves at home."

They got busy, opening packs, spreading bedrolls on bunks. Immediately thereafter, they started to assemble heavy machine guns, howitzers, even a nuclear blaster.

"You, there!" The accented voice squawked indignantly from a loudspeaker in the wall. "I see that. I got video. You not put guns together here."

Graaborg looked up from his inspection of a live fission shell. "Obscenity you," he said pleasantly. "Who are you, anyway?"

"I executive officer. I tell captain."

"Go right ahead. My orders say that according to treaty, as long as we stay in our assigned part of the ship, we're under our own discipline. If your captain doesn't like it, let him come down here and talk to us." Graaborg ran a thumb along the edge of his bayonet. A wolfish chorus from his men underlined the invitation.

No one pressed the point. The cruiser lumbered into space, rendezvoused with her task force, and went into nonspatial drive. For several days, the Norron army contingent remained in its den, more patient with such stinking quarters than the Kolreshites could imagine anyone being. Nevertheless, no spaceman ventured in there; meals were fetched at the galley by Norron squads.

Graaborg alone wandered freely about the ship. He was joined by Commander von Brecca of Ostarik, the head of the Double Kingdom's naval liaison on this ship: a small band of officers and ratings, housed elsewhere. They conferred with the Kolreshite officers as the necessity arose, on routine problems, rehearsal of various operations to be performed when Earth was reached a month hence—but they did not mingle socially. This suited their hosts.

The fact is, the Kolreshites were rather frightened of them. A spaceman does not lack courage, but he is a gentleman among warriors. His ship either functions well, keeping him clean and comfortable, or it does not function at all and he dies quickly and mercifully. He fights with machines, at enormous ranges.

The ground soldier, muscle in mud, whose ultimate weapon is whetted steel in bare hands, has a different kind of toughness.

Two weeks after departure, Graaborg's wrist chronometer showed a certain hour. He was drilling his men in full combat rig, as he had been doing every "day" in spite of the narrow quarters.

"Ten-SHUN!" The order flowed through captains, lieutenants, and sergeants; the bulky mass of men crashed to stillness.

Major Graaborg put a small pocket amplifier to his lips. "All right, lads," he said casually, "assume gas masks, radiation shields, all gun squads to weapons. Now let's clean up this ship."

He himself blew down the wall with a grenade.

Being perhaps the most thoroughly trained soldiers in the universe, the Norron men paused for only one amazed second. Then they cheered, with death and hell in their voices, and crowded at his heels.

Little resistance was met until Graaborg had picked up von Brecca's naval command, the crucial ones, who could sail and fight the ship. The Kolreshites were too dumfounded. Thereafter the nomads rallied and fought gamely. Graaborg was handicapped by not having been able to give his men a battle plan. He split up his forces and trusted to the intelligence of the noncoms.

His faith was not misplaced, though the ship was in poor condition by the time the last Kolreshite had been machine-gunned.

Graaborg himself had used a bayonet, with vast satisfaction.

M'Katze Unduma entered the office in the Witch Tower. "You sent for me, your lordship?" he asked. His voice was as cold and bitter as the gale outside.

"Yes. Please be seated." Margrave Hans von Thoma Rusch looked tired. "I have some news for you."

"What news? You declared war on Earth two weeks ago. Your army can't have reached her yet." Unduma leaned over the desk. "Is it that you've found transportation to send me home?"

"Somewhat better news, your excellency." Rusch leaned over and tuned a telescreen. A background of clattering robots and frantically busy junior officers came into view.

Then a face entered the screen, young, and with more life in it than Unduma had ever before seen on this sullen planet. "Central Data headquarters—Oh, yes, your lordship." Boyishly, against all rules: "We've got her! The *Bheoka* just called in . . . she's ours!"

"Hm-m-m. Good." Rusch glanced at Unduma. "The *Bheoka* is the superdreadnought accompanying Task Force Two. Carry on with the news."

"Yes, sir. She's already reducing the units we failed to capture. Admiral Sorrens estimates he'll control Force Two entirely in another hour. Bulletin just came in from Force Three. Admiral Gundrup killed in fighting, but Vice Admiral Smitt has assumed command and reports three-fourths of the ships in our hands. He's delaying fire until he sees how it goes aboard the rest. Also—"

"Never mind," said Rusch. "I'll get the comprehensive report later. Remind Staff that for the next few hours all command decisions had better be made by officers on the spot. After that, when we see what we've got, broader tactics can be prepared. If some extreme emergency doesn't arise, it'll be a few hours before I can get over to HQ."

"Yes, sir. Sir, I . . . may I say—" So might the young Norron have addressed a god.

"All right, son, you've said it." Rusch turned off the screen and looked at Unduma. "Do you realize what's happening?"

The ambassador sat down; his knees seemed all at once to have melted. "What have you done?" It was like a stranger speaking.

"What I planned quite a few years ago," said the Margrave.

He reached into his desk and brought forth a bottle. "Here, your excellency. I think we could both use a swig. Authentic Terrestrial Scotch. I've saved it for this day."

But there was no glory leaping in him. It is often thus, you reach a dream and you only feel how tired you are.

Unduma let the liquid fire slide down his throat.

"You understand, don't you?" said Rusch. "For seven centuries, the Elephant and the Whale fought, without being able to get at each other's vitals. I made this alliance against Earth solely to get our men aboard their ships. But a really large operation like that can't be faked. It has to be genuine— the agreements, the preparations, the propaganda, everything. Only a handful of officers, men who could be trusted to . . . to infinity"—his voice cracked over, and Unduma thought of war prisoners sacrificed, hideous casualties in the steel corridors of spaceships, Norron gunners destroying Kolreshite vessels and the survivors of Norron detachments which failed to capture them—"only a few could be told, and then only at the last instant. For the rest, I relied on the quality of our troops. They're good lads, every one of them and, therefore adaptable. They're especially adaptable when suddenly told to fall on the men they'd most like to kill."

He tilted the bottle afresh. "It's proving expensive," he said in a slurred, hurried tone. "It will cost us as many casualties, no doubt, as ten years of ordinary war. But if I hadn't done this, there could easily have been another seven hundred years of war. Couldn't there? Couldn't there have been? As it is, we've already broken the spine of the Kolreshite fleet. She has plenty of ships yet, to be sure, still a meance, but crippled. I hope Earth will see fit to join us. Between them, Earth and Norstad-Ostarik can finish off Kolresh in a hurry. And after all, Kolresh *did* declare war on you, had every intention of destroying you. If you won't help, well, we can end it by ourselves, now that the fleet is broken. But I hope you'll join us."

"I don't know," said Unduma. He was still wobbling in a new cosmos. "We're not a . . . a hard people."

"You ought to be," said Rusch. "Hard enough, anyway, to win a voice for yourselves in what's going to happen around Polaris. Important frontier, Polaris."

"Yes," said Unduma slowly. "There is that. It won't cause any hosannahs in our streets, but . . . yes, I think we will continue the war, as your allies, if only to prevent you from massacring the Kolreshites. They can be rehabilitated, you know."

"I doubt that," grunted Rusch. "But it's a detail. At the very least, they'll never be allowed weapons again." He raised a sardonic brow. "I suppose we, too, can be rehabilitated, once you get your peace groups and psychotechs out here. No doubt you'll manage to demilitarize us and turn us into good plump democrats. All right, Unduma, send your Civilizing missionaries. But permit me to give thanks that I won't live to see their work completed!"

The Earthman nodded, rather coldly. You couldn't blame Rusch for treachery, callousness, and arrogance—he was what his history had made him—but he remained unpleasant company for a Civilized man. "I shall communicate with my government at once, your lordship, ånd recommend a provisional alliance, the terms to be settled later," he said. "I will report back to you as soon as ... ah, where will you be?"

"How should I know?" Rusch got out of his chair. The winter night howled at his back. "I have to convene the Ministry, and make a public telecast, and get over to Staff, and— No. The devil with it! If you need me inside the next few hours, I'll be at Sorgenlos on Ostarik. But the matter had better be urgent!"

THE STARS GO OVER THE LONELY OCEAN

I've known Poul Anderson for—ye gods, for over twenty years. We've sat up late into the night, sometimes drinking and singing, sometimes talking of more serious matters. Once in a great while, when the mood is right, Poul will offer a toast: "Long live freedom and damn the ideologies!"

That line comes from Robinson Jeffers.

Jeffers was born in Pittsburgh in 1887; from 1916 to his death in 1962 he lived in the rugged seacoast hills near Carmel. The *Britannica* entry says Jeffers "viewed civilization from his tower and found it contemptible. Using violent imagery, he expressed what were perhaps the bitterest views of any major poet writing in his time."

Well, yes; but his views are more complex than that. Jeffers believed that civilizations inevitably decline through becoming introverted—an observation made in the '30s, and which hasn't exactly been rendered invalid by events since that time.

A few years ago the U.S. Postal Service issued a Jeffers commemorative stamp. Inflation made it obsolete about as soon as it was printed; but that hasn't happened with his poetry. This was (obviously) written in 1940 or early '41.

THE STARS GO OVER THE LONELY OCEAN

by Robinson Jeffers

Unhappy about some far off things
That are not my affair, wandering
Along the coast and up the lean ridges,
I saw in the evening
The stars go over the lonely ocean,
And a black-maned wild boar
Plowing with his snout on Mal Paso Mountain.

The old monster snuffled, "Here are sweet roots,
Fat grubs, slick beetles and sprouted acorns.
The best nation in Europe has fallen,
And that is Finland,
But the stars go over the lonely ocean,"
Said the old black-bristled boar,
Tearing the sod on Mal Paso Mountain.

"The world's in a bad way, my man,
And bound to be worse before it mends;
Better to lie up in the mountain here
Four or five centuries,
While the stars go over the lonely ocean,"
Said the old father of wild pigs,
Plowing the fallow on Mal Paso Mountain.

"Keep clear of the dupes that talk democracy
And the dogs that bark revolution,
Drunk with talk, liars and believers.
I believe in my tusks.
Long live freedom and damn the ideologies,"
Said the gamey black-maned boar
Tusking the turf on Mal Paso Mountain.

THE TRUE HORROR
OF SOVIET INTERNAL EXILE

From Dissent to Docility

Victor Herman is the author of *Coming Out of the Ice*, which tells of his eighteen years of prison and exile in the Soviet Union. Mr. Dohrs is professor of geography at Wayne State University. Neither is a part of the science fact/science fiction community in which I move, so it is not surprising that I never met either of them.

Thus I have no anecdotes about the authors. This is probably as well. Their story speaks for itself.

Lest we become lost in contemplation of our faults; lest we forget that at the very least we have the freedom to publish this book; it is well that we look in the face the true enemy of liberty in these closing decades of the Second Millennium. . . .

There are two threats to freedom. The one which concerned John Stuart Mill, and which occupies the time and energies of the American Civil Liberties Union, is the threat from "within"; the threat posed by our own government; and certainly republics have fallen to their own armies and police.

More commonly, nations lose their liberties to their neighbors; aye, and more than liberty. Certainly the twentieth century shows conquest from without as fatal as tyranny from within. (Hannah Arendt observed that the totalitarian rules as a foreign prince in his own country.)

Indeed, Soviet Communism has the dubious record of having enslaved and murdered more people than any previous despotate of history; yet few weep for the victims. There are just too many of them. They become a faceless blur, a mass of humanity so large that we cannot think of it as human. Solzhenitsyn has tried to tell us of them; to make them come alive, so they will not have died in vain; but again the sheer mass overwhelms. Repetitious, said one critic. Will that critic some day enter the Gulag?

Die Gedanken, Sie sind frei. The thoughts are free, no one can make me repent my thoughts—

We may cry that in hope. Herman and Dohrs tell us the truth of it.

THE TRUE HORROR
OF SOVIET INTERNAL EXILE

From Dissent to Docility

by Victor Herman and Fred E. Dohrs

•

The prisoner is sentenced to five years of internal exile."

"The prisoner is sentenced to eight years of internal exile."

These words have been heard recently in Moscow courts where, after a travesty of a trial, the accused Soviet citizen is convicted of such crimes as "malicious hooliganism," or "anti-Soviet behavior." Americans know these prisoners as dissidents.

Being required to live at a specific place within the Soviet Union doesn't sound like such a terrible punishment. After all, it's a huge country, and exile couldn't be that bad. It certainly hasn't the ominous sound of "prison" or "prison camp at hard labor."

However mild "internal exile" may sound to Americans, the facts of such exile are grim and almost hopeless for the political prisoner. The total control apparatus required to make internal exile effective puts pressure on the prisoner from the moment of arrest.

But even before the arrest, the regime—the Communist Party and the KGB—has already decided the guilt and probably the sentence. Once arrested, the prisoner loses the few rights he may have had before. He must turn in his internal passport and working papers—the absolute essentials for living in the USSR. He is jailed immediately and can have no communication at all with the outside. The "one telephone call" allowed by the American system of justice does not exist in the Soviet Union. He may be held in the local jail or transported many miles to await further action.

Family and friends are not informed either of his where-abouts or of the charges against him. Nor may they communicate with him.

For days, weeks, or months, nothing may happen. He simply remains in jail. Delay is part of the system or pressures to soften him up for interrogation. Perhaps the thugs in the system will work him over a little—or they may just leave him alone, letting him wonder what will happen next. Only when the official who signed the arrest order decides to take further action can the next step, usually a trial or a semblance of a trial, take place.

For the more prominent dissidents—usually those known to Western news people and arrested in Moscow or Leningrad, the showplace cities—there may be a public announcement of the time and place of the trial and a statement of the charges. For the hundreds and thousands of others, unknown to foreigners, whether in the major cities or elsewhere in the Soviet Union, information is rarely given out prior to the trial, and often not even then.

Because "guilt" has already been determined, the trial itself is largely irrelevant. Only occasionally are family or friends allowed in the courtroom, which is "packed" with the Party faithful or those seeking Party favors. In some cases—often involving dissidents from the many national minorities seeking freedom from both Soviet and Russian control—the trial may be held in secret. Nothing is known before or after it. The individual simply disappears.

Whether or not the defendant uses the official lawyer suppled by the regime makes little difference, because the issue of guilt or innocence is never in doubt. The only question is the nature and severity of the sentence.

Where family or friends are admitted to the trial, it is usually the first time they have seen the prisoner since his arrest, which may have been months before. During the trial, direct communication is usually forbidden. It is only after sentencing that any contact is allowed between the sentenced prisoner and his family or friends. He may talk with them briefly. Sometimes a package of food, clothing, and money may be passed to the prisoner, for his transport and exile. Then come heart-rending farewells, and the prisoner is returned to jail.

The prisoner does not learn the place of his exile at this time. Selection of the place of exile is usually based on several considerations, including the length of sentence and the health and strength of the prisoner. Often, the deciding factor is whether the regime wants him to survive the sentence. There are many places in Siberia and elsewhere where a sentence of exile is tantamount to a death sentence.

With the place of exile determined, the prisoner begins his trip. If it is relatively close, the trip may be made with no stopovers. For more distant places, the journey may take days or weeks, with stopovers at local jails along the way. He remains completely under the control of the MVD—the Ministry of Internal Affairs, a branch of the KGB—and is guarded by well-armed MVD personnel.

Finally, he arrives with his meager possessions at the place of exile, which may be a fairly remote Siberian village deep in the forests where the only activity is timber-cutting and logging. Reporting to the local MVD office—there are MVD offices everywhere—he is taken to the Commandant and turns in the official paper specifying the place and term of exile.

The Commandant gives him an assignment form which states the conditions of his exile at this location: that he must stay within the limits of the village or such work areas in the forest as may be designated; that infringements of these restrictions could lead to a long-term sentence (up to twenty years) as a prisoner (not an exile) at hard labor. The prisoner signs the paper agreeing to these terms. He really has no choice.

Now he is "free," the Commandant tells him, to begin his new life, and he will be expected to report to the MVD once a week. He is given another official form which identifies him as a convicted criminal assigned for exile in this area. This serves as his only identity document—a substitute for his internal passport—during the period of his exile. The Commandant suggests he might find work cutting timber in the nearby forest. He is then dismissed and leaves the building, "free" for the term of his sentence.

"Free" for what? Even "free *from* what? He has no job, no place to live, no assurance even of the chance to obtain food, in a small and obviously very poor Siberian village.

But, as the Commandant said, he is "free" to do or not to do what he wants. The regime will not force him to do anything except stay in this place for the duration of his sentence. There is no requirement to work, but if he doesn't he will be regarded as a "parasite," making it difficult if not impossible to get enough food to live. And if he didn't work during exile, he would later be sentenced to "hard labor" for a long term. So he is "free" to work if he can find a job. Or "free" to die, which would not be difficult in these surroundings.

He is also "free" to live where he wishes or is able to find shelter. There is no requirement to live in any particular place so long as he stays within his limits. With a long severely cold and bitter Siberian winter only weeks away, it is clear that he soon will be "free" to freeze to death.

Without question he realizes, indeed he knows, that he *is* relatively free. He thinks of the others, the countless now nameless and faceless who were sentenced to long terms in prison and slave-labor camps, working themselves to death under far worse conditions than the poverty of a village in the Siberian forests.

He may start wondering again, as he did during the weeks in prison before the trial, whether his personal bid for freedom—his individual dissidence—has been worth it. He had a pretty good job, a place to live—not much of one, but a place—a family and friends. Yet the injustices of the system rankled, became a gnawing obsession, and he spoke out, he wrote of freedom—real freedom and justice in the Soviet Union.

He understood perfectly well the possibility, indeed the likelihood, of arrest, prison, slave labor, or exile when he first began to express his views about the regime openly. When they came to get him it should not have been a surprise, but it certainly was a shock.

And now in the squalid village he was "free." Was it worth

it? The process of breaking a man—less brutal than in the past, but undeniably efficient—was beginning to work on him.

But to stand there with the cool of a Siberian evening fast coming on was no solution to the immediate problem of staying alive. Shelter, any shelter, was needed.

The villagers, meanwhile, were not unaware of the presence of a new exile. Many of them were the sons or daughters of those exiled a generation or more ago. Others had been exiles themselves but, following completion of their terms, had for a variety of reasons decided to stay on here, despite the poor conditions of their existence. It may not be the best life possible, but clearly it is not the worst. They were alive, and countless others were not.

Because this village, like most Soviet villages, existed at a near poverty level, a new exile couldn't expect much. However, he might not be warmly welcomed, but he wouldn't be turned away—particularly if he could work, or if he had money. For many of the more recent exiles were from substantial families, or had held well-paying jobs: many had some money, often much more than most of the villagers.

The first requirement is shelter for the night. He goes to the nearest house (hut or hovel would be more accurate) and asks if he can sleep inside, on the floor with the cow and the pigs if necessary. He will take little space and will work, do whatever is asked, for the chance of a place to sleep. The peasant, standing at the door of his crowded one-room hut with his toddlers and the chickens running about on the dirt floor, is compassionate, but firm.

"You can see for yourself, comrade, we have no space. With the cold nights coming on, we bring the cow and calf and the pigs inside too, so we're full up. You might try Yuri Petrovich down the street. He has fewer children and a larger house."

If he can offer money, a place may be made for him, even on the stove where the family sleeps. With enough money, he may even displace a younger family member, who goes back to sleeping on the floor.

After several stops at other huts, he gets a place—sleeping with a cow in a rude shed attached to a one-room house. For the moment, for the night, he has a place to sleep and is grateful to his host for the roof and the warmth of the cow.

Food is another matter. A village family may be willing to share its simple and often limited fare for one meal or even two. Beyond that, especially for a new exile who is unknown and untested, it may be difficult. Unless of course the exile has money; but under these conditions, even money may not be as important as food in hand. The constant nagging concern of every peasant is, "Will there be enough for the family through the winter?"

For the new exile, this may be the emergency for which the dwindling food supply his family gave him at the time of parting had been planned. Rusks of carefully dried bread are the staple of this emergency food supply. And if he is lucky, there may still be a piece of cheese or sausage saved for just such a time. Relieving his hunger with the rusks, he drifts off to sleep against the warm side of the cow, thinking: This is only shelter. Tomorrow, there must be work.

The pale sun was barely over the horizon when the trucks roared over the ruts in the village street. They came to haul the men out to their work in the forests where the timber-cutting was. The exile joined them, a helping hand pulled him up into the back of the truck, and, along with twenty others, he headed for the woods.

After the others had gone to their work in the woods, he approached the foreman and asked for a job. "Sure you can have a job cutting timber, but can you do the work?" the foreman laughed, not unkindly, looking at his pale, uncal-loused, city-bred hands. For years they had done no manual labor heavier than using a pen, pencil, or typewriter. He had not even been active in sports.

Most of the dissidents these days come from essentially white-collar, middle-class backgrounds and jobs. Anti-regime voices are rare among manual laborers, factory workers, and peasants.

"If you can cut and stack six cubic meters a day, you'll get four rubles. Twenty-five workdays a month," the foreman continued. "Can you do it?"

He shrank a bit under the direct but friendly question from the foreman. Could he? He doubted it. He hardly even knew how to swing an axe, much less to handle a bow saw. But was there a choice? He could inquire about a less physically demanding job—something in the camp office perhaps, or tallying the logs as they are loaded for shipment.

If he had money—a lot of money—he could try to sweeten his request for an easier job like bookkeeping or something else for which he was at least fairly well equipped. And, with luck, he could buy or bribe his way along.

Lacking money, he could only make a stab at lumberjacking. He seized the axe in his unaccustomed fingers and trudged in his city shoes into the woods.

So it went. Survival as an exile requires ready adaptation to a new and grim situation. Many victims of Soviet oppression in all of its forms have been able to survive, but many more have gone under.

After months or a year or more of adapting, a new groove, a way of living a little above survival, is established in the village. A better place to live is found or even built, with help from the villagers. A small garden is planted, bringing a modest food supply—potatoes, cabbage, little else; but still, something to be put aside for the long Siberian winter.

A routine closely in harmony with the Siberian seasons develops. In Siberia, the weather rules. It dictates a long semi-hibernation through the worst parts of the winter, almost sealed in the hut, close to the stove. The deep and heavy mud of the spring and fall cause a different kind of isolation. And then there is the short Siberian summer, with its long, warm days and twilight through the night. A life very close to the primitive rhythms of nature.

I'm not much more than an animal, the exile thinks to himself. But it's not really a bad life—I eat and sleep and work—and I'm alive! This last point was heavily underscored one day deep in the forest. While doing a survey line with a team, well beyond their own working area, they came on another large crew cutting timber. But these men were different—a slave gang from a forced-labor camp. He had heard talk in the village about such a camp some kilometers away, but it was a shock when he actually *saw* them. They like himself, were political prisoners, but they had been sentenced to long years at hard labor rather than exile.

With each working team of ten or so, there were two well-armed guards and two savage watchdogs. The guards, alerted by the dogs' barking, waved his crew away, but he had been close enough to see the prisoners' thin, haggard faces, eyes without hope, and bodies emaciated from overwork and hunger. These men were working out their lives, and for most of them there was no hope, no prospect of a tomorrow when their sentences might end and they might be allowed to lead the relatively free life of an exile.

There, he thought, but for the grace of God, go I. And for a moment, he was grateful to the Communist Party for giving him such a light sentence.

Some time later, as he lay on his warm stove, he realized that he was no longer thinking like a dissident. He had become an exile, a Siberian working out his sentence, with few thoughts about anything except his very simple and uncomplicated routine existence. Nothing else really mattered. He realized he thought less and less about his family, and indeed he rarely heard from them now. There was almost no communication from his old friends, the handful of dissidents he had known, the old group.

And rarely, anymore, did he think about any future beyond the years of his exile, which still stretched out before him. Returning to home and to do his old job—if he could get it back, which was unlikely—seemed so remote he could hardly even imagine it. And he knew that Moscow and Leningrad and the other big cities would undoubtedly be off-limits for him the rest of his life.

He was, in a way, shocked by the nature and level of his thoughts. No longer the bright intellectual who had thought to change the Soviet system—the system that now provided him with the simple necessities of his life. But he was intelligent enough to know what had happened to him over the months and years of his exile. He had been beaten by the Soviet system.

He was no longer a dissident. He was not even against the

regime anymore. They had beaten him, as they had beaten countless others before him. He could not admit, even to himself, that he had been *broken* by the system. That would be too much for the small part of his mind which still thought within the old frame of reference. It wouldn't allow him to admit final defeat. To be broken would be degrading.

And he was still a man in spite of everything that had been done to him. There was still some pride. He had *not* been broken by the system. And he, a soft city-dweller with smooth pale hands, had beaten the forest and the trees. He felt his rough, calloused hands, with their broken, dirty, untrimmed nails. By God, those hands could work!

As he drifted off to sleep, he thought only that tomorrow was another day. But he was content, and knew he would never go back.

He was home.

Once again, the Soviet system had won over the dissident. They had stilled a dissident voice and gained a docile worker, willing to produce and live at a bare subsistence level. He needed no guards, no dogs, and no expensive non-productive apparatus. After all, he was "free"!

Unless the prisoner was to be worked to death, the exile system was better and cheaper than slave labor.

And in the outside world, almost no one knew or cared.

Why should they change such an effective system?

SWISS MOVEMENT

> A well regulated militia, being necessary to the security
> of a free State, the right of the people to keep and bear arms,
> shall not be infringed.—Second Article of Amendment to
> the Constitution of the United States of America.

The Swiss Confederacy last fell to a conqueror when Napoleon's army carried Liberty, Equality, and Fraternity at bayonet point across Europe. Even then the "Helvetian Republic" enjoyed considerable autonomy within the new French Continental System.

Since that time the Swiss have built their defense on a single principle: armed neutrality. And when they say armed, they mean armed.

Like the Roman Republic of old, the Swiss army is the Swiss nation. Conscription is universal; there are no exceptions. None. Not for theological students and priests, not for the most conscientious of conscientious objectors. Every male citizen of Switzerland serves in the army from age eighteen until he is fifty. For the first few years his training is intense; for the next dozen years, he will report annually; and from age thirty five to fifty he will be in the standby reserve, liable to military call at any time.

Moreover, from age eighteen until age fifty he keeps his military weapons at home. They are liable to military inspection at any time, and God help the citizen whose equipment is not in good order. (One obvious consequence of this policy is that Swiss society is well armed; there are no gun control laws. There are also few armed robberies.)

Thus do the Swiss defend their liberties.

There are some who say the price is too high; that the obligations of universal military service outweigh the benefits of freedom. The Swiss do not agree. To them, military service is not an onerous duty. It is a privilege. To be sure, it is a privilege which must not be refused; but a privilege nonetheless.

There are no constitutional reasons why the United States could not employ the Swiss system of universal military training.

The courts have repeatedly held conscription to be within the powers of Congress, and the Second Amendment implies the power to issue regulations for governing the militia.

Nor could it be claimed that universal conscription is undemocratic. Most of the great democracies throughout history were defended by conscripts, and indeed most only fell when they turned from the draft to a "voluntary" military. It is difficult to enslave a democracy with citizens in arms; while a professional army may well be loyal to its officers, and often thinks contemptible the citizens it defends. Professionals have a near monopoly on the effective means of violence; they thus have a constant temptation to rob the paymaster rather than fight for him.

Libertarians object that conscription is itself an unjustifiable imposition on liberty. Robert Heinlein once said that a nation which must be defended by conscripts is not worth defending. One doubts that he really meant that, since not long after he volunteered to be returned to active duty in a time when we still had the draft; one may after all be more patriotic than libertarian, and given the alternatives in this imperfect world many libertarians shrink from following their arguments to their final conclusion.

The other objection one hears is that we cannot entrust the safety of the state to its citizens; that the Swiss system would turn us into an armed camp. *Some* groups (which ones depend upon who is talking) would abuse their privileges and use their weapons to enslave others. . . .

We would certainly be armed under the Swiss system; but travelers in Switzerland do not feel themselves within the oppressive confines of a garrison state; and Swiss society is made up of groups which at one or another time had as much reason to oppress each other as any in history. One wonders if the famous Swiss tolerance of language and religious differences is not at least in part due to the knowledge that all the linguistic and religious groups are well armed and well trained. . . .

Vinicoff and Martin show another possible Swiss defense in this story of the near future.

SWISS MOVEMENT

by Eric Vinicoff and Marcia Martin

The highway between Munich and Border Station Nineteen wound through benighted woods and solemn hills. Few automobiles traveled it, since most of the post's supplies and personnel came and went by jetcopter. But General Ober owned a vintage '82 Porsche, and he indulged his love of driving at every opportunity. Thus it was that he sped along the two-lane road, returning to the post after a staff meeting in Heidelberg.

He let his mental auto-pilot guide the Porsche while he mulled over his new assignment. The Premier wanted an incident. Not that there was any real danger of outside intervention—the world was not going to come to the aid of Switzerland after the Collapse of 1992—yet even a flimsy provocation would serve to lessen international rumblings.

It should not be difficult to fake an attack on Nineteen; Swiss Ski Patrol uniforms and weapons are already stockpiled for the operation. Secrecy is the key. Who can I trust to help me in this? Berfeld?

Twin lights in the rear scanner screen caught his attention. A Volkswagen electric mini-bus drew alongside the Porsche. It was filled to overflowing with a blond-haired family.

So the war finally begins. I am glad. Hauggard argues that the Swiss cannot be conquered because of their tenacity and excellent defensive location, but that kind of thinking harkens back to the days of troop warfare. With CBMs to batter them—not to mention fighters, bombers, attack jetcopters, glider-landing air cavalry and robo-tanks—I wager the end will be swift and satisfactory. At best we can defeat them, and at worst—destroy them.

The Volkswagen honked its horn gaily, and General Ober honked back. It was good to see people unaffected by the grimness of military life.

Atomic weapons are another advantage we have over the Swiss. We do not dare use them, of course; an A-assault on Switzerland would pollute half the water in Central Europe, and much of the air as well. But perhaps the threat of atomic warfare would cause—

He never saw the woman beside the driver of the Volkswagen open her window. He never saw the tow-headed girl in the back seat hand her mother a tangerine-sized globe of dark plastic. He never saw the mother depress a button in the side of the ball and toss it across the gap between the two vehicles.

In fact, no single, final, distinctive sight marked for General Ober his passage from life to death. The Porsche burst into orange and black around him, then it crashed through a stand of somber oaks.

Laughing and smiling still, the blond-haired family drove on.

GOVERNMENT CENTRAL,
HEIDELBERG, NOREUROPA

"I've called this emergency meeting," said the Premier, "to consolidate our Switzerland campaign." He glared at his seven department heads spaced around the circular conference table. "Einerson, where is your report on the Basel Institute? Why hasn't it been forwarded to me?"

Gunnar Einerson, the Head of Military Intelligence, knew he was being upbraided. He gripped his lucky stone firmly and replied, "Two of my best operatives are investigating now, Premier. I expect them back in three days. But I tell you, the Swiss wouldn't destroy the Institute just to keep it out of our hands. They're saner than that."

"We must be certain!" Premier Kosti shouted. His mercurial temper was merely a pose, a political tool for intimidating subordinates. Beneath it lay an organic computer untainted by emotion. "The mining bacteria they cultivate there is worth more than everything else in the country combined!"

Then the Premier listened carefully to his earphone monitor. Anger brought redness to his face.

"General Ober's automobile was just found wrecked along

the highway to Border Station Nineteen," he announced. "That means our plan for creating an incident with Switzerland was *not* put into effect! Our schedule is set back days . . . maybe weeks!"

No sympathy for Ober—just wrath at the untimeliness of his death, Gunnar observed. Then an equally unpleasant thought came to him. "Premier, you're assuming he died accidentally?"

Kosti was irritated at being wrenched from his own dark calculations. "Of course! What else? He lost control of that ludicrous racing car and crashed!"

Gunnar's hunch crystallized into a certainty. He used his station's phone link to call the police in Munich and order that some tests be made.

Frederico Martinelli, late of Noreuropan Military Intelligence, lay collapsed over the washstand of a shabby apartment in downtown Basel—on the left bank of the Rhine and less than nine hundred meters from the Institute. Hans Bergenholm decided from the stiffness of the corpse that it had been there for many hours.

Operatives never become friendly with other operatives—it is too chancy—but you were pleasant to work with, Frederico Martinelli. Good-bye.

Hans examined the husky Latin body for clues, but he found none. Nor did a look around the bathroom reveal anything. Frederico held a toothbrush in one dead hand, so Hans placed a small dab of toothpaste from the uncapped tube onto the washstand and sniffed it. All he could detect was mint overpowering enough to hide any more subtle aroma.

He looked closely at the tube and smiled. At the base, where only the most discerning observer would have seen it, a tiny puncture mark marred the slick plastic. *Something fatal injected into the toothpase? How baroque! Someone goes to great lengths to make his murders look accidental.*

But who? Who explains why, how and everything else. Not the Swiss, surely. Their espionage service is such a pitiful little thing, and very carefully watched. If they were good enough to kill a skilled operative like Frederico, we would know it.

Perhaps someone wants to deprive Noreuropa of Switzer-land—and the Basel Institute. France? Balkania? The Soviet Union? It could be anyone. Fortunately I can leave that particular complication to Gunnar. My problems are to complete the assignment and stay alive. In that order.

Hopefully I do not have to start over quite from scratch. If only Frederico kept his diary up to date and well-hidden.

Hans quickly found the floor tile which was not as firmly secured in place as its fellows. He pushed it away, removed a cunningly inserted chunk of floorboard and pulled out the small black notebook.

He opened it, flipping to the final entry. The writing was in German—computer cryptography had eliminated fancy cyphers.

SWISS SECURITY IS A FARCE. I PROBED B. I. LAST NIGHT. NO DETECTION. I DESCENDED INTO THE TOP-SECRET LEVEL AND CHECKED THE SHIPPING RECORDS FOR T. S. CULTURES. IT OCCURRED TO EINERSON THAT TAILORED BACTERIA MIGHT HAVE WAR POTENTIAL.

NONE ARE GOING TO MILITARY POSTS. HOWEVER, MUCH TO MY SURPRISE AND CONCERN, I LEARNED THAT ALMOST ALL OF THE NON-COMMERCIAL STRAINS ARE BEING DISPATCHED TO NATIONAL SERVICE TRAINING CENTERS.

Hans, too, was surprised. Of all the countries in Europe, only Switzerland retained compulsory military training for its citizens—Sweden had abandoned the practice upon incorporating with Noreuropa. Every Swiss man and woman took a year of training at the age of nineteen. The National Service Centers were only quasi-military operations, however; they could hardly be key points in the Swiss defense plans. Why, then, were they receiving shipments of special biocultures from Basel? He read on.

THE ONLY OTHER SIZABLE SHIPMENTS OF T. S. STRAINS ARE MONTHLY ORDERS SENT TO THE HOROLOGICAL LABORATORY IN NEUCHATEL.

WE MUST INVESTIGATE THERE NEXT.

FINAL SUMMATION ON TROOP DEPLOYMENT (ADDEN-
DUM FOR EINERSON).

MILITARY FORCES ARE IN DEFENSIVE ALIGNMENT FOR
A NOREUROPAN ATTACK, BUT THE SWISS DO NOT APPEAR
TO TAKE THE THREAT SERIOUSLY. PUBLIC OPINION IS
THAT NO INVASION WILL TAKE PLACE. ERGO, I ASSUME
THEY PLAN TO ACCEPT INCORPORATION.

Hans shook his head. His own spying had confirmed that
the Swiss did *not* plan to accept incorporation.

Then why are they so confident of their safety?

*I wish I could call Gunnar for orders. This personal-contact-
only procedure may work wonders for security, but it is hell on
operatives stuck in the field with broken assignments. Technically I know I should finish up on the Institute operation, but
these new loose ends look more important.*

Only one question remained; which to investigate first-the
Training Centers or the Horological Laboratory.

GOVERNMENT CENTRAL
HEIDELBERG, NOREUROPA

". . . mercury fulminate, most likely," reported the voice
from Munich police central. "We found traces of the bomb
casing—our lab is studying them now. All we know for sure
is that it wasn't an amateur job. Most—"

Premier Kosti's fist slammed a button on the arm of his
throne-like chair, and the voice died. "The Swiss!" he muttered. "So this is how they defend themselves!" He smiled
thinly. "General Ober supplies us with our incident after
all.

"If the Swiss think that treacherously killing one general
will deter us, let them learn how wrong they are! Kroger,
bring our forces to combat readiness! I'll give the Swiss one
last opportunity to incorporate willingly! If they refuse, we
invade!"

High General Kroger, more comfortable in his military
environment then at these Council sessions under the eye of
the Premier, mumbled softly, "I will, ah . . . attend to it at

once, sir." He activated his com link and began whispering orders.

"Einerson," the Premier continued, "I want no more automobile crashes involving important government officials! Arrange guards for every citizen with an O clearance or higher! Further, I want every Swiss national in Noreuropa arrested—every vacationer, businessman, embassy worker and so on! Every Swiss national! Interrogate them! Find out what happened to General Ober, who ordered it and why!"

Gunnar wondered how, with so many soldiers committed to the Swiss invasion, he would be able to muster guards for every important man and woman in Noreuropa—and then send others after the Swiss nationals. "Yes, Premier," he sighed.

In the central section of Neuchatel, occupying an entire block all by itself, stood the ugly concrete box of the Swiss Horological Laboratory. Founded in 1796 by the *Federation des Fabricateurs de Montres*, it was bought by the Swiss government during the money troubles of 1992. In its early days the laboratory had worked solely to improve the art of watchmaking. By the Twenty-first Century, however, SHL operated in every genre of micromanipulation. SHL microtools could be found functioning superiorly in every nation on Earth. They were the *ne plus ultra* of their field.

A Swiss Army truck entered the SHL garage at ten minutes after midnight. Guards gave it a cursory examination, then they sent it down to the bottom level garage—where the highest security was maintained.

The truck bore one item of unexpected cargo—Hans Bergenholm.

Confident in his "borrowed" Swiss Army sergeant's uniform, Hans marched along a gleaming corridor and peered into room after room. In each one technicians labored over banks of micromanipulatory equipment, performing incomprehensible tasks. Hans knew by the number of signs urging caution and soldiers on patrol that he was in a top-secret area.

Inside the last room of the corridor something caught his eye which stopped him abruptly. A crate marked BASEL INSTITUTE—FRAGILE sat on the floor.

"INTRUDER ALERT!" An electronically amplified voice reverberated through the corridor. "INTRUDER ALERT! LOOK FOR A MAN IN A SERGEANT'S UNIFORM. HE IS AN IMPOSTOR!"

So they went to load a new cargo into the truck and found the driver. Time for another change of costume. Hans slipped quietly into the workroom containing the Basel Institute crate. The small white cubicle was dominated by a roundtable micromanipulation station. Concentric rings of controls wound around the rim—nine seats faced them, but only one was occupied. A rotating work platform stood elevated in the center. From the ceiling sprouted lights, television cameras, waldoes and other tools.

The workroom's occupant, a huge man with short black hair, was engrossed in a televised image of his work-in-progress. By the look of him he had not even heard the alert.

Hans slashed the man across the back of the neck, then he quickly shut the sliding door and donned his third outfit of the night. Before departing, however, he eyed the object on the work platform.

It was to all appearances a perfectly normal portable FM radio—a Revox model which Hans had often seen in shop windows. The backplate was in place, but he had interrupted the process of inserting the second of four holding screws.

Hans put the radio in his coat pocket—there would hopefully be time to examine it later. It appeared to be the next link in a mysterious, confusing chain.

Feet pounded down the corridor toward the workroom. Hans put his back to the wall beside the door. When two armed guards charged into the room, he caught the second one through with a blow similar to that which had felled the technician. The result was the same.

Hans stepped out into the passageway—empty—and paused by the door. The first guard had turned at the sound of his crumpling fellow; now he moved cautiously into the corridor. Hans smiled and thumbed the DOOR SHUT button.

While the guard wrestled with the power door, Hans tore the FN submachine gun from his hands and smashed down on the brown-capped head with it. Then he walked calmly back toward the garage. The weapon he hid under his bulky lab coat.

Several contingents of soldiers hurried past him. *So long as the hare remains one step ahead of the hounds, he is safe. If only my luck will hold a little longer.*

He entered the garage office prepared to deal permanently with whoever stood between him and escape, but the place was empty. *Scouring the level for me, most likely.* He hunted around the control panels until he found the automatic lift sequencer. Activating it, he stepped into the garage proper.

"There he is!" someone shouted. "Get him!" Slugs from at least two FNs drove Hans to cover behind a truck's front end. He returned fire with his own stolen weapon. A squad of soldiers spread out to trap him.

Hans looked around desperately. The garage lift entrance was grinding open, but fifty meters of bare concrete lay between it and him. Directly behind him sat a military motorcycle-cum-sidecar. Hans dug into his memory, and his heart jumped. The cycle did not require a key!

He dove into the saddle and started the fuel-cell-powered motor. Hunched over as much as possible, he still took a long, shallow bullet graze across his upper back. The pain almost caused him to fall off the cycle. More streams of nickel alloy whipped past his ear.

Wheels spun on concrete, grabbed, and Hans shot across the garage into the lift. Just barely in time, too; the portal almost shut on his posterior.

The ride up took much too long for his sore nerves. He could feel blood on his back and pain spreading through his body. *What can they do to me in here? Gas? Ultrasonics? Hidden guns?*

But apparently the Swiss had not taken any of those precautions for, when the lift reached ground level, Hans remained conscious and intact. The guards there had been warned. Four submachine guns opened up on him as he accelerated into the street, but the soldiers could not gauge the speed of the hurtling cycle well in the darkness. Bullets tore chunks of ice and macadam from the roadway on every side of Hans. Then he was out of range.

Dawn is already on the horizon. I must get away from here quickly. Abandon the cycle. Tend my back. Then examine the radio and attempt to solve this mad riddle.

*   *   *

In the Security Section of SHL, two high-ranking Swiss officers turned away from the television screen they had been watching. One nodded to the other and said, "It was a tightrope between being too easy to penetrate and actually killing the Noreuropan operative—but I think we walked it successfully."

"Will he understand what he saw?" pondered the other. "If not, everything we've done is useless."

"Then," responded the first officer, "both sides will 'reap a whirlwind' as the saying goes."

Hans retrieved his suitcase at the Neuchatel train station an hour after dawn. He slipped into the men's lavatory and donned fresh clothing. His torn, dirty and blood-stained lab coat went into the dump chute. A clumsily placed bandage covered the equally clumsily cleaned wound on his back—working on one's own back with just a shaving mirror for guidance is not easy.

Procuring a map in the lobby, he sat down on a hard bench and hunted for the nearest National Service Training Center. He found one outside of Lipsze, fifty kilometers south and east of Neuchatel, almost on the Italian border. Lipsze was scarcely more than a village, yet it had a train station, so Hans bought a ticket. With over an hour before departure, he ordered a hearty breakfast at the station restaurant. He sat by a window where he could watch the monorail cars pulling away from the platform.

First Hans fought back drowsiness with food and *café au lait*, then he brought out the radio.

Looks absolutely normal. He studied every centimeter of it carefully. No hidden switches. No unusual fittings. He flipped the ON-OFF knob and tuned in station after station. *Whatever else it does, it certainly works well as a radio.*

Then Hans found the unmarked setting between FM and FM stereo. A streamer of white vapor began to leak from the radio's speaker. He caught one sniff of the gas and frantically twisted the switch back to FM. Using a napkin, he fanned the fumes away.

Nerve gas! This is a murder weapon!

Eighteen hours later, Hans gained the top of a hill over-looking the Lipsze National Service Training Center. He shut off the motor of his rental snowmobile and used its field scanner to put a closeup image of the camp on the dashboard screen. He watched it, shivering. *Why, oh why did I not phone ahead and reserve a closed cabin model?* Even a rented warm-suit turned up to full power was not equal to the biting night.

Dawn remained hours off, but there was a full moon by which Hans could see. The layout of barracks around a central court appeared like any other military camp. Soldiers patrolled beyond the outer fence. Floodlights added their puddles of illumination to the scene. Hans sat back and waited.

The zealous young heroes who wish to join Military Intelligence should be here now. Our work is not all high living and romantic adventure. Most of it is sitting and waiting—cold, boring, unglamorous waiting.

A truck arrived at the main gate shortly after sunrise. Hans, half-frozen, recognized the Army vehicle as one he had seen in the SHL garage. Presumably it bore a cargo of micro-machined products.

Are they all radios, or a selection of equally innocent-looking devices? What purpose do they serve? And why are they brought here? Hans laughed at himself. These were the questions to which he himself was supposed to be learning the answers, not asking them of the grim Aesir.

The truck parked in the court, and young people in brown Army uniforms—civilian youths taking their year of training—started to unload small packages. These were borne into a high-roofed storehouse.

Elsewhere on the field, the early morning instruction pro-gram was beginning. Trainees worked in squads of twenty, directed by older men and women, garbed not in Army brown, to Hans' surprise, but in black, unadorned warm-suits.

The training procedures also startled him. Judo, karate and wrestling were normal enough, but ... one team was *stalking* another, a gigantic game of hide-and-seek played seriously, according to unknown rules. Another team hunched around the hood of a demonstration car while its instructor tinkered with the engine. Another team was receiving small 35mm cameras from an SHL box. Its instructor stood atop one of several discarded crates, lecturing them.

Another team dug holes and planted devices in them— carefully. Another team was being frisked by its instructor, who unearthed an impressive stack of concealed weapons. Another team practiced scaling the two-story wall of the storehouse—using some form of grippers which fitted on their hands and feet. Another team issued from the main gate and scattered into the hillside woods. Two more teams paused by the gate, obviously waiting to go after them.

Hans was fascinated. *This is no military training center; in fact, it seems to have little to do with soldiering. But I do recall something similar—the M. I. institution at Jarlsberg. A training school for spies. Is this where Switzerland produces operatives so good that we have never spotted them in the field?*

But nobody is that good. Operatives do not carry on their activities in a vacuum. If they were gathering information in other nations, we would know it. Another thing: the training down there is too specialized. No espionage skills, no spy techniques. Just the "commando" end of the business. In fact ...

It all came together. *A secret training academy—not for operatives, but for people who can kill even a man like Frederico who knew every dirty trick in the business, for people who use props like gas bombs disguised as radios, for ... assassins.*

GOVERNMENT CENTRAL
HEIDELBERG, NOREUROPA

Gunnar picked up the top flimsy from a stack on the arm of his chair and waved it at Premier Kosti. "They've been coming in all day, Premier. For example—" He began to read from the sheet:

"REPORT: POLICE, UNIFIED BERLIN. IN PURSUANCE OF
COUNCIL SECURITY DIRECTIVE 208. WE SOUGHT TO AR-
REST THOSE SWISS NATIONALS IN OUR JURISDICTION.

"CASE ONE: LE JOI, FRANCES E., AGE 26, FEMALE, RESI-
DENCE IN ZERMATT, SWITZERLAND. STATED PURPOSE OF
VISIT—PURCHASING GOODS FOR HER PHOTOGRAPHIC SHOP.

"SERGEANTS FRITZ MEULLER AND JON KURTZMAN AR-
RESTED THE AFOREMENTIONED AT 0730 ON JANUARY 17
AT HER HOTEL ROOM. THEY WERE ENROUTE TO POLICE
CENTRAL, WITH HER IN THE PRISONER SECTION OF THEIR
PATROL CAR, AT 0750 (COM CALL CONFIRMATION).

"THE VEHICLE WAS FOUND, AT 1050, WRECKED IN A FIELD
OUTSIDE OF OUR JURISDICTION. SERGEANTS MEULLER
AND KURTZMAN WERE SEATED WITHIN, DEAD FROM BRO-
KEN NECKS APPROPRIATE TO SUCH AN ACCIDENT. NO
TRACES OF THE PRISONER REMAINED.

"CASE TWO—"

"Enough." Kosti's voice was deadly calm. "You tell me they
all read that way, and I believe you. Every Swiss national in
Noreuropa has gone into hiding. Those who were arrested
managed to escape through 'accidents.' Accidents!" he screamed.
"They weren't accidents! They weren't ordinary citizens, either! Soldiers, Einerson! Soldiers sent to ruin us from within!
Are our key men and women guarded?"

"Yes, Premier." Gunnar wiped sweat from his forehead.
"But I disagree about the nationals being soldiers. They
aren't. They can't be. You know how carefully we checked
them before issuing travel visas. None of them have ever
belonged to the Swiss military. Each has a *bona fide* history
running back to his or her teens."

"What else can they be?" the Premier shrieked.

Gunnar shook his head. "I don't know, Premier. I just don't
know."

*A training school for assassins. Bio-warfare cultures from
Basel. Special equipment from SHL. Graduates go from here
to kill spies like Frederico and . . . who else?* Hans sat back in
his snowmobile and pondered a hundred questions.

Motive was the major mystery. *Killing an operative is not going to put Noreuropa off; the Swiss must know that. I wonder what their program is.*

Watching trainees scatter into the woods below him. Hans knew where that data could be obtained.

He crept down the hillside toward the camp, intent on a stalk of his own. From the bare ridge summit he prowled through increasing numbers of leafless trees until the ground leveled off and he found himself moving amid thick woods.

Away to his right a branch quivered and dropped its burden of snow. A slight sound, most men would not have heard it. But Hans' life had often hinged on such sounds; he was sensitive to them. He fell onto his belly and crawled in that direction.

Hans peered through the branches of a fat, concealing bush. At first he saw nothing unusual near the noise-making tree. A snowdrift lay up against the northern side of the trunk—that was all. No footprints, no movements, no sounds; only silence and stillness. Whoever had upset the snow was well hidden.

So Hans waited. Patience was the gift of maturity to operatives; attempts to drill it into the young almost always fell short of total success. After a long but unmeasured amount of time, the snowdrift moved. A lithe figure in white began to crawl away from the tree.

Ten meters separated the stalker and his prey. Hans knew he could get no closer without alerting the trainee anyway, so he crashed through the underbrush and dove full upon the back of the other man. That worthy, having heard the first twig snap in Hans' leap, half-turned to fend him off.

A silent struggle ensued, as neither wished to advertise his presence. The trainee still believed that he was fighting one of his fellows.

Hans struck out with a paralyzing blow before the trainee realized differently. The Swiss youth had fought frantically and with skill, but he did not have the fine edge of coordination which experience brings. Slinging the limp body over his shoulder, Hans moved cautiously up the hillside.

He dumped his unconscious cargo into the snowmobile seat and pulled off the white helmet. A pale face appeared, with red lips and straw-blond hair. *Hans Bergenholm, you must be getting old not to have recognized those curves, even through a warm-suit.*

Exposure to the morning chill brought the girl around. She took her disconcerting situation calmly, which made Hans happy. A professional himself, he preferred dealing with professionals. "You're not one of the teachers," she said flatly. "Who are you?"

Hans watched carefully the tensing of her neck muscles. "Please don't," he requested softly. "I'm fifty pounds heavier than you, more skilled, and I already am what you are training to be."

She relaxed. "So you're an . . . operative. Noreuropa?"

"Yes. Now let me explain the rules of the game. I have the key, so you can't start the snowmobile. There are no handy blunt instruments. I patted you down for weapons and found none. If you try to scream, I'll have to coldcock you. Finally, we're far enough away from your assassination academy to eliminate the possiblity of visitors. We can, therefore, have a serious discussion."

There is only one point at which to stop talking in an interrogation—the beginning. The girl stared impassively.

"That won't work either," Hans said. "I'd hate to have to hurt you."

"Would you really?" The girl's voice dripped scorn. "I bet you'd enjoy it! My name's Andrea, Andrea Deneuve! I'm not talking because of your threat, you repulsive old man, but because I've something to say! So long as a single Swiss citizen lives we'll never be conquered! Take *that* back and tell it to your horrible old Premier!

"Switzerland has *always* been free! We survived Caesar, Charlemagne, Napoleon, Bismarck, Hitler and Drachek! We'll survive your Premier!"

Hans replied, "Switzerland can't possibly withstand our military machine. Your mountains and harsh winters and brave soldiers won't save you, just as Germany's 'Fortress Europe' didn't save her from the Allied invasions during

World War Two. You've nö choice. You either accept incorporation, or lose a devastating and futile war.

"Joining Noreuropa isn't like becoming a slave province of ancient Rome. We put strict controls on resource use, of course, but they're necessary. That's why Noreuropa exists; to insure, by means of a united Europe, the best exploitation of our limited natural resources. Since Africa and Asia and the Americans are hoarding, we must make do with what little we have."

The girl's cheeks flushed with suppressed rage, and she prepared a retort. Hans was pleased with his ploy. By drawing her into a political argument, he had gotten past her half-trained caution. *Keep this going long enough, Hans, and she might say something useful.*

"We don't need Noreuropa to keep us from wasting resources!" the girl spat out. "We budget ourselves quite carefully! After all, *our* scientists developed the mining bacteria! You've no right to tell us how to live! We've always *been* free, and we'll always *be* free!"

Hans countered, "You'll only lose the privilege of betraying Europe by foolish unilateral activity. Home rule will be maintained, except in situations which concern Noreuropa as a whole. Your civil rights will be respected.

"Think of what you'll gain; a share of our advanced technology, our social services, our military security, our common pool of resources—everything that comes from belonging to a large and wealthy nation."

"We'll manage on our own, thank you," the girl said bitterly. "Why not offer your benefits to some other country— one willing to be bought!"

Hans decided that the time was ripe to steer her into a more profitable vein. "We don't want to invade your lovely nation, but a unified Europe leaves no room for dissidents— and a unified Europe is what we need today."

"That's what *you* say!" she replied hotly. "Who appointed Noreuropa the mastermind of Europe's future?"

Hans sighed. "If the nations on this continent won't act rationally, then someone must . . ."

"Is Noreuropa fit to play Messiah?" The girl—Andrea—

was close to angry tears. "Noreuropa, who 'saves' Europe by armed conquest? If any nation deserves that role, it's us! Switzerland has lived without war for over twelve hundred years—a span *you* would end! We don't march our armies about and preach peace like you; for centuries we've maintained a sys—" She stopped abruptly, silenced by the fear of saying too much.

GOVERNMENT CENTRAL
HEIDELBERG, NOREUROPA

High General Kroger raised his eyes from the reports he had been reading and announced, "Here is the, ah ... response from Berne to our final demand for incorporation, sir. A Swiss diplomatic messenger just delivered it to our, ah ... embassy there, and they are relaying." He shook his head in disbelief at what he was hearing through the earphone.

The other department heads and Kosti stared at him.

"Well, out with it!" the Premier roared.

Kroger looked distinctly uncomfortable. "Sir, I, ah ... do not understand this!"

"WHAT ... DOES ... THE ... NOTE ... SAY?!"

"Sir," Kroger replied unhappily, "the sum of the Swiss, ah ... communiqué is one word: Drachek."

The Head of Military Intelligence found it incredible that a man could turn so red without bursting, but Kosti managed the feat. While the Premier fumed, Gunnar thought. *Drachek, the Slav leader who almost turned his people into a world power before he was caught in the Purge of '99. How in the name of Odin does he relate to this puzzle?*

Gunnar punched the number of M. I. Central Files on his armrest com. "Rayna," he said, "run a correlation program for Drachek-Switzerland, Drachek-Noreuropa and Drachek-present situation *inter* Noreuropa *et* Switzerland. I want data, and I want it fast!" He broke off the call.

Premier Kosti was ranting again. "This final piece of insolence is too much! Kroger, initiate Operation Checkmate! Since we haven't heard properly from Switzerland, Switzerland shall hear properly from us!"

The High General smiled happily and began whispering into his com. Throughout the room a wave of excited discussion grew. Kosti's wrath became savage anticipation.

Suddenly Kroger gave out a high-pitched squawk of rage. "What?!" he demanded of the com. "Begin a full search at once! The saboteurs must be caught! And when I get to the bottom of this, Colonel, someone down there will lose more than rank!"

Kroger looked up to find every eye in the room on him. "What is it?" asked the Premier with ominous calm.

The High General had trouble speaking. At first nothing came out but squeaking sounds. Then: "Premier Kosti, there has been an, ah . . . explosion in the com-center. It is being investigated. But this will mean a, ah . . . delay in dispatching the invasion orders."

"Use another radio!" The Premier was furious. "Use a telephone! Send an officer in a fast jet! Do anything but weary me with further delays!"

"Unfortunately, it is, ah . . . not that simple, sir," Kroger replied. "The orders must be transmitted through a RASDAX discriminator, otherwise they won't be, ah . . . accepted as authentic. An ordinary, ah . . . radio or telephone won't do. Our auxiliary com-center is being prepared for use, but all of our com-techs were, ah . . . on duty when the explosion occurred. More are being flown in from Bonn, but, ah . . . it will be hours, perhaps days, before the orders can be transmitted.

"As for, ah . . . sending a messenger, only one officer has the authority to initiate Operation Checkmate—the, ah . . . High General. Personal verification is necessary."

Premier Kosti pointed a bone-thin arm at Kroger. "Then go! Deliver the invasion orders personally! But when you return . . . I WANT TO KNOW HOW THE SWISS PENETRATED GOVERNMENT CENTRAL'S SECURITY WEB AND SABOTAGED OUR COM-CENTER!"

High General Kroger bowed stiffly and exited.

"You won't get out of the country, you know," Andrea said. The morning sun rode a little higher in the sky, and the snowmobile was almost bearable.

"Then why not humor me," Hans suggested. "Tell me about your alma mater, the assassination school."

Silence.

"In that case, let me tell you. Switzerland has nineteen National Service Training Centers. My luck would have to be improbably good for me to stumble upon your one and only murder academy. Further, both the Basel Institute and SHL are sending materials to *all* the centers." Hans noted a flickering of Andrea's expression—all he needed to confirm his fantastic suspicion—and continued, "Everything I've seen so far points to a large operation.

"Which is why you're coming to Noreuropa with me. A handful of killers could be coped with, but the thought of what you Swiss might be doing scares me. No wonder you murdered Frederico. Our interrogators will get the whole truth out of you."

"And what do you think that truth is?" she sneered.

Hans swallowed. His assumptions were based on tenuous evidence, to say the least. But they appeared to be the only possible explanation. By hitting her with them and observing the reaction, he would know for sure.

"At the age of nineteen every Swiss citizen enters an NST center for one year. But they don't learn to soldier, do they? They learn to kill! Every man and woman in this lovely, pastoral country is a trained assassin!"

The sentence sounded incredible to Hans even as he uttered it, but her eyes acknowledged that he had spoken the truth.

A drug from Hans' kit . . . Andrea, a comatose sleepwalker incapable of speech . . . by snowmobile to Lipsze . . . new clothes . . . Herr Kleibman and his "disturbed" daughter . . . by train to Geneva . . . Air France to Paris, then Lufthansa to Heidelberg . . . an antidote injection . . .

GOVERNMENT CENTRAL
HEIDELBERG, NOREUROPA

Premier Kosti and Gunnar Einerson were alone in the

Council chamber, discussing the unexplained jet crash that had taken the life of High General Kroger—before he could deliver his orders—when Hans rushed his female prisoner into the room. They went at once to Gunnar's chair and stood quietly beside him; Hans to the right, Andrea to the left.

The Head of Military Intelligence switched on his computer vocal input terminal. The government's cybernetic complex was often called on by the Council for analysis and synthesis; Gunnar wanted it to compile data.

He then asked for Hans' report. Both he and Kosti stared curiously at Andrea, but the question of her presence could wait. The report, in view of everything that had happened, was urgent.

Hans' recitation required more than twenty minutes; at the end of it he could hardly hear himself over Kosti's mutterings of protest. Andrea stood silently through the entire monologue, listening carefully and studying the faces of the three men.

The Premier immediately activated his own computer terminal and asked, "Is Bergenholm lying?"

"Voice and bio-scanner analyses indicate no conscious attempts at falsehood," the baritone pseudo-voice replied.

"Keep monitoring," ordered the Premier. "Report any lies."

Then he muttered to himself. "Now I see Switzerland's game." Turning to Hans, he continued aloud, "Fearing the unknown is natural, Bergenholm, but surely you don't think even a *nation* of knife-in-the-back killers can defeat our forces?"

"Haven't they already?" Gunnar shot back before Hans could answer. The Head of Military Intelligence was frowning. "Every move we make, they block. They don't have to fight our soldiers; they can keep us from ever launching an attack."

Hans looked at Andrea, who was smiling like a blond-haired Mona Lisa, and said, "You've been a bit too docile through all of this. I get the feeling you wanted to come with me. You haven't so much as a poisoned fingernail, so you're obviously not here to kill anyone. You must have something to tell us. Out with it!"

But Andrea shook her head, saying nothing.

Gunnar thrust his left hand into his suit pocket and grasped his lucky stone for courage. Then he said, "Premier, I did some digging, and I believe I know how the Slav leader Drachek relates to all of this."

"I'm listening," Kosti growled.

All eyes were on Gunnar as he began speaking. "The Foreign Office had certain hints in the months just before the purge. Like us, Drachek wanted to annex Switzerland to obtain the Basel Institute. In light of our own difficulties I investigated the 'purge' carefully, and I learned something very disturbing: the men who became the post-purge leaders of Balkania didn't direct or carry out the killings! In fact, to this day no one knows who did! But I doubt it's a coincidence that the new regime had no hostile interest in Switzerland!"

The Premier, whatever his faults, was not stupid. "Swiss assassins! What a brilliant method of self-defense! No need to battle armies—just murder the leaders who threaten you! I wonder how long they've been at it?"

"You can't be serious—" Hans began, only to be cut off by Gunnar.

"A very long time, Premier," Gunnar stated. "I reached the same conclusion as you, but *before* I heard Hans' report. So I probed deeper and found no less than *seven* instances where assassinations or 'accidents' saved Switzerland from foreign aggression—the earliest taking place almost four centuries ago. In 1914, for example both Austria-Hungary and Germany were ready to expand through conquest. Switzerland lay on their borders, an inviting target. But one assassination, cleverly blamed on a fanatic group, started World War One. Both countries lost interest in Switzerland

"In 1943 Hitler was trying to conquer all of Europe— including, eventually, Switzerland. But an 'attempted assassination' that 'failed' turned the little man with the mustache against his most capable generals and lost World War Two for him.

"In 1985 the French—"

"Wait a minute!" Hans interrupted. "If they're that good, I should be dead now! I must have been *allowed* to see what I saw in Switzerland and *allowed* to escape!"

"So Switzerland wants us to know about her assassins," said the Premier. He was speaking thoughtfully instead of shouting—a sign of extreme concern. "Ober, the escape of the nationals, Kroger, our comcenter and Bergenholm's experiences; we're being warned. But why do we deserve a warning when Hitler, Drachek and the others didn't?"

Gunnar was ready with an answer to that. "Because Noreuropa's resource conservation program is vital to Europe, and the Swiss know it! Likewise our program for European unification. Remember Hans' report, his interrogation of Mme. Deneuve? She practically said as much. Switzerland needs Europe, and Europe needs Noreuropa. The Swiss want to stop our invasion, but they don't want us destroyed."

The three men looked to Andrea for confirmation or rejection of Gunnar's theory, but she was attentively studying the ceiling.

"Destroyed?" Hans asked Gunnar. "How can the Swiss assassins destroy us? I don't see this great danger you're hinting at."

"That's because you're blind!" Gunnar replied angrily. "Consider the condition Noreuropa would be in if all of our leaders, administrators, high-ranking officers, important technicians and scientists were killed! Consider our economy shattered by the loss of key personnel, our government inactive, our military beheaded, our whole society paralyzed! Lastly, consider the fact that anybody who tried to put the pieces back together would become a target—and everybody would know it! The results would be worse than the Collapse; we would be prey for France or Balkania or just about anyone else!"

Silence filled the room.

Gunnar eyed Andrea as though she were a chess problem that he could not solve, then he said to the Premier, "I suppose they have it all down to a science. They probably use computers to analyze target countries; put in a desired goal— like preventing an invasion of their homeland—and get out a list of those who must die."

"Computer, attention!" the Premier rapped out. "Given the stated Swiss capabilities for warfare by assassination, calculate our most favorable strategy *in re* invading Switzerland."

Eight seconds passed; an incredibly long time for the cybernetic complex. Then the pseudo-voice replied, "Null program. There are no favorable strategies."

Gunnar nodded. He had reached the same conclusion immediately upon hearing his operative's report. But outrage and disbelief could be read in Hans' face. The Premier appeared lost in thought. Andrea smiled.

"The Swiss have discovered the most efficient form of warfare," Gunnar said in an admiring tone. "They defend their independence by killing two thousand leaders—the right ones—rather than two million troops. Warfare by assassination is easier, more humane and less expensive. Moreover, it produces little property damage. But for seven thousand years no one has seen the obvious—because leaders aren't likely to use a form of warfare in which they're the prime targets."

Gunnar stopped his general lecturing and turned to face the Premier. "But now the Swiss have begun it, and every nation will have to copy them. We'll train assassins." He laughed.

"What is so humorous?" Kosti demanded.

"We're heading for a pragmatic era of world peace!" Gunnar chuckled. "With leaders as targets—and pitifully accessible to expert killers—who will dare start wars? Peace through fear; I think that's the greatest joke in human history!" He laughed again, briefly, then stopped.

No one answered him.

Hans said to Gunnar, "But if we train assassins right away, ours can neutralize theirs. Then our military superiority—"

"A veteran operative should know better," Gunnar replied shortly. "It doesn't work that way. Assassins can't stalk assassins; they need traceable targets. The kind of war you suggest would be mutually devastating—at best. Since Switzerland has such a lead on us, I doubt we would do even that well."

Gunnar laboriously lifted and looked under every corner of

the Swiss trap, hoping to find a flaw. But he could find none.

Ordinary protective measures had failed to stop the assassins. Not surprisingly, since it was almost axiomatic that a skilled assassin held the advantage over his target. The killer could strike at will—whenever the odds most favored him. Extraordinary precautions? A few key men could be thoroughly closeted away, but only a few. And they would not be able to operate very efficiently under wraps. Nor could absolute safety be guaranteed.

Gunnar took a deep breath, faced the Premier squarely and began, "The Swiss have shown us by demonstration and historical example that we'll be destroyed if we invade Switzerland. We're being warned off. I don't think we can dispute the proof; therefore I suggest you cancel Operation Checkmate permanently. Even if we conquered Switzerland we couldn't hold it. Remember what a relative handful of French Resistance fighters did to the Nazis during World War Two, then consider our troops in a nation of killers!"

The Premier said nothing. Gunnar studied his expression. *He is worried, afraid. No one likes to face death. But he is not totally convinced. If he decides to launch the invasion, Noreuropa will suffer cruelly.*

The bleep of the Premier's com unit startled everyone except Andrea. "Premier Kosti!" came an overwrought underling's voice. "Premier, emergency security reports are coming in from all over Noreuropa! Government officials, military commanders, important businessmen; almost every citizen under Military Intelligence special protection has been the victim of a grotesque joke—"

"So it begins," Andrea said, breaking her silence at last. She stepped over to Kosti's chair and flicked off the com. "I can explain much better than he can, Premier. You see, we've arranged a final demonstration of the effectiveness of warfare by assassination. After this, you'll have to make a decision."

Outrage and confusion held the three men rigid. Andrea went on, "Herr Einerson, you're the Head of Military Intelligence—the Noreuropan best equipped to ferret out assassination plots. And here we are in your most secure area. Are you safe?"

"Of course he is," Hans grated. "You were carefully scanned at the door—you haven't any SHL devices hidden away."

Andrea smiled broadly. "Herr Einerson, you have a certain notorious good luck charm in your pocket. Would you bring it out, please, and show it to us?"

Gunnar brought out his stone and stared at it.

"Now open it," she ordered.

Gunnar saw that his small cube of obsidian was bisected by a hairline—one he knew should not be there. He pulled at both sides, and the "lucky stone" fell apart. Within lay a carefully folded slip of paper.

He unfolded the slip. His hands shook only slightly—a testament to iron control.

"Not only here," Andrea said cheerfully, "but in every military installation in every city; everywhere in Noreuropa similar notes are being read. Over three thousand, two targets per assassin. I'm pleased to hear they're having the desired effect."

"What does it say?!" the Premier screamed at Gunnar.

The latter's lips formed the ghost of a smile as he replied, "It reads: 'BOOM—YOU ARE DEAD.' "

Premier Kosti bowed his ancient head and wept.

The JIGSAW MAN

When I conceived this anthology, I naturally supposed that Larry Niven would do a story for it. After all, we are friends and partners, with three collaborations in print and two more in preparation. Moreover, I knew that Larry had strong ideas about liberty.

Oddly enough, though, he couldn't think of a proper story. It may be that his feelings on the subject are too strong.

There remained "Jigsaw Man," written years ago, but as relevant today as when it was first done.

One chief enemy of liberty is greed. Barbarians lust after the wealth of defenseless civilizations. Within the society, the greedy few may plunder the powerless many. We understand the motive all too well. Recall from Dr. Faustus: "I, sir? I am Covetousness, begot by an old churl in a leathern bag."

In the days of kings, many friends of liberty put their trust in the people. Could we but establish democracy, we would insure freedom forever and aye.

Even in those times men of wisdom doubted the certainty of the proposition; and few would think it true today. Tocqueville tells us that avarice is a plague to which all democracies are perilously susceptible. The citizens collectively seem no more devoted to freedom than were the kings, and indeed are no less passionate in their demands than were the aristocrats. The lure of plunder can be as attractive to a majority as to kings.

And if the plunder is life itself . . .

THE JIGSAW MAN
by Larry Niven

In A.D. 1900, Karl Landsteiner classified human blood into
four types: A, B, AB, and O, according to incompatibilities.
For the first time it became possible to give a shock patient a
transfusion with some hope that it wouldn't kill him.

The movement to abolish the death penalty was barely
getting started, and already it was doomed.

Vh83uOAGn7 was his telephone number and his driving
license number and his social security number and the number of his draft card and his medical record. Two of these had
been revoked, and the others had ceased to matter, except for
his medical record. His name was Warren Lewis Knowles. He
was going to die.

The trial was a day away, but the verdict was no less certain
for that. Lew was guilty. If anyone had doubted it, the persecution had ironclad proof. By eighteen tomorrow Lew would be
condemned to death. Broxton would appeal the case on some
grounds or other. The appeal would be denied.

The cell was comfortable, small, and padded. This was no
slur on the prisoner's sanity, though insanity was no longer
an excuse for breaking the law. Three of the walls were mere
bars. The fourth wall, the outside wall, was cement padded
and painted a restful shade of green. But the bars which
separated him from the corridor, and from the morose old
man on his left, and from the big, moronic-looking teenager
on his right—the bars were four inches thick and eight
inches apart, padded in silicone plastics. For the fourth time
that day Lew took a clenched fistful of the plastic and tried to
rip it away. It felt like a sponge rubber pillow, with a rigid
core the thickness of a pencil, and it wouldn't rip. When he let
go it snapped back to a perfect cylinder.

"It's not fair," he said.

The teenager didn't move. For all of the ten hours Lew had
been in his cell, the kid had been sitting on the edge of his

bunk with his lank black hair falling in his eyes and his five o'clock shadow getting gradually darker. He moved his long hairy arms only at mealtimes, and the rest of him not at all.

The old man looked up at the sound of Lew's voice. He spoke with bitter sarcasm. "You framed?"

"No, I—"

"At least you're honest. What'd you do?"

Lew told him. He couldn't keep the hurt innocence out of his voice. The old man smiled derisively, nodding as if he'd expected just that.

"Stupidity. Stupidity's always been a capital crime. If you *had* to get yourself executed, why not for something important? See the kid on the other side of you?"

"Sure," Lew said without looking.

"He's an organlegger."

Lew felt the shock freezing on his face. He braced himself for another look into the next cell—and every nerve in his body jumped. The kid was looking at him. With his dull dark eyes barely visible under his mop of hair, he regarded Lew as a butcher might consider a badly aged side of beef.

Lew edged closer to the bars between his cell and the old man's. His voice was a hoarse whisper. "How many did he kill?"

"None."

"?"

"He was the snatch man. He'd find someone out alone at night, drug him and take him home to the doc that ran the ring. It was the doc that did all the killing. If Bernie'd brought home a dead donor, te doc would have skinned *him* down."

The old man sat with Lew almost directly behind him. He had twisted himself around to talk to Lew, but now he seemed to be losing interest. His hands, hidden from Lew by his bony back, were in constant nervous motion.

"How many did he snatch?"

"Four. Then he got caught. He's not very bright, Bernie."

"What did you do to get put here?"

The old man didn't answer. He ignored Lew completely, his shoulders twitching as he moved his hands. Lew shrugged and dropped back in his bunk.

It was nineteen o'clock of a Thursday night.

The ring had included three snatch men. Bernie had not yet been tried. Another was dead; he had escaped over the edge of a pedwalk when he felt the mercy bullet enter his arm. The third was being wheeled into the hospital next door to the courthouse.

Officially he was still alive. He had been sentenced; his appeal had been denied; but he was still alive as they moved him, drugged, into the operating room.

The interns lifted him from the table and inserted a mouthpiece so he could breathe when they dropped him into freezing liquid. They lowered him without a splash, and as his body temperature went down they dribbled something else into his veins. About half a pint of it. His temperature dropped toward freezing, his heartbeats were further and further apart. Finally his heart stopped. But it could have been started again. Men had been reprieved at this point. Officially the organlegger was still alive.

The doctor was a line of machines with a conveyor belt running through them. When the organlegger's body temperature reached a certain point, the belt started. The first machine made a series of incisions in his chest. Skillfully and mechanically, the doctor performed a cardiectomy.

The organlegger was officially dead.

His heart went into storage immediately. His skin followed, most of it in one piece, all of it still living. The doctor took him apart with exquisite care, like disassembling a flexible, fragile, tremendously complex jigsaw puzzle. The brain was flashburned and the ashes saved for urn burial; but all the rest of the body, in slabs and small blobs and parchment-thin layers and lengths of tubing, went into storage in the hospital's organ banks. Any one of these units could be packed in a travel case at a moment's notice and flown to anywhere in the world in not much more than an hour. If the odds broke right, if the right people came down with the right diseases at the right time, the organlegger might save more lives than he had taken.

Which was the whole point.

*   *   *

Lying on his back, staring up at the ceiling television set, Lew suddenly began to shiver. He had not had the energy to put the sound plug in his ear, and the silent motion of the cartoon figures had suddenly become horrid. He turned the set off, and that didn't help either.

Bit by bit they would take him apart and store him away. He'd never seen an organ storage bank, but his uncle had owned a butcher-shop . . .

"Hey!" he yelled.

The kid's eyes came up, the only living part of him. The old man twisted round to look over his shoulder. At the end of the hall the guard looked up once, then went back to reading.

The fear was in Lew's belly; it pounded in his throat. "How can you stand it?"

The kid's eyes dropped to the floor. The old man said, "Stand what?"

"Don't you know what they're going to *do* to us?"

"Not to me. They won't take me apart like a hog."

Instantly Lew was at the bars. "Why not?"

The old man's voice had become very low. "Because there's a bomb where my right thighbone used to be. I'm gonna blow myself up. What they find, they'll never use."

The hope the old man had raised washed away, leaving bitterness. "Nuts. How could you put a bomb in your leg?"

"Take the bone out, bore a hole lengthwise through it, build the bomb in the hole, get all the organic material out of the bone so it won't rot, put the bone back in. 'Course your red corpuscle count goes down afterward. What I wanted to ask you. You want to join me?"

"Join you?"

"Hunch up against the bars. This thing'll take care of both of us."

Lew had backed up against the opposite set of bars.

"Your choice," said the old man. "I never told you what I was here for, did I? I was the doc. Bernie made his snatches for me."

Lew had backed up against the opposite set of bars. He felt them touch his shoulders and turned to find the kid looking dully into his eyes from two feet away. Organleggers! He was surrounded by professional killers!

"I know what it's like," the old man continued. "They won't do that to me. Well. If you're sure you don't want a clean death, go lie down behind your bunk. It's thick enough."

The bunk was a mattress and a set of springs mounted into a cement block which was an integral part of the cement floor. Lew curled himself into fetal position with his hands over his eyes.

He was sure he didn't want to die *now*.

Nothing happened.

After a while he opened his eyes, took his hands away and looked around.

The kid was looking at him. For the first time there was a sour grin plastered on his face. In the corridor the guard, who was always in a chair by the exit, was standing outside the bars looking down at him. He seemed concerned.

Lew felt the flush rising in his neck and nose and ears. The old man had been playing with him. He moved to get up. . . .

And a hammer came down on the world.

The guard lay broken against the bars of the cell across the corridor. The lank-haired youngster was picking himself up from behind his bunk, shaking his head. Somebody groaned; and the groan rose to a scream. The air was full of cement dust.

Lew got up.

Blood lay like red oil on every surface that faced the explosion. Try as he might, and he didn't try very hard, Lew could find no other trace of the old man.

Except for the hole in the wall.

He must have been standing . . . right . . . there.

The hole would be big enough to crawl through, if Lew could reach it. But it was in the old man's cell. The silicone plastic sheathing on the bars between the cells had been ripped away, leaving only pencil-thick lengths of metal.

Lew tried to squeeze through.

The bars were humming, vibrating, though there was no sound. As Lew noticed the vibration he also found that he was becoming sleepy. He jammed his body between the bars, caught in a war between his rising panic and the sonic stunners which might have gone on automatically.

The bars wouldn't give. But his body did; and the bars were slippery with . . . He was through. He poked his head through the hole in the wall and looked down.

Way down. Far enough to make him dizzy.

The Topeka County courthouse was a small skyscraper, and Lew's cell must have been near the top. He looked down a smooth concrete slab studded with windows set flush with the sides. There would be no way to reach those windows, no way to open them, no way to break them.

The stunner was sapping his will. He would have been unconscious by now if his head had been in the cell with the rest of him. He had to force himself to turn and look up.

He was *at* the top. The edge of the roof was only a few feet above his eyes. He couldn't reach that far, not without . . .

He began to crawl out of the hole.

Win or lose, they wouldn't get him for the organ banks. The vehicular traffic level would smash every useful part of him. He sat on the lip of the hole, with his legs straight out inside the cell for balance, pushing his chest flat against the wall. When he had his balance he stretched his arms toward the roof. No good.

So he got one leg under him, keeping the other stiffly out, and *lunged*.

His hands closed over the edge as he started to fall back. He yelped with surprise, but it was too late, the top of the courthouse was moving! It had dragged him out of the hole before he could let go. He hung on, swinging slowly back and forth over empty space as the motion carried him away.

The top of the courthouse was a pedwalk.

He couldn't climb up, not without purchase for his feet. He didn't have the strength. The pedwalk was moving toward another building, about the same height. He could reach it if he only hung on.

And the windows in that building were different. They weren't made to open, not in those days of smog and air conditioning, but there were ledges. Perhaps the glass would break.

Perhaps it wouldn't.

The pull on his arms was agony. It would be so easy to let go. . . . No. He had committed no crime worth dying for. He refused to die.

Over the decades of the twentieth century the movement continued to gain momentum. Loosely organized, international in scope, its members had only one goal: to replace execution with imprisonment and rehabilitation in every state and nation they could reach. They argued that killing a man for his crime teaches him nothing; that it serves as no deterrent to others who might commit the same crime; that death is irreversible, whereas an innocent man may be released from prison if his innocence can be proven. Killing a man serves no good purpose, they said, unless for society's vengeance. Vengeance, they said, is unworthy of an enlightened society.

Perhaps they were right.

In 1940 Karl Landsteiner and Alexander S. Wiener made public their report on the Rh factor in human blood.

By mid-century most convicted killers were getting life imprisonment or less. Many were later returned to society, some "rehabilitated," others not. The death penalty had been passed for kidnapping in some states, but it was hard to persuade a jury to enforce it. Similarly with murder charges. A man wanted for burglary in Canada and murder in California fought extradition to Canada; he had less chance of being convicted in California. Many states had abolished the death penalty. France had none.

Rehabilitation of criminals was a major goal of the science/art of psychology.

But—

Blood banks were worldwide.

Already men and women with kidney diseases had been saved by a kidney transplanted from an identical twin. Not all kidney victims had identical twins. A doctor in Paris used transplants from close relatives, classifying up to a hundred points of incompatibility to judge in advance how successful the transplant would be.

Eye transplants were common. An eye donor could wait until he died before he saved another man's sight.

Human bone could *always* be transplanted, provided the bone was first cleaned of organic matter.

So matters stood in mid-century.

By 1990 it was possible to store any living human organ for any reasonable length of time. Transplants had become routine, helped along by the "scalpel of infinite thinness," the laser. The dying regularly willed their remains to organ banks. The mortuary lobbies couldn't stop it. But such gifts from the dead were not always useful.

In 1993 Vermont passed the first of the organ bank laws. Vermont had always had the death penalty. Now a condemned man could know that his death would save lives. It was no longer true that an execution served no good purpose. Not in Vermont.

Nor, later, in California. Or Washington. Georgia. Pakistan, England, Switzerland, France, Rhodesia . . .

The pedwalk was moving at ten miles per hour. Below, unnoticed by pedestrians who had quit work late and night owls who were just beginning their rounds, Lewis Knowles hung from the moving strip and watched the ledge go by beneath his dangling feet. The ledge was no more than two feet wide, a good four feet beneath his stretching toes.

He dropped.

As his feet struck he caught the edge of a window casement. Momentum jerked at him, but he didn't fall. After a long moment he breathed again.

He couldn't know what building this was, but it was not deserted. At twenty-one hundred at night, all the windows were ablaze. He tried to stay back out of the light as he peered in.

The window was an office. Empty.

He'd need something to wrap around his hand to break that window. But all he was wearing was a pair of shoesocks and a prison jumper. Well, he couldn't be more conspicuous than he was now. He took off the jumper, wrapped part of it around his hand, and struck.

He almost broke his hand.

Well . . . they'd let him keep his jewelry, his wristwatch and diamond ring. He drew a circle on the glass with the ring, pushing down hard, and struck again with the other hand. It *had* to be glass; if it was plastic he was doomed.

The glass popped out in a near-perfect circle.

He had to do it six times before the hole was big enough for him.

He smiled as he stepped inside, still holding his jumper. Now all he needed was an elevator. The cops would have picked him up in an instant if they'd caught him on the street in a prison jumper, but if he hid the jumper here he'd be safe. Who would suspect a licensed nudist?

Except that he didn't have a license. Or a nudist's shoulder pouch to put it in.

Or a shave.

That was very bad. Never had there been a nudist as hairy as this. Not just a five o'clock shadow, but a full beard all over, so to speak. Where could he get a razor?

He tried the desk drawers. Many businessmen kept spare razors. He stopped when he was halfway through. Not because he'd found a razor, but because he knew where he was. The papers on the desk made it all too obvious.

A hospital.

He was still clutching the jumper. He dropped it in the wastebasket, covered it tidily with papers, and more or less collapsed into the chair behind the desk.

A hospital. He *would* pick a hospital. And *this* hospital, the one which had been built right next to the Topeka County courthouse, for good and sufficient reason.

But he hadn't picked it, not really. It had picked him. Had he ever in his life made a decision except on the instigation of others? Friends had borrowed his money for keeps, men had stolen his girls, he had avoided promotion by his knack for being ignored. Shirley had bullied him into marrying her, then left him four years later for a friend who wouldn't be bullied.

Even now, at the possible end of his life, it was the same. An aging body snatcher had given him his escape. An engineer had built the cell bars wide enough apart to let a small man squeeze between them. Another had put a pedwalk along two convenient roofs. And here he was.

The worst of it was that here he had no chance of masquerading as a nudist. Hospital gowns and masks would be the minimum. Even nudists had to wear clothing sometime.

The closet?

There was nothing in the closet but a spiffy green hat and a perfectly transparent rain poncho.

He could run for it. If he could find a razor he'd be safe once he reached the street. He bit at a knuckle, wishing he knew where the elevator was. Have to trust to luck. He began searching the drawers again.

He had his hand on a black leather razor case when the door opened. A beefy man in a hospital gown breezed in. The intern (there were no human doctors in hospitals) was halfway to the desk before he noticed Lew crouching over an open drawer. He stopped walking. His mouth fell open.

Lew closed it with the fist which still gripped the razor case. The man's teeth came together with a sharp click. His knees were buckling as Lew brushed past him and out the door.

The elevator was just down the hall, with the doors standing open. And nobody coming. Lew stepped in an punched O. He shaved as the elevator dropped. The razor cut fast and close, if a trifle noisily. He was working on his chest as the door opened.

A skinny technician stood directly in front of him, her mouth and eyes set in the utterly blank expression of those who wait for elevators. She brushed past him with a muttered apology, hardly noticing him. Lew stepped out fast. The doors were closing before he realized that he was on the wrong floor.

That damned tech! She'd stopped the elevator before it reached bottom.

He turned and stabbed the Down button. Then what he'd seen in the one cursory glance came back to him, and his head whipped around for another look.

The whole vast room was filled with glass tanks, ceiling height, arranged in a labyrinth like the bookcases in a library. In the tanks was a display more lewd than anything in Belsen. Why, those things had been *men!* and *women!* No, he wouldn't look. He refused to look at anything but the elevator door. *What was taking that elevator so long?*

He heard a siren.

The hard tile floor began to vibrate against his bare feet. He felt a numbness in his muscles, a lethargy in his soul.

The elevator arrived ... too late. He blocked the doors open with a chair. Most buildings didn't have stairs: only alternate elevators. They'd have to use the alternate elevator to reach him now. Well, where was it? ... He wouldn't have time to find it. He was beginning to feel really sleepy. They must have several sonic projectors focused on this one room. Where one beam passed the interns would feel mildly relaxed, a little clumsy. But where the beams intersected, here, there would be unconsciousness. But not yet.

He had something to do first.

By the time they broke in they'd have something to kill him for.

The tanks were faced in plastic, not glass: a very special kind of plastic. To avoid provoking defense reactions in all the myriads of body parts which might be stored touching it, the plastic had to have unique characteristics. No engineer could have been expected to make it shatterproof too!

It shattered very satisfactorily.

Later Lew wondered how he managed to stay up as long as he did. The soothing hypersonic murmur of the stun beams kept pulling at him, pulling him down to a floor which seemed softer every moment. The chair he wielded became heavier and heavier. But as long as he could lift it, he smashed. He was knee deep in nutritive storage fluid, and there were dying things brushing against his ankles with every move; but his work was barely a third done when the silent siren song became too much for him.

He fell.

And after all that they never even mentioned the smashed organ banks!

Sitting in the courtroom, listening to the drone of court-room ritual, Lew sought Mr. Broxton's ear to ask the question. Mr. Broxton smiled at him. "Why should they want to bring that up? They think they've got enough on you as it is. If you beat *this* rap, then they'll persecute you for wanton destruction of valuable medical sources. But they're sure you won't."

"And you?"

"I'm afraid they're right. But we'll try. Now, Hennessey's about to read the charges. Can you manage to look hurt and indignant?"

"Sure."

"Good."

The prosecution read the charges, his voice sounding like the voice of doom coming from under a thin blond mustache. Warren Lewis Knowles looked hurt and indignant. But he no longer felt that way. He had done something worth dying for.

The cause of it all was the organ banks. With good doctors and a sufficient flow of material in the organ banks, any taxpayer could hope to live indefinitely. What voter would vote against eternal life? The death penalty was his immortality, and he would vote the death penalty for any crime at all.

Lewis Knowles had struck back.

"The state will prove that the said Warren Lewis Knowles did, in the space of two years, willfully drive through a total of six red traffic lights. During that same period the same Warren Knowles exceeded local speed limits no less than ten times, once by as much as fifteen miles per hour. His record had never been good. We will produce records of his arrest in 2082 on a charge of drunk driving, a charge of which he was acquitted only through—"

"Objection!"

"Sustained. If he was acquitted, Counselor, the Court must assume him not guilty."

"REPENT, HARLEQUIN!"
SAID THE TICKTOCKMAN

I first met Harlan Ellison at the Seattle World Science Fiction Convention. He is unlikely to recall the incident. I was a mere fan, an aerospace engineer turned graduate student; while Harlan was greatly (and deservedly) proud of being the convention's toastmaster, a job he performed with skill and gusto.

I next got involved with him many years later when he suckered me into becoming President of SFWA, something I wouldn't have believed possible that anyone could do to me. After that our paths began to cross more frequently. Harlan has a reputation—God knows it's well deserved—for being irascible, feisty, rude, and intolerant. But while that's all true, he can also be a dedicated and generous friend.

Harlan is the only person I know who can dominate a conversation from four thousand miles away. Whenever a dozen science fiction writers gather together, a Harlan story will be amongst them.

Harlan Ellison's dedication to the cause of freedom is well known. He has participated in dozens of fund raisers, rallies, walks, talks, and lawsuits. He was thus one of the first potential contributors I thought of when I planned this book.

He took the request seriously. For several weeks he considered what he might say in an anthology devoted to freedom, and more than once he called to discuss topics and ideas.

Then one day he called again. He had thought about the subject long and hard, and the more he thought the more he believed "Repent, Harlequin" was his most powerful statement on freedom; as powerful as he had ever done, and perhaps as good as he would ever do.

"REPENT, HARLEQUIN!"
SAID THE TICKTOCKMAN
by Harlan Ellison

There are always those who ask, what is it all about? For those who need to ask, for those who need points sharply made, who need to know "where it's at," this:

> *"The mass of men serve the state thus, not as men mainly, but as machines, with their bodies. They are the standing army, and the militia, jailors, constables, posse comitatus, etc. In most cases there is no free exercise whatever of the judgment or of the moral sense; but they put themselves on a level with wood and earth and stones; and wooden men can perhaps be manufactured that will serve the purpose as well. Such command no more respect than men of straw or a lump of dirt. They have the same sort of worth only as horses and dogs. Yet such as these even are commonly esteemed good citizens. Others—as most legislators, politicians, lawyers, ministers, and office-holders—serve the state chiefly with their heads; and, as they rarely make any moral distinctions, they are as likely to serve the Devil, without intending it, as God. A very few, as heroes, patriots, martyrs, reformers in the great sense, and men serve the state with their consciences also, and so necessarily resist it for the most part; and they are commonly treated as enemies by it."*
> —Henry David Thoreau, "Civil Disobedience"

That is the heart of it. Now begin in the middle, and later learn the beginning; the end will take care of itself.

But because it was the very world it was, the very world they had allowed it to *become*, for months his activities did not come to the alarmed attention of The Ones Who Kept The

Machine Functioning Smoothly, the ones who poured the very best butter over the cams and the mainsprings of the culture. Not until it had become obvious that somehow, someway, he had become a notoriety, a celebrity, perhaps even a hero for (what Officialdom inescapably tagged) "an emotionally disturbed segment of the populace," did they turn it over to the Ticktockman and his legal machinery. But by then, because it was the very world it was, and they had no way to predict he would happen—possibly a strain of disease long-defunct, now, suddenly, reborn in a system where immunity had been forgotten, had lapsed—he had been allowed to become too real. Now he had form and substance.

He had become a *personality*, something they had filtered out of the system many decades before. But there it was, and there *he* was, a very definitely imposing personality. In certain circles—middle-class circles—it was thought disgusting. Vulgar ostentation. Anarchistic. Shameful. In others, there was only sniggering: those strata where thought is subjugated to form and ritual, niceties, proprieties. But down below, ah, down below, where the people always needed their saints and sinners, their bread and circuses, their heroes and villains, he was considered a Bolivar; a Napoleon; a Robin Hood; a Dick Bong (Ace of Aces); a Jesus; a Jomo Kenyatta.

And at the top—where, like socially-attuned Shipwreck Kellys, every tremor and vibration threatens to dislodge the wealthy, powerful and titled from their flagpoles—he was considered a menace; a heretic; a rebel; a disgrace; a peril. He was known down the line, to the very heart-meat core, but the important reactions were high above and far below. At the very top, at the very bottom.

So his file was turned over, along with his time-card and his cardioplate, to the office of the Ticktockman.

The Ticktockman: very much over six feet tall, often silent, a soft purring man when things went timewise. The Ticktockman.

Even in the cubicles of the hierarchy, where fear was generated, seldom suffered, he was called the Ticktockman. But no one called him that to his mask.

You don't call a man a hated name, not when that man,

behind his mask, is capable of revoking the minutes, the hours, the days and nights, the years of your life. He was called the Master Timekeeper to his mask. It was safer that way.

"This is *what* he is," said the Ticktockman with genuine softness, "but not *who* he is. This time-card I'm holding in my left hand has a name on it, but it is the name of *what* he is, not *who* he is. The cardioplate here in my right hand is also named, but not *whom* named, merely *what* named. Before I can exercise proper revocation, I have to know *who* this *what* is."

To his staff, all the ferrets, all the loggers, all the finks, all the commex, even the mineez, he said, "Who is this Harlequin?"

He was not purring smoothly. Timewise, it was jangle.

However, it *was* the longest speech they had ever heard him utter at one time, the staff, the ferrets, the loggers, the finks, the commex, but not the mineez, who usually weren't around to know, in any case. But even they scurried to find out.

Who is the Harlequin?

High above the third level of the city, he crouched on the humming aluminum-frame platform of the air-boat (foof! air-boat indeed! swizzleskid is what it was, with a tow-rack jerry-rigged) and he stared down at the neat Mondrian arrangement of the buildings.

Somewhere nearby, he could hear the metronomic left-right-left of the 2:47 P.M. shift, entering the Timkin roller-bearing plant in their sneakers. A minute later, precisely, he heard the softer right-left-right of the 5:00 A.M. formation, going home.

An elfin grin spread across his tanned features, and his dimples appeared for a moment. Then, scratching at his thatch of auburn hair, he shrugged within his motley, as though girding himself for what came next, and threw the joystick forward, and bent into the wind as the air-boat dropped. He skimmed over a slidewalk, purposely dropping a few feet to crease the tassels of the ladies of fashion, and—inserting thumbs in large ears—he stuck out his tongue,

rolled his eyes and went wugga-wugga-wugga. It was a
minor diversion. One pedestrian skittered and tumbled, sending parcels everywhichway, another wet herself, a third
keeled slantwise and the walk was stopped automatically by
the servitors till she could be resuscitated. It was a minor
diversion.

Then he swirled away on a vagrant breeze, and was gone.
Hi-ho.

As he rounded the cornice of the Time-Motion Study Building, he saw the shift, just boarding the slidewalk. With
practiced motion and an absolute conservation of movement,
they sidestepped up onto the slow-strip and (in a chorus line
reminiscent of a Busby Berkeley film of the antediluvian
1930s) advanced across the strips ostrich-walking till they
were lined up on the expresstrip.

Once more, in anticipation, the elfin grin spread, and there
was a tooth missing back there on the left side. He dipped,
skimmed, and swooped over them; and then, scrunching
about on the air-boat, he released the holding pins that
fastened shut the ends of the home-made pouring troughs
that kept his cargo from dumping prematurely. And as he
pulled the trough-pins, the air-boat slid over the factory
workers and one hundred and fifty thousand dollars' worth of
jelly beans cascaded down on the expresstrip.

Jelly beans! Millions and billions of purples and yellows
and greens and licorice and grape and raspberry and mint
and round and smooth and crunchy outside and soft-mealy
inside and sugary and bouncing jouncing tumbling clittering
clattering skittering fell on the heads and shoulders and
hardhats and carapaces of the Timkin workers, tinkling on
the slidewalk and bouncing away and rolling about underfoot
and filling the sky on their way down with all the colors of joy
and childhood and holidays, coming down in a steady rain, a
solid wash, a torrent of color and sweetness out of the sky
from above, and entering a universe of sanity and metronomic
order with quite-mad coocoo newness. Jelly beans!

The shift workers howled and laughed and were pelted,
and broke ranks, and the jelly beans managed to work their
way into the mechanism of the slidewalks after which there

was a hideous scraping as the sound of a million fingernails rasped down a quarter of a million blackboards, followed by a coughing and a sputtering, and then the slidewalks all stopped and everyone was dumped thisawayandthataway in a jack-straw tumble, still laughing and popping little jelly bean eggs of childish color into their mouths. It was a holiday, and a jollity, an absolute insanity, a giggle. But . . .

The shift was delayed seven minutes.

They did not get home for seven minutes.

The master schedule was thrown off by seven minutes.

Quotas were delayed by inoperative slidewalks for seven minutes.

He had tapped the first domino in the line, and one after another, like chik chik chik, the others had fallen.

The System had been seven minutes' worth of disrupted. It was a tiny matter, one hardly worthy of note, but in a society where the single driving force was order and unity and equality and promptness of clocklike precision and attention to the clock, reverence of the gods of the passage of time, it was a disaster of major importance.

So he was ordered to appear before the Ticktockman. It was broadcast across every channel of the communications web. He was ordered to be *there* at 7:00 dammit on time. And they waited, and they waited, but he didn't show up till almost ten-thirty, at which time he merely sang a little song about moonlight in a place no one had ever heard of, called Vermont, and vanished again. But they had all been waiting since seven, and it wrecked *hell* with their schedules. So the question remained: Who is the Harlequin?

But the *unasked* question (more important of the two) was: how did we get *into* this position, where a laughing, irresponsible japer of jabberwocky and jive could disrupt our entire economic and cultural life with a hundred and fifty thousand dollars' worth of jelly beans.

Jelly for God's sake *beans!* This is madness! Where did he get the money to buy a hundred and fifty thousand dollars' worth of jelly beans? (They knew it would have cost that much, because they had a team of Situation Analysts pulled off another assignment, and rushed to the slidewalk scene to sweep up and count the candies, and produce findings, which disrupted *their* schedules and threw their entire branch at least a day behind.) Jelly beans! Jelly . . . *beans?* Now wait a second—a second accounted for—no one has manufactured jelly beans for over a hundred years. Where did he get jelly beans?

That's another good question. More than likely it will never be answered to your complete satisfaction. But then, how many questions ever are?

The middle you know. Here is the beginning. How it starts:

A desk pad. Day for day, and turn each day. 9:00—open the mail. 9:45—appointment with planning commission board. 10:30—discuss installation progress charts with J.L. 11:45—pray for rain. 12:00—lunch. *And so it goes.*

"I'm sorry, Miss Grant, but the time for interviews was set at 2:30, and it's almost five now. I'm sorry you're late, but those are the rules. You'll have to wait till next year to submit application for this college again." *And so it goes.*

The 10:10 local stops at Cresthaven, Galesville, Tonawanda Junction, Selby and Farnhurst, but not at Indiana City, Lucasville and Colton, except on Sunday. The 10:35 express stops at Galesville, Selby and Indiana City, except on Sundays & Holidays, at which time it stops at . . . *and so it goes.*

"I couldn't wait, Fred. I had to be at Pierre Cartain's by 3:00, and you said you'd meet me under the clock in the terminal at 2:45, and you weren't there, so I had to go on. You're always late, Fred. If you'd been there, we could have sewed it up together, but as it was, well, I took the order alone . . ." *And so it goes.*

Dear Mr. and Mrs. Atterley: in reference to your son Gerold's constant tardiness, I am afraid we will have to suspend him from school unless some more reliable method can be instituted guaranteeing he will arrive at his classes on time. Granted he is an exemplary student, and his marks are high, his constant flouting of the schedules of this school makes it impractical to maintain him in a system where the other children seem capable of getting where they are supposed to be on time *and so it goes.*

YOU CANNOT VOTE UNLESS YOU APPEAR AT 8:45 A.M.

"I don't care if the script is *good*, I need it Thursday!"

CHECK-OUT TIME IS 2:00 P.M.

"You got here late. The job's taken. Sorry."

YOUR SALARY HAS BEEN DOCKED FOR TWENTY MINUTES TIME LOST.

"God, what time is it, I've gotta run!"

And so it goes. And so it goes. And so it goes. And so it goes goes goes goes goes tick tock tick tock tick tock and one day we no longer let time serve us, we serve time and we are slaves of the schedule, worshippers of the sun's passing; bound into a life predicated on restrictions because the system will not function if we don't keep the schedule tight.

Until it becomes more than a minor inconvenience to be late. It becomes a sin. Then a crime. Then a crime punishable by this:

EFFECTIVE 15 JULY 2389 12:00:00 midnight, the office of the Master Timekeeper will require all citizens to submit their time-cards and cardioplates for processing. In accordance with Statute 555-7-SGH-999 governing the revocation of time per capita, all cardioplates will be keyed to the individual holder and—

What they had done, was to devise a method of curtailing the amount of life a person could have. If he was ten minutes late, he lost ten minutes of his life. An hour was proportionately worth more revocation. If someone was consistently tardy, he might find himself, on a Sunday night, receiving a communique from the Master Timekeeper that his time had run out, and he would be "turned off" at high noon on Monday, please straighten your affairs, sir, madame or bisex.

And so, by this simple scientific expedient (utilizing a scientific process held dearly secret by the Ticktockman's office) the System was maintained. It was the only expedient thing to do. It was, after all, patriotic. The schedules had to be met. After all, there *was* a war on!

But, wasn't there always?

"Now that is really disgusting," the Harlequin said, when

Pretty Alice showed him the wanted poster. "Disgusting and *highly* improbable. After all, this isn't the Day of the Desperado. A *wanted* poster!"

"You know," Pretty Alice noted, "you speak with a great deal of inflection."

"I'm sorry," said the Harlequin, humbly.

"No need to be sorry. You're always saying 'I'm sorry.' You have such massive guilt, Everett, it's really very sad."

"I'm sorry," he repeated, then pursed his lips so the dimples appeared momentarily. He hadn't wanted to say that at all. "I have to go out again. I have to *do* something."

Pretty Alice slammed her coffee-bulb down on the counter. "Oh for God's *sake*, Everett, can't you stay home just *one* night! Must you always be out in that ghastly clown suit, running around an*noy*ing people?"

"I'm—" He stopped, and clapped the jester's hat onto his auburn thatch with a tiny tingling of bells. He rose, rinsed out his coffee-bulb at the spray, and put it into the drier for a moment. "I have to go."

She didn't answer. The faxbox was purring, and she pulled a sheet out, read it, threw it toward him on the counter. "It's about you. Of course. You're ridiculous."

He read it quickly. It said the Ticktockman was trying to locate him. He didn't care, he was going out to be late again. At the door, dredging for an exit line, he hurled back petulantly, "Well, *you* speak with inflection, *too!*"

Pretty Alice rolled her pretty eyes heavenward. "You're ridiculous." The Harlequin stalked out, slamming the door, which sighed shut softly, and locked itself.

There was a gentle knock, and Pretty Alice got up with an exhalation of exasperated breath, and opened the door. He stood there. "I'll be back about ten-thirty, okay?"

She pulled a rueful face. "Why do you tell me that? Why? You *know* you'll be late! You *know it!* You're *always* late, so why do you tell me these dumb things?" She closed the door.

On the other side, the Harlequin nodded to himself. *She's right. She's always right. I'll be late. I'm always late. Why do I tell her these dumb things?*

He shrugged again, and went off to be late once more.

*   *   *

He had fired off the firecracker rockets that said: I will attend the 115th annual International Medical Association Invocation at 8:00 P.M. precisely. I do hope you will all be able to join me.

The words had burned in the sky, and of course the authorities were there, lying in wait for him. They assumed, naturally, that he would be late. He arrived twenty minutes early, while they were setting up the spiderwebs to trap and hold him. Blowing a large bullhorn, he frightened and unnerved them so, their own moisturized encirclement webs sucked closed, and they were hauled up, kicking and shrieking, high above the amphitheater's floor. The Harlequin laughed and laughed, and apologized profusely. The physicians, gathered in solemn conclave, roared with laughter, and accepted the Harlequin's apologies with exaggerated bowing and posturing, and a merry time was had by all, who thought the Harlequin was a regular foofaraw in fancy pants; all, that is, but the authorities, who had been sent out by the office of the Ticktockman; they hung there like so much dockside cargo, hauled up above the floor of the amphitheater in a most unseemly fashion.

(In another part of the same city where the Harlequin carried on his "activities," totally unrelated in every way to what concerns us here, save that it illustrates the Ticktockman's power and import, a man named Marshall Delahanty received his turn-off notice from the Ticktockman's office. His wife received the notification from the gray-suited minee who delivered it, with the traditional "look of sorrow" plastered hideously across his face. She knew what it was, even without unsealing it. It was a billet-doux of immediate recognition to everyone these days. She gasped, and held it as though it were a glass slide tinged with botulism, and prayed it was not for her. Let it be for Marsh, she thought, brutally, realistically, or one of the kids, but not for me, please dear God, not for me. And then she opened it, and it *was* for Marsh, and she was at one and the same time horrified and relieved. The next trooper in the line had caught the bullet. "Marshall," she screamed, "Marshall! Termination, Marshall!

OhmiGod, Marshall, whattl we do, whattl we do, Marshall omigodmarshall . . ." and in their home that night was the sound of tearing paper and fear, and the stink of madness went up the flue and there was nothing, absolutely nothing they could do about it.

(But Marshall Delahanty tried to run. And early the next day, when turn-off time came, he was deep in the Canadian forest two hundred miles away, and the office of the Ticktockman blanked his cardioplate, and Marshall Delahanty keeled over, running, and his heart stopped, and the blood dried up on its way to his brain, and he was dead that's all. One light went out on the sector map in the office of the Master Timekeeper, while notification was entered for fax reproduction, and Georgette Delahanty's name was entered on the dole roles till she could remarry. Which is the end of the footnote, and all the point that need be made, except don't laugh, because that is what would happen to the Harlequin if ever the Ticktockman found out his real name. It isn't funny.)

The shopping level of the city was thronged with the Thursday-colors of the buyers. Women in canary yellow chitons and men in pseudo-Tyrolean outfits that were jade and leather and fit very tightly, save for the balloon pants.

When the Harlequin appeared on the still-being-constructed shell of the new Efficiency Shopping Center, his bullhorn to his elfishly-laughing lips, everyone pointed and stared, and he berated them:

"Why let them order you about? Why let them tell you to hurry and scurry like ants or maggots? Take your time! Saunter a while! Enjoy the sunshine, enjoy the breeze, let life carry you at your own pace! Don't be slaves of time, it's a helluva way to die, slowly, by degrees . . . down with the Ticktockman!"

Who's the nut? Most of the shoppers wanted to know. Who's the nut oh wow I'm gonna be late I gotta run . . .

And the construction gang on the Shopping Center received an urgent order from the office of the Master Timekeeper that the dangerous criminal known as the Harlequin was atop their spire, and their aid was urgently needed in apprehending him. The work crew said no, they would lose time on their construction schedule, but the Ticktockman managed to pull the proper threads of governmental webbing, and they were told to cease work and catch that nitwit up there on the spire; up there with the bullhorn. So a dozen and more burly workers began climbing into their construction platforms, releasing the a-grav plates, and rising toward the Harlequin.

After the debacle (in which, through the Harlequin's attention to personal safety, no one was seriously injured), the workers tried to reassemble, and assault him again, but it was too late. He had vanished. It had attracted quite a crowd, however, and the shopping cycle was thrown off by hours, simply hours. The purchasing needs of the system were therefore falling behind, and so measures were taken to accelerate the cycle for the rest of the day, but it got bogged down and speeded up and they sold too many float-valves and not nearly enough wegglers, which meant that the popli ratio was off, which made it necessary to rush cases and cases of spoiling Smash-O to stores that usually needed a case only every three or four hours. The shipments were bollixed, the transshipments were misrouted, and in the end, even the swizzleskid industries felt it.

"Don't come back till you have him!" the Ticktockman said, very quietly, very sincerely, extremely dangerously.

They used dogs. They used probes. They used cardioplate crossoffs. They used teepers. They used bribery. They used stiktytes. They used intimidation. They used torment. They used torture. They used finks. They used cops. They used search&seizure. They used fallaron. They used betterment incentive. They used fingerprints. They used the Bertillon system. They used cunning. They used guile. They used treachery. They used Raoul Mitgong, but he didn't help much. They used applied physics. They used techniques of criminology.

And what the hell: they caught him.

After all, his name was Everett C. Marm, and he wasn't much to begin with, except a man who had no sense of time.

* * *

"Repent, Harlequin!" said the Ticktockman.

"Get stuffed!" the Harlequin replied, sneering.

"You've been late a total of sixty-three years, five months, three weeks, two days, twelve hours, forty-one minutes, fifty-nine seconds, point oh three six one one one one microseconds. You've used up everything you can, and more. I'm going to turn you off."

"Scare someone else. I'd rather be dead than live in a dumb world with a bogeyman like you."

"It's my job."

"You're full of it. You're a tyrant. You have no right to order people around and kill them if they show up late."

"You can't adjust. You can't fit in."

"Unstrap me, and I'll fit my fist into your mouth."

"You're a non-conformist."

"That didn't used to be a felony."

"It is now. Live in the world around you."

"I hate it. It's a terrible world."

"Not everyone thinks so. Most people enjoy order."

"I don't, and most of the people I know don't."

"That's not true. How do you think we caught you?"

"I'm not interested."

"A girl named Pretty Alice told us who you were."

"That's a lie."

"It's true. You unnerve her. She wants to belong; she wants to conform; I'm going to turn you off."

"Then do it already, and stop arguing with me."

"I'm not going to turn you off."

"You're an idiot!"

"Repent, Harlequin!" said the Ticktockman.

"Get stuffed."

So they sent him to Coventry. And in Coventry they worked him over. It was just like what they did to Winston Smith in *1984*, which was a book none of them knew about, but the techniques are really quite ancient, and so they did it to Everett C. Marm, and one day quite a long time later, the Harlequin appeared on the communications web, appearing elfin and dimpled and bright-eyed, and not at all brain-washed, and he said he had been wrong, that it was a good, a very good thing indeed, to belong, to be right on time hip-ho and away we go, and everyone stared up at him on the public screens that covered an entire city block, and they said to themselves, well, you see, he was just a nut after all, and if that's the way the system is run, then let's do it that way, because it doesn't pay to fight city hall, or in this case, the Ticktockman. So Everett C. Marm was destroyed, which was a loss, because of what Thoreau said earlier, but you can't make an omelet without breaking a few eggs, and in every revolution a few die who shouldn't, but they have to, because that's the way it happens, and if you make only a little change, then it seems to be worthwhile. Or, to make the point lucidly:

"Uh, excuse me, sir, I uh, don't know how to uh, to uh, tell you this, but you were three minutes late. The schedule is a little, uh, bit off."

He grinned sheepishly.

"That's ridiculous!" murmured the Ticktockman behind his mask. "Check your watch." And then he went into his office, going *mrmee, mrmee, mrmee, mrmee.*

KISS THEM GOODBY

The theory of compulsory public education was an investment in the future. It is good for the Republic that its future citizens have skills; that they be able to support themselves; that we have no "proletarians" in our society. (In Rome, the Proletarian Century consisted of those citizens who had no property or skills, and contributed nothing to the Republic but their progeny.)

But compulsion always brings problems. It is *always* an inroad on liberty. Sometimes one must compel; sometimes liberty can be preserved no other way. But one ought always to be clear about what one is doing, particularly when compulsion is "for your own good."

John Stuart Mill in *On Liberty* had wise words on public education:

If the government would make up its mind to require for every child a good education, it might save itself the trouble of providing one. It might leave to parents to obtain the education where and how they pleased, and content itself with helping to pay the school fees of the poorer classes of children, and defraying the entire school expenses of those who have no one else to pay for them.

The objections which are urged with reason against State education do not apply to the enforcement of education by the State, but to the State's taking upon itself to direct that education; which is a totally different thing. That the whole of any large part of the education of the people should be in State hands, I go as far as anyone in deprecating. All that has been said of the importance of individuality of character, and diversity in opinions and modes of conduct, involves, as of the same unspeakable importance, diversity of education. A general State education is a mere contrivance for molding people to be exactly like one another; and as the mold in which it casts them is that which pleases the predominant power in the government, whether this be a monarch, a priesthood, an aristocracy, or the majority of the existing generation; in proportion as it is efficient and successful, it establishes a despotism over the mind, leading by natural tendency to one over the body.

An education established and controlled by the State should only exist, if exist at all, as one among many competing experiments, carried on for the purpose of example and stimulus, to keep the others up to a certain standard of excellence.

Mill goes on to say that the State might fairly test children at an early age to see if they can read, and if they remain illiterate, fine their parents.

We have not taken his advice. Instead, we have established an enormous state school system. When I was young, the schools were all locally controlled. There was no such thing as a federal education system, and indeed the topic of "federal aid to education" was hotly debated. Many thought the Constitution forbade federal funding—or control—of local schools.

One argument in favor of federal aid to education was that the illiteracy rate in the United States was nearly 15 percent. It was said that our schools were shockingly poor; the Soviets had a much better system; and we needed federal intervention to create "schools fit for the atomic age." Moreover, it would be painless; for a one-time payment of a few billion dollars invested wisely in research, planning, equipment, and classrooms, we would have schools to be proud of.

Somehow, despite increasingly massive doses of federal aid, the schools didn't get better. Recently, with illiteracy officially estimated as in excess of 30 percent. I heard that all our education problems would vanish with the creation of a Federal Department of Education. We can all hope so.

Meanwhile, because our schools are public, and federally

funded, we have conflict of rights. Whether or not compulsory busing is justified, it cannot be denied that liberty suffers in the name of racial equality.

So far everyone has been lucky. There have been several schoolbus accidents, but no disasters.

As a general rule John Carr, my long-suffering associate, does first reading of unsolicited submissions for these anthologies. We get a lot of those; John reads them all, very carefully, because even when a story is not suitable we can hope to discover talented new writers. Of course most of what he reads is simply bad. (John W. Campbell used to boast that as editor of *Analog* he had read more bad science fiction than anyone in the world.)

Mr. Carr, therefore, gets understandably blasé about new stories; thus, when he interrupts me to show me a submission I should look at immediately, I expect something out of the ordinary. This is one he insisted I read quickly, and it did not disappoint me.

KISS THEM GOODBY

by C. Bruce Hunter

Director Jaffey was wheezing when he reached the second-floor landing. He thought to himself that he was ten years too old and twenty pounds too heavy to be running up and down stairs like this. He stood on the landing for several seconds and waited for his heart to stop pounding before he trudged down the hall toward Myrick's office.

It was a typical government office building, with rows of impressively titled doors separated by walls of almost indescribably neutral color. Harsh afternoon sunlight came directly through a window at the end of the hall, projecting an elongated pattern of light and dark bars on the floor. The building seemed almost empty except for the uproar coming from an open door at the end of the hall.

Jaffey homed in on the noise without bothering to read the

doors along the way. The sound of bureaucratic confusion drew him like a beacon, leaving no doubt of his destination. Still out of breath, he stormed into the outer office, announcing himself as he charged through the door.

"Can't you people make *anything* work around here?"

"Good morning, sir," a startled secretary said, juggling a stack of papers to keep from dropping them. "The elevator's been out all . . ."

"Where's Myrick?" the Director snapped. His shortness of breath made the words sound sharper than he meant them to sound.

"He's in the conference room. Shall I announce . . ." Her words trailed off as he rushed past her and through the open door.

There was an air of panic in the conference room. A large table in the center of the room was the focus of attention. A dozen people darted frantically around it, sifting through stacks of paper, yelling questions and instructions. Some were locked in heated arguments. Others, hands cupped over ears, tried to talk into telephones.

"What the hell have you people done?" Jaffey demanded. His voice was loud and sharp. Twelve years in politics had taught him how to take charge of this kind of situation. He stiffened and waited for the reaction.

Myrick's head bobbed up from behind a large stack of blueprints. Light from the window behind him reflected off the beads of sweat that had formed on his bald head. The others jumped to attention for a moment, then pretended to return to their work, leaving Myrick to face the music.

"We're working on it, sir," Myrick stammered. He reached for his collar, as if to straighten the necktie he had removed hours before. his lips tensed in anticipation.

"Bull! Don't stall me, boy." Jaffey lapsed into the slight Texas drawl he affected whenever he was reaching for maximum impact. "You know how important this thing is? The President has his job on the line. H.E.W. could go right down the drain. And you're *working on it?*"

"It wasn't anything we did," Myrick said, trying to remember where his tie was. "Something just went haywire."

"Well, you had by God better find out what it was, and you don't have much time."

Myrick's face reddened, and the color quickly spread up and across his bald head. The urgency in the Director's voice needed no explanation. Myrick's unit was the logical place to lay the blame. If he expected to get out of this thing in one piece, he was going to have to find some quick answers.

He tried to choose his words carefully. "We're going over the circuits now, and we have crews examining the terminals."

"How long?" Jaffey asked with more than a little impatience.

"We've been at it for six hours. If anything major was wrong we would have found it by now. It has to be something small, but checking out all the fine points in the system could take two or three days."

"Have you tested the machinery?"

"That was the first thing we did. Right after it happened we sent one of the test dummies through. Everything worked perfectly. Then we shut down the machinery, and we've been testing circuits since then."

Jaffey realized there was no point in staying here. These damned technicians probably had absolutely no understanding of the situation. All they knew was their transistors. The whole country was about to fall apart, and all they could do was test their damned circuits.

"I'm flying back to Washington," he snapped, trying to wrap up the conversation as quickly as possible. "The President wants my report in person." He paused to let that sink in. "When I get back you had better have your stuff together."

Jaffey tried to pack as much tension as possible into the last words, then he turned and rushed out of the room before Myrick had a chance to reply.

The Director waited nervously. He was playing with the button he had twisted off his coat sleeve five minutes earlier and counting the *fleurs-de-lis* on the wallpaper. His first count had been two hundred seventy-six, not counting the portion of the wallpaper that was covered by a large roll-top desk. He estimated that the desk covered a dozen and a half more.

Jaffey was a little too numb to think about the problem any more, and he was now reaching for anything he could find to distract himself.

A secretary finally emerged from the inner office and announced, "President Stewart will see you now."

Jaffey found that he was not really prepared for the words he had waited over an hour to hear. He took a deep breath, stood up and walked slowly toward the President's office, unaware that the button had rolled across the floor and disappeared under the roll-top desk.

The President sat behind a massive desk at one end of the room. His face was lined, and his jowls sagged in a way that made him look much older than his fifty-four years. He glared impatiently at Jaffey and snapped, "Well? What happened?"

Jaffey swallowed hard before answering.

"They're still trying to puzzle it out, Mr. President."

"Do those idiots know what they've done?" The President's voice broke slightly. "We finally reach a breakthrough in the busing problem—our one chance to make some real progress. We go through hell to sell it to the people. We sink millions in it. And they ruin the whole thing in three minutes."

Jaffey's political savvy began to overcome his fatigue and numbness. Obviously the President needed to be placated, and the Director searched his mind for an expedient response.

"Once they find out what went wrong, they might be able to reverse the process. We might not actually lose anyone."

"It's too late." The President's voice reflected the anguish that showed in his eyes. "They've already started impeachment proceedings. And there's a bill on the floor of the House to dismantle H.E.W.. Even if we do get everyone back alive, it won't help. Every bigot in the country has been praying for an opportunity like this. Now that they have it, they're not about to let go."

"Maybe we can put the blame on Myrick. It's bound to be his fault anyway." Jaffey's logical mind was busily sorting out the alternatives.

"Sure." The President considered the suggestion for a moment. "But that won't do any good, either. He's just a low-level civil servant in a high-level job. It's going to take more than his head to satisfy the country. No. Everyone involved in this thing is finished, and there's nothing we can do about it."

The director's mouth started getting dry when he realized how few alternatives were left. "What about the telephone company? Everybody's against them. All we have to do is. . ."

"Don't you think I've considered that?" the President stared blankly at his desk. "The telephone company is going to be here forever. They're big enough to ride even this out. Anyway, this thing is out of their ball park. It's political all the way. We're the ones who are going to have to pay for it."

Jaffey was silent for several seconds. He couldn't think of anything else to try.

"Then what can we do?"

"Nothing." President Steward paused for a long time. "Just find out what went wrong."

The Director pushed his way through the crowd. It had started with a few picket signs, but they had soon been pushed to the background as more and more demonstrators assembled in the street and the park beyond. They milled around restlessly and waited for something to happen.

National Guardsmen stood in formation around the building's entrance, and others watched nervously from the roof.

When Jaffey reached the front rank, he held up his ID card to a corporal who looked at it and called a captain. The captain examined the card, then passed Jaffey through the ranks.

"Do your men have control of the situation?" the Director asked as they climbed the steps at the front of the building.

The captain looked around to be sure none of his troops could hear. "No way. If it comes to bloodshed, most of my men will probably side with the mob. It's all I can do to keep them in formation now."

"But they're trained for this sort of thing." Jaffey's voice was thin. He could imagine any number of possible developments, none of them pleasant.

"They're trained to keep order." The captain's words came

slowly. "They've never been up against anything like this, and I don't think they know how to handle it."

For the first time Jaffey noticed how young the captain looked. If he'd been in civilian clothes, Jaffey would have made him to be no more than eighteen or nineteen years old.

It was a sobering thought, and the Director tried to put it out of his mind as he entered the building and made for the stairs without even trying the elevator.

This time the outer office was empty. He walked unannounced and unnoticed into the conference room. A bank of phones had been installed along one wall, and a Guardsman stood at the window nervously watching the scene below.

Orderly stacks of paper had become a crumpled mountain on the conference table, and the technicians frantically shuffled through them to find the papers they needed. A small group huddled in the corner, arguing about something that could not be heard over the general noise in the room.

People constantly moved back and forth between the conference table and the telephones, as bits of information were relayed and instructions received.

Myrick stood in the middle of it all, surrounded by staff members waiting their turn to talk to him. His tie was still missing and his shirt had become wet. When he saw Jaffey come in, he brushed his staff aside and took a half-step forward. "How does it look?"

Jaffey was in no mood for small talk. "The government won't be overthrown, but the rest of us are finished. How do you *think* it looks?" He did not wait for an answer to what was obviously not a question. "What have you got?"

"I don't think we'll ever know."

"Don't get smart."

"I'm serious. I went through the system myself about an hour ago—from here to Kansas City and back. There were no problems at all. Whatever happened the first time must have been a fluke. It will probably never happen again, and we'll probably never find out what went wrong."

Myrick slumped into the nearest chair. "It was a perfect system. No time lost in transportation. We could send the kids anywhere we wanted to, meet any quotas. And the telephone lines can handle all the traffic we could generate. The cost is nominal. It was perfect."

"And the first time we put it into practice we lose eleven children." Jaffey's nostrils flared.

"Just be glad we found out they weren't coming out at the other end," Myrick said, rubbing his palms together. "We had another fifty children lined up to enter the terminal. We would have sent them all through if the Kansas City operator hadn't cut in to ask when we were going to start sending."

"Then what do we say happened to them?" Jaffey stared at the floor.

"What *can* we say? We're leaving the terminals on 'receive' hoping that some of them will come walking out, but there's no real chance of that. They're just gone, and that's all we can say."

"So they just disappeared without a trace. Is that it?"

"Not exactly without a trace," Myrick mumbled as if he didn't want to say what came next. "We got a report from a Nashville television station. Seems a man there called in to complain. His TV screen went blank for a few seconds. Then a boy's face flashed across the screen. The man said it looked like the boy was screaming."

Jaffey shuddered. They were both silent for a long time. Finally Myrick asked, "Where do we go from here?"

"Nowhere," Jaffey's voice at last held no emotion. "We've done all we . . ."

They both jerked as a telephone crashed to the floor. The room became quiet as everyone turned to look.

"What's going on?" Myrick demanded.

"I was talking to the White House . . ." The secretary's voice trembled to a stop. She stood with her back pressed against the wall, staring at the phone she had dropped.

"What is it?" Myrick repeated.

". . . the line went dead for a second. . . . Then I heard a little girl scream."

MacDonough's Song

I have always tried to include poetry in my anthologies. Unfortunately, none submitted for this book seemed quite appropriate. So, I thought, I will turn to the classics. I mentioned this to Poul Anderson. A few days later he sent a note suggesting "MacDonough's Song," by Kipling, as particularly appropriate.

He couldn't possibly have known that I had already chosen it, and indeed had copied it out the night before his letter came.

A week later I was discussing the book with David Friedman, and mentioned that I was going to publish a poem by Robinson Jeffers. "Ah," said David. "But you really must include 'MacDonough's Song' by Kipling. Do you know it?"

Whereupon we proceeded to recite the poem in unison.

Kipling was born in India, and after schooling in England, returned there. When in 1889 he left India the second time he was enormously popular at home, and after Poet Laureate Alfred Lord Tennyson died in 1892, Kipling became "the unofficial Poet Laureate of England." There are a number of rumors concerning why he never officially received the post. The mildest is that Queen Victoria was offended by the poem "Widow of Windsor" ("Walk wide of the Widow of Windsor, for half of creation she owns . . ."). A more interesting story whose validity I've never been able to check is that Kipling was the anonymous author of the scurrilous ballad "The Bastard King of England," about Henry VIII, and Victoria resented *that* (although why she'd be tender in concern for Henry Tudor I don't know).

The *Britannica* entry for Kipling, alas, says that in 1895 (when Kipling and his wife were in settled residency in the United States), he made it known that he would accept neither knighthood nor the post of Poet Laureate. I prefer the rumors.

MACDONOUGH'S SONG
by Rudyard Kipling

"AS EASY AS A B C"—A DIVERSITY OF CREATURES

Whether the State can loose and bind
  In Heaven as well as on Earth:
If it be wiser to kill mankind
  Before or after the birth—
These are matters of high concern
  Where State-kept schoolmen are;
But Holy State (we have lived to learn)
  Endeth in Holy War.

Whether The People be led by The Lord,
  Or lured by the loudest throat;
If it be quicker to die by the sword
  Or cheaper to die by the vote—
These are things we have dealt with once,
  (And they will not rise from their grave)
For Holy People, however it runs,
  Endeth in wholly Slave.

Whatsoever, for any cause,
  Seeketh to take or give
Power above or beyond the Laws,
  Suffer it not to live!
Holy State or Holy King—
  Or Holy People's Will—
Have no truck with the senseless thing.
  Order the guns and kill!
  Saying—after—me:—

Once there was The People—Terror gave it birth;
Once there was The People and it made a Hell of Earth.
Earth arose and crushed it. Listen, O ye slain!
Once there was The People—it shall never be again!

LIPIDLEGGIN'

I am tempted to repeat the Thoreau quote on what to do if someone is determined to do you good; but perhaps it is time to look again at John Stuart Mill's *On Liberty:*

> . . . it is a proper office of public authority to guard against accidents. If either a public officer or anyone else saw a person attempting to cross a bridge which had been ascertained to be unsafe, and there were no time to warn him of his danger, they might seize him and turn him back, without any real infringement of his liberty; for liberty consists in doing what one desires, and he does not desire to fall into the river. Nevertheless, when there is not a certainty, but only a danger of mischief, no one but the person himself can judge of the sufficiency of the motive which may prompt him to incur the risk: in this case, therefore (unless he is a child, or delirious, or in some state of excitement or absorption incompatible with the full use of the reflecting faculty), he ought, I conceive, to be only warned of the danger; not forcibly prevented from exposing himself to it.
>
> Similar considerations, applied to such a question as the sale of poisons, may enable us to decide which among the possible modes of regulation are or are not contrary to principle. Such a precaution, for example, as that of labeling the drug with some word expressive of its dangerous character, may be enforced without violation of liberty: the buyer cannot wish not to know that the thing he possesses has poisonous qualities. But to require in all cases the certificate of a medical practioner would make it sometimes impossible, always expensive, to obtain the article for legitimate uses.

In the Servile State, liberty is not important. The State begins by telling you how it will help you; how it will "protect and serve, and guard men from harm." But soon you find that if you accept the State as benefactor, you must also accept its conditions.

F. Paul Wilson is an M.D. in general practice. Although the AMA's computers monthly send him invitations to join, he has refused membership on liberterian grounds. This story was sent to me by an old friend for my amusement well before I conceived this anthology.

LIPIDLEGGIN'

by F. Paul Wilson

Butter.

I can name a man's poison at fifty paces. I take one look at this guy as he walks in and say to myself, "Butter."

He steps carefully, like there's something sticky on the soles of his shoes. Maybe there is, but I figure he moves like that because he's on unfamiliar ground. Never seen his face before and I know just about everybody around.

It's early yet. I just opened the store and Gabe's the only other guy on the buying side of the counter, only he ain't buying. He's waiting in the corner by the checkerboard and I'm just about to go join him when the new guy comes in. It's wet out—not raining, really, just wet like it only gets up here near the Water Gap—and he's wearing a slicker. Underneath that he seems to have a stocky build and is average height. He's got no beard and his eyes are blue with a watery look. Could be from anywhere until he takes off the hat and I see his hair: it's dark brown and he's got it cut in one of those soupbowl styles that're big in the city.

Gabe gives me an annoyed look as I step back behind the counter, but I ignore him. His last name is Varadi—sounds Italian but it's Hungarian—and he's got plenty of time on his hands. Used to be a PhD in a philosophy department at some university in upstate New York 'til they cut the department in half and gave him his walking papers, tenure and all. Now he does part-time labor at one of the mills when they need a little extra help, which ain't near as often as he'd like.

About as poor as you can get, that Gabe. The government giraffes take a big chunk of what little he earns and leave him near nothing to live on. So he goes down to the welfare office where the local giraffes give him food stamps and rent vouchers so he can get by on what the first group of giraffes left him. If you can figure that one out . . .

Anyway, Gabe's got a lot of time on his hands, like I said, and he hangs out here and plays checkers with me when things are slow. He'd rather play chess, I know, but I can't stand the game. Nothing happens for too long and I get impatient and try to break the game open with some wild gamble. And I always lose. So we play checkers or we don't play.

The new guy puts his hat on the counter and glances around. He looks uneasy. I know what's coming but I'm not going to help him out. There's a little dance we've got to do first.

"I need to buy a few things," he says. His voice has a little tremor in it and close up like this I figure he's in his mid-twenties.

"Well, this *is* a general store," I reply, getting real busy wiping down the counter, "and we've got all sorts of things. What're you interested in? Antiques? Hardware? Food?"

"I'm not looking for the usual stock."

(The music begins to play)

I look at him with my best puzzled expression. "Just what is it you're after, friend?"

"Butter and eggs."

"Nothing unusual about that. Got a whole cabinet full of both behind you there."

(We're on our way to the dance floor)

"I'm not looking for that. I didn't come all the way out here to buy the same shit I can get in the city. I want the real thing."

"You want the real thing, eh?" I say, meeting his eyes square for the first time. "You know damn well real butter and real eggs are illegal. I could go to jail for carrying that kind of stuff!"

(We dance)

Next to taking his money, this is the part I like best about dealing with a new customer. Usually I can dance the two of us around the subject of what he really wants for upwards of twenty or thirty minutes if I've a mind to. But this guy was a lot more direct than most and didn't waste any time getting down to the nitty gritty. Still, he wasn't going to rob me of a little dance. I've got a dozen years of dealing under my belt and no green kid's gonna rob me of that.

A dozen years . . . doesn't seem that long. It was back then that the giraffes who were running the National Health Insurance program found out that they were spending way too much money taking care of people with diseases nobody was likely to cure for some time. The stroke and heart patients were the worst. With the presses at the Treasury working overtime and inflation getting wild, it got to the point where they either had to admit they'd made a mistake or do something drastic.

Naturally, they got drastic.

The President declared a health emergency and Congress passed something called "The National Health Maintainance Act" which said that since certain citizens were behaving irresponsibly by abusing their bodies and thereby giving rise to chronic diseases which resulted in consumption of more than their fair share of medical care at public expense, it was resolved that, in the public interest and for the public good, certain commodities would henceforth and hereafter be either proscribed or strictly rationed. Or something like that.

Foods high in cholesterol and saturated fats headed the list. Next came tobacco and any alcoholic beverage over 30 proof.

Ah, the howls that went up from the public! But those were nothing compared to the screams of fear and anguish that arose from the dairy and egg industry which was facing immediate economic ruin. The Washington giraffes stood firm, however—it wasn't an election year—and used phrases like "bite the bullet" and "national interest" and "public good" until we were all ready to barf.

Nothing moved them.

Things quieted down after a while, as they always do. It helped, of course, that somebody in one of the drug companies had been working on an additive to chickenfeed that would take just about all the cholesterol out of the yolk. It worked, and the poultry industry was saved.

The new eggs cost more—of course!—and the removal of most of the cholesterol from the yolk also removed most of the taste, but at least the egg farmers had something to sell.

Butter was out. Definitely. No compromise. Too much of an "adverse effect on serum lipid levels," whatever that means. You use polyunsaturated margarine or you use nothing. Case closed.

Well, almost closed. Most good citizen-type Americans hunkered down and learned to live with the Lipid Laws, as they came to be known. Why, I bet there's scads of fifteen-year-olds about who've never tasted real butter or a true, cholesterol-packed egg yolk. But we're not all good citizens. Especially me. Far as I'm concerned, there's nothing like two fried eggs—fried in *butter*—over easy, with bacon on the side, to start the day off. *Every* day. And I wasn't about to give that up.

I was strictly in the antiques trade then, and I knew just about every farmer in Jersey and Eastern Pennsylvania. So I found one who was making butter for himself and had him make a little extra for me. Then I found another who was keeping some hens aside and not giving them any of that special feed and had him hold a few eggs out for me.

One day I had a couple of friends over for breakfast and served them real eggs and toast with real butter. They almost strangled me trying to find out where I got the stuff. That's when I decided to add a sideline to my antiques business.

"I figured New York City to be the best place to start so I let word get around the antique dealers there that I could supply their customers with more than furniture. The response was wild and soon I was making more money running butter and eggs than I was running Victorian golden oak.

I was a lipidlegger.

Didn't last, though. I was informed by two very pushy fellows of Mediterranean stock that if I wanted to do any lipid business in Manhattan, I'd either have to buy all my merchandise from their wholesale concern, or give them a very healthy chunk of my profits.

I decided it would be safer to stick close to home. Less volume, but less risky. I turned my antique shop up here by the Water Gap—that's the part of North Jersey you can get to without driving by all those refineries and reactors—into a general store.

A dozen years now . . .

"I heard you had the real thing for sale," the guy says.

I shake my head. "Now where would you hear a thing like that?"

"New York."

"New York? The only connection I have with New York is furnishing some antique dealers with a few pieces now and then. How'd you hear about me in New York?"

"Sam Gelbstein."

I nod. Sam's a good customer. Good friend, too. He helped spread the word for me when I was leggin' lipids into the city.

"How you know Sam?"

"My uncle furnished his house with furniture he bought there."

I still act suspicious—it's part of the dance—but I know if Sam sent him, he's all right. One little thing bothers me, though.

"How come you don't look for your butter and eggs in the city? I hear they're real easy to get there."

"Yeah," he says and twists up his mouth. "They're also spoiled now and again and there's no arguing with the types that supply it. No money-back guarantees with those guys."

I see his point. "And you figure this is closer to the source."

He nods.

"One more question," I say. "I don't deal in the stuff, of course"—still dancing—"but I'm just curious how a young guy like you got a taste for contraband like eggs and butter."

"Europe," he says. "I went to school in Brussels and it's all still legal over there. Just can't get used to these damned substitutes."

It all fit, so I go into the back and lift up the floor door. I keep a cooler down there and from it I pull a dozen eggs and a half-kilo slab of butter. His eyes widen as I put them on the counter in front of him.

"This is the real thing?" he asks. "No games?"

I put out an English muffin, split it with my thumbs and drop the halves into the toaster I keep under the counter. I know that once he tastes this butter I'll have another steady customer. People will eat ersatz eggs and polyunsaturated margarine if they think it's good for them, but they want to know the real thing's available. Take that away from them and suddenly you've got them going to great lengths to get what they used to pass up without a second thought.

"The real thing," I tell him. "There's even a little salt added to the butter for flavor."

"Great!" He smiles, then puts both hands into his pockets and pulls out a gun with his right and shield with his left. "James Callahan, Public Health Service, Enforcement Division," he says. "You're under arrest, Mr. Gurney." He's not smiling anymore.

I don't change my expression or say anything. I just stand there and look bored. But inside I feel like someone's wrapped a length of heavy chain around my guts and hooked it up to a high-speed winch.

Looking at the gun—a little snub-nosed .32—I start to grin.

"What's so funny?" he asks, nervous and I'm not sure why. Maybe it's his first bust.

"A public health guy with a gun!" I'm laughing now. "Don't that seem funny to you?"

His face remains stern. "Not in the least. Now step around the counter. After you're cuffed we're going to take a ride to the Federal Building."

I don't budge. I glance over to the corner and see a deserted checkerboard. Gabe's gone—skittered out as soon as he saw the gun. Mr. Public Health follows my eyes.

"Where's the red-headed guy?"

"Gone for help," I tell him.

He glances quickly over his shoulder out the door, then back at me. "Let's not do anything foolish here. I wasn't crazy enough to come out here alone."

But I can tell by the way his eyes bounce all over the room and by the way he licks his lips that, yes, he was crazy enough to come out here alone.

I don't say anything, as he fills in the empty space. "You've got nothing to worry about, Mr. Gurney," he says. "You'll get off with a first offender's suspended sentence and a short probation."

I don't tell him that's exactly what worries me. I'm waiting for a sound: the click of the toaster as it spits out the English muffin. It comes and I grab the two halves and put them on the counter.

"What are you doing?" he asks, watching me like I'm going to pull a gun on him any minute.

"You gotta taste it," I tell him. "I mean, how're you gonna be sure it ain't oleo unless you taste it?"

"Never mind that." He wiggles the .32 at me. "You're just stalling. Get around here."

But I ignore him. I open a corner of the slab of butter and dig out a hunk with my knife. Then I smear it on one half of the muffin and press the two halves together. All the time I'm talking.

"How come you're out here messin' with me? I'm small time. The biggies are in the city."

"Yeah." He nods slowly. He can't believe I'm buttering a muffin while he holds a gun on me. "And they've also bought everyone who's for sale. Can't get a conviction there if you bring the 'leggers in smeared with butter and eggs in their mouths."

"So you pick on me."

He nods again. "Somebody who buys from Gelbstein let slip that he used to connect with a guy from out here who used to do lipidlegging into the city. Wasn't hard to track you down." He shrugs, almost apologizing. "I need some arrests to my credit and I have to take 'em where I can find 'em."

I don't reply just yet. At least I know why he came alone:

he didn't want anyone a little higher up to steal credit for the bust. And I also know that Sam Gelbstein didn't put the yell on me, which is a relief. But I've got more important concerns at the moment. I press my palm down on top of the muffin until the melted butter oozes out the sides and onto the counter, then I peel the halves apart and push them toward him.

"Here. Eat."

He looks at the muffin all yellow and drippy, then at me, then back to the muffin. The aroma hangs over the counter in an invisible cloud and I'd be getting hungry myself if I didn't have so much riding on this little move.

I'm not worried about going to jail for this. Never was. I know all about suspended sentences and that. What I *am* worried about is being marked as a 'legger. Because that means the giraffes will be watching me and snooping into my affairs all the time. And I'm not the kind who takes well to being watched. I've devoted a lot of effort to keeping a low profile and living between the lines—"living in the interstices," Gabe calls it. A bust could ruin my whole way of life.

So I've got to be right about this guy's poison.

He can't take his eyes off the muffins. I can tell by the way he stares that he's a good-citizen type whose mother obeyed all the Lipid Laws as soon as they were passed, and who never thought to break them once he became a big boy. I nudge him.

"Go ahead."

He puts the shield on the counter and his left hand reaches out real careful, like he's afraid the muffins will bite him. Finally, he grabs the nearest one, holds it under his nose, sniffs it, then takes a bite. A little butter drips from the right corner of his mouth, but it's his eyes I'm watching. They're not seeing me or anything else in the store . . . they're sixteen years away and he's ten years old again and his mother just fixed him breakfast. His eyes are sort of shiny and wet around the rims as he swallows. Then he shakes himself and looks at me. But he doesn't say a word.

I put the butter and eggs in a bag and push it toward him.

"Here. On the house. Gabe will be back any minute with the troops so if you leave now we can avoid any problems." He lowers the gun but still hesitates. "Catch those bad guys in the city," I tell him. "But when you need the real thing for yourself, and you need it fresh, ride out here and I'll see you're taken care of."

He shoves the rest of the muffin half into his mouth and chews furiously as he pockets his shield and gun and slaps his hat back on his head.

"You gotta deal," he says around the mouthful, then lifts the bag with his left hand, grabs the other half muffin with his right, and hurries out into the wet.

I follow him to the door where I see Gabe and a couple of the boys from the mill coming up the road with shotguns cradled in their arms. I wave them off and tell them thanks anyway. Then I watch the guy drive off.

I guess I can't tell a Fed when I see one, but I can name anybody's poison. Anybody's.

I glance down at the pile of newspapers I leave on the outside bench. Around the rock that holds it down I can see where some committee of giraffes has announced that it will recommend the banning of Bugs Bunny cartoons from the theatres and the airwaves. The creature, they say, shows a complete disregard for authority and is not fit viewing for children.

Well, I've been expecting that and fixed up a few mini-cassettes of some of Bugs' finest moments. Don't want the kids around here to grow up without the Wabbit.

I also hear talk about a coming federal campaign against being overweight. Bad health risk, they say. Rumor has it they're going to outlaw clothes over a certain size. That's just rumor, of course . . . still, I'll bet there's an angle in there for me.

Ah, the giraffes. For every one of me there's a hundred of them.

But I'm worth a thousand giraffes.

GIVE ME LIBERTY

Robert Heinlein is a devoted patriot and extraordinarily loyal friend. He is not often embarrassed by anything.

Once, however—

In those days I was an engineer working in the space program. Recall that Mr. Heinlein is also a graduate engineer, and that Ginny Heinlein has been a professional chemist.

Many years ago, when Robert lived in Colorado Springs, I visited him in his self-designed home at 1776 Broadmoor Avenue. I had obtained a splendid room in the Broadmoor Hotel (in those days at least one of the world's truly great hotels) and took a taxi to Mr. Heinlein's home. We went to dinner in his car (a classic black 1948 Cadillac, the elegant sort of car they don't make any more) and returned to his home, where we sat talking late into the night.

I had an appointment with North American Air Defense Command (NORAD) for the next morning, and at 2:00 A.M. we reluctantly decided to end what had been a thoroughly enjoyable evening. It had been snowing since 6:00 the previous evening. Mr. Heinlein called a taxi, which duly came, and I boarded it; but it was unable to climb out of his driveway.

At this point my host reluctantly revealed a dread secret. His house, which had no guest room and *obviously* had no facilities in which guests could stay overnight, had in its living room hidden beds and curtains for privacy, and in concealed cabinets were new toothbrushes, pajamas, socks, linen, and other amenities for travelers caught without luggage. . . .

I stayed the night. In the morning he undertook to drive me to NORAD. The abandoned taxi sat forlornly in his driveway, but he wasn't concerned. "My car has steel lugs in the tires," he said. "It will have no difficulty climbing the hill."

We entered his car. He started it and warmed it thoroughly. Then he put it into gear.

It didn't move.

Repeated efforts produced the same result. Noise of straining engine, but no motion. We produced various theories about what was wrong with the transmission, then abandoned the attempt and went inside to sit at the breakfast table. I called NORAD and postponed my appointment—obviously, since taxis could not reach me, and the Heinlein car was inoperative.

Robert offered breakfast. He apologized that it would be a bit skimpy since they had run out of bacon the previous day. We had coffee and contemplated the sad state of the world—

When Ginny came from the kitchen carrying toast and jam and flapjacks and bacon and eggs—

"Bacon?" Robert inquired.

"I went to the store," Ginny said.

"But the car," we protested. "It's not working."

"Oh, that. The steel lugs in the tires were frozen to the driveway. I poured hot water on them," said Ginny.

In the late '50s and early '60s, Robert and Ginny Heinlein put much time and treasure trying to convince the nation to look to its defenses. They published an advertisement which has since become known as "the Patrick Henry drive." They mailed thousands of reprints, made public speeches, mailed petitions to the White House, all directed toward keeping this nation strong.

There was no visible effect on U.S. policies.

One other result was that Robert ceased work on a book which he then called *The Heretic* and which was later published under the title *Stranger in a Strange Land*.

Instead he wrote another prizewinner.

Robert does not often explain his works; but here he tells us what he had in mind when he wrote *Starship Troopers;* and he also has much of importance to say about freedom.

GIVE ME LIBERTY
By Robert Heinlein

Starship Troopers outraged my readers. I still can't see how that book got a Hugo. It continues to get lots of nasty "fan"

mail and not much favorable fan mail ... but it sells and
sells and sells and sells, in eleven languages. It doesn't slow
down—four new contracts just this year. And yet I almost
never hear of it save when someone wants to chew me out
over it. I don't understand it.

The criticisms are usually based on a failure to understand
simple indicative English sentences, couched in simple words—
especially when the critics are professors of English, as they
often are. (A shining counter example, a professor who can
read and understand English, is one at Colorado College—a
professor of *history*.)

We have also some professors of English who write science
fiction but I do not know of one who formally reviewed or
criticized *Starship Troopers*. However, I have gathered a
strong impression over the years that professors of English
who write and sell science fiction average being much more
grammatical and much more literate than their colleagues
who do not (cannot?) write saleable fiction.

Their failures to understand English are usually these:

1. "Veteran" does not mean in English dictionaries or in
this novel solely a person who has served in military forces. I
concede that in commonest usage today it means a war
veteran ... but no one hesitates to speak of a veteran
fireman or veteran school teacher. In *Starship Troopers* it is
stated flatly and more than once that nineteen out of twenty
veterans are *not* military veterans. Instead, 95% of voters are
what we call today "former members of federal civil service."

Addendum: The volunteer is not given a choice. He/she
can't win a franchise by volunteering for what we call civil
service. He volunteers ... then for two years plus-or-minus
he goes where he is sent and does what he is told to do. If he is
young, male, and healthy, he may wind up as cannon fodder.
But there are long chances against it.

2. He/she can resign at any time other than during combat—
i.e., 100% of the time for 19 out of 20; 99% + of the time for
those in the military branches of federal service.

3. There is *no* conscription. (I am opposed to conscription
for any reason at any time, war or peace, and have said so
repeatedly in fiction, in nonfiction, from platforms, and in

angry sessions in think tanks. I was sworn in first in 1923, and have not been off the hook since that time. My principal pride in my family is that I know of not one in over two centuries who was drafted; they all volunteered. But the draft is involuntary servitude, immoral, and unconstitutional no matter what the Supreme Court says.)

4. Criticism: "The government in *Starship Troopers* is militaristic." "Militaristic" is the adjective for the noun "militarism," a word of several definitions but not one of them can be correctly applied to the government described in this novel. No military or civil servant can vote or hold office until after he is discharged and is again a civilian. The military tend to be despised by most civilians and this is made explicit. A career military man is most unlikely ever to vote or hold office; he is more likely to be dead—and if he does live through it, he'll vote for the first time at 40 or older.

"That book glorifies the military!" Now we are getting somewhere. It does indeed. Specifically the P.B.I., the Poor Bloody Infantry, the mudfoot who places his frail body between his loved home and the war's desolation—but is rarely appreciated. "It's Tommy this and Tommy that and chuck him out, the brute!—but it's 'thin red line of heroes when the guns begin to shoot.' "

My own service usually doesn't have too bad a time of it. Save for very special situations such as the rivers in Nam, a Navy man can get killed but he is unlikely to be wounded . . . and if he is killed, it is with hot food in his belly, clean clothes on his body, a recent hot bath, and sack time in a comfortable bunk not more than 24 hours earlier. The Air Force leads a comparable life. But think of Korea, of Guadalcanal, of Belleau Wood, of Viet Nam. The H-bomb did not abolish the infantryman; it made him essential . . . and he had the toughest job of all and should be honored.

Glorify the military? Would I have picked it for my profession and stayed on the rolls the past 56 years were I not proud of it?

I think I know what offends most of my critics the most about *Starship Troopers*: It is the dismaying idea that a voice in governing the state should be earned instead of being handed to anyone who is 18 years old and has a body temperature near 37°C.

But there ain't no such thing as a free lunch.

Democracies usually collapse not too long after the plebs discover that they can vote themselves bread and circuses ... for a while. Either read history or watch the daily papers; it is now happening here. Let's stipulate for discussion that some stabilizing qualification is needed (in addition to the body being warm) for a voter to vote responsibly with proper consideration for the future of his children and grandchildren—and yours. The Founding Fathers never intended to extend the franchise to everyone; their debates and the early laws show it. A man had to be a stable figure in the community through owning land or employing others or engaged in a journeyman trade or *something*.

But a few pay any attention to the Founding Fathers today—those ignorant, uneducated men—they didn't even have television (have you looked at Monticello lately?)—so let's try some other "poll taxes" to insure a responsible electorate:

a) Mark Twain's "The Curious Republic of Gondor"—if you have not read it, *do* so.

b) A state where anyone can buy for cash (or lay-away installment plan) one or more franchises, and this is the government's sole source of income other than services sold competitively and non-monopolistically. This would produce a new type of government with several rabbits tucked away in the hat. Rich people would take over the government? Would they, now? Is a wealthy man going to impoverish himself for the privilege of casting a couple of hundred votes? Buying an election today, under the warm-body (and tombstone) system is much cheaper than buying a controlling number of franchises would be. The arithmetic on this one becomes unsolvable ... but I suspect that paying a stiff price (call it 20,000 Swiss francs) for a franchise would be even less popular than serving two years.

c) A state that required a bare minimum of intelligence and education—e.g., step into the polling booth and find that the computer has generated a new quadratic equation just for you. Solve it, the computer unlocks the voting machine, you vote. But get a wrong answer and the voting machine fails to unlock, a loud bell sounds, a red light goes on over that booth—and you slink out, face red, you having just proved yourself too stupid and/or ignorant to take part in the decisions of the grownups. Better luck next election! No lower age limit in this system—smart 12-yr-old girls vote every election while some of their mothers—and fathers—decline to be humiliated twice.

There are endless variations on this one. Here are two: *Improving the Breed*—No red light, no bell . . . but the booth opens automatically—empty. *Revenue*—You don't risk your life, just some gelt. It costs you a 1/4 oz troy of gold in local currency to enter the booth. Solve your quadratic and vote, and you get your money back. Flunk—and the state keeps it. With this one I guarantee that no one would vote who was not interested and would be most unlikely to vote if unsure of his ability to get that hundred bucks back.

I concede that I set the standards on both I.Q. and schooling too low in calling only for the solution of a quadratic since (if the programming limits the machine to integer roots) a person who deals with figures at all can solve that one with both hands behind him (her) and her/his eyes closed. But I just recently discovered that a person can graduate from high school in Santa Cruz with a straight-A record, be about to enter the University of California on a scholarship . . . but be totally unable to do simple arithmetic. Let's not make things too difficult at the transition.

d) I don't insist on any particular method of achieving a responsible electorate; I just think that we need to tighten up the present warm-body criterion before it destroys us. How about this? For almost a century and a half women were not allowed to vote. For the past sixty years they have voted . . . but we have not seen the enormous improvement in government the suffragettes promised us.

Perhaps we did not go far enough. Perhaps men are still corrupting government . . . so let's try the next century and a half with males disenfranchised. (Fair is fair. My mother was past forty before she was permitted to vote.) But let's not stop there; at present men outnumber women in elective offices, on the bench, and in the legal profession by a proportion that is scandalous.

Make males ineligible to hold elective office, or to serve in the judiciary, elective or appointed, and also reserve the profession of law for women.

Impossible? That was *exactly* the situation the year I was born, but male instead of female, even in the few states that had female suffrage before the XIXth Amendment, with so few exceptions as to be unnoticed. As for rooting male lawyers out of their cozy niches, this would give us a pool of unskilled manual laborers—and laborers are very hard to hire these days; I've been trying to hire one at any wages he wants for the past three months, with no success.

The really good ones could stay on as law clerks to our present female lawyers, who will be overworked for a while. But not for long. Can you imagine female judges (with no male judges to reverse them) permitting attorneys to take six weeks to pick a jury? Or allowing a trial to ramble along for months?

Women are more practical than men. Biology forces it on them.

Speaking of that, let's go whole hog. Until a female bears a child her socio-economic function is male no matter how orthodox her sexual preference. But a woman who is mother to a child *knows* she has a stake in the future. So let's limit the franchise and elegibility for office and the practice of law to mothers.

The phasing over should be made gentle. Let males serve out their terms but not succeed themselves. Male lawyers might be given as long as four years to retire or find other jobs while not admitting any more males into law schools. I don't have a candidate for President but the events of the last fifty years prove that anybody can sit in the Oval Office; it's just that some are more impressive in appearance than others.

Brethren and Sistern, have you ever stopped to think that *there has not been one rational decision out of the Oval Office for fifty years?*

An all-female government could not possibly be worse than what we have been enduring. Let's try it!

"I have sworn upon the altar of God eternal hostility against every form of tyranny over the mind of man."—Thomas Jefferson, 1800 A.D.

SQ

A few days after I was elected President of the Science Fiction Writers of America, I presided over an annual meeting held in the San Francisco Bay Area. SFWA badly needed restructuring. The publications required attention. We needed a handbook for new members. The Nebula procedures wanted a hard look. And so forth.

Thus the discussions were lively; and I noted that one lady in particular was full of constructive suggestions, and moreover, when she suggested something ought to be done, there would as often as not be two or three to volunteer to undertake the onerous work. After half an hour of this I could stand it no longer. When she suggested that she would see one task to completetion, I said, "And you are . . . ?

"Le Guin," she replied.

Thus did I meet the author of *The Dispossessed*, which in the following year won both the Nebula and Hugo awards; sadly, the second-place winner was *The Mote in God's Eye*.

The late Hannah Arendt was as brilliant a friend as liberty ever had. One of her last works was a study of Eichmann; and she subtitled it "The Banality of Evil." Tyrants always pose as friends of the people; but they do not always pose as masters, as Ursula Le Guin brilliantly shows. . . .

SQ

By Ursula K. Le Guin

I think what Dr. Speakie has done is wonderful. He is a wonderful man. I believe that. I believe that people need beliefs. If I didn't have my belief I really don't know what would happen.

And if Dr. Speakie hadn't truly believed in his work he couldn't possibly have done what he did. Where would he have found the courage? What he did proves his genuine sincerity.

There was a time when a lot of people tried to cast doubts on him. They said he was seeking power. That was never true. From the very beginning all he wanted was to help people and make a better world. The people who called him a power-seeker and a dictator were just the same ones who used to say that Hitler was insane and Nixon was insane and all the world leaders were insane and the arms race was insane and our misuse of natural resources was insane and the whole world civilization was insane and suicidal. They were always saying that. And they said it about Dr. Speakie. But he stopped all that insanity, didn't he? So he was right all along, and he was right to believe in his beliefs.

I came to work for him when he was named the Chief of the Psychometric Bureau. I used to work at the UN, and when the World Government took over the New York UN Building they transferred me up to the thirty-fifth floor to be the head secretary in Dr. Speakie's office. I knew already that it was a position of great responsibility, and I was quite excited the whole week before my new job began. I was so curious to meet Dr. Speakie, because of course he was already famous. I was there right at the dot of nine on Monday morning, and when he came in it was so wonderful. He looked so kind. You could tell that the weight of his responsibilities was always on his mind, but he looked so healthy and positive, and there was a bounce in his step—I used to think it was as if he had rubber balls in the toes of his shoes. He smiled and shook my hand and said in such a friendly, confident voice, "And you must be Mrs. Smith! I've heard wonderful things about you. We're going to have a wonderful team here, Mrs. Smith!"

Later on he called me by my first name, of course.

That first year we were mostly busy with information. The World Government Presidium and all the Member States had to be fully informed about the nature purpose of the SQ Test, before the actual implementation of its application could be eventualized. That was good for me too, because in preparing all that information I learned all about it myself. Often, taking dictation, I learned about it from Dr. Speakie's very lips. By May I was enough of an "expert" that I was able to prepare the "Basic SQ Information" pamphlet for publication just from Dr. Speakie's notes. It was such fascinating work. As soon as I began to understand the SQ Test Plan I began to believe in it. That was true of everybody in the office, and in the Bureau. Dr. Speakie's sincerity and scientific enthusiasm were infectious. Right from the beginning we had to take the Test every quarter, of course, and some of the secretaries used to be nervous before they took it, but I never was. It was so obvious that the Test was *right*. If you scored under 50 it was nice to know that you were sane, but even if you scored over 50 that was fine too, because then you could be *helped*. And anyway it is always best to know the truth about yourself.

As soon as the Information service was functioning smoothly Dr. Speakie transferred the main thrust of his attention to the implementation of Evaluator training, and planning for the structurization of the Cure Centers, only he changed the name to SQ Achievement Centers. It seemed a very big job even then. We certainly had no idea how big the job would finally turn out to be!

As he said at the beginning, we were a very good team. Dr. Speakie valued my administrative abilities and put them to good use. There wasn't a single slacker in the office. We all worked very hard, but there were always rewards.

I remember one wonderful day. I had accompanied Dr. Speakie to the Meeting of the Board of the Psychometric Bureau. The emissary from the State of Brazil announced that his State had adopted the Bureau Recommendations for Universal Testing—we had known that that was going to be announced. But then the delegate from Libya and the delegate from China announced that their States had adopted the Test too! Oh, Dr. Speakie's face was just like the sun for a minute, just *shining*. I wish I could remember exactly what he said, especially to the Chinese delegate, because of course China was a very big State and its decision was very influential. Unfortunately I do not have his exact words because I was changing the tape in the recorder. He said something like, "Gentlemen, this is a historic day for humanity." Then he began to talk at once about the effective implementation of the Application Centers, where people would take the Test, and the Achievement Centers, where they would go if they scored over 50, and how to establish the Test Administrations and Evaluations infrastructure on such a large scale, and so on. He was always modest and practical. He would rather talk about doing the job than talk about what an important job it was. He used to say, "Once you know what you're doing, the only thing you need to think about is how to do it." I believe that that is deeply true.

From then on, we could hand over the Information program to a subdepartment and concentrate on How to Do It. Those were exciting times! So many States joined the Plan, one after another. When I think of all we had to do I wonder that we didn't all go crazy! Some of the office staff did fail their quarterly Test, in fact. But most of us working in the Executive Office with Dr. Speakie remained quite stable, even when we were on the job all day and half the night. I think his presence was an inspiration. He was always calm and positive, even when we had to arrange things like training 113,000 Chinese Evaluators in three months. "You can always find out 'how' if you just know the 'why'!" he would say. And we always did.

When you think back over it, it really is quite amazing what a big job it was—so much bigger than anybody, even Dr. Speakie, had realized it would be. It just changed everything. You only realize that when you think back to what things used to be like. Can you imagine, when we began planning Universal Testing for the State of China, we only allowed for 1,100 Achievement Centers, with 6,800 Staff! It really seems like a joke! But it is not. I was going through some of the old files yesterday, making sure everything is in order, and I found the first China Implementation Plan, with those figures written down in black and white.

I believe the reason why even Dr. Speakie was slow to realize the magnitude of the operation was that even though he was a great scientist he was also an optimist. He just kept hoping against hope that the average scores would begin to go down, and this prevented him from seeing that universal application of the SQ Test was eventually going to involve everybody either as Inmates or as Staff.

When most of the Russian and all the African States had adopted the Recommendations and were busy implementing them, the debates in the General Assembly of the World Government got very excited. That was the period when so many bad things were said about the Test and about Dr. Speakie. I used to get quite angry, reading the *World Times* reports of debates. When I went as his secretary with Dr. Speakie to General Assembly meetings I had to sit and listen in person to people insulting him personally, casting aspersions on his motives and questioning his scientific integrity and even his sincerity. Many of those people were very disagreeable and obviously unbalanced. But he never lost his temper. He would just stand up and prove to them, again, that the SQ Test did actually literally scientifically show whether the testee was sane or insane, and the results could be proved, and all psychometrists accepted them. So the Test-Ban people couldn't do anything but shout about freedom and accuse Dr. Speakie and the Psychometric Bureau of trying to "turn the world into a huge insane asylum." He would always answer quietly and firmly, asking them how they thought a person could be "free" if he suffered under a delusional system, or was prey to compulsions and obsessions, or could not endure contact with reality? How could those who lacked mental health be truly free? What they called freedom might well be a delusional system with no contact with reality. In order to find out, all they had to do was to become testees. "Mental health *is* freedom," he said. " 'Eternal vigilance is the price of liberty,' they say, and now we have an infallible watchdog to watch for us—the SQ Test. *Only the testees can be truly free!*"

There really was no answer they could make to that except illogical and vulgar accusations, which did not convince the delegates who had invited them to speak. Sooner or later the delegates even from Member States where the Test-Ban movement was strong would volunteer to take the SQ Test to

prove that their mental health was adequate to their responsibilities. Then the ones that passed the Test and remained in
office would begin working for Universal Application in their
home State. The riots and demonstrations, and things like
the burning of the Houses of Parliament in London in the
State of England (where the Nor-Eurp SQ Center was housed),
and the Vatican Rebellion, and the Chilean H-Bomb, were
the work of insane fanatics appealing to the most unstable
elements of the populace. Such fanatics, as Dr. Speakie and
Dr. Waltraute pointed out in their Memorandum to the
Presidium, deliberately aroused and used the proven instability
of the crowd, "mob psychosis." The only response to mass
delusion of that kind was immediate implementation of the
Testing Program in the disturbed States, and immediate
amplification of the Asylum Program.

That was Dr. Speakie's own decision, by the way, to re-
name the SQ Achievement Centers "Asylums." He took the
word right out of his enemies' mouths. He said, "An asylum
means a place of *shelter*, a place of *cure*. Let there be no
stigma attached to the word 'insane,' to the word 'asylum,' to
the words 'insane asylum'! No! For the asylum is the haven of
mental health—the place of cure, where the anxious gain
peace, where the weak gain strength, where the prisoners of
inadequate reality assessment win their way to freedom!
Proudly let us use the word 'asylum.' Proudly let us go to the
asylum, to work to regain our own God-given mental health,
or to work with others less fortunate to help them win back
their own inalienable right to mental health. And let one
word be written large over the door of every asylum in the
world—'WELCOME!' "

Those words are from his great speech at the General
Assembly on the day World Universal Application was de-
creed by the Presidium. Once or twice a year I listen to my
tape of that speech. Although I am too busy ever to get really
depressed, now and then I feel the need of a tiny "pick-me-
up," and so I play that tape. It never fails to send me back to my
duties inspired and refreshed.

Considering all the work there was to do, as the Test scores
continued to come in always a little higher than the Psycho-

metric Bureau analysts estimated, the World Government Presidium did a wonderful job for the two years that it administered Universal Testing. There was a long period, six months, when the scores seemed to have stabilized, with just about half of the testees scoring over 50 and half under 50. At that time it was thought that if 40 per cent of the mentally healthy were assigned to Asylum Staff work, the other 60 per cent could keep up routine basic world functions such as farming, power supply, transportation, etc. This proportion had to be reversed when they found that over 60 per cent of the mentally healthy were volunteering for Staff work, in order to be with their loved ones in the Asylums. There was some trouble then with the routine basic world functions functioning. However, even then contingency plans were being made for the inclusion of farmlands, factories, power plants, etc., in the Asylum Territories, and the assignment of routine basic world functions work as Rehabilitation Therapy, so that the Asylums could become totally self-supporting if it became advisable. This was President Kim's special care, and he worked for it all through his term of office. Events proved the wisdom of his planning. He seemed such a nice wise little man. I still remember the day when Dr. Speakie came into the office and I knew at once that something was wrong. Not that he ever got really depressed or reacted with inopportune emotion, but it was as if the rubber balls in his shoes had gone just a little bit flat. There was the slightest tremor of true sorrow in his voice when he said, "Mary Ann, we've had a bit of bad news I'm afraid." Then he smiled to reassure me, because he knew what a strain we were all working under, and certainly didn't want to give anybody a shock that might push their score up higher on the next quarterly Test! "It's President Kim," he said, and I knew at once—I knew he didn't mean the President was ill or dead.

"Over fifty?" I asked, and he just said quietly and sadly, "Fifty-five."

Poor little President Kim, working so efficiently all that three months while mental ill health was growing in him! It was very sad and also a useful warning. High-level consultations were begun at once, as soon as President Kim was

committed, and the decision was made to administer the Test
monthly, instead of quarterly, to anyone in an executive
position.

Even before this decision, the Universal scores had begun
rising again. Dr. Speakie was not distressed. He had already
predicted that this rise was highly probable during the transition period to World Sanity. As the number of the mentally
healthy living outside the Asylums grew fewer, the strain on
them kept growing greater, and they became more liable to
break down under it—just as poor President Kim had done.
Later, when the Rehabs began coming out of the Asylums in
ever-increasing numbers, this stress would decrease. Also
the crowding in the Asylums would decrease, so that the
Staff would have more time to work on individually orien-
tated therapy, and this would lead to a still more dramatic
increase in the number of Rehabs released. Finally, when the
therapy process was completely perfected, including preven-
tive therapy, there might be no Asylums left in the world at
all! Because everybody will be either mentally healthy or a
Rehab, or "neonormal," as Dr. Speakie liked to call it.

It was the trouble in the State of Australia that precipi-
tated the Government Crisis. Some Psychometric Bureau
officials accused the Australian Evaluators of actually falsifying Test returns, but that is impossible since all the computers are linked to the World Government Central Computer
Bank in Keokuk. Dr. Speakie suspected that the Australian
Evaluators had been falsifying *the Test itself*, and insisted
that they themselves all be tested immediately. Of course he
was right. It had been a conspiracy, and the suspiciously low
Australian Test scores had resulted from the use of a false
Test. Many of the conspirators tested higher than 80 when
forced to take the genuine Test! The State Government in
Canberra had been unforgivably lax. If they had just admitted it everything would have been all right. But they got
hysterical, and moved the State Government to a sheep
station in Queensland, and tried to withdraw from the World
Government. (Dr. Speakie said this was a typical mass psychosis: reality-evasion, followed by fugue and autistic with-
drawal.) Unfortunately the Presidium seemed to be paralyzed.

Australia seceded on the day before the President and Presidium were due to take their monthly Test, and probably they were afraid of overstraining their SQ with agonizing decisions. So the Psychometric Bureau volunteered to handle the episode. Dr. Speakie himself flew on the plane with the H-Bombs, and helped to drop the information leaflets. He never lacked personal courage.

When the Australian incident was over, it turned out that most of the Presidium, including President Singh, had scored over 50. So the Psychometric Bureau took over their functions temporarily. Even on a long-term basis this made good sense, since all the problems now facing the World Government had to do with administering and evaluating the Test, training the Staff, and providing full self-sufficiency structuration to all Asylums.

What this meant in personal terms was that Dr. Speakie, as Chief of the Psychometric Bureau, was now Interim President of the United States of the World. As his personal secretary I was, I will admit it, just terribly proud of him. But he never let it go to his head.

He was so modest. Sometimes he used to say to people, when he introduced me, "This is Mary Ann, my secretary," he'd say with a little twinkle, "and if it wasn't for her I'd have been scoring over fifty long ago!"

He truly appreciated efficiency and reliability. That's why we made such a good team, all those years we worked together.

There were times, as the World SQ scores rose and rose, that I would become a little discouraged. Once the week's Test figures came in on the readout, and the *average* score was 71. I said, "Doctor, there are moments I believe the whole world is going insane!"

But he said, "Look at it this way, Mary Ann. Look at those people in the Asylums—3.1 billion inmates now, and 1.8 billion Staff—but look at them. What are they doing? They're pursuing their therapy, doing rehabilitation work on the farms and in the factories, and striving all the time, too, to *help* each other toward mental health. The preponderant inverse sanity quotient is certainly very high at the moment;

they're mostly insane, yes. But you have to admire them. They are fighting for mental health. They will—they *will* win through!" And then he dropped his voice and said as if to himself, gazing out the window and bouncing just a little on the balls of his feet, "If I didn't believe that, I couldn't go on."

And I knew he was thinking of his wife.

Mrs. Speakie had scored 88 on the very first American Universal Test. She had been in the Greater Los Angeles Territory Asylum for years now.

Anybody who still thinks Dr. Speakie wasn't sincere should think about that for a minute! He gave up everything for his belief.

And even when the Asylums were all running quite well, and the epidemics in South Africa and the famines in Texas and the Ukraine were under control, still the work load on Dr. Speakie never got any lighter, because every month the personnel of the Psychometric Bureau got smaller, since some of them always flunked their monthly Test and were committed to Bethesda. I never could keep any of my secretarial staff any more for longer than a month or two. It was harder and harder to find replacements, too, because most sane young people volunteered for Staff work in the Asylums, since life was much easier and more sociable inside the Asylums than outside. Everything so convenient, and lots of friends and acquaintances! I used to positively envy those girls! But I knew where my job was.

At least it was much less hectic here in the UN Building, or the Psychometry Tower as it had been renamed long ago. Often there wouldn't be anybody around the whole building all day long but Dr. Speakie and myself, and maybe Bill the janitor (Bill scored 32 regular as clockwork every quarter). All the restaurants were closed, in fact most of Manhattan was closed, but we had fun picnicking in the old General Assembly Hall. And there was always the odd call from Buenos Aires or Reykjavik, asking Dr. Speakie's advice as Interim President about some problem, to break the silence.

But last November 8, I will never forget the date, when Dr. Speakie was dictating the Referendum for World Economic Growth for the next five-year period, he suddenly interrupted

himself. "By the way, Mary Ann," he said, "how was your last
score?"

We had taken the Test two days before, on the sixth. We
always took the Test every first Monday. Dr. Speakie never
would have dreamed of excepting himself from Universal
Testing regulations.

"I scored twelve," I said, before I thought how strange it
was of him to ask. Or, not just to ask, because we often
mentioned our scores to each other; but to ask *then*, in the
middle of executing important World Government business.

"Wonderful," he said, shaking his head. "You're wonderful,
Mary Ann! Down two from last month's Test, aren't you?"

"I'm always between ten and fourteen," I said. "Nothing
new about that, Doctor."

"Someday," he said, and his face took on the expression it
had when he gave his great speech about the Asylums,
"someday, this world of ours will be governed by men fit to
govern it. Men whose SQ score is zero. Zero, Mary Ann!"

"Well, my goodness, Doctor," I said jokingly—his intensity
almost alarmed me a little—"even *you* never scored lower
than three, and you haven't done that for a year or more
now!"

He stared at me almost as if he didn't see me. It was quite
uncanny. "Someday," he said in just the same way, "nobody
in the world will have a quotient higher than fifty. Someday,
nobody in the world will have a quotient higher than thirty!
Higher than ten! The Therapy will be perfected. I was only
the diagnostician. But the Therapy will be perfected! The
cure will be found! Someday!" And he went on staring at me,
and then he said, "Do you know what my score was on
Monday?"

"Seven," I guessed promptly. The last time he had told me
his score it had been seven.

"Ninety-two," he said.

I laughed, because he seemed to be laughing. He had
always had a puckish sense of humor that came out unex-
pectedly. But I thought we really should get back to the
World Economic Growth Plan, so I said laughingly, "That
really is a very bad joke, Doctor!"

"Ninety-two," he said, "and you don't believe me, Mary Ann, but that's because of the cantaloupe."

I said, "What cantaloupe, Doctor?" and that was when he jumped across his desk and began to try to bite through my jugular vein.

I used a judo hold and shouted to Bill the janitor, and when he came I called a robo-ambulance to take Dr. Speakie to Bethesda Asylum.

That was six months ago. I visit Dr. Speakie every Saturday. It is very sad, he is in the McLean Area, which is the Violent Ward, and every time he sees me he screams and foams. But I do not take it personally. One should never take mental ill health personally. When the Therapy is perfected he will be completely rehabilitated. Meanwhile, I just hold on here. Bill keeps the floors clean, and I run the World Government. It really isn't as difficult as you might think.

THE RIGHT TO PUNISHMENT

by Jerry Pournelle

This was originally written to be the introduction to Ursula Le Guin's story; but it became so long that it was manifestly unfair to do that to her. It remains closely related to "SQ."

The enemies of freedom need not wear the Gorgon's Mask; or if they do, it will not be the Medusa of the ancient inscriptions, raw head and bloody bones, frightful grin and protruding tongue; it will be the Medusa of later times: as Russel Kirk has described her, "a frigid beauty, the mask of a woman beyond good and evil ... a faint sensual smile creeping upon the lips, a hint of terror or of pain haunting the eyes. The Anatolian monster that haunted the early Greeks through their dreams has become the incarnation, in art, of concupiscence struck down in the moment of its evil perfection."

Certainly the Gorgon of today seduces as often as she terrifies. Soviet tanks roll through the streets of Budapest and Prague and the KGB does its bloody work at 5 Dzerzhinsky Street right enough; but the Gorgon can put on a different mask, and stroll the halls of Westminster or Capital Hill seducing us with tales of kindness.

As with, for example, the various Mental Health Acts.

For centuries the English cherished the right of *habeas corpus*. This is a writ of command, from a judge to a jailor, demanding that the jailor appear before the judge and state why the subject of the writ has been imprisoned; and if no proper answer can be made, the prisoner must then and there be released. Were this all, the writ would be of little use; what made it such a powerful instrument of freedom was the very limited number of returns considered proper. It was not enough that someone was imprisoned at the whim of the monarch. It took judge and jury acting with proper procedure.

Then a few years ago it was argued that this was all very well for criminals, but what of mental patients? Was it not a gross travesty to force them to endure a trial? To parade their infirmities before a judge and jury in a public courtroom? Surely liberty is not well served by such barbaric practices. ...

And so, in England, Parliament enacted various Mental Health Acts. One of them made it a proper return to *habeas corpus* that the "patient" was held on orders of a board consisting of two licensed psychiatrists and the governor of a duly registered mental hospital or asylum. Indeed, it was sufficient to present properly witnessed signatures to commitment papers; the imprisoned person need not be brought to court at all. (Why subject a sick person to the terrors of a courtroom?)

And all was well. Except for disturbing rumors.

Item: There was resident in Sherwood Forest a dotty old man, retired on military pension, who "practiced the ancient and honorable arts of animal husbandry, to wit, the keeping of hens." He lived in seclusion in a shack well away from any other human habitation, which was as well, because he shared his quarters (other than his kitchen and a small sleeping compartment) with his chickens.

Moreover, he was an eccentric. He liked talking with such children as found their way to his lonely stones. It was never contended that he did them any harm; merely that he enjoyed their company, and they his, and they were willing to endure the unsavory air and general slovenliness of his shack. One of his young guests was the child of a public health official. He spoke at home of his elderly friend, and in due course the father came uninvited to inspect, and was turned away as a trespasser.

The next official visit came in the dead of night. Two police constables and a psychiatrist, acting on a "warrant" procured from public health officers, broke in his door about midnight; they seized him, put him in handcuffs, and dragged him away, while others set fire to his unsanitary quarters.

His sanity hearing was held less than an hour later. Two psychiatrists and the governor of a local mental health hospital found him to be "in an agitated state, with delusions of persecution, and if released he would be a danger to himself. He is severely disturbed. . . ." There were other findings in a similar vein. The result was that he was taken (for his own protection) to the local mental health hospital (a private institution, but paid by the Treasury to care for involuntary patients), and there he was locked away.

Daily did he protest to his keepers. In particular he demanded that a letter be taken to his Member of Parliament. And daily was he calmed, spoken to in soothing tones, told that his M.P. would certainly be told. . . .

Many months passed; but eventually the M.P. *was* told; and being the nephew of this retired war hero (Victoria Cross), he asked a Question in Parliament; the Minister of Health was forced to investigate; a new sanity hearing was arranged; and lo, the old man was found to be quite sane (if a bit eccentric) and his anger—aye, anger and hatred—directed to those who had imprisoned him seemed well justified.

Item: There was a gentleman, owner of a small business, whose wife was admitted to hospital for surgery under the National Health scheme. In due course she was discharged. She believed, and her husband believed, that she was entitled to further treatment; that indeed she was in need of further treatment, and this was being denied because she and her husband were Tories, vocal opponents of "socialized medicine," agitators for the abolition of the national health scheme.

Time passed. The gentleman made a nuisance of himself. He sent letter after letter to the director of the local hospital, to the Minister of Health, to his Member of Parliament, to the newspapers, and to everyone he thought might listen to his case.

And at midnight of a Wednesday he heard a knock at the door; opening it he admitted two police constables and a police psychiatrist, who proceeded to take him in handcuffs to the local hospital, where its director sat with two psychiatrists. . . .

He too was found to be in an agitated condition, etc., etc.

It took him less time to arrange for Questions in Parliament; new hearings were held; and to the chagrin of the local medical boards, not only was he found to be sane, but his wife entitled to further treatment. . . .

Item: A gentleman declined to sell his field to the local County Council. Eminent domain was invoked; the field was forcibly taken. He complained. Bitterly, and often, and eventually he too was taken before a hospital governor and two psychiatrists—

This one has an uglier ending. After several years he escaped and somehow persuaded officials to reopen his case. It was found that two of those who sat on the board that committed him had heavy financial interests in the scheme that caused his field to be taken, and indeed one had become rich as a result; and that the field was improperly seized.

Unfortunately by this time the man really was quite mad. It is thought that he was sane enough before the affair began, but perhaps not.

Thus may liberty succumb to the lure of kindness. Had these people been treated as *criminals;* had it been thought they were being punished; then it is unlikely they would even have been brought to trial. We understand safeguards against punishment. We are not always so canny when it is our wish to do good.

Another argument is made: Criminals, or at least many of them, are ill. This is self-evident. If they were not sick, they wouldn't be criminals.

We should not punish people for being sick. We should instead cure them.

The case of the "mentally disordered sex offender" seems particularly clear. Certainly these are "sick people" and it smacks of the snake pit and the rack to punish them. At the same time, we certainly do not want them wandering about in society molesting children.

California therefore adopted a number of new laws. One

made it a valid return to *habeas corpus* that the prisoner was held as a "mentally disordered sex offender" on order of a board of psychiatrists at a state mental hospital. Thus the offender could be kept until cured of antisocial tendencies.

Item: A man was convicted of indecent exposure. The circumstances were not entirely clear; certainly he had exposed himself to some children, but he was very drunk at the time. In any event he was arrested, and persuaded to plead guilty to the misdemeanor charge. It was a first offense.

Indecent exposure is a sex offense. He was thus sent to Atascadaro State Hospital, where a board of psychiatrists adjudged him a "mentally disordered sex offender" and ordered him held on indefinite commitment.

A year passed. Then another. Then a third. He was again tested, again found to be a "mentally disordered sex offender," and in addition it was found that he "was hostile and uncooperative and not responding to treatment." Furthermore, it was unlikely that he would *ever* respond to treatment. He was incurable, and he was taking up a bed in an already overcrowded hospital, using up expensive and valuable state medical resources—

His case was reviewed carefully, and it was indeed found that he was incurable. Since he was incurable there was no point in treating him. Since there was no point in treating him, he should not be in the state hospital at all. But since he *was*, after all, a "mentally disordered sex offender," he could not be released. He was therefore transferred to San Quentin.

He had received a life sentence for indecent exposure.

Eventually some law professors, among them my very conservative mentor Kenneth Cole, heard of his plight. Funds were raised. A federal writ of *habeas corpus* was obtained.

The plea made was simple: that the man had a right to be *punished*, and society had a right to punish him; but to hold him in San Quentin forever for a misdemeanor crime was unjust; to say that he was being "rehabilitated" was ridiculous; and to say he received "rehabilitation" rather than "punishment" *for his own good* was monstrous.

Eventually sanity prevailed, although those who argued

the man's case were accused of wanting to release sex maniacs upon the community.

A final item: Every now and again one sees news accounts of psychiatrists who have devised tests that will pick out, from a classroom of children, those who will become violent criminals. Sometimes this is promised at surprisingly early ages.

The suggestion is always made that we act on those predictions.

Kipling gave the right advice on how to deal with that monstrous idea. Order the guns. . . .

Editor's introduction to:

THE LOOKING GLASS OF THE LAW

Kevin O'Donnell is a comparative newcomer to the science fiction scene; and he has a unique problem. People don't believe he exists.

For years Barry Malzberg used the pseudonym "K.M. O'Donnell," and a lot of fans know that; so when a real O'Donnell appears on the scene—

Many and many a year ago when I was a graduate student in psychology, I worked as assistant to Dr. Albert Ax, who had built the world's most sophisticated polygraph. One of my tasks was to construct an even better machine.

Ax worked marvels. His famous paper "On the physiological differentiation between fear and anger" remains a classic, and was the beginning of modern scientific "lie detection." We had high hopes in those days. We were, after all, working with vacuum tubes and mechanical recording pens (which often sprayed ink all over us). Our best amplifiers were horribly noisy; and the only way to change analog (continuous) signals to digital data that a computer could work with involved mechanical stepping switches and other horrors. But, one day, we knew, electronic science would advance; and that would be that. We'd have polygraphs that could do the kinds of things the popular press (and the CIA) thought Ax could do in 1954.

I left that field; but I note that despite transistors and large-scale integrated circuits and infinitely more sensitive amplifiers and transducers, polygraphs are not all that much more reliable— as instruments for detecting truth—than they were in my student days. Thus the courts rightfully distrust them.

But suppose—suppose one day a really reliable polygraph became possible. . . .

THE LOOKING GLASS OF THE LAW

by Kevin O'Donnell, Jr.

They stopped the bus at the corner of Sherman and Whalley. A burly patrolman wearing the helmet and jodhpurs of a motorcycle cop was first on. With impartial interest, he studied the forty-seven passengers, who, after bored nods, returned to the conversations they'd suspended. The driver muttered something about his schedule and the cop said, "Sure, buddy. Sorry."

He walked down the aisle, scanning the faces that reflected the frail light. "You, ma'am," he said, pointing to a white-haired woman with three shopping bags. She smiled cheerfully and bustled to the front, where two more policemen chatted on the steps. One led her away. "You." A friendly wino blinked through his personal fog. Helping him to his feet, the cop faced him in the right direction and patted him on the shoulder. "And you." He stood above a middle-aged man with shaggy hair and an air of nervous good-fellowship.

"Officer," said George Hennesy, speaking rapidly, "I'm on my way to work. I'm a night watchman, and if I don't get there by—"

"We'll write you an excuse, sir. Please come along."

Praying that he wouldn't have to leave the soft foam seat, Hennesy stared up into patient blue eyes. "Please get somebody else, huh?"

"Sir, I'd hate to have to use this on you." Big-knuckled fingers plucked a dart gun from its leather holster. With a glance at Hennesy, the cop spun the dial to "Obedience." "Sir?"

"You win." When he raised his hands, the sleeves of his ragged blue jacket slid down, baring bony wrists.

"No need for that, sir." Chuckling, he let Hennesy precede him; when he got to the door, he laid an engaging grin upon the remaining passengers. His hearty voice caromed off the rear windows: "I'm sorry we had to delay you. We appreciate your co-operation and your good will—we couldn't do it without you. Thanks, and good night."

As they swung down onto the crowded sidewalk, somebody stuck his head through a window and hollered, "Way to be, offsir—keep up the good work, y'hear?" The bus moved away to a rumble of agreement.

"Jesus," said Hennesy, bitter at having been singled out, "they really love you guys."

"They got reason to, sir." A group of old men swirled past them and he held Hennesy's arm so they wouldn't be separated. "Ten years ago, that bus—and these sidewalks—woulda been deserted. All the people woulda been home, hiding under their beds. They ain't afraid no more, which is how come they love us." Shy astonishment crept over his wind-burned face as he added, "It's sort of a nice feeling, y'know? Now, c'mon, you got a date with The Machine."

Just my fucking luck, thought Hennesy as his thin soles scraped on the broken asphalt. *Twenty-eight more hours and I'd've been golden. Now Helen's gonna be unhappy, and disappointed, when I get home. Again.* His stomach full of weary hopelessness, he walked towards the Police Department van. There was no line before the entrance, but an inset light burned redly. Resigned to his fate, he fell into an at-ease stance and waited for the minutes to pass. When the old lady came out of the darkness to stand behind him, he turned to the cop in puzzled anger. "Hey, what is this? I was the last one off; I oughta be the last one through."

"Sorry." His silver helmet shimmered in the sodium light. The leather gloves in his hand were black and thick. He slapped them idly against the side of his leg. "She had to check her bags, sir—and anyway, you gotta get to work, right?"

"Yeah, I suppose so." The red glow shifted to emerald green and a figure stumbled out the van's side door.

"In you go, sir," ordered the cop, gesturing with his chin.

"Ah, Christ." He went up three dirt-encrusted steps and pushed on the aluminum door. It swung open at his touch, as had those of the other Machines through which he'd passed. Stepping in, he looked for differences. None. The Machines were all alike, right down to the scuffed green paint on the metal floor. A wall of heavy blue rubber blocked his path. While he glared at it, an amplified voice blasted: "Please insert your arms into the holes."

"All right, already!" Six times he'd gone through the routine; six times the same neutral voice had directed him. The least the cops could do was have a different tape at each Machine. He sighed, and thrust his hands into the holes in the rubber. Velvet-covered steel bands contracted on his wrists and sucked them inwards. The previous subject had been taller than Hennesy, so the holes were high, but The Machine made a smooth adjustment and softened his discomfort. Behind him, another wall rose out of the floor. Inching up to his back, it leaned against him with an even, immobilizing pressure. The forewall retreated from his face, leaving him a pocket of greasy air to breathe and depthless darkness to probe.

As he had six times before, Hennesy made a solemn vow to visit the Hall of Records and register to vote. The machines were killing him—that one was squeezing his head harder than any of the others had—and to his way of thinking, it was all the fault of those lunatics in Congress who'd repealed the fourth and fifth amendments. Them and their cronies in state legislatures around the country who'd decided that overkill was the answer to the crime problem. *I'm gonna register, and I'm gonna vote, and I'm gonna vote for anybody who runs against any of those bastards. Even if it's a chimpanzee, I'll vote for him.*

Two hundred and forty-nine sensors had wormed their way through his clothing to take up listening posts next to his skin. Their metal ears were cold, and he shivered. He felt the needles jab into his forearms and cursed. *What the hell does New Haven need ten of these monsters for?* A Machine processed an average subject in ten minutes. Allowing for delays, balks, and the occasional individual who had to be manhandled into place, it could interrogate five people an hour. One hundred twenty a day. Forty-three thousand, eight hundred a year. Ten Machines upped that last number to four hundred thirty-eight thousand, or one hundred thousand more than the population of New Haven County. *Jesus God,* he thought, *they won't even leave 'em in one place and give a sucker an even chance. Naw, they gotta keep moving 'em around, so you never know where you shouldn't oughta go.*

His knees buckled as the truth serums hit him; the manacles held him upright. The ebony before his eyes acquired a texture, deep and soft. It separated into patterns and shapes, became three-dimensional, whirled and twirled. In matching time pulsed the paternal voice he'd learned to despise: HAVE YOU DONE ANYTHING WRONG IN THE LAST THIRTY DAYS?

Took him right back to third grade, when the nuns used to drag them down to the church on Friday afternoons and make them stand in long shadowed lines, shuffling in and out of confessionals where hoarse-tongued priests gave them advice and penance, and sent them out to sin no more. Dimly, he watched himself say, "Yes." The sensors soaked up physiological data and relayed it to the computer. A jury of semiconductors confirmed his honesty.

ON MORE THAN ONE OCCASION?

"No."

WAS THAT ONE OCCASION ILLEGAL AS WELL AS WRONG?

Hah, hah, he could beat the rap, all he had to do was say *No* so loudly and clearly that The Machine would have to know he believed it himself, and then it would let him free, because it wasn't allowed to fuck around with morality, only with legality. And Helen wouldn't know anything about it, and he wouldn't have to hurt her. Again. He lifted his head, cleared his throat, smiled at the thought of fooling The Machine, and said, "Yes."

DESCRIBE THE CIRCUMSTANCES—

whadIsay? Jet black sculptures jeered him.

—AS FULLY AND AS COMPLETELY—

ohmydeargod, that stuff really does loosen your tongue. He giggled.

—AS POSSIBLE.

"It was Wednesday, March 19, and it was raining cats and dogs and I was waiting for a bus that wouldn't come for another thirty-three minutes, so I went into Macy's to get out of the rain and the cold. It was really crowded and all the salesgirls were busy, they weren't paying any attention to me, and the aisles were dense with shoppers—I held my wallet 'cause I was afraid somebody'd try to steal it—and I looked at my watch. Had thirty-one minutes to go. I walked around, looking at all the things on display, wishing that I had the money to buy something for my wife Helen just 'cause it was pretty and not 'cause she needed it. There was this ashtray, from Taiwan, carved out of black and white marble, so thin that if you held it up to the light you could look through it and see the shadows of your fingers. I knew she'd love it. It was small enough to go into my pocket. It fit very nice, no bulges, no sags. I left the store and didn't pay for it." Night figures paused in their dance to applaud his recital; he felt himself grin and bow repeatedly.

WHAT WAS THE PRICE OF THE ASHTRAY?

He wanted to protest that he couldn't possibly remember the exact number of dollars and cents that an unaffordable luxury would have cost if he had paid for it, but the serum opened the shell of his memory and pulled out the pearl: "Twenty-nine ninety-eight."

THANK YOU.

"You're welcome." He heard clicks and hums in the area behind the wall and he knew what they meant, but he didn't care because the people in the shadows had taken up their ballet again.

HAVE YOU DONE ANYTHING ELSE IN THE LAST THIRTY DAYS WHICH MIGHT QUALIFY AS ILLEGAL? DESCRIBE ANY INSTANCE OF WHICH YOU ARE DOUBTFUL. THE COMPUTER WILL JUDGE.

Did the dancers pause? He opened his mouth to scoff but words trickled out. "Well, the other day, April 7, that was Monday, I was walking along and I found this wallet. No ID's or nothing. I thought about turning it in to the police, but my own wallet was pretty decrepit, so I decided to keep it."

THAT IS NEITHER WRONG NOR ILLEGAL. YOU MAY KEEP IT. IS THERE ANYTHING ELSE?

He swooped through the long halls of his memories. In niches along the walls glowed abstract designs. His eyes tasted their colors, reveled in the brightness. Only two were scarlet, and he'd recounted them already. "No."

VERY GOOD. THE RECORDS INDICATE THAT YOU HAVE NOT PRE-VIOUSLY CONFESSED THIS CRIME. THEREFORE, YOU HAVE BEEN FINED ACCORDING TO THE USUAL FORMULA. IN ONE MOMENT YOU WILL BE PUNISHED. WHEN YOU ARE YOURSELF AGAIN, REMEMBER THIS MACHINE. YOU CAN NEVER ESCAPE FROM IT; YOU CAN NEVER HIDE FROM IT. ONLY OBSERVANCE OF THE LAW CAN SAVE YOU.

He hummed a little tune to himself, pleased that it was almost over. His first session had been much longer. The portion of his mind that wasn't watching the ballerinas wondered what form his punishment would take.

SHOPLIFT! His hands were gloved with frost; froze; crystal-lized; erupted with agonizing needles of ice. Whimpering, he hung from the manacles.

SHOPLIFT! The ice melted; the skin raced from white to red. Hot! Blisters bubbled and burst; baked flesh disintegrated; the bones themselves began to char.

SHOPLIFT! The gloom grew whiskery and beady-eyed with rats that scurried to his fingers and nibbled at the living flesh. Blood oozed, then dripped, then spurted. Sharp teeth ripped his hands apart and absconded with the pieces.

THAT IS ALL. SHOULD YOU WISH TO APPEAL THIS COURT'S DECI-SION, A TRANSCRIPT WILL BE PROVIDED UPON REQUEST. GO NOW, AND BREAK THE LAW NO MORE.

The restraining pressure eased; cool air washed over his back and began to dry the shirt that stuck to sweaty skin. The manacles opened and the weight of his arms dragged them free. He staggered to the exit door, but couldn't operate the knob. A policeman outside heard his fumbling and opened it for him.

"This way, sir." He took him by the arm and led him to a row of cots. The colors of the street corner light were height-ened to an alien intensity. Hennesy sank down with numb relief. A gentle wind took chatter from the sidewalk and offered it to him, but he couldn't understand it. The cop paused for a moment before asking, "You were on the bus, sir?"

"Right." Before the Machine he would have been voluble in his outrage; after it, he could only attempt to repeat the word. "Ri . . ."

"Well, sir," said the officer as he ripped a ticket from a booklet, "Here's a pass entitling you to one free bus ride. And this is your excuse, for your employer."

"Thanks." He tucked them into his jacket pocket, and stared up at the sky. It showed stars, which he hadn't seen often. He watched them wink at each other across the great space they defined. He envied them their freedom.

The serums had spent themselves, and their effects were fading. He grew aware of a black man on the cot next to his. Short and thin, thirtyish and ugly, he was bent double. His tender hands cupped his balls; he moaned sporadic intervals. When he felt Hennesy's gaze, he looked up. "Hey, dude—what'd they get you for? What'd they do?"

Hennesy shrugged. "Shoplifting. They fined me, and gave me a dose of aversion therapy."

"Hunh! Me too. But, shit, she's my own wife, man! Caught her stepping out with my for-mer best friend . . . whupped her some, then strapped her to the bed and showed her who her man *is*. Man's got a right, don't he?" He rubbed himself gently. "That muhfucking therapy felt like a gahdamn *mule* kicked me—sheeyit, they say I won't be able to use this for another six weeks. Now I ask you, what the hell am I going to *do* with myself, man? I mean, this here is worse than the fucking *slammer*. Can you dig it?"

"Yeah, it's a bitch." He opened his hands to his eyes and his body was amazed at their wholeness. His mind had expected nothing else, but his body *knew* they had been destroyed. Three times. "Don't know how I'm gonna pay off that fine, though."

"They already hit your bank account?"

"Two milliseconds after the fine came down."

"How much?"

"Hell . . . four times twenty-nine ninety-eight. What's that, a hundred something? I ain't got it."

"So mug somebody, deposit the bread, and lie low for thirty days."

"Uh-uh. I got a job. Besides, they caught me once, for beating on somebody who was bugging my wife—don't plan to face an assault rap ever again." A shudder raced the memory through his body. He'd never screamed so loud in his life. Being skinned alive had not been pleasant. "That therapy is bad shit."

"Don't I know it." The black man groaned as he sat up. "Hey, looky there."

"Where?"

"The Machine, dude. Who went in after you?"

"Some old lady, don't know who she is. Looks like a grandmother. Why?"

"Well look and see for yourself."

He squinted through the yellow light. The van squatted on the asphalt like a blue beetle. A wisp of greasy brown smoke rose through a vent in its roof.

"Damn!" The black voice trembled with anger and fear. "Wonder what the hell *she* did."

Hennesy shook his head and looked away. He'd go register to vote in the morning. He *would*. Unless . . .

NO MORE PENCILS, NO MORE BOOKS

Ye shall know the truth, and the Truth shall make you free.

Nearly twenty years ago, *Blackboard Jungle* was a horror story.

Now it's a bit old-fashioned, a bit too hopeful.

John Morressy's story is, just now, a horror story, science fiction, a picture of an improbable future. . . .

NO MORE PENCILS, NO MORE BOOKS

by John Morressy

It wasn't first-timer's shakes. Colby was long past that. All the same, he felt the lightness in his belly and the tightness in his throat, and the creeping feeling that everyone else in the car knew just where he was going on this gloomy Monday morning.

He leaned back, took a deep breath, and directed his gaze out the window of the silent, rocking train, trying to keep his nerves calm. They were well into the city now, speeding along behind the protective fence, just above ground level. Colby's eyes flicked automatically from burned-out window to window, from one rubble heap to the next, searching out danger signs. He saw nothing. The light rain was falling steadily, and he guessed that the rubble rats had stayed in shelter. They'll all be in school today, keeping dry, he thought. Just my luck.

The train climbed, moved smoothly along, safely above roof level for the next two miles, then slowed for the main transfer point. Colby took his bag and moved out with the others, not too fast and not too slow, trying to damp his rising excitement.

Even at this early hour, most of the passengers were heading for the eight-car Business District and Midtown shuttles, where there were almost as many guards as riders. Colby headed for the special shuttle marked Inner City No. 3. The gateman checked his identification, took a quick look in his bag, and passed him through without a word. The inside guard gave Colby a just-perceptible smile and said, "Good luck, buddy."

"Thanks," Colby replied. His voice was hoarse, but he did not want to clear his throat in the guard's hearing.

The shuttle was a small electric with seats for twelve. It carried no guard. Colby was alone in it for a few minutes before a tall husky man entered and took the seat behind him. The newcomer gave Colby a quick glance but said nothing. Two more men entered. They stretched out as comfortably as the seats permitted, folded their arms, and went to sleep. Colby tried to do the same. He could not sleep. He kept thinking of the school at Greenbelt, where he could be right now. It was not too late; they would still have to take him back.

This was a bad way to be thinking, he knew. A man made his decisions and then he stuck with them. The move to Inner City No. 3 was a free choice, made with full knowledge of the gains and losses entailed. A little tougher, perhaps, especially in the beginning, but he'd been trained for it. And, here, he could count on support. There was nothing to worry about.

With nine men aboard, the shuttle pulled out of the station, down the ramp to the street. The ride was silent and surprisingly smooth. At one bumpy stretch Colby took a quick look outside and saw a pile of burned-out cars, real old-style gassers, in a tumbled roadside heap. They had probably been set up as a barrier during the night and thrust aside by an early patrol. He closed his eyes again. A loud thump brought him upright as something heavy crashed on the roof of the shuttle. None of the others stirred. He leaned back, shut his eyes, and kept them shut until the ride was over.

He was feeling better, more confident, when the shuttle pulled into the learning compound. The others filed out, mumbling a word now and then but generally silent, and he trailed along. At the first checkpoint he was given a locker number and sent down a short corridor. He changed quickly, relieved himself, and drank two glasses of water to moisten his throat.

A wiry little man entered the locker room and called Colby's name. When Colby replied, the man approached and held out his hand.

"I'm Ed Mills. I'm the assistant principal here," he said.

"Glad to meet you, Mr. Mills."

"Sorry I wasn't able to get together with you sooner, Colby. Things have been hectic here. If you have any questions about routine or schedules, or any of the operations, I'll try to answer them. Any questions at all, I'm here to help."

"Mr. Oakland explained things pretty well, sir. I've read all the orientation material he gave me. I've memorized the ground plan and the schedules."

"That's good. And you're familiar with the monitor we use?"

"I've logged sixty hours on the M-6 and eighty hours on the M-6A, sir."

"Good, good," Mills said, obviously pleased. "I have to remember that I'm dealing with an experienced teacher."

"This is my first Inner City hitch, sir."

"It's not as bad as some people like to make it sound. We've got a tight ship here, Colby, and a good crew. You'll meet them later. Now, do you have any questions? The kids will be finished breakfast and morning medication in five minutes. You'd better be in place when they get out."

"No questions, sir. I'll head for my room."

"Remember one thing, Colby, and you'll be all right. Once you're behind that monitor, you're the boss. Never forget it, and never let them forget it. If something has to be done, do it. We'll back you up." Mills extended his hand once again. "Good luck, Colby."

Colby settled into place behind his monitor. Everything he needed to run a class was there at his fingertips, all the information before his eyes. He set the classroom lights high, dimmed his own, turned on the speakers, and waited for his class to enter. At precisely 8:30 the access door slid back and they began to saunter in. A few stared at him, others elaborately ignored him. The PSMs shuffled unaware to their places. When every student was at his proper console, still half asleep and sluggish from breakfast and his medication, Colby switched on the morning sports readout. The class settled down, and the room was quiet.

Second and third periods went by without an incident. Inner City wasn't supposed to be this quiet. Colby knew. He began to wonder what was going on. Perhaps one of the pill men had taken pity on the new teacher and overdosed everyone. He had heard of that being done. Or maybe the kids had a surprise planned for him.

The morning continued to go so well that Colby let his vigilance slip. He made the mistake of keeping his eyes on the monitor screen for too long. When he looked up, a fist was coming straight for his face.

He didn't flinch. He had been warned of this trick. The fist slammed into the plexine barrier and slowed, impact absorbed harmlessly. It stopped six inches from Colby's face. The kid looked at him with eyes cold as stones.

Colby stayed cool. He let the kid curse him out for a few seconds; then he cut the incoming speaker and let the kid stand there working his mouth without a sound coming through to the teacher's side.

That was a point for Colby. When he turned the speaker on again, he found that some of the others in the classroom were applauding, whistling, and stamping their feet to show approval. One of the PSMs struggled to his feet and went into a slow lurching dance. A kid in the front row began to spar playfully with the one who had thrown the punch at Colby.

Colby let them go on for a time to work off some of the morning's pent-up energy. So far, no harm was being done. But this playful mood did not last long. When he saw knives, Colby knew that things had gone far enough. He hit two switches, fast. His amplified voice boomed into the room, cutting through the uproar.

"I'm locked on both of you. You use the knives, I use the stinger," he said.

The kids studied each other and then him. Colby kept his finger lightly resting on the white button. Slowly, with the greatest disdain they could pack into each movement, they put away the knives. They slouched to their places and slumped into the consoles.

Colby ran a quick readout of names. One thing he had learned was to get the names of the troublemakers right away. The one who had thrown the punch was Santos. The other one, the boxer, was Turner.

Santos sat glaring at him. Colby lowered his eyes to study the monitor screen. When he looked up, Santos's eyes were still fixed on him.

The kid was a hard case, he thought. Hell, they were all hard cases here. Even the PSMs, the quiet ones who spent most of the day nodding and staring into space, were dangerous when they came out of their fog. This wasn't a greenbelt prep school, where kids smiled at the teacher and carried their own reader deck. This was Inner City No. 3, where kids carried weapons. If they smiled, it was a sure sign they were getting ready to use them. No teacher could afford to forget that.

Colby switched to the speaker on Santos's console and said, "What's the matter, Santos? Your reader broken?"

"Not yet, general."

"Then get to work."

"Up yours, general."

"Get to work, Santos."

Santos pulled off his boot. Still looking straight at Colby, he brought the steel-tipped heel down hard on the reader screen. Those screens were made of a plexine tougher than the barrier that divided teachers from their classes, but Santos was not trying to break the reader, he was out for Colby. Colby knew it, and knew that he had to react. He locked the stinger on Santos.

"Hit the reader once more and you get stung," he said.

Santos brought the boot heel down, and Colby tapped the white button. Santos straightened like an icicle, then slumped in his seat. The boot dropped from his twitching fingers.

The room was very still. Colby ran a quick individual scan

of all consoles. The PSMs, still deep under from their morning's dosage, were vegetables. The others all had their readers on, and some were making a pretense of following the bright images that capered across the screen in the day's reading assignment.

Colby felt better, with a sense that he was in control now. These kids had seen that a greenie could use the stinger as well as any I.C. old-timer.

They stayed put after that. Seeing someone stung always took the fight out of them for a time. The room was relatively peaceful for the remainder of the fifth period.

The bell rang at 11:30, the signal for shouts and stomping. Even a few of the PSMs showed signs of life. It was lunchtime for class 3-12A, and for Colby as well. He watched them file out, keeping his eyes on the corridor cameras to make sure the lanes remained clear and the traffic flowed smoothly. Once he saw the cafeteria doors locked behind class 3-12A, Colby was on his own, free until 12:15.

Colby took the teachers' passage to the dining room. It was shorter and faster than using the corridors, and he had to show his pass at only two checkpoints.

He was looking around the room for a place to sit when a stocky black man at the center table beckoned to him, saying, "Over here, buddy. Time you got to meet your colleagues."

Five men sat at the table. There was one empty place, and Colby settled into it, looked around the ring of faces, and said, "Thanks. My name's Tom Colby."

The others were all in their late twenties or early thirties. They were burly men, Colby's size or bigger. Their presence seemed to crowd the room. All were clean-shaven, with close-cropped hair, and all wore standard light-blue teaching fatigues like Colby's. They moved with the smooth easy grace of athletes.

"I'm Howard," said the man who had called him. He looked to be the oldest of the group, as well as the biggest. He wore senior instructor's stripes with seven hitch marks. Pointing to the man at his left, Howard went around the table clockwise. "This is Lehman, Wood, Bakersfield, and Hunter."

From across the table, Wood asked, "You're Young's replacement, aren't you?"

"That's right," Colby replied.

"Yeah, I saw you in the shuttle this morning. Wondered who you were."

Bakersfield laughed and shook his head. "Lucky you, Colby. You got Santos and his whole zoo to keep you busy."

"It's not bad so far. Most of the class are on permanent medication."

"The ones who aren't can kill you. You used the stinger this morning. I picked up the static on the monitor."

"Santos was pushing pretty hard. I gave him a touch of it."

"That was smart," Howard said. "Most new guys wait too long before they use the stinger. They lose the initiative. I'd tell every new teacher to use it the first day."

"You're not new at this, are you, Colby?" Wood asked. "I heard that Young's replacement was coming from another school."

"I taught at Greenbelt No. 31 for two years," Colby said.

"You moved here from a Greenbelt school . . . what the hell did you do, Colby, lose your mind?"

"Just got greedy," Colby said blandly, and they laughed at his answer. He smiled and said, "What I really mean is, I needed extra money. Greenbelt schools are nice easy places to teach, sure, but it takes a long time and a lot of payoffs to get anywhere. My wife's going to have a baby in the fall, and we're hurting for money, so I volunteered for an I.C. hitch."

"You won't get rich here, buddy," said Lehman, and Wood added, "No, but you might get hurt."

Colby enumerated on his fingers as he said, "Inner City Teaching Corps means a pay differential, promotion preference, early retirement, total medical, full insurance . . . that's pretty good."

"It has to be. The work is rotten."

"What about endorsements, Colby? From what I hear, you can pick up a lot of endorsement money in the greenbelts," Bakersfield said.

"Not until you're there a while. I was starving."

Bakersfield raised an eyebrow and looked at him in disbelief. "Starving? At Greenbelt No. 31?"

"Well, all right, not starving, but I just couldn't get out of the hole. They'd only run a twelve-period day, but every teacher has to supervise a student activity, and everyone has a weekend study group. There's no money for that until you get to supervisory level. I couldn't hold down a part-time job, and my wife couldn't get any kind of work at all. There's nothing out there that isn't sewed up. I'm still paying off the people I had to bribe to get the job in the first place."

"Things sure have changed. When my father was in school, there was a shortage of teachers. Never had to bribe people to get an interview in those days," Howard said.

Bakersfield laughed. "You still don't—if it's an interview for Inner City No. 3."

"So now you're here. Think you can handle this ratpack after all that time in Greenbelt?" Wood asked.

"I went back and took the full course at Quantico. Four months ICTC Basic, eight weeks advanced. Came out first in my class."

"Young was pretty good, too, but they got him," Wood said.

"How?"

Howard answered. "Somebody waited for him in the teachers' passage. Caught him off-guard and put a knife into him. Seventeen times."

"How'd they get into the corridor?"

"Nobody knows. So don't get careless between checkpoints."

"Maybe nobody can prove it yet, but it was Santos," said Wood. "I covered that class last week, while they were looking for a replacement, and I could see it right away. The kid's dangerous."

"Santos is a hard case," Colby said. "He didn't give me much choice about using the stinger."

Wood went on as if he had not heard. "He's like a steel brick: hard as hell and all sharp edges. And he's smart, too, don't let him fool you. Everybody else in that class is a moron, but Santos has brains. He should be on permanent medication. Keep him doped up and the whole school will be better off."

"He'll be getting out soon, won't he?" Bakersfield asked.

"End of next term, if he doesn't screw up again," Howard said. "He's just waiting out a diploma so he'll be eligible for unemployment benefits. That's the only reason any of these kids are here."

"Kids? Santos is as old as you are, Howard."

"They shouldn't give that class a new guy. Santos will eat Colby alive." said Wood.

Without looking up from his coffee cup, Colby said evenly, "I'll handle Santos. Nobody has to worry about me."

Hunter, silent until now, looked around the table and said irritably, "Why the hell are we talking about Santos? It's lunchtime. You're getting me sick. Who watched the playoff last night?"

Lunch kept everyone calm for a time, and the seventh and eighth periods passed with nothing more than a few minor scuffles. Colby cooled them with a warning. The kids looked at Santos, still appearing groggy from the morning's jolt, and decided to stay in their consoles and watch the science cartoons.

Today's ninth and tenth periods were set aide for a sex-education hollie, a weekly routine at all I.C. schools. Everyone from the superintendent on down knew that I.C. kids needed sex education as much as they needed classes in vandalism, but the life-sized, full-color holographic projections kept them quiet. There was some ethical objection to the practice, mostly from local preachers and neolibertarians, but the pious warning tacked on the end of each hollie served to satisfy everyone else. The sex hollies gave the teachers a chance to catch their breath and get through the afternoon, and that was all anyone really cared about.

Urging and threats were unnecessary now. Every student was in his console before the bell rang. Colby activated the hollie matrix, dimmed the lights, and turned the class over to his automatic monitors. Ten minutes into the period, his intercom buzzed. It was Howard.

"How's it going, Colby?"

"Everybody's studious all of a sudden."

"They always are. We take our break these two periods.

You go as soon as Wood gets back. He'll lock his monitor into yours when he leaves, and you reverse it when it's your turn."

"Right. Where do I go, the dining room?"

"That's where most of us head. Be careful in the passage."

"I hear you, Howard. Thanks."

Ninth period flowed unnoticed into the tenth. At 2:40, Colby's intercom buzzed once again, this time with a message from Wood, who was leaving on his break. As they spoke, the backup monitor flashed the diagram of Wood's class.

Colby scanned both monitors quickly, then sat back to await Wood's return. At 2:45, restless, he arose, scanned the monitors again, and then did a visual check of his room.

Santos and two others were missing. They showed on the monitor, but their consoles were empty. There was no way of telling how long they had been gone.

Colby grabbed the intercom and hit the all-channels over-ride. "Three students missing from 3-12A. They've found a way to bypass the monitor. I'm going to check the passage."

"Don't go in that passage alone!" Howard's voice thundered.

"Wood's on his break. He could need help," Colby said, cutting the switch before Howard could respond.

The lights in the passage were out. Colby flashed his handbeam in both directions, saw nothing, and headed for the dining room. Just beyond the first checkpoint, his light caught the cluster of struggling forms.

"Hang on, Wood!" he shouted.

Wood went down before he could reach him, and the three turned to face Colby. Two had knives, the third carried a club, and Colby had only the flashlight. He kept it to one side, at arm's length, aimed into their eyes, and moved in on them.

The passage was narrow. They had no way to surround him, and if two came at him simultaneously, they would only crowd each other. Santos fell back, and the other knife wielder, one hand before him to shield his eyes from the light, came forward to close with Colby.

He was eager, but not very good. Colby dodged his thrust and kicked hard at his kneecap. The kid screamed and went down. One more kick and he was out. Santos and the other one hesitated. Colby snatched up the fallen knife and moved in on them. Santos threw his knife down and both kids turned to run. Howard and Bakersfield were waiting for them.

The hollie ended with the standard warning, which drew the customary catcalls and whistling. Colby raised the lights. Two minutes later, the bell rang to end tenth period. The kids, all laughing and grinning except for the PSMs, filed out for dinner. If anyone noticed that Santos and the others were missing, he gave no sign of it.

Colby kept an eye on both monitors, his and Wood's, until the cafeteria doors closed behind their classes. When he entered the passage to the dining room, he noticed that the lights were working again.

Wood and Howard came in halfway through the period. Wood had a bandage on his hand and a bruise on his forehead, but he flashed Colby a big grin. Howard only nodded. They brought their trays to Colby's table.

"Thank's, Colby," said Wood. "They had me boxed in. If you hadn't come along, I would have gotten what Young got."

Colby shrugged off his gratitude. "It could have been me in that corridor, and if it was, you'd have come in to help. That's what ICTC is all about, isn't it?"

"All the same, you saved my skin. How'd you know they were there?"

"Dumb luck. I just happened to do a visual check, and they were missing. I can't figure out how they did it, though."

"I told you Santos was smart, didn't I? He figured out a way to override all the monitors in his console. He also managed to unscramble the locks on the faculty-access doors. He could've caused a hell of a lot of trouble."

"Sure could. What'll they do with him?"

"Permanent socializing medication, as of right now. This was his tenth offense, so it's automatic—no appeal," said Wood contentedly.

Howard added, "They'll keep him on here for another two years. Student stipend's only half what he'd get on unemployment. So that hits him in the pocket, where it really hurts."

"What about the others?"

"I recommended the same thing." Howard bit off a piece of roll, sipped his coffee, and off-handedly asked, "You didn't hear me say anything about not going into the passage, did you, Colby?"

Colby glanced at him quickly, but Howard was looking away. Colby looked to Wood for guidance. Wood closed his eyes and shook his head once, slowly.

"Not go in . . . ? Gee, I don't recall hearing that," Colby said.

Howard turned to him and nodded, as if Colby had given the proper response. "I figured you didn't hear. I guess your intercom's out of order."

"I guess so," Colby said.

Howard emptied his coffee cup and set it down. "That's good," he said. "If you disobeyed a direct order, I'd have to report it, and that would look bad, this being your first day and all. I want you to have a nice clean record, Colby. We want you to stick around."

"I don't know, Howard. I hear that all these Greenbelt guys are soft," said Wood. He looked from one to the other, then broke into a grin and began to laugh.

"I heard that, too, but this one's learning fast," Howard said. "He'll make a good teacher someday."

THE CIVIL RIGHTS DILEMMA

by Jerry Pournelle

No person shall be held to answer for a capital, or otherwise infamous crime, unless on a presentment or indictment of a grand jury, except in cases arising in the land or naval forces, or in the militia, when in actual service in time of war or public danger; nor shall any person be subject for the same offense to be twice put in jeopardy of life or limb; nor shall be compelled in any criminal case to be a witness against himself, nor deprived of life, liberty, or property, without due process of law: not shall private property be taken for public use, without just compensation.   —Fifth Article of Amendment, Constitution of the United States of America.

Without civil society there can be no civil rights. Self-evident as this may seem, our courts do not always act as if they realize it.

The Fifth Amendment devotes only fourteen words (out of a total of 107) to self-incrimination; but to most U.S. citizens, that right is the very cornerstone of our liberties.

Not everyone agrees. The argument against "the Fifth" begins with the premise that before there can be liberty, there must be a social order; if the society does not survive then freedom won't either. This is most often invoked in time of war—hot war or cold war—and since the 1950s is an argument in bad repute, largely because no rational debate on the subject is possible. The defenders of "the Fifth" chant "McCarthyism," the audience shrinks away in horror, and thought ends.

Yet the case against "the Fifth," at least as it has been interpreted in the U.S., is fairly strong. No less a friend to freedom than Sidney Hook—who is certainly no right-winger—has written powerfully against it. Jeremy Bentham thought protection against self-incrimination absurd. "The innocent may be protected against torture in other ways," he said. "The law as presently constituted protects only the guilty." What argument is there in favor of a law that protects criminals? That it is hard on the criminal to be required to give evidence against himself? Bentham called that "the old woman's argument."

For all that, friends of liberty shudder at the alternative. It is all too easy to force a man to confess; Solzhenitsyn shows us a hundred ways, each more horrifying than the last.

Yet surely there is a path between the horrors of the gulag on the one side, and our present situation on the other; for we have taken little Willie's "I don't gotta tell nobody nuthin' " and made it a chief principle of constitutional law.

Self-incrimination is not the only privilege subject to abuse; and certainly one can find horror stories enough.

As an example, take a recent case in California: a male student approached a young married woman in order, in his words, "to socialize with her." She rebuffed his advances; and in sight of her husband he tore a steel leg from a cafeteria table and proceeded to bludgeon her to death. The husband pursued when the man left the scene, and followed him to a place where the police subsequently arrested him. He was read his "rights" and waived them, declining counsel.

Police officers questioned the "suspect"; they asked if he was not ashamed of himself; if his family would be proud of him; and he dictated and signed a full confession. During the course of the confession he asked to see his mother; the context suggests that he wanted her to hear him express regret for the murder.

In subsequent appeal he was granted a new trial; his request for his mother was tantamount to a request for counsel, and at that moment the interrogation had to cease.

Query: Has liberty been well served? Whose liberty? In this case the victim seems to have been deprived of her rights—and her husband invited to avail himself of something more primitive than the King's Justice. What the courts seem to be telling him is that he cannot expect justice from the People of California, but must instead turn to his relatives, clan, lodge, or gang. . . .

Consider an elderly couple, Jewish if you like, in one of the threatened districts of, say, New York. They live in fear. They cannot walk the streets of their neighborhood; they are afraid to shop for groceries, although they have no choice;

they are afraid to enter their apartment on their return for fear they will encounter a burglar.

At night they live huddled together behind a well-barricaded door, hoping that no one will break in the door and attack them, but knowing that precisely that has happened to their neighbors.

Query: Are they more or less free in the United States today than they would have been in Berlin of 1938? Have they any more "right" to walk the streets? Have they any less terror of the barbarian in the night? Have they any less reason to fear senseless hatred, sadism, mutilation, death?

Sirhan B. Sirhan was found by police with the gun that killed Senator Kennedy still in his hand; the hand, gun and all, was under the foot of Roosevelt Greer. It cost the taxpayers of California some $20 million to give Sirhan "a fair trial." Has liberty been well served?

Harry Jaffa points out that "no American statesman ever violated the ordinary maxims of civil liberties more than did Abraham Lincoln, and few seem to have been more careful of them than Jefferson Davis. Yet the cause for which the one slighted these maxims was human freedom, while the other, claiming to defend the forms of constitutional government, found in those forms a ground for defending and preserving human slavery."

Jaffa continues by quoting Lincoln himself.

And this issue embraces more than the fate of these United States. . . . It forces us to ask: "Is there, in all republics, this inherent and fatal weakness? Must a Government, of necessity, be too *strong* for the liberties of its own people, or too *weak* to maintain its own existence?"

Are all the laws *but one* to go unexecuted, and the Government itself go to pieces, lest that one be violated?

The dilemma has never been better stated. Without civil

society there can be no civil liberty; without effective law enforcement there can be no rights. Our present-day judicial absurdities lead inevitably to private revenge; to acts of rebellion. *Must* we, for justice, turn to the Godfather? Was *that* ordained by the Constitution?

RAID

I've never met Ted Butler, and I've been unable to get him on the telephone; thus I can't say much about him. His address lists him as living in the Seattle area; to be exact in the suburb where I very nearly bought a house, way back when I worked for Boeing and we had to bootleg space research on weekends. I wish I had bought there; the area has grown enormously, and I expect an old farmhouse would be worth a lot of money. There are times, too, when I miss Seattle. "I'd like to have seasons again," I say to my wife.

She, being very practical, says, "Remember the time in Seattle when we went out of town for a week and missed summer? You need webbed feet to live in Seattle."

Understand, she grew up there, and most of her relatives still live there, and for all I know we're related to Ted Butler, who remains hardy enough to endure the land where they Keep Washington Green.

In a state of nature, says Thomas Hobbes, life is "solitary, poor, nasty, brutish, and short." Without a social order to preserve rights, one lives in a war of each against all; it is therefore necessary to compromise. Freedom cannot live outside society.

Of course one can go too far in compromising liberty to preserve the society. Liberty will inevitably conflict with social policy. Sometimes the social policies are thought to be of overriding importance. . . .

RAID

by Ted D. Butler

Snow crunched under their feet in the darkness as Lt. Orloff
escorted Representative Karnes toward the front of the duplex.
They crouched down and scuttled behind the fence till they
reached the technician manning the sensors.

"Anything yet?" asked Karne's companion.

The technician pushed down a wool muffler from his mouth.
"Just finishing the adjustments for walls and insulation now,
lieutenant. It'll be a little longer."

Karnes broke the ensuing silence with a whispered question. "Do you go out on these often?"

"We find ourselves out in this," he waved at the snow
covered ground, "about once a week now. Used to be more
often, but people are learning they must obey the law." He
stopped as the technician raised his hand.

"Sir, they are definitely breaking the law in the left side of
that building." At Orloff's nod he turned back to his gear and
spoke softly into a microphone.

Orloff turned back to Karnes. "The judge is standing by
and we have a fax machine in the truck. We should have a
warrant in just a few minutes."

They waited in silence, then the snow crunched behind
them as another officer trotted up and handed Lt. Orloff a
plastic-wrapped paper.

The lieutenant assured himself the paper bore a copy of the
judge's signature, then gave the signal for the E officers
around the building to move in.

The night filled with the sound of pounding feet and
panting lungs as the police rushed the building from all
sides. There sounded a loud whuff accompanied by the noise
of splintering wood as the front door yielded to an air bomb.

Karnes trotted more slowly after the police. As he arrived
in the door opening he saw a young man vaulting the back of
a couch. He was clubbed down by a burly officer. A pretty

young woman sat unmoving on the couch a look of terror on her face.

There was a flash as the technician, armed with a camera now, recorded the scene, then busied himself with measurements of the room's air.

Karnes stepped to Orloff's side and gestured toward the big officer. "Is it necessary to be so harsh?"

The lieutenant glanced toward where the man was being roughly handcuffed. "He was trying to destroy evidence." He considered Karne's face for a moment then went on, "It was because of criminals like these that Tynan's wife died of pneumonia last winter." He paused. "But you're right, I'd hate to see him get into trouble. I'll speak to him about being too violent."

The woman on the couch started to sob as a matron helped her up and guided her into a back room. Karnes noticed the man had already disappeared.

"Where is she being taken?" he asked.

Orloff was searching the room with his eyes as he answered curtly, "They'll have to be dressed warmly for the trip downtown."

Karnes glanced around the room. The two young people were obviously just setting up housekeeping. Newlyweds? He touched Orloff's arm. "What sentence will they get?"

The lieutenant spotted what he was looking for and started toward it as he answered, "Well, this is obviously a first offense and they're young. On the other hand, Judge Branden likes examples." He stopped moving and considered. "They'll probably be exposed in the wilderness for seven days." Karnes must have looked horrified, because the other put up his hand. "Oh, they'll be given plenty of non-energy survival gear. They're healthy and they're young. They'll survive. But," he went on in angry triumph, "they'll think twice about breaking the law again. Besides, look what those criminals did." The energy policeman's face bore a look of outrage as he pointed at a device on the wall.

Karnes walked over and looked as Orloff continued. "Don't

feel sorry for them. Feel sorry for the others that'll suffer because of them later this winter."

The thermostat read a hideous seventy-five degrees Fahrenheit.

FREEDOM IN THE WAKE OF HEGEL AND MARX

If one political fact seems certain in this uncertain age, it is that communist regimes are tyrannies. Solzhenitsyn describes in *The Gulag Archipelago* a system of studied cruelty that can only be called beastly, savagery unequaled in human history and continuing to this day.

George Orwell warned long ago of the dangers of the planned economy. "In a world in which the State is the sole employer, dissent means starvation."

Truisms. Platitudes. Communism has failed. Communist regimes destroy freedom. They don't even produce economic goods. (Recurrent iron curtain joke: "Rejoice, comrades, the communists have taken over the Sahara Desert." "I had not heard. What happened?" "Ah, for ten years, nothing; then they announced a shortage of sand.")

On any criterion other than the contemptible worship of pure power, communism has failed; yet Western intellectuals continue their flirtations. "The only enemies are to the right; there is no enemy to the left" is routinely taught in political science and philosophy classes across the United States as if it were self-evident truth. Why?

We live in a world made by ideas. Marcuse's *One Dimensional Man* is one of the most difficult and incomprehensible works ever penned; but it changed the lives of many of our brightest students. Eric Fromm has never been easy to read; but he reached mass audiences, and had his effect on intellectuals from New York to Dubuque.

In this essay, Dr. Stefan T. Possony analyzes the wellsprings at which Fromm and Marcuse drank; and he does them the courtesy of taking them seriously.

Stefan T. Possony grew up in Vienna between World Wars. His father was a lead tenor with the Viennese State Opera, and

Possony grew up among the Viennese intelligentsia. He received his doctorate from the University of Vienna when he was barely twenty. He went immediately into journalism, where he was associated with the anti-Nazi newspapers. His political work brought him to the attention of the Gestapo, and after Hitler's annexation of Austria, Steve fled to Czechoslovakia—which didn't remain a haven for very long.

As the panzers rolled into Prague, Steve went to Paris, where he was associated with the Air Ministry. He acquired a prodigious reputation as an intelligence specialist; but his warnings were not heeded, and France fell to the blitzkrieg. After many adventures Possony and his wife escaped from France to North Africa, and from there to the United States, where he was immediately put to work in military intelligence. He spent the remainder of World War II in the Pentagon.

He continued in intelligence work after 1945, and received a medal for predicting—accurately—the first Soviet atom bomb tests. He also became a professor of political science at George Washington University. That led to his appointment as a senior fellow with Stanford University's Hoover Institution on War, Revolution, and Peace, where he remained until his retirement a couple of years ago.

He is co-author with William Kintner and Robert Strausz-Hupe of *The Protracted Conflict*, which many think the most important book ever written on the cold war. He is also co-author, with Jerry Pournelle, of *The Strategy of Technology*, which is used as a textbook in the U.S. Air Force's War College.

This essay is not easy reading; but it is the most important in this book.

FREEDOM IN THE WAKE OF HEGEL AND MARX
by Stefan T. Possony

Freedom calls for institutions, such as elections, free speech, an effective opposition, and many more; and for an electorate which neither is given to extremism, nor aims at the destruction of democracy.

It would seem that this context is too narrow if current problems of freedom are to be considered.

To survive and prosper, freedom needs to grow. But how can freedom be enlarged? In past times, the answer was easy: eliminate oppressive institutions, laws, and practices, and replace despotic rulers. Given the absence of unfreedom, the chances were that the citizens would utilize the opportunities that were given to them as free peoples, and that freedom would advance.

Contemporary observers may remark that optimism is unwarranted: freedom shrinks whenever the citizens do not behave and vote rationally, or even reasonably; whenever legislatures act stupidly and destructively; and whenever governments are usurped by power-hungry types whose interest in good government and effective administration is far weaker than their interest in being reelected.

During the last thirty years or so the very possibility of freedom in industrial-technological societies has been questioned. Why? Because in such a society alienation on an ever expanding scale is thought unavoidable; and because alienated man allegedly neither is able to handle freedom, nor desires it. The freedom that exists in such societies is described as purely formal: elections no longer are selections of the best, if they ever were, and they are artfully manipulated by unknown professionals.

We are told that the evil of vanishing freedom will disappear only if it is eradicated by revolution. What type of revolution? A revolution which destroys alienation and its causes.

So what *is* alienation? The cancer of freedom. *The Oxford Universal Dictionary* provides more prosaic definitions: action of estranging; transferring of ownership; diversion of anything to a different purpose (1828); derangement of mental faculties; and insanity (1482).

"Alienable" goes back to 1611 and "alienate" to 1513. Sociologists and psychologists use the word in the sense of human powerlessness, and inability to "find oneself." Others think that an alienated person is estranged or split from himself or herself; that such an individual is dominated by somebody else or by an alien force; that life has lost meaning; that hope is gone; and that interpersonal relations no longer work satisfactorily. Alienation is not considered to be a neurosis or a depression. It is a psychological state caused largely by social circumstances.

No doubt, a morbidity like alienation exists, and it may be attributable to or be aggravated by social conditions. The notion, however, that mental and psychological disturbances occur which are due *exclusively* to social or socioeconomic causes seems unwarranted. Many disturbances happen independently from socioeconomic events.

The incidence of alienation fluctuates according to the rule that one doesn't catch shellshock if one is not shot at, and that, therefore, shellshocks are frequent only during war. But even if there are "epidemics" of shellshocks and alienation, only small percentages of the population are affected.

A short history of the alienation theory may help to explain what we are talking about. We ignore early authors like Plotinus, St. Augustine, and Ludwig Feuerbach.

In 1931 the Marx-Engels Institute at Moscow (founded in 1922) published a thick bundle of manuscripts which Karl Marx had written some ninety years earlier. The writings of young Marx were startling and surprised the Marxists.

Since the volumes of the Moscow Institute were practically unobtainable through the book trade, a German publisher quickly brought out a large and cheap printing (1932). The *Frühschriften* became a sensation, and Marx's posthumous book was a success among non-Marxists. The customary interpretation of Marx for which Engels, Kautsky, and Lenin had been responsible was shown to be reductionist and falsely oriented to a primitive and superficial materialism which simply was not contained in the texts which Marx produced during his younger years.

The success centered mainly on a piece entitled "Economics and Philosophy" written in 1844, when Marx was twenty-six years of age.

In 1931, when *Frühschriften* were printed, David Ryazanov, Director of the Institute, was thrown into the Lubianka and vanished into the Gulag. The Institute was renamed the Marx-Engels-Lenin institute. Allegedly Ryazanov, Member of the Academy of Sciences, had plotted with the Mensheviks. He had indeed maintained contacts with Marx scholars outside the U.S.S.R., but that was his only crime. However, Stalin and his ideology experts were highly suspicious of what young Marx had written.

Siegfried Landshut, the German editor of the mss., wrote in 1953: "Official Soviet Marx scholars never took notice of these early writings." Ryazanov was liquidated in 1938, and the Institute was renamed the Institute of the USSR Central Executive Committee for Marx-Engels-Lenin-Stalin. (It will soon become clear below why the Stalinists tabooed young Marx.)

The so-called Frankfurt School of Marxist scholars, who were contemptuous of the Marx interpretations which Moscow was dishing out, took it upon themselves to publicize what young Marx had been saying. Soon Hitler put a stop to this activity, and the Frankfurters went to America. This was the best that could ever happen to "alienation": introduced mainly by Erich Fromm and Herbert Marcuse, who had both been in on the discovery of the manuscripts and who took delight in sprinkling Marx with the baptismal water of Sigmund Freud, the word became fashionable. As Freudians discovered sex symbols in pencils and trees, and pears and pussycats, so socialists saw alienation behind every difficulty. Fromm extended alienation from a crippler of the proletariat to the threat against all classes. The new concept was nourished richly by the energies of alienated and concerned American intellectuals. Marx and Freud had been "unacceptable" for decades. Suddenly, under the ministrations of the Frankfurters, they made a political career in America.

In 1965, Adam Schaff, member of the Central Committee of the Polish CP, asked whether alienation could occur under socialism. He answered his tantalizing question affirmatively. Party theoreticians in Hungary and Czechoslovakia agreed with him. In the USSR, long after Stalin's demise, the problem continued to be pointedly ignored. A contributor to *Bolshaya Entsiklopedia* explained that "alienation" referred to past history, that's all. A *Philosophical Dictionary* published in the GDR (without date, about 1970 or later) asserted that alienation is eliminated by the ending of exploitation and oppression. Meaning: it does not exist behind the Berlin Wall. This remark was added: "This does not mean that all manifestations of alienation disappear automatically." The leadership of the party is needed to "change the people of the socialist society into the real masters of their destiny." Marx would have laughed at this sly insinuation by a Stalinist bureaucrat.

This sequence has an ironic side-history. In 1923, Georg Lukacs wrote *History and Class Consciousness*, the only significant contribution to philosophy and theory a Marxist ever made after Marx. As a party member he was promptly attacked by Sinovyev, then "boss" of the Third International, who never read the book. Outside the communist universe, Martin Heidegger's book of 1927, which made this philosopher world-famous, was, in part, directed against Lukacs. (This was the starting point of the temporary connection, mainly in France, between Marxism and existentialism.)

Lukacs did a surprisingly good job in *anticipating* what was contained in Marx's unpublished papers, which were to start the alienation excitement nine years later. Accused of being a "revisionist," he was forced to stop selling his book; he capitulated weakly.

During 1930–31 Lukacs was in Moscow and studied the *Frühschriften* in the Institute's files. Had Ryazanov told Lukacs about "Economics and Philosophy" in 1922, and did he in 1931 tip him off so that he could organize fast mass publication in Germany? Lukacs escaped several times being purged, but he was "demoted" from philosophy and serious work on Marx, and relegated to literature. Lukacs died in 1971. Forbidden to reach out for the top problems during the forty years which remained to him, he never again reached the high plateau which he had attained in 1923. Without a conspiracy between Ryazanov and Lukacs, the *Frühschriften* would not have seen the light of day within Stalin's lifetime; and they might have disappeared. Ryazanov was the foremost and indeed only true Marxologist in the Soviet Union. Precisely for that reason, he became the victim with whom Stalin began the purges exterminating the honest ideological communists of 1917.

Incidentally, it is interesting to speculate on who might have taken the initiative in imposing censorship on Marx. Who among those *apparatchiki* was able to understand Marx's philosophical language? Who perceived the fatal significance of the discovery? N.I. Bukharin is a likely suspect.

Marx's theories on alienation came in two versions. In the first, Marx regarded divisions of labor, especially the division into manual and mental labor, and private property as the twin causes of man's alienation from his true nature. The second version asserted that human relations are falsified through reification, notably the transformation of human labor into a commodity for the market, and of production into an activity fully determined, not by utility, but by profit. Furthermore, social contacts connected with production are reduced into impersonal and monetary arrangements. Commodities and money payments, in particular wages, are "fetishes" which hide and distort human relationships.

Alienation also appears as self-alienation, which is connected to labor: that what man produces he alienates from himself. The individual thus is the author of his alienation but he has no alternative, since he must eat. Self-alienation also refers to the realities which an individual cannot handle. Self-alienation obviously contains an element of human freedom, but Marx did not follow this lead.

Alienation is steadily increasing, and as a consequence of reification, people fall prey to false consciousness.

In *Das Kapital* much of this was compressed into the concept of exploitation of the proletariat by the capitalist class.

The main effect of alienation (or exploitation) is that the person so afflicted is an "object," not a subject of the social process which concerns him. He is not his own master but is run by impersonal, blind, and alien forces. He is tormented by the misery and monotony of his work from which he is unable to free himself. This requires change: misery must be overcome by "enlarged reproduction," and alienation by restoring human relationships to their natural directness and satisfactions.

The Frankfurters in America, taking some cues from Freud's *Discomfort in Culture* (1930), added psychological effects like frustration, suppression of desires, unhappiness; and loss of meaning, norms, and "dimensions" of living. A woman writer from East Germany produced this formula: "Nothing pleases me." Socialism was seen as the cure, but this idea was left unfinished in confused rhetoric.

Much of Marx's thinking on alienation was romantic and illusionary, for example his notion that an unalienated individual is at one with the community, and that in a true democracy private and public interests would be identical. Neither such an individual nor such a community ever existed or would be desirable. Marx did not notice that in case of identity of interests, no majority-minority votes, and therefore no democracy, would be needed. As to the overcoming of alienation, Marx himself made the point that a self-realizing individual is unalienated.

Marx himself faded out his worry about division of labor, and the Frankfurters did not ascribe all psychological and mental disturbances to socioeconomic conditions and institutions. But Marx's linking of alienation and exploitation to private property, and his widely known thesis that exploitation consists in denying most of the surplus to the manual worker who produced it, was a *departure* from his original insights.

The psychologization of alienation brought Marx to life in Western Europe and the U.S. In Fromm's variant, alienation dehumanized not only the proletariat, as Marx had stated, but society as a whole. Fromm proclaimed the *Frühschriften*, with their emphasis on alienation, as the fundamental exposition of Marx's doctrine.

It is unnecessary to waste time showing that Marx's own analysis of capitalism does not bear out the notion of private property being the chief cause of alienation. It would be more intelligent to attribute alienation to poverty, which, of course, denotes lack of property. Certainly, there are instances of private property directly or indirectly producing alienation. Emile Durkheim's *anomie* is an undisputed generator of alienation in many forms and evidently can infect any institution. Indeed, all institutions pass through phases of anomy and most "die" of it. Hence it may be assumed that property causes alienation *whenever it is anomic*. But whenever property is properly designed and functions efficiently, it does *not* cause alienation. The absence of property results in unhappiness and signifies lack of freedom and capabilities for self-realization.

Interestingly enough, Marx knew better than his followers or his detractors believed of him. The purpose of history is not communism but the self-realization of man. The ending of exploitation through expropriating the expropriators means nothing unless man realizes himself. Communism is neither a situation (*Zustand*), nor an ideal. It is instead the "real movement which terminates the current condition"—a condition characterized by the defect of self-alienation. Through the mere abolition of private property communism would only generalize and complete private property, and the condition of the working man (i.e., alienation) would be extended to *all* men. Such communism would be motivated by envy and urges to equalize, yet equality is no political requirement for communism.

As the community becomes the "general capitalist," the result would be that man does not go beyond private property but falls back behind it. The personality would be annihilated, and the exclusive dominion of the economy would entail the "complete loss of man."

The purpose is instead to redo the relations between humans so that "man would become the highest being for man." The relation of man to man should involve nothing but the "direct expression of their individual existence." Man needs to be freed from the compulsions of material life and become "a being which determines itself." When this occurs the community will become "the reality of the moral idea." This was the destiny of man—this *was* "communism," as Marx saw it in the wake of Hegel.

Marx's text, it should be obvious, was bound to cause apoplexy in the Kremlin. Fromm should have emphasized Marx's unexpected thoughts in his discussions of alienation in the *Frühschriften*. Yet he left private property as an intact target, and added competition as an institution-to-be-abolished. His analysis was loaded with socialist clichés—a typical case of false consciousness.

This still leaves open the question of how alienation and self-alienation (i.e., unmanageable reality) can be overcome.

As observed before, peoples and societies are not infected as a whole, only small numbers are significantly affected. The percentages tend to be higher among the elites and counter-elites both of the upper and the lower "classes," and among minority groups which feel, or are, persecuted. Those who deem their work to be necessary, stick to their chores, ignore the chatter of gloom and doom, and keep the society going. The alienated among the juveniles, well known since Goethe's Werther, used to be lovesick. At present they may be drug-addicted or terroristic. They tend to be self-liquidating either by growing up and solving their crisis, or by suicide. The violent and criminal types tend to provoke their destruction unless instincts of self-preservation take over.

The alienated among the elites also start in their youth. Their chief problem is to seek meaning. If they don't find it, they will tend toward an ineffectual and problematic life. If they do find meaning, usually in their later teens, they gravitate toward rebellion. When they reach the mid-twenties, they either turn toward reform or revolution, or toward evolution or conservation.

Those types of alienation are primarily psychological, and they recur and disappear with each generation. However, socioeconomic troubles may increase the incidence. Conditioning for alienation, for example through art, pulp production, media sensationalism, and the manipulation of "hero" models, may push vulnerable youngsters into chaotic behavior. Most return to normalcy, some destroy themselves.

What about those whose alienation is due to structural and procedural defects and to anomy of the institutions?

In 1842 Marx enumerated a "psychological law": "The theoretical intellect (Geist) which liberated itself changes into will and turns against the reality which exists without it." Thus, the conflict is given a new dimension by the Geist altering itself. Negativity (which includes alienation) acts productively and provides impulses. The self- realization of man is a process in the course of which man poses himself through his self-consciousness. For Hegel, with Marx copying him, self-consciousness is the essense of the "human being," and all alienation consists in the alienation of the self-consciousness. Meaning: It is in the head. (In German, self-consciousness has a connotation of self-reliance and self-confidence.)

Being a problem of thought, albeit with existential roots, it is potentially soluble by learning, persuasion, and intellectual progress and creation.

However, Marx also argued that the self-realization of man (society as a whole) can be accomplished only through the self-liquidation (Selbst-Aufhebung) of the proletariat.

In all this, the movement of the idea is the implementation of philosophy, and thinking must surpass thinking and transcend itself. (Feuerbach's untranslatable: das sich im Denken ueberbietende Denken.) Going beyond thinking, Voltaire's Candide turned to gardening and Goethe's Faust ended his long career in alienation by building a canal.

The spirit is decisive, provided the idea leads to improvements of the reality. But those improvements are effective only if they emanate from creative thought.

Marx pointed to the conclusion of Hegel's Phenomenology: the objective is "absolute knowledge" which consists of history conceived as conscious organization and science based upon knowledge as it exists and emerges. History happens by realizing the idea. "Philosophy cannot materialize without abolishing the proletariat, and the proletariat cannot liquidate itself without realizing philosophy," Marx added.

Hegel and Marx did a wonderful job in befuddling the reader. Perhaps a recapitulation will help in reducing the confusion.

The term "proletariat" should not be interpreted in the Marxist tradition of "classes" and "class struggles." Here the term simply means persons who are poor, are poorly paid for their work, and in their existence are dependent upon other people. Marx used the word "class," but his emphasis was on "self," especially self-alienation and self-realization, its negation.

Alienation is an integral part of the dialectic movement of the spirit. This movement is directed toward human self-determination and the fulfillment of human nature. Alienation is overcome by self-consciousness; not by actions of strangers, but by actions of one's own mind.

The movement or the process which leads to the human goal, while it is propelled by alienation, will be successful because the spirit is intrinsically free. It is in the nature of the spirit that it must alienate itself in order to find itself again. "Precisely this movement is what constitutes freedom." By coming back onto itself the spirit is freeing itself. Thinking is the only sphere where the spirit can be "absolutely free and with itself, and from where all alienness can vanish."

Materialism means to think in terms of the real mover, which, according to Hegel and in *this* text also according to Marx, is the idea as it manifests itself in the process of history.

"The ability to be with itself in the negative denotes the freedom of man, and the spirit's coming to itself can be regarded as man's highest goal."

Unless the dialectic is stopped, which is impossible, alienation is constantly produced and constantly negated. It is therefore part of life, and neither a symptom nor a cause of man's self-alienation. However, it should be added, alienation can be prolonged if the movement of the idea slows or is slowed down.

The Hegel-Marx theorem indicates that the decisive conflicts occur "in the spirit" or in the realm of ideas. Hegel's and Marx's major error is that "idea" is used in the singular. If, as is necessary, ideas are visualized in the plural, with several of them engaging in contradictory self-realizations, the dia-

lectic becomes far more complicated and the battlefield ceases
to be uni-dimensionally in the spirit.

The question now arises: What is the foremost form of
alienation as the antithesis in a dialectic cycle, and what is
its major cause?

Poverty, lack of economic security, debilitating anxieties,
and lack of personal freedom are the main forms of alienation, and lack of self-consciousness and inability for self-
realization are its major causes. Personal reductions, difficulties in relations between humans, and also various types
of addictions, obsessions, and compulsions, all merging into
bondage, may be viewed as effects of economic institutions
in anomy.

Poverty and most variants of economic shortages are due to
insufficiency of capital and investment, and result in lack of
growth or regression which lead to human suffering. Most of
these deficiencies are not due to the lack of potentials and
capabilities but to erroneous policies which in turn are attributable to false consciousness.

Marx's theory of capital must be interpreted on the basis of
Hegel—Lenin knew this and wrote the point down explicitly.
If he had known the *Frühschriften*, he would not have fallen
into the trap which became known as "Leninism." Anyway,
the older Marx conceived of capital as the "subject" of history.
This concept also was rooted in his early writings, but it took
body only in *Das Kapital*. Obviously, capital was substituted
for the spirit, and was the result of Marx's attempt to make
Hegel, who was standing on his head, to stand on his feet.
Marx sensed that capital is vulnerable to anomy, much of
which is mediated by false consciousness. He did not realize
that his substitution was a reification of the idea or the *Geist*,
and that he handled capital as a "fetish," not as a factor
moved by reason and effort under conditions of chance and
risk.

As capital was wrongly upgraded to be the prime mover,
not only of the economy, but of all history, political oppres-

sion was downgraded, and the role of political power, especially of the bureaucracy as the producer of multifaceted
alienation, was not seen. Political power is alienated from
itself when it has no other purpose than self-perpetuation
and aggrandizement, when the power holders regard the
state and its facilities as their own personal property, and
when the formulae of state and government are mystifications.
In 1841 and 1842 Marx was much concerned with the state,
i.e., with political power. Years later he and Engels ended up
with the idea that the state would wither away. While the
party ideologues did not abandon this slogan, Marx neglected
the problem. Since no one else was thinking about the problem, state and bureaucracy remained unrecognized as primary producers of alienation.

Naturally, alienated political power is in part derived from
the alienation which exists among the population. Just as an
alienated leadership and its bureaucracy cause and stimu-
late alienation among the "ruled," so the latter transmit
their alienation to the former, and aggravate the alienated
condition of the rulers. Alienation therefore may grow through
the interaction between "high" and "low" alienated groups,
and the process could continue indefinitely.

In his comments on Hegel's philosophy of the state, Marx
described the state as the "private property" of the bureaucracy, in which the purposes of the state are diverted into
private goals. He also pointed to the urge of government
leaders to divinize themselves and the state (which they do
by ordering the veneration of new idols, fetishes, beliefs, and
missions). But he failed to argue that repressive political
power—which need not but usually does include economic
repression—is the strongest promoter of alienation.

As the alienation the bureaucracy has propagated is reflected back, the bureaucracy will be seized by progressive
alienation which in turn causes anomy in the apex of
leadership.

A "regime" does not go out of business because individual
leaders become senile and die; nor because younger leaders
are rash fools. It disappears because the executives of the
bureaucracy impose new ideals, and because the emergence

of new fetishes is inevitably followed by dethronization of the old leaders who blundered and failed due to disturbances in their consciousness: They lacked comprehending knowledge (*begreifendes Wissen*) and dynamic knowledge of themselves.

The spirit (or intellect) is constantly busy searching for truth and tends to reexamine beliefs, expectations, goals, and hopes. For a short or long time it may accept the idols which the political authority presents, and it may switch to new idols prescribed by rulers; or it may reject the novelties. As the spirit learns (which is in its nature), false consciousness is recognized. Thereafter man continues his quest for self-realization, regardless of the signals the power-holders are sending. This process re-creates conditions wherein the spirit, namely its critical knowledge, and alienation interact dialectically and freely. If the spirit frees itself from power-possessing false consciousness, alienation cannot be static; instead it transforms itself into one of the movers of renewed and accelerated social process.

Unfortunately, false consciousness is resistant and tough. It does not embody a few random errors but is derived from an entire system which is strongly structured. Its principles are hard to attack, and they involve a world view which is tightly held together. Marx spoke about "the lie of the principle" which is difficult to detect. False consciousness is a profound danger to the spirit, especially if it is paired with "unhappy consciousness" (Hegel). It is antagonistic to the spirit, and does not necessarily exist in a dialectic relationship with rational self-consciousness, nor with personal self-realization. False consciousness threatens the spirit, and hinders its autonomous movement, thereby alienating freedom and twisting it into a caricature of itself. Hegel discovered false consciousness but he failed to see its importance and scope. Marx imitated him. Neither considered that systematic self-critique is the proper weapon against this threat. Marx's followers of the 20th century established exercises of self-criticism as a sham and mockery of the spirit.

What does it all mean?

Anomic state structures and incapable and oppressive governments (leadership, bureaucracy, and legislation) cause alienation in human relations and promote false consciousness among political groups. Alienation, false consciousness, and lies of principle tend to remain concealed for a long time during which the spirit does not come to itself and historical crises cannot be stopped.

Nevertheless, despite anomy, spontaneous movements toward self-correction start without fail.

Alienation also tends to correct itself, in particular when human relationships are widely felt to be unsatisfactory.

If the contents of consciousness have become plainly wrong, attempts arise to eliminate false consciousness. At some point those who are made to suffer from dictatorial tyrants, or from numerous deceptively democratic legislative and bureaucratic despots, realize that they suffer needlessly. At the same moment consciousness may change. However, for so long as the false consciousness does not overcome itself, and regardless of whether alienation is substantially reduced, the crisis continues. The spirit defends itself against falsehood. By contrast, it is characteristic of false consciousness that it protects falsehood through concealment, forgery, and reduction.

Anomy and alienation are perennial. Hence the correction of procedures and institutions is one of our daily chores. False consciousness accentuates anomy upon which it feeds, and delays and disturbs self-correction.

Freedom is based on the comprehension of freedom and its development, and of its negations and dangers. To overcome the threat of unfreedom—oppression or political slavery— freedom must be promoted by the negation of the negation. That is, the threats to freedom must be negated: primarily, to paraphrase Marx, with the weapon of criticism, and secondarily—if still necessary—with the criticism of weapons.

It must be understood that while freedom is entirely compatible with modern technologies and economies and is indispensable for their effectiveness, it cannot without destroying itself be linked to false consciousness, nor coexist with threats which are not self-liquidating but are self-promoting.

The Stalinists realized from the first that as theoretician of alienation Marx is an enemy of Stalinism, and that the whole complex of alienation needs to be concealed lest it invalidate the legitimacy of the dictatorship, which claims to be derived from Marx.

The neo-Marxists from the Frankfurt School living in the U.S. used the alienation argument in opposition to Stalinism, but they misinterpreted Marx on private property and communism (socialism), which they recreated as fetishes of the present epoch. Thus, they promoted a rejuvenated Western Marxism which gave ideological assistance to socialist parties, aggressive radicals, and terrorist groups. By exaggerating the seriousness and endurance of alienation and hiding its positive aspects, they unwittingly covered up far worse forms of "bondage" such as gulags, extermination camps, and genocides. Unintentionally, they weakened the will of democratic states to survive. Only a few voices were heard to explain that the socialism and communism proclaimed by Stalinism are a mystification.

In recent years, alienation was modernized by fear-arousing theories about limits to growth, the end of resources, destruction of life, caused by industry; as well as holocausts brought about by profit-seeking capitalists. By acting on fantasies, real dangers are veiled. Policies may be enacted to make prophecies of doom self-fulfilling.

In this chaos, the U.S. has been sticking to a basic concept of freedom formulated 200 years ago. It never looked closely at the negation, paid little attention to alienation, ignored false consciousness, and nixed all thinking on negation of negation. Hence America does not see the negation at work in the USSR, nor the alienation of the CPSU from Marx. This has been the most grievous of our intelligence blunders.

American democracy has produced entire sets of idols. It was captivated by the fetish of elections with distorted issues and meaningless choices between masked personalities. Large segments of the American electorate and its "political class" are afflicted by false consciousness. Therefore they vote bad governments and bad legislatives into office, who spread anomy into all institutions which still function effectively.

The U.S. even neglected to equip itself with the semantics

and concepts required to analyze the *real* challenges of our time.

The United States is fumbling in its efforts to keep freedom alive by restimulating self-realization and self-determination as the crucial tasks and achievements of free men.

What in particular are American leaders alienated from? Perhaps many are alienated from genuine values. But I don't really believe this. The paradox is rather that far from being alienated from their false consciousness, which blinds them to so many problems and threats and opportunities, and makes them adore so many fetishes, they actually are enamored with the myths and old-fashioned ideas they are carrying in their heads. Spiritual self-correction has been suspended, and no one calls for a crash program to revise and modernize the ideas which tested poorly on experience. That's what has been happening in the U.S., where the idols of communism are kept on their pedestal to salve bad conscience—not about our failures—but about our unique achievements.

THE HORRIBLE HISTORY OF JONES

Chesterton is best described as a crusty old individualist, an orthodox individualist whose friends included Shaw and Wells as well as Hilaire Belloc; and if you have never seen his heroic poem "Lepanto," it is worth a very long trip to find.

He once defined freedom as the right "to be our potty little selves." It is as good a definition as any I've heard.

I blush to say it, but I did not know "the Horrible History of Jones" when I conceived this book. Fortunately I brought David Friedman here to Chaos Manor to show him how easily one may write with my friend Ezekial (who happens to be a computer); and the text David chose for practice was "Jones."

Thus we may all share it. Hardly anyone writes doggerel like this nowadays.

THE HORRIBLE HISTORY OF JONES
by Gilbert Keith Chesterton

> Jones had a dog; it had a chain;
> Not often worn, not causing pain;
> But as the I.K.L. had passed
> Their "Unleashed Cousins Act" at last,
> Inspectors took the chain away;
> Whereat the canine barked "hurray!"
> At which, of course, the S.P.U.
> (Whose Nervous Motorists Bill was through)
> Were forced to give the dog in charge,
> For being Audibly at Large.
> None, you will say, were now annoyed,
> Save haply Jones—the yard was void.

But something being in the lease
About "alarms to aid police,"
The U.S.U. annexed the yard
For having no sufficient guard;
Now if there's one condition
The C.C.P. are strong upon
It is that every house one buys
Must have a yard for exercise;
So Jones, as tenant, was unfit,
His state of health was proof of it.
Two doctors of the T.T.U.'s
Told him his legs, from long disuse,
Were atrophied; and saying "So
From step to higher step we go
Till everything is New and True."
They cut his legs off and withdrew.
You know the E.T.S.T.'s views
Are stronger than the T.T.U.'s;
And soon (as one may say) took wing
The Arms, though not the Man, I sing.
To see him sitting limbless there
Was more than the K.K. could bear.
"In mercy silence with all speed
That mouth there are no hands to feed;
What cruel sentimentalist,
O Jones, would doom thee to exist—
Clinging to selfish Selfhood yet?
Weak one! Such reasoning might upset
The Pump Act, and the accumulation
Of all constructive legislation;
Let us construct you up a bit—"
The head fell off when it was hit:
Then words did rise and honest doubt,
And four Commissioners sat about
Whether the slash that left him dead
Cut off his body or his head.
An author in the Isle of Wight
Observed with unconcealed delight

A land of old and just renown
Where Freedom slowly broadened down
From Precedent to Precedent . . .
And this, I think, was what he meant.

Editor's introduction to:

IDENTITY

A. E. Van Vogt is an amazing chap. He's been publishing since the '40s—oops, according to the *SF Encyclopedia,* his first story, "Black Destroyer," was in *Astounding* in 1939. Incidentally, "Black Destroyer" and another done in that time period were the basis for his recently settled claims against the motion picture *Alien.*

But although Van has been publishing for forty years, he looks no older than I do; indeed, he's in very good shape for a man *my* age. He's an active writer, lecturer, and partygoer.

His "Weapons Shop" stories were powerful statements about freedom, as well as some of the best "sense of wonder" stories ever written.

"Identity" previously appeared in the program book of the 1978 CHATTACON SF Convention where Van was guest of honor. I am pleased to offer its first professional publication.

IDENTITY

by A.E. Van Vogt

A few minutes ago a man said to me: "Who are you? What are you doing here?"

That startled me . . . I didn't know. I hadn't even thought about it.

Now, I'm sitting here on this bench. And I have a feeling that something is wrong. And maybe I should go somewhere. But where?

What am I doing here? Who am I?

Vaguely, I remember I was walking. And then the man—middle-aged, with dark eyes and dark hair, wearing a giba suit—came from behind a tree, stopped, and asked the questions. At the moment it didn't really occur to me that he was addressing me. So I just walked on.

Recalling him, I glance back the way I had come, hoping to see him again. But there is no one visible in that direction.

What I do see is a high fence that extends into the distance to my left, and is presently lost among the trees of the park. On my side of the fence, to my right is a single, large, white building.

There is a street on the other side of the fence. A street and pretty Plexiglas buildings. Light reflects back to me from the glass. People are passing by on the street a few yards away. Some of them glance at me, but of course none come over since they are on the other side of the fence.

As that awareness strikes me, I have an odd thought: That middle-aged man was inside the fence, as I am. Why did he walk over and say what he did?

Of course, at the time I was walking also. Maybe—a sudden possibility occurs—I'm trespassing. Perhaps these are the grounds of the large, white building. . . . Who are you? What are you doing here? These questions, it seems to me, are exactly what a caretaker or guard would ask an intruder.

I climb to my feet as I have this realization. Swiftly, I walk toward the white building. I'm hopeful now. But also puzzled. Because, since I didn't answer him at the time, why did he accept my presence without any further challenge?

The entrance of the building comes into my view as I round the corner. I see that several levels of steps lead up to a number of doors. I run up the steps. It is as I approach the doors on the final level that I see a sign. It reads: HAVE YOU CHECKED WHAT'S IN YOUR POCKETS?

I come to a teetering stop, shocked.

Because, suddenly, I think of what has happened as being a sequence of events. That man spoke to me on purpose. He knew my condition. He knew my condition. He knew I had no idea who I was. Knew it before I did.

The sign in front of me tells me instantly that there have been others in my strange state. The words, for Dlid's sake, are carved into the marble.

Even as I have these thoughts, I am fumbling in my pockets, one after the other. You'd think that they would have put the message in the pouch pocket of my heavy gourton blouse. But, instead, I find it in the left back pocket of my slacks.

It's a small envelope. I open it and remove the contents, a folded sheet of permadocum. I unfold the sheet, and read:

> Friend: You were convicted of a serious crime. You were offered a choice: transportation for five years to the prison planet, Arcturus VIII, or change of identity, with the privilege of remaining on earth. You chose change of identity. Your new identity is: Patricia Martin. Your age, 23. Your marital status, single. Your future residence: Apartment 6, Building 4238, City 231. Your job is with Metro Idiom Archenetics, Building 4497, City 231 (about a block from where you will be living). When you are ready for the next step, please enter this building and obtain your I.D. card and two credit cards. Good luck.

"Patricia Martin." I spoke the name aloud, savoring it. "Hey," I said then, "hey!"

I straightened. Walking tall, I opened the door, and entered the building. The immediate interior was a lobby, but I could see several large rooms branching off. An arrow pointed to one of them. As I walked in that direction I realized—

It was really great to know again who I was.

I was pretty sure I had never had such a thought before.

DEFENDING AND EXTENDING
THE FREEDOM TO INNOVATE

Dr. John McCarthy is the director of the Artificial Intelligence Laboratories at Stanford University. A short, intense man with a thick beard and hands that never cease moving, he is one of the most stimulating and original thinkers I have ever met.

We don't normally think of freedom to innovate as basic; yet in one sense, all other freedoms rest on it. Societies have the freedoms they can afford: witness that across this land we have bashed down the high curbings at street corners, installing ramps to give the handicapped in their wheelchairs the right to use our streets. (For they may have previously had the *legal* right to the streets, but what use was that so long as it was physically impossible?)

Note that we could not, thirty years ago, have afforded to bash down those curbs; and had anyone proposed those ramps as a fundamental right, he would have been laughed down.

If we can continue to increase the wealth of this nation; if, through use of space, and solar power satellites, and innovative technologies, we can grow rich enough; then I fully expect to see new freedoms for everyone; for the poor the right to go places and do things that today not even the wealthiest can afford.

Technology is the most liberating force in history. In 1800 the kings of the Earth had no "right" to travel from California to New York in a matter of hours; nor to penicillin, nor color television, nor false teeth, nor Band-aids, nor good light to read by at night; today all those things are taken for granted even by the wretched— at least in the United States.

New sources of energy, new technology for producing wealth; these will liberate the earth more surely than any ideology. We need only the freedom to innovate.

DEFENDING AND EXTENDING
THE FREEDOM TO INNOVATE
by John McCarthy

This article is about what makes it possible for people to invent new things and get them used. There are some threats to the freedom to innovate and also some opportunities to use computer technology so that good ideas will be invented more easily and accepted more quickly.

In the good old days, an inventor had only to worry about whether his invention was worthwhile, whether it had already been invented, getting money to develop it, getting a patent that would stand up in court, and getting people to buy his product once it was on the market. There were quite a few successful inventors, and many American and European companies are named for the inventors of their original products.

Many people think that a major obstacle to invention is that companies buy up inventions and suppress them. Perhaps it has happened, but it can't amount to much. Tales of the everlasting light bulb and the gasoline pill have appeared in print since the 1920s. One could imagine that these suppression efforts were totally successful, but then one has to say why foreign companies anxious to break into the American market don't step out of line, why companies go bankrupt without trying to save themselves by introducing the forbidden better products, and why "socialist" countries not motivated by profit don't have them. I can't think of anything being marketed today that was developed many years ago but suppressed until recently by a company owning the invention.

However, there is evidence of government suppression of new technology. When an innovation is totally suppressed, we cannot be sure that it would have been a success had it been allowed. Therefore, the clearest cases are when an innovation has been allowed in some countries and suppressed in others. The British government has suppressed several inventions that are in use in the U.S. Presently citizens band radios are forbidden in Britain (also in Japan, where most of them are made), and so were acoustic couplers that permit computer terminals to use ordinary telephones to communicate with computers. For some years, public time-sharing in Japan was a monopoly of the government telephone company.

Electronic funds transfer has the potential of eliminating violent crime for money, because a robber cannot safely demand that you transfer money to his account. It can also greatly reduce theft by making it hard for the fence to transfer money to the thief. It is being hampered though not totally suppressed in the U.S., and our regulations for new drugs have become so hard to satisfy that many are used for years in Europe before being allowed in the U.S. On a related topic, many drugs that require prescriptions in the U.S. are available over the counter in other countries. I am not aware of a study showing that other countries have suffered for their more liberal policy.

Several centuries ago, and more recently in oriental societies, inventors had a much harder time, and in some countries hundreds of years often went by without significant invention. Since most people saw no innovation in their lifetimes, they often believed that society and technology had always been as they saw it. In Europe, innovation was discouraged by a legend of a Golden Age when things had been better and a belief that present people and things were degenerate remnants of the past. (One thing that might have encouraged such ideas is the fact that cropland loses its fertility with time unless it can be fertilized, so there were always tales of the bigger crops of past times). Many societies, like the medieval Catholic church and Japan between 1637 and 1868, had explicit objections to any innovation as corrupting the pure principles that had been established.

Innovation is easiest when there are many possible supporters of it. The inventor of a new household gadget, to take an easy case, can go to dozens of manufacturers any one of which can decide to make it. In traditional societies or present planned societies, there may be only one person who can say yes or no to an idea in a given field. If he says no, that's it. The Russians are always saying that someone in Russia invented something first, but the idea was rejected there and developed in the West. They criticize the person who rejected the good idea but don't criticize the system which permits one person or bureaucracy to kill an idea. Perhaps many of the ideas they referred to, as was the fate of what became the Xerox copier, were rejected by many companies in the West before one took it up and made it successful.

However, it won't work simply to make everyone more receptive to all new ideas, because almost all new ideas are bad, and when bureaucrats are told by their superiors to be more receptive to new ideas, they sometimes give money to their relatives, and usually tend to back ideas similar to those the other bureaucrats are backing, so that there will be less criticism when the idea fails. Someone risking his own money often pays the best attention to the likely success of the idea and how well the project is going.

If the same function can be provided by a device sold in the store and a system that requires a monopoly to work, the gadget is often preferable even at considerably greater cost, and it is likely to be available much sooner. An example is the telephone-answering machine which provides the same service that telephone companies are just beginning to offer as part of the electronic telephone exchanges. Most likely it could always have been done better centrally but wasn't.

Unfortunately, not every worthwhile innovation takes the form of a gadget that anyone can make and sell and anyone can buy or not as he chooses. When streetcars, home electricity, piped gas and telephones were invented in the late nineteenth century, they all required local monopolies for success. The companies had to get franchises from cities and towns, and some of the benefits of competition were necessarily lost. Inventions that require franchises today have a harder time, because having the idea and the money to back it doesn't carry weight with people who want everything studied endlessly at the expense of the backers or who believe that groups distinguished by misfortune rather than potential contribution should share the hoped-for gravy. Hundreds of millions that have been invested in research aimed at recovering minerals from the ocean bottoms and may never pay off, because our government has forbidden sea mining while the U.S. tries to negotiate an unnecessary "law of the sea" treaty.

The United States has been better than other countries about freedom to innovate. As a result many inventions originate in the U.S., and until recently the U.S. had the highest standard of living. However, movements for the suppression of innovation have been strong in the U.S. since the late 1960s, and this is one of the reasons why our standard of living increased slowly enough so that some European countries have passed us and has even declined in the last two years.

The attacks and restrictions on innovation are part of the larger move toward increased regulation and planning. Regulators and advocates of regulation like to think of the battle as between the public interest (represented by themselves) and the companies (usually referred to as monopolies whether they are or are not) greedily "pushing" unneeded goodies on a passive public. However, we prefer to regard the battle as between the public's right to buy whatever technology makes possible and the desire of the "public policy community" to decide what is good for the public.

Here are two typical and rather mild statements from a recent article on "Social analysis of computing":

> It is hard to believe that the public could best be served by rapid development of a poorly understood technology.

> With such meager systematic attention, it is hard to believe that important understandings about the long-term and more subtle social features of computing will be acquired before inappropriate commitments are made.

The trouble is that no inventor can ever be sure of how his invention will be used. Indeed most are overoptimistic about what good the invention will do; otherwise they wouldn't work so hard. What saves us is that the public isn't as childlike as planners like to imagine them. Not even children are as childlike as some planners like to imagine them. They can try something offered for sale and stop using it if it doesn't suit them. Few things, if any, meet the classical criteria of an addictive drug—bad for you, but once hooked, you're hooked for life. Almost always, people choose reasonably well among the options available to them. Moreover, when someone thinks people have chosen badly, he may be wrong. Some of the reasons may not be expressed in words but may still be valid.

There are two separable questions (1) When are general decisions by social scientists or politicians about what people should buy and use likely to be better than the decisions the individuals concerned will make on the spot? (2) When do people have a *right* to make their own decisions even if they may be mistaken? A good slogan might be, "Unless there is very strong evidence to the contrary, each person should be regarded as the best judge of his own welfare."

While the 1970s were bad years for innovations and *laisser innover* acquired the ill repute of *laisser faire* in liberal circles, there is good reason to hope that the 1980s will be better. At least politicians of both parties are worried about the recent lack of innovation and investment in innovation in America, and "the re-industrialization of America" has become a popular slogan.

It isn't only products that benefit from there being many possible adopters of innovation. The existence of different states and countries is helpful in getting a hearing for legal innovations. For example, since about the 1930s it has been legal in California to make a right turn on a red light after stopping if the traffic permits. The rule gradually spread and recently the Feds coerced the last two states into adopting it by threatening to withhold highway money. It's nice that this good rule prevails in the whole country, but this seems to be killing the goose that laid the golden egg. Without freedom for states to differ, California couldn't have tried out the rule in the first place. The next innovation may have a far harder time.

Ideally, anyone who thinks he has a better way of doing something should be able to get it objectively considered by a person or group with the ability to investigate the matter thoroughly and the power to adopt it. Would-be innovators often imagine that someone somewhere has the power to do what they want if only they could get his ear. They often find kings, dictators, and communist countries fascinating, because they imagine that the obstacles they see at home could be overcome by a stroke of a pen.

Often there is no one with the power to adopt the proposal. When there is, he or they are often swamped with other proposals.

When an innovation is proposed, it usually requires the support of many people before it can be adopted widely. For some kinds of innovation, a lot depends on who proposes it. The fuzzier the criteria, the more innovation is limited to the existing authorities. It would be difficult for a nonprofessional who was not a public official or politician to get a paper proposing a change in foreign policy accepted by the magazine *Foreign Affairs*, and if it were published, it would probably not be taken seriously.

The opposite extreme is mathematics and physics, in which a paper can be submitted to any of dozens of journals by anyone in the world. The writer is often unknown by reputation to the referee to whom the editor sends the paper. If the referee says the result is correct and significant, the paper will be published. In 1905, an obscure employee of the Swiss patent office submitted four papers to the German physics journal *Annalen der Physik*. All four were published, and one of them introduced the theory of relativity. Within a few years these papers made Albert Einstein's reputation as the world's leading physicist.

The possibility of innovation in social and political matters can be extended to more people if these subjects become more objective. Once the best time to plant crops was a matter of religion in some countries, and I suppose you could get in trouble for making unorthodox statements about it. A second problem is that issues are like horses; their owners hope to ride them to power. A politician won't easily pay much attention to an argument from some nobody that his winning issue is unsound.

Eventually, we may hope to extend mathematical treatment to social issues, but it is much farther away than many social scientists believe. Successful theories must be based on logical rather than numerical or statistical relations. In the limit, an unknown person could provide a computer-checked proof that a new policy would be better than the present policy.

Attitudes toward innovation

Many factors in society encourage or discourage invention, and here are a few of each.

First, the society should consider invention a good thing, which hasn't always been true. Second, potential inventors should have access to many different sources of backing. In a feudal or semifeudal society like pre-Meiji Japan or the Soviet Union today, a potential inventor belongs to an organization and if his immediate bosses don't like the idea or it doesn't apply to their activity, he is out of luck. Many successful American inventors try many backers before they find one. Third, unless it is possible to make a lot of money from a successful invention, there won't be backers, because most inventions fail. Fourth, a substantial part of the public must like new things and be eager to try them out.

On the other hand, overly powerful planners discourage invention. They make their plan, perhaps taking into account many sources of information, but once it is made, they want to carry it out, and they regard new ideas that don't fit into the plan as a nuisance—to be stamped out or at least to be delayed until the next plan. Invention is also discouraged if groups are considered to have a right to a share of the market, so that competition is disallowed. Unrealistic demands for guaranteed safety discourage invention, since an invention that costs a few tens of thousands to develop may cost millions for required safety studies. The latest discouragement is *technology assessment*. The idea is that the social effect of the invention should be completely determined before the invention is allowed to be sold.

The point isn't that innovations cannot turn out badly. They often do. The point is the reaction to the prospect that they might.

We can stop using DDT or use it more sparingly if it turns out to harm useful animals. Those who had bumper stickers labeled "Damn Deadly Toxin," however, bear part of the responsibility for the large increase in malaria deaths in backward countries after use of DDT was stopped. We can spray asbestos-covered surfaces with plastic now that it has been determined that asbestos fibers increase significantly the amount of lung cancer if breathed.

The problem is demanding unreasonable criteria for safety and/or for not injuring anyone's economic interests, or at least the interests of favored groups.

There seem to be several motivations, and often they coexist in the same person.

1. There are safety objections to specific technologies. Sometimes this is justified, or if not justified, then simply mistaken as to the facts. Sometimes, however, the objection survives an admission that the facts were wrong, and sometimes it depends on ignoring the hazards of the older technologies.

Thus Consumer's Union and Ralph Nader have opposed the use of microwave ovens, especially by children, on the theory that microwatts of microwave leakage might harm people. Their statements don't compare this danger, which they admit is unsupported by experimental evidence, with the hundreds of people who are killed and injured every year from accidents with conventional cooking. If their opposition caused the lesser use of microwave ovens in the U.S. than in Japan, we can estimate (on the basis of the *Statistical Abstract of the United States*) that their position has caused the deaths of several children a year since the early 1970s. Of course, if the danger of microwaves is substantial, they have saved some children, but every year that goes by with no report at all of injury from microwave ovens makes this increasingly unlikely.

The most important example of applying differing standards applied to old and new ways of doing things is nuclear energy. A few days after the Three Mile Island accident, which injured no one, the *New York Times* reported eleven coal miners killed in an accident. Another story somewhat later reported four killed by a wood stove that caught fire. It has recently turned out that well-insulated houses accumulated carbon monoxide, formaldehyde and radon, the latter sometimes to levels illegal in uranium mines, and yet the government continues its campaign for superinsulation. The current evidence is that it is safer to produce the energy than to superinsulate houses. Applying different standards to different technologies is natural as long as people continue to think about issues mainly in a qualitative rather than a quantitative way. While there are more concerning nuclear energy than can be taken up in this article, most of the opposition involves applying different standards to it and other sources of energy.

2. During the 1960s and 1970s there developed a strong ideology that everything could be done better if planned on a national scale. In the case of innovation, this led to the idea of technology assessment, and the Congress's Office of Technology Assessment. The idea was that the potential effects of every innovation should be examined before it was used. Unfortunately, we cannot agree even on the effects of past innovations—let alone future ones. Some people think that the invention of the automobile was a disaster for the U.S., and if we had only taken the time to think about it, we would have done something quite different. However, they can't agree on what would have been done differently. The evidence is otherwise, since other countries, in which large-scale use of cars is more recent, haven't been able to think of any path that is much different from ours or that is regarded as having worked out better.

3. An argument frequently used for preventing an innovation is that if even a test is permitted, irresistible momentum may be created. This was one of the main environmentalist arguments against developing the American supersonic transport even to the stage of testing. The argument amounts to a confession that the public may evaluate the results of the test differently from the environmentalists, and therefore the public shouldn't have that opportunity.

4. Economic regulation as a way of protection against competition has an older history. Regulating the rates truckers may charge, the products they can carry, and the routes they can operate on goes back to the 1930s. Even when Congress has legislated that the only objections be on safety grounds, it is routine for companies to file safety objections to delay competitive products. There is no penalty for this even if the objection is ruled trivial.

The regulators have invariably asserted more power than the Congressional debates indicate Congress thought it was giving them, but it has been very difficult for Congress to bring itself to slap them down. This is because once an interest is established, it can contribute to incumbent campaigns.

5. The environmental movement, which started reasonably, developed leaders with a taste for power. With three million alligators in Florida, they resist removing alligators from the list of endangered species, because it might signal an environmental retreat.

6. A preference for a specific technology may make a person attack all rivals. Some of the enthusiasm for solar energy takes this form.

It may be a mistake to try to make too much sense of all this. Once a person has taken sides, he may favor a proposal if made by the "good guys" that he would oppose if made by the "bad guys." He may even switch sides on a proposed technology in order to maintain his conception of who is good and bad. The switch of the Sierra Club on nuclear energy in 1975 can be given this interpretation.

Computers and innovation

Many people say that technology is changing the world faster and faster, and people can't adapt to it. This is wrong. In fact, the inventions brought into use since World War II, such as TV, jet travel and the pill, have affected daily life much less than those adopted between 1890 and 1920, such as electric lights, piped-in gas, telephones, automobiles, and mechanical refrigeration, affected the life of that time. For most people, computers, nuclear energy, lasers, and DNA are just names in the news, because no one cares whether his electric bill was prepared by a typist or a computer or whether the light goes on because of burning coal or fissioning uranium.

Since people take health and prosperity as only their just deserts, maybe the lack of technological innovation in daily life has contributed to the anti-technological beliefs. This lack is temporary, because cheap information processing will lead to many more popular inventions.

A wave of innovations coming from computer technology can be expected between now and the end of the century. The use of computers for large-scale scientific and business computations has already changed these activities, but the use of computer facilities in daily life will be much more important.

We don't refer to the personal computers already on the market. They are an interesting hobby and useful for small business, but most people don't need a lot of straight computation, however cheap. The real changes will come when home computers or just home computer terminals are connected by telephone to all the repositories of information in our society.

To begin with, everyone can have immediate access to all the books in the Library of Congress (perhaps 30 million) without needing even one bookshelf. Already the cost of storing the information on computer disk files is less than that of storing it on library shelves. The cost of getting it into computer form is large, but the main problem is creating the library and dealing with copyrights, etc. Maintaining the library seems to be a natural monopoly, but having multiple copies of it wouldn't be very expensive if the resulting competition would be useful.

Access to existing kinds of books, magazines and newspapers is important, but keeping the information in computer form will transform publication. At present, 80 to 90 percent of the cost of a book is in printing, distribution and advertising. With computer publication, almost all of the costs will be the actual preparation of the material, which means that much of what the reader pays can go to the author. Moreover, something can be published simply by typing it into the computer system and declaring the file public. If the author has to rent the file space for a book, this will come to less than a dollar a month.

Since readers can have programs notify them automatically when something new by a favorite author appears, famous authors won't need publishers. A journalist specializing in enetgy or in the affairs of a particular foreign country won't necessarily need a newspaper or magazine if he has acquired a public. Much smaller publics with specialized interests can exist. Of course, no one will decide what to read by looking in the grand catalog file; library catalogs are already too big. People will find things of interest through "magazines" whose editors have a reputation for selecting interesting stuff and getting their writers to write for their public. Reviews will be important.

The standards of controversy will improve, because when someone is attacked, the reader will be able to ask whether he has an answer. Present controversial style depends for many of its effects on the fact that it is rarely possible for the reader or listener to hear an immediate answer. When this is impossible, the attacker will have to take it into account.

An important start on the computer library can be made by getting the government to keep the information that is supposed to be available to the public in computer files that anyone can access from anywhere in the country. This includes the laws and regulations published in the Federal Register, but also information required by the Freedom of Information Act. Now much of this information is in reading rooms in Washington, and only organizations can afford to dig it out.

Besides the information in newspapers, books and magazines, everyone can have immediate access to airline schedules and availability of seats, and the same information for movies, plays and concerts. Stores will keep catalogs in computer file, so that a person or a program acting for him will be able to find the "best buy" very quickly.

Computer technology has already helped electronic innovation by making the design process easier and more objective. An engineer can design a computer using a computer-aided design system without the aid of draftsmen. One man can design circuitry that formerly required several. Moreover, the design can be simulated, and potential backers can have a greater assurance that the design will work if built. In the case of integrated circuits, the design in the computer can be carried all the way to making the masks that are used to produce the circuit.

This technology is gradually being extended to mechanical design. When an inventor can design and simulate an automobile engine without leaving his computer terminal, and can also generate the computer instructions for the machining and automatic assembly, we will see many more new engines than we see now. Moreover, the simulations will make convincing a potential backer more of an objective matter and less of an exercise in salesmanship.

Extending this ability to simulate to social organizations so that proposed changes can be evaluated objectively is a much longer-term goal.

While there are many attacks on freedom to innovate, maybe there isn't too much to worry about in the long run. Unless freedom to innovate is suppressed in all countries, the few that preserve it will eventually dominate the world intellectually. If the use of innovations is encouraged in some countries and prevented in others, then the former will come to dominate the world physically as well. Therefore, maybe we shouldn't think mainly defensively but should put almost all of our effort into considering ways in which the ability to innovate can be extended.

Of course, it would be nice if one of the countries that preserved freedom to innovate was the United States. Maybe we will return to our traditional attitude:

Let it be tried. If it works out badly we can always change it.

For freedom to survive, mankind must survive.

In this day and time that is not a trivial observation. Consider how vulnerable we are. As Robert Heinlein said years ago, the earth is just too small and fragile a basket for the human race to keep all its eggs in.

Look at what can happen to us. In addition to wars and famines, which could destroy our proud technologies and put us back into the stone age, there are natural catastrophes. *Lucifer's Hammer* was a novel (a best-selling one, I say with some pride) about a comet striking the Earth. Shortly after it was published, Nobel prizewinner Luis Alverez demonstrated that an event much like *Hammer* was probably responsible for the extinction of the dinosaurs.

The earth itself can last at most another four billion years. That seems a long time; but the human race could easily outlast the earth and sun. To do that, we must learn to live in space.

This generation has the resources for that. This generation can do it. Perhaps the next will not be so fortunate. Roberto Vacca's *The Coming Dark Age* describes several ways in which our civilization could collapse, not suddenly and with a bang, but suddenly enough that space travel becomes impossible. And after that, there may be wars and rumors of wars. . . .

If we go to space, we can assure the blessings of liberty to ourselves and our posterity for a very long time to come. That seems a very worthwhile goal for any generation.

—Jerry Pournelle (Member, L-5 Society Board of Directors)

THE L-5 SOCIETY
by Robert A. Heinlein

If science fiction is simply fun to you, skip this. But if you believe as I do that our race can and will and *must* spread out into space, stick around.

The L-5 Society's sole purpose is to place a colony at LaGrange Point #5, the one trailing the Moon at 60 degrees.

Sounds silly? It does to us, too, on gloomy days. We are about as far along as Willy Ley and von Braun and Goddard were in the thirties ... but one generation later, Neil Armstrong stepped down on Luna.

And things move faster today. Technology doubles every seven years. We could build that city in space today ... but we'll be able to build it faster, easier, more economically in the nineties. Or (I'm an optimist!) in the eighties. I have already lived from horse and buggy to space shuttle; I cannot believe that human progress will come to a sudden stop. Space will be colonized.

Space *will* be colonized—although possibly not by us. If we lose our nerve, there are plenty of other people on this planet. The construction crews may speak Chinese or Russian, Swahili or Portugese. It does not take "good old American know-how" to build a city in space. The laws of physics work just as well for others as they do for us.

I don't think we've lost our nerve. We can put a construction crew of our own up there ... and space is big enough for everyone—all races, all languages. We need never be crowded again.

L-5 Society dues are $20/year ($15 for students) and include the monthly magazine *L-5 News* with all the latest space news, data not in newspapers and which must be dug out from technical journals and specialized sources—our editors do it for you. The Society supplies other services too, but I'm not going to list them, as the L-5 Society was not organized to serve or amuse its members.

ITS SOLE PURPOSE IS TO FOUND THE FIRST COLONY
IN SPACE.

How's your nerve? Are your eyes on the stars? Send in your dues and join us.

Welcome aboard!

Robert A. Heinlein (Member, L-5 Society Board of Directors)
FOR THE MEMBERSHIP COMMITTEE
L-5 Society
1620 N. Park
Tucson, Arizona 85719

FULL FREEDOM

The late Willy Ley was listed as "Science Editor" of *Galaxy Science Fiction*; mostly he wrote a column. After he died—tragically, a few weeks before Eagle landed in the Sea of Tranquillity—the post was vacant, until I began doing a science fact column. The column was popular, and somewhere along the line I was asked if I wanted to be on the masthead as "Science Editor."

Heaven knows the duties weren't onerous. Sometimes Editor Jim Baen would call me—I recall a couple of questions about some of John Varley's first published works—and the few rare times I went to New York I was impressed into slogging the slush pile (editorial slang for doing first reading of unagented and unsolicited manuscripts)—but mostly I did nothing at all to justify the title. That was all right, because I got nothing out of it except a couple of free lunches and a press pass.

Then one day there appeared "Jogging up Main Street" by Thomas Wylde. The story was well written, and contained a plausible concept that just happens to violate a couple of conservation laws. The *Galaxy* staff hadn't asked my opinion because they'd seen nothing wrong with the story—but a lot of readers did, and they weren't slow about telling the "Science Editor" what they thought. . . .

It was only after I'd bought this story out of *my* slush pile and was speaking to Mr. Wylde on the telephone that I realized he was the author of that piece.

Technology plus freedom can produce an interesting society. Oddly enough, there is not much science fiction set in such a world.

Thus I was delighted to get this story, of a world and time when freedom, if not exactly free, can still be reasonable. . . .

FULL FREEDOM
by Thomas Wylde

"Heads up," said the computer.

The ready-room squawk-box crackled, and everyone tensed. Then the computer said, "Team one, gate one. Go now."

I caught the message through the headset, plugged into a game of Powergate. I looked across the ready room at Doris. She was grinning, eager as usual. We were team one.

I tapped in my personal HOLD code and unplugged.

"Go get 'em, Local," said Brad.

"Yeah," said Sylvie. "Enjoy it while you can. You go on the Remote board in the morning."

"Don't remind me," I said.

Sure, Remote is interesting—full of fast changes and nervous sweat—but Local is more personal, more satisfying. You're right *there*, on the scene. Besides, in between assignments you get to hang around the ready room and play Powergate or Ping-Pong or some other intellectual pursuit.

I caught up to Doris at gate one.

"Last mission of the day, anyway," I said.

"Don't you like your work?" she said, eyes wide.

Gate one was a jet chopper, this time. We got the briefing en route.

We were headed for the crackling dry mountains north of the city. It seems a Full Freedom had been out hiking, found himself at the edge of a precipitous canyon, and took it into his head to roll down. He'd got himself halfway down, wedged under a boulder, and started a little brush fire with his power cutter. Remote Monitor had done what he could, but the guy's suit wasn't responding—control failure most likely.

Remote had seen the 2F come up to the cliff, naturally. (The fellow's puffing breath and pounding heart had flagged down the computer.) And Remote could see what the clown was about to do. (You get so you can almost see their little minds whirling around, thinking up mischief.) But Remote couldn't do anything to stop him. That's the law.

You can't stop a Full Freedom from doing anything legal.

Sometimes you can't even advise the idiot.

And even when the Remote Monitor can get a word in sideways, a headstrong 2F nearly always ignores it. But for the kind of heavy-duty premiums those Full Freedom policy holders pay out, you kinda hate to spoil their day.

Doris and I checked each other's power suits while the chopper circled and sprayed retardant on the fire. The Angeles Forest, at least, was safe for another few hours.

The guy in the downed suit looked little worse for wear. We dropped to the ground beside him and I checked his vitals while Doris set up a portajack to ease the boulder off the guy.

We had him on his feet in three minutes, limping slightly— the suit had taken most of the weight. (In fact, the strain had temporarily fouled the Remote takeover circuits.)

We gave him some imitation orange juice and an aspirin.

He complained that the rescue chopper was too loud, so I sent it away to hover behind the next ridge.

"We can take you to the hospital," said Doris.

The guy shook his head. He was about fifty, with graying hair and a red, sweat-streaked face. "No time," he said. "Gotta meeting at six-thirty. I'll wear the medi-suit tonight for an hour or so."

"Fine," I said. I wanted to get on out of there. "You want a lift back to town?"

The guy shook his head again, then power-jumped to the next ridge, right into the teeth of the chopper's propwash. In a moment he had disappeared into the smog-hazy brush.

"And thank *you*," Doris yelled after him.

I grinned. "Don't you like your work?"

"Rich bastards."

"Make the world go round," I said. "Anyway, those Full Freedom guys pay our salary."

"Such as it is," she said.

I called the chopper back and we jumped for the sling.

On the way back I turned the radio down and asked Doris to marry me again. She smiled and shook her head.

"Why not?"

'My accountant says marriage would screw up my taxes."

"I'll pay the difference."

She shrugged. "I'll tell him, but he's very strict."

By the time we checked back in the shift was over, so we climbed out of the power suits and turned them in. The readouts were okay, but the chopper guy wanted to know about the extra klicks.

"Customer request," I told him, then explained in detail. I knew they were grilling Doris about the same matter. The Company doesn't care that much, but the customers resent anyone in a power suit who isn't paying Full Freedom rates. Even Local troubleshooters.

We were an hour late getting out of there, and by that time all we wanted to do was grab some grub and hit the sack.

We were shift-jumping tomorrow, to get on the new schedule, and I wanted all the sleep I could get before climbing behind a Remote board. For that reason—and maybe 'cause she'd turned me down again—I put Doris on hold. And from the way she was thrashing about in bed, I just might have hit a nerve. Good.

The Remote board is merely a stationary parasite suit, plus ancillaries. The Full Freedom folks hate the very *idea* of the parasite suit, but its necessity has been demonstrated time and again. The 2F folk just keep on grumbling. Well, it's what they do best. . . .

Doris was also plugged into the Remote board, about five places down from me. Remotes don't work in teams. Generally, anything one Remote in a parasite suit can't handle is a job for a Local team.

Business was brisk. I monitored all cases flagged by the computer, and any suit parameter—temperature, power drain, noise level, customer vitals—can trigger a red flag. The computer also monitors external ambience—what we call the "scene"—for key threat words spoken in conversation. The computer even keeps an ear out for *sarcasm*, and that's how I came to be plugged into a middle-aged executrix at the bitter end of a four-martini lunchbreak.

The woman's companion had (according to the replay) just remarked, "Of course the rose was plastic."

Immediately the woman (a paid-up Full Freedom with special library access—Freedom of Information) became irritated. She contemplated (according to power suit "muscle" monitors) throwing the contents of her as yet untouched water glass in the man's face.

The creep across the way—excuse me—the *gentleman* in jeopardy was another Full Freedom—and a paranoid, at that—with a microsecond threat response rider on his policy. Unfortunately, microsecond response meant low-order discrimination circuits. (He couldn't afford the deluxe package, and he was one of those Full Freedom bozos who relied on Legal Branch to sort things out de facto.)

"Take it easy," I whispered in her ear.

("Stay the hell out of it,") she subvocaled back. ("This is a private conversation. Uh, code five blue nine green. Scram!")

"Sorry," I said. "Send-away code is topped by a violence flag."

I used the parasite suit to override and relax her tightening arm "muscles."

I said, "Don't you know how much water *costs*?"

("It's worth it.")

"His suit," I said, "will eat you alive before you can blink."

("Is this what I pay premiums for?") she asked.

"Just remember he won't feel a thing."

"What's the matter, dear?" the man was saying.

("Bastard.")

I didn't like his smile either, but that was no reason to damage a couple of power suits—not to mention innocent bystanders and assorted furniture.

"Be careful what you say," I whispered. "Don't get *his* Remote riled."

For all I knew somebody alongside me was already monitoring the guy—Doris, maybe.

We spent the next few minutes on the razor's edge of Conflict of Interests.

("Just get me out of here with some dignity,") the lady said finally. ("I'll make it worth your while.")

"I'm not allowed to accept gratuities," I told her. "But I'll see what I can do. Relax!"

I used the parasite suit to take full control of her, then—
when she whispered, ("Ready.")—I launched her under the
table and let her yank the guy's legs out from under him. His
power suit demolished the chair in surprised response, but by
the time he'd scrambled to his feet we were jumping out the
door and into a taxi.

I left her in the taxi. (There are some Full Freedom ladies
who wouldn't be caught dead *jumping* up the road.) She was
exhilarated, breathless, and full of thanks. It made me feel
good.

But not good enough to enjoy my next call, which came up
immediately and put me fully *inside*—emergency priority
w/o formal invitation—a businessman with a gun to his head.

Did the fool actually think he could fire a bullet right
through the suit?

I jerked his arm down, but wasn't quick enough to prevent
the guy from firing a shot through the ceiling of his house. I
left the computer to calculate the bullet's trajectory and take
action (in case any Full Freedom policy holders were in the
vicinity of the predicted impact zone).

I administered a downer to the guy, again without permission, and laid him out on the floor. Together we stared up at
the bullet hole in the ceiling.

It was a very big hole. . . .

It occurred to me the guy *knew* what he was doing. The
load in that bullet might just have been heavy enough to
create a fatal concussion. The slug wouldn't have got through,
but the suit couldn't have dealt effectively with all those
joules.

"Relax," I told the man, letting my grip on his suit loosen
as the drug took effect (it's hard to relax in a vise).

I blinked out of the circuit long enough to see if the
Company would send a Local team to the scene, or if they
wanted me to walk the guy in myself.

The downer was doing its job quite well, so the decision was
made. He was my baby.

After a few minutes of deep breathing and soothing talk
(his breath, my rap), I got him to his feet and into the
bathroom to wash his face.

It was then, as we faced the mirror, that I got a chance to see that it was the same man we'd pried out from under a boulder the day before.

"You're a busy guy," I told him.

He was mellow enough by then to say, "You betcher ass, chief."

"Call me Bob," I said.

The Company has a policy about names. They want the customer to think he's dealing with live human beings (which is sometimes even true), so they encourage us to divulge to the client a name. (Any name—it doesn't have to be our *real* name. Sometimes I use "Rusty" or "Jackson" or "Billy." Bob is my real name.)

The man said, "I'm coming apart, Bob."

"Let's go get some counseling, pal."

"It won't do any good." He laughed in a way that set off my own red flags. "Besides, I can't afford it. Not any more."

And there was the crux of his problem.

He could no longer afford the premiums on his Full Freedom policy. And he didn't want to continue life among the rabble.

It was significant (I think) that he tried to kill himself *before* his policy ran out.

He must have known we'd stop him. (Suicide is still illegal, though there are ways around that, if you wanna fill out that many forms.)

Maybe he was just testing us. . . .

When he'd rested a bit, I took him out onto the street and jumped him to the emergency hospital. I admit I was showing off a little, pushing his suit to the max (and beyond—I had so much failure prediction built into the parasite suit that I could safely run his ass ragged).

He loved it, of course—it was the kind of trip every Full Freedom geek has in mind when he signs up, but he never has a chance to learn to do it for himself. (Besides, if any 2F bozo tried it there'd be a dozen flags down and a very loud-talking Remote on his back.)

After I'd explained this excursion from Company policy, the guy wanted to know why I didn't get a Remote on *my* back. Fleas on top of fleas, he wanted. I told him our recursive policy stopped before the Remote's parasite suit—no fleas on *our* backs, thank God. . . .

. . . only supervisors . . .

I left him in a hospital corridor, too doped up to make a nuisance of himself, and went back to my duties.

At the end of the shift I had to explain (in horrifying detail) why I thought it necessary to rush the man to the hospital in so reckless a manner.

Doris didn't bother to wait for me. By the time I got to the apartment, she was already finished with dinner.

"Thanks for waiting," I said, hypothetically triggering about a million sarcasm flags.

"Don't mention it," she said coolly.

Later I found out she *had* been called in to Remote the guy in the restaurant, the one I'd dumped on the floor for the lady. The male client refused to pay for the table Doris had wrecked in a moment of rage. It made her look bad.

Tonight it was her turn to sleep while I thrashed about. . . .

Day two on the Remote board, and Doris was way the hell down at the end of the row. Fine with me.

I spent the morning getting rich idiots out of trouble and plugging ignorant folk into Freedom of Information playbacks.

I ate lunch with Brad in the ready room.

He said, "You got Doris on your back again."

"No such luck," I said. "In fact, I may have to get a court order to eat dinner with her tonight. She stays strictly away from my back."

He was about to reply when the computer said, "Heads up."

We waited for the call, then Brad relaxed. "I'm up next, I think."

I chewed absently on my vending-machine sandwich, then realized what I was doing and quickly swallowed. It's not a good idea to keep any portion of these sandwiches in your mouth for very long. The poor darlings are so nutritionally balanced it's all they can do to hold together long enough to get pried from the machine.

I passed Doris on the way back to the Remote board. My

God, she'd even scheduled herself for a different lunchbreak.
She was working herself into a serious pout. I stayed way
back.

The board was busy all afternoon. I had just jumped a
foolish woman out of a tricky part of town when the Remote
board supervisor cut into the circuit and squelched my good-
bye lecture.

"Got one for you, Bob," said the supervisor. "Asked for you
by name."

"I'm flattered."

"Team one," she said. "Local. Gate six. Go now."

As I climbed out of the parasite suit I glanced down the
line. Doris had reported back from lunch. Now she too was
getting loose. It was gruesome.

A parasite suit is so ugly, every time I see somebody
struggling with one—getting in or out—I think of man-eating
crab lice. At least you don't have to go out on the street
wearing one.

Troubleshooter suits are smooth by comparison, though
tool-studded and spiny with exoskeleton. Full Freedom suits
are actually rather pretty, color-coordinated, even semitrans-
parent. Some 2F suits change color spontaneously, like a
chameleon, either matching local color or diverging as much
as possible. (You ought to see a partyful of Stand-Out! suits
going through their paces.)

Doris didn't say a word until we were en route—aboard
another jet chopper.

She said: "Move over, 'Jackson.' "

I moved. "Sorry to crowd you, lady. This wasn't my idea,
you know."

It turned out to be the request of our new friend, the
suicidal businessman.

"Look," I told her, "if it'll make you feel any better, I'll
withdraw my offer of marriage."

"What a relief, 'Rusty.' "

"Cuteness just explodes out of your every pore."

"My new perfume, 'Billy.' "

"I thought it was aftershave lotion, 'Butch.' "

She wouldn't even dignify that one with a nasty look, so I
concerned myself with the briefing.

This time our friend had grabbed some hostages and barricaded himself in his hillside mansion. (It turned out the house whose ceiling he'd shot up wasn't his, but belonged to a former lover. This poor wienie was really deep in the soap-opera end of life.)

We circled once and the chopper kicked us out over the front lawn. It was a nice big place, twentieth-century lush—but turned out it was rented, though. Our friend was overextended in a number of ways.

Doris and I split up and prowled the grounds before going inside. We'd been "requested," but that's no reason to abandon caution. Maybe he just wanted to take us to hell with him.

There were no cops, of course. *Much* too early. The Company doesn't like to advertise this sort of Full Freedom abuse. (Except in an extremely cagy manner to potential customers. . . .)

The Remote man on the case hadn't been able to act because of the precarious situation of the hostages. The playback told us there were three of them—pre-school children—which our friend had snagged in the street out front of another hillside mansion. (Some folks are just plain careless with their children. Full Freedom folk tend to think they can buy their way out of any difficulty. I've seen downtown pillheads take more precautions.)

I left Doris lurking outside some French doors around back, then I went up to the front entrance and plugged my power suit comm set into the house comm set.

"Hello," I said. "We meet again."

"Nice to see you," he said. I supposed he had viddy on the porch.

I raised my head to give him a better look at my face. I smiled reassuringly (right out of the manual). "Looks like we got a little situation here."

"I'd say so."

A pair of nice fat understatements. The dude had three wet kids in there standing in the bathtub, wrapped with bare electrical wire. The switch was in his hands, but we couldn't just reach in with a parasite suit and save the day. He held a jiggle switch, and there was no way a Remote operator (or anyone else, for that matter) was going to slide into that Full Freedom suit without setting off the current.

"Come on inside," he said through the porch speaker. "But walk real slow."

"You got it."

I came in through the unlocked door. The Remote Monitor kept me updated and guided me to the bathroom in question. It was downstairs, adjacent to guest quarters.

"I'm just outside the door," I announced. "Can I come in?"

"Wait a minute." There was a sweaty pause, then he said, "Where's your partner?"

"Out back."

"Is he armed?"

"Of course she is," I said, telling the truth just like it says in the manual. (Actually it says tell the truth unless it's better not to—no fool, that manual.) "I'm armed, too, pal, and there's nothing either of us can do about that. It comes with the suit."

We waited while he ran that one through his brain. The playback update from Remote was busy scanning the interior of the bathroom. The possibility of simply shutting down his house current had been taken care of. He'd dragged in a half-dozen big Ni-Cad batteries out of his car. There was every reason to believe they were fully charged (though you can imagine they were pretty old). The kids looked scared, shivering in the bathtub, afraid to squirm around or touch the wires wound around them.

I could see the suspect in the playback, reflected in the mirror. He was fully dressed, sitting on the toilet with the jiggle switch balanced on his fingertips. If he got any jumpier we could all go home, remembering to call the meat wagon on the way.

"Okay," he said, and I canceled the playback to concentrate on real time.

"I can come inside?" I asked hopefully.

"Wait a minute."

Dammit. I was sitting on enough nervous energy to *melt* the goddamn door. "Come on, pal. Let me in so we can have a little chat."

Get 'em talking (says the manual). Get in as close as possible and wear their ears off.

I subvocaled to Doris. I wanted her inside the house. She popped the French doors and stepped silently inside.

"Hey!" the guy yelled. He must have had an alarm terminal in there.

"It's okay," I said quickly. "She's just going to get in a little closer, so she can help you."

"Don't fool with me!"

"Relax, pal, or it'll all be over."

"For them, maybe, but not for me."

"Them" meant the kids, presumably.

"Don't delude yourself," I said, still poised a millimeter in front of the door. "Full Freedom or not, there's no way you can keep a troubleshooter's suit from coming right through you. And lest you forget, there's a furniture-eating Remote guy on your case, and the instant those kids are out of the equation—one way or the other—he's going to be on you and in you and all around you."

There was another drooling pause, then he said, "She can come inside. As a matter of fact, I want *her* to come into the bathroom—not you."

Now what? Maybe he had a little hanky-panky in mind, though the esteemed manual hints primly that suicidal types are pretty much lacking in sexuality—at least at the very brink of suicide.

Which brought up an interesting question: Was suicide really his goal?

Doris jammed herself into my back, coming to an abrupt halt outside the door. I could see she was eager, as usual.

Whatever pain she was to me at home, on duty she was all the partner anyone could ask for.

("He wants you inside,") I subvocaled.

("I heard through Remote. I'm ready, Bob.")

I got a "Bob" finally. This must be serious. . . .

"Is she out there?" he yelled.

Doris yelled "yes" back at him, then subbed to me: ("Any ideas?")

("Play by ear, I guess. Be careful, protect the kids, watch your ass, and so forth.")

She nodded, and I got out of her way.

Our friend suddenly got real tricky and demanded a Freedom of Information scan from Doris's suit, showing that she was alone at the door and that I was way across the hall. Then he popped the lock on the bathroom door, and Doris went slowly inside.

I continued to watch the scene from the Remote viewing camera on Doris's suit. The first thing the guy said, after relocking the door, was: "Take off your power suit."

"I can't do *that!*" she said.

But we both heard the Remote supervisor in our ears, giving the go-ahead. Doris swung about nervously (or pretended to move nervously), giving us all a good look at the children. They seemed all right—but scared and wet and tired of this stupid game.

Doris shucked her power suit, leaving it standing by itself in a corner. Then the guy sat her down with her back against the bathroom door and handed *her* the jiggle switch.

"You'll be very careful, I'm sure," he told her. "All I have to do is yell *Boo* and you'll trip the switch."

That was true enough. Doris sat very still while he got out of his Full Freedom suit and into her more powerful troubleshooter's suit. I waited just outside the door, but not touching it, lest my jittery, power-assisted muscles give the door a shake—and flip Doris across the room.

Once the guy had the suit on, he simply waved bye-bye and crashed through a wall beside the medicine dispenser. The move was so sudden and unexpected that Doris almost fried the kids.

The supervisor was yelling *Get him! Get him!* loud enough to reach me without a radio. A portion of my field of vision flared into a diagram of the house, with the fugitive's present course mapped in red.

His troubleshooter's suit was still hooked up to Remote sensing, but there was no way to get physical control with a parasite suit. And how do you suppose the guy knew that?

I hated to think about the report I'd have to make when all this was over.

For the present, at least, my course was clear, and I started running through walls in the shortest route of pursuit. In a moment we were both out in the chaparral behind the house and jumping for the nearest ridgeline.

The guy was crazy, of course. How the hell did he expect to get away with it? He couldn't hide, not with the Remote sensing of the suit turned on, and he couldn't escape the Company force—the dreaded Security Branch—which contained (just barely) some of the meanest ladies and gentlemen you'd ever want to avoid in a dark alley (or in broad daylight, for that matter).

Hell, he couldn't even hope to escape *me*.

Our power suits might be equal in strength and dexterity, but a lot depends on the jockey. I was gaining steadily on him.

We thrashed and jumped through half a dozen crackling canyons. The jet chopper had lifted from the lawn and come around in pursuit. It was maneuvering frantically in the narrow canyons, trying for a clear shot to spray out a load of StikiStuf, which can grapple a man in an ordinary Full Freedom power suit and make his life a misery. An inexperienced man in a troubleshooter's suit is probably just as vulnerable, but it didn't look as if we'd get a chance to find out this time.

The chopper stood off at a distance, thoroughly frustrated. The man on the ground—yours truly—was once again the preferred tool here.

So we jumped and scrambled and sweated halfway across Hollywood Sign National Park. Finally he got himself in a jam and tried to jump up a cliff too high. He smacked into the loose rock about two-thirds of the way up, but couldn't stick. He plucked hopelessly at the sage, then dropped onto his back in the spiny manzanita. He squirmed about, rolled over, saw me coming fast, and hopped to his feet, more stunned than hurt.

"Get back!" his loudspeaker shrieked. "I'll set this mountain on fire!"

I stopped a few meters from him and asked the Remote supervisor for an update on the guy's vitals. The poor jerk was in lousy shape, his heart on the nasty verge of fibrillation, his breath fast and shallow and full of stinging smog.

"I mean it!" he yelled.

"Don't let him rest!" the supervisor said. "*Climb* on him!"

The chopper was noisily poking near. I waved it off.

"Let's take a break," I told the guy. "There's no way you can just walk out of this."

"Jump him!" yelled the supervisor.

("In a minute,") I said.

"I can do a lot of damage," the guy said. "Stay away from me."

"What are you afraid of?"

For a moment his mike was open and all I heard was his scraping, strangulating breath. Then he said, "I don't want to go back."

"We're not going to hurt you."

He laughed in a pointless, end-of-life manner that made me wince. I said, as soothingly as I could through the loudspeaker: "I'll take you back personally. Nobody else has to—"

"Not that!" he yelled. "I don't care about back *there*."

"Then back where?"

"Back to normal. Back to regular. I don't want to go back to being . . . ordinary. Full Freedom is—"

"Bullshit," I said. "Full Freedom is just a stupid *game*. A Full Freedom idiot is just *that much* different—" I held my fingers a few centimeters apart —"from the average guy. There's nothing legal you can do in a suit that any bozo on the street can't do with a moment's effort. Full Freedom is just a goddam gimmick, an expensive geegaw to fool the rich idiots into thinking they're special."

"I don't believe that," he said, after several seconds' silence.

"You just forgot what it was like," I said. "Besides, while you were busy living it up in your ridiculous Full Freedom suit, the aforementioned bozo on the street was helping himself to a life that was getting better by the second. And don't think those big-buck premiums you and your upper-crust buddies have been paying out haven't helped a whole hell of a lot. We been feeding off you clowns for years."

All this time, while I jabbered and scolded, I was also

creeping closer to the guy. By the time he unwrapped his brain long enough to notice anything, it was too late. He muttered halfheartedly: "I thought I told you to stay—"

But I closed the gap with one jump and got him in an old-fashioned bear hug. The harder his suit tried to break the grip, the harder I squeezed.

The next thirty minutes were pretty boring, and I nearly dozed off, while the two suits twined and struggled and drained their powerpaks. In the end we were locked tight in our loveless embrace, suits dead, dim Low Power lights flashing slowly, waiting for Security Branch to chopper in and airlift us in a clump back to headquarters.

They gave my suit a quick charge and I was able to unlock my grip. By the time they pulled the man out of Doris's suit he was half dead.

Well, they could fix *that*. (The guy was still, believe it or not, a valued and paid-up Full Freedom policy holder.)

I limped back to the ready room. Doris was waiting for me there, having seen to the return of the children. There were no criminal charges under consideration.

"I heard your little speech," she said.

"It was just general palaver, like the manual says."

She winked. "Good luck with the debriefing."

I gotta admit I was a little nervous about the debriefing. I don't think what I told that man in the bush was inaccurate, but it wasn't the sort of statement the Company wants to release as public policy.

After all, there are a lot more up-and-coming freedom-craving idiots out there, and a lot more Full Freedom policies to hawk. We need the money, all of us, if things are ever going to equal out in this world.

At least we're headed in the right direction. You'll see what I mean when you get a troubleshooter's suit of your own. But be patient. Freedom ain't cheap.

DODKIN'S JOB

When I began this book, I knew I wanted this story for it.

Actually it's a bit more complicated than that. I recalled the story from *Astounding* of a long time ago; but I remembered neither title nor author, nor date of publication. Just this marvelous story about the horrors of bureaucracy—alienation and *anomie* with a vengeance—and an angry man trying to fight the system. . . .

Somehow John Carr ran down the story from my description. I can't think how.

Jack Vance is often described as "widely traveled." I'm in a position to know he's been to South Africa: I was there on a journalistic assignment some years ago, and a South African official asked me if they should issue a visa to a science fiction writer named Jack Vance.

Why ask me? I wondered, but they *had* asked me. "What do you want to know about him?"

"Is he honest? Will he write of what he sees, rather than what he expected to see?"

"Great glory, yes," I said. And that apparently was sufficient. I have never understood that incident; but then I left the Republic of South Africa with the firm and fixed opinion that I don't know how to run their country. I am not at all certain *they* know what they're doing either, but I'm *very* certain I don't know. When you have a nation of tribes, some barely above the Stone Age (and some ready to denounce you for "cultural aggression" if you attempt to bring them *out* of the Stone Age), then your best course of action is not obvious. Preserving freedom in South Africa must at the least take account of (1) what has happened to the black republics across the continent, and (2) the fact that some of the tribes resident there would be delighted to reenslave other tribes. . . .

Jack Vance is known as one of the most interesting writers in the field. This is one of his earliest stories, but it has never gone out of date.

DODKIN'S JOB

by Jack Vance

The theory of Organized Society (as developed by Kinch, Kolbig, Penton, and others) yields such a wealth of significant information, revealing manifold intricacies and portentous projections, that occasionally it is well to consider its deceptively simple major premise (here stated by Kolbig):

> When self-willed microunits combine to form and sustain a durable macrounit, certain freedoms of action are curtailed.

> This is the basic process of Organization.

> The more numerous and erratic the microunits, the more complex must be the structure and function of the macrounit—hence the more pervasive and restricting the details of Organization.
> —from Leslie Penton, *First Principles of Organization*

The general population of the City had become forgetful of curtailed freedoms, as a snake no longer remembers the legs of its forebears. Somewhere someone has stated, "When the discrepancy between the theory and practice of a culture is very great, this indicates that the culture is undergoing rapid change." By such a test the culture of the City was stable, if not static. The population ordered their lives by schedule, classification, and precedent, satisfied with the bland rewards of Organization.

But in the healthiest tissue bacteria exist, and the most negligible impurity flaws a critical crystallization.

Luke Grogatch was forty, thin and angular, dour of forehead, with a sardonic cast to his mouth and eyebrows and a sideways twist to his head as if he suffered from earache. He was too astute to profess nonconformity; too perverse to strive for improved status; too pessimistic, captious, sarcastic, and outspoken to keep the jobs to which he found himself assigned. Each new reclassification depressed his status; he disliked each new job with increasing fervor.

Finally, rated as *Flunky/Class D/Unskilled*, Luke was dispatched to the District 8892 Sewer Maintenance Department and from there ordered out as night-shift swamper on Tunnel Gang Number 3's rotary drilling machine.

Reporting for work, Luke presented himself to the gang foreman, Fedor Miskitman, a big, buffalo-faced man with flaxen hair and placid blue eyes. Miskitman produced a shovel and took Luke to a position close up behind the drilling machine's cutting head. Here, said Miskitman, was Luke's station. Luke would be required to keep the tunnel floor clean of loose rock and gravel. When the tunnel broke through into an old sewer, there would be scale and that detritus known as "wet waste" to remove. Luke was to keep the dust trap clean and in optimum adjustment. During the breaks he would lubricate those bearings isolated from the automatic lubrication system and he was to replace broken teeth on the cutting head whenever necessary.

Luke inquired if this was the extent of his duties, his voice strong with an irony the guileless Fedor Miskitman failed to notice.

"That is all," said Miskitman. He handed Luke the shovel. "Mostly it is the trash. The floor must be clean."

Luke suggested to the foreman a modification of the hopper jaws which would tend to eliminate the spill of broken rock; in fact, went Luke's argument, why bother at all? Let the rock lie where it fell. The concrete lining of the tunnel would mask so trivial a scatter of gravel.

Miskitman dismissed the suggestion out of hand: the rock must be removed. When Luke asked why, Miskitman told him, "That is the way the job is done."

Luke made a rude noise under his breath. He tested the shovel and shook his head in dissatisfaction. The handle was

too long, the blade too short. He reported this fact to
Miskitman, who merely glanced at his watch and signaled to
the drill operator. The machine whined into revolution and
with an ear-splitting roar made contact with the rock.
Miskitman departed, and Luke went back to work.

During the shift he found that if he worked in a half-crouch
most of the hot, dust-laden exhaust from the machine would
pass over his head. Changing a cutting tooth during the first
rest period he burned a blister on his left thumb. At the end
of the shift a single consideration deterred Luke from declaring himself unqualified: he would be declassified from
Flunky/Class D/Unskilled to *Junior Executive*, with a corresponding cut in expense account. Such a declassification would
take him to the very bottom of the Status List, and so could
not be countenanced; his present expense account was barely
adequate, covering nutrition at a Type RP Victualing Service, sleeping space in a Sublevel 22 dormitory, and sixteen
Special Coupons per month. He took Class 14 Erotic Processing, and was allowed twelve hours per month at his recreation club, with optional use of bar-bells, table-tennis
equipment, two miniature bowling alleys, and any of the six
telescreens tuned permanently to Band H. Luke often
daydreamed of a more sumptuous life: AAA nutrition, a suite
of rooms for his exclusive use, Special Coupons by the bale,
Class 7 Erotic Processing, or even Class 6, or 5: despite
Luke's contempt for the High Echelon he had no quarrel with
High Echelon perquisites. And always as a bitter coda to the
daydreams came the conviction that he might have been
enjoying these good things in all reality. He had watched his
fellows jockeying; he knew all the tricks and techniques: the
beavering, the gregarization, the smutting, knuckling, and
subuculation. . . . Why not make use of this knowledge?

"I'd rather be Class D Flunky," sneered Luke to himself.

Occasionally a measure of doubt would seep into Luke's
mind. Perhaps he merely lacked the courage to compete, to
come to grips with the world! And the seep of doubt would
become a trickle of self-contempt. A Nonconformist, that's
what he was—and he lacked the courage to admit it!

Then Luke's obstinacy would reassert itself. Why admit to

Nonconformity when it meant a trip to the Disorganized House? A fool's trick—and Luke was no fool. Perhaps he was a Nonconformist in all reality; again, perhaps not—he had never really made up his mind. He presumed that he was suspected; occasionally he intercepted queer side-glances and significant jerks of the head among his fellow workers. Let them leer. They could prove nothing.

But now ... he was Luke Grogatch, Class D Flunky, separated by a single status from the nonclassified sediment of criminals, idiots, children, and proved Nonconformists. Luke Grogatch, who had dreamed such dreams of the High Echelon, of pride and independence! Instead—Luke Grogatch, Class D Flunky. Taking orders from a hay-headed lunk, working with semiskilled laborers with status almost as low as his own: Luke Grogatch, flunky.

Seven weeks passed. Luke's dislike for his job became a mordant passion. The work was arduous, hot, repellent. Fedor Miskitman turned an uncomprehending gaze on Luke's suggestions and arguments. This was the way things were done—his manner implied—always had been done, and always would be done.

Fedor Miskitman received a daily policy directive from the works superintendent which he read to the crew during the first rest break of the shift. These directives generally dealt with such matters as work norms, team spirit, and cooperation; pleas for a finer polish on the concrete; warnings against off-shift indulgence which might dull enthusiasm and decrease work efficiency. Luke usually paid small heed, until one day Fedor Miskitman, pulling out the familiar yellow sheet, read in his stolid voice:

PUBLIC WORKS DEPARTMENT. PUBLIC UTILITIES DIVISION
AGENCY OF SANITARY WORKS. DISTRICT 8892
SEWAGE DISPOSAL SECTION

Bureau of Sewer Construction and Maintenance
Office of Procurement

Policy Directive: 6511 Series BV96

Order Code:	GZP—AAR—REG
Reference:	G98—7542
Date Code:	BT—EQ—LLT
Authorized:	LL8—P—SC 8892
Checked:	48
Counterchecked:	92C

From: Lavester Limon, Manager, Office of Procurement
Through: All construction and maintenance offices
To: All construction and maintenance superintendents
Attention: All job foremen
Subject: Tool longevity, the promotion thereof
Instant of Application: Immediate
Duration of Relevance: Permanent

Substance: At beginning of each shift all hand-tools shall be
             checked out of District 8892 Sewer Maintenance
             Warehouse. At close of each shift all hand-tools
             shall be carefully cleaned and returned to District
             8892 Sewer Maintenance Warehouse.

                    Directive reviewed and transmitted:
                        Butry Keghorn, General
                        Superintendent of Con-
                        struction, Bureau of
                        Sewer Construction
                        Clyde Kaddo, Superinten-
                        dent of Sewer Mainte-
                        nance

As Fedor Miskitman read the "Substance" section, Luke
expelled his breath in an incredulous snort. Miskitman finished, folded the sheet with careful movements of his thick
fingers, looked at his watch. "That is the directive. We
are twenty-five seconds over time; we must get back to
work."

"Just a minute," said Luke. "One or two things about that
directive I want explained."

Miskitman turned his mild gaze upon Luke. "You did not understand it?"

"Not altogether. Who does it apply to?"

"It is an order for the entire gang."

"What do they mean, 'hand-tools'?"

"These are tools which are held in the hands."

"Does that mean a shovel?"

"A shovel?" Miskitman shrugged his burly shoulders. "A shovel is a hand-tool."

Luke asked in a voice of hushed wonder: "They want me to polish my shovel, carry it four miles to the warehouse, then pick it up tomorrow and carry it back here?"

Miskitman unfolded the directive, held it at arm's length, and read with moving lips. "That is the order." He refolded the paper and returned it to his pocket.

Luke again feigned astonishment. "Certainly there's a mistake."

"A mistake?" Miskitman was puzzled. "Why should there be a mistake?"

"They can't be serious," said Luke. "It's not only ridiculous, it's peculiar."

"I do not know," said Miskitman incuriously. "To work. We are late one minute and a half."

"I assume that all this cleaning and transportation is done on Organization time," Luke suggested.

Miskitman unfolded the directive, held it at arm's length, read. "It does not say so. Our quota is not different." He folded the directive and put it in his pocket.

Luke spat on the rock floor. "I'll bring my own shovel. Let 'em carry around their own precious hand-tools."

Miskitman scratched his chin and once more reread the directive. He shook his head dubiously. "The order says that all hand-tools must be cleaned and taken to the warehouse. It does not say who owns the tools."

Luke could hardly speak for exasperation. "You know what I think of that directive?"

Fedor Miskitman paid him no heed. "To work. We are over time."

"If I was general superintendent—" Luke began, but Miskitman rumbled roughly.

"We do not earn perquisites by talking. To work. We are late."

The rotary cutter started up; seventy-two teeth snarled into gray-brown sandstone. Hopper jaws swallowed the chunks, passing them down an epiglottis into a feeder gut which evacuated far down the tunnel into lift-buckets. Stray chips rained upon the tunnel floor, which Luke Grogatch must scrape up and return into the hopper. Behind Luke two reinforcement men flung steel hoops into place, flash-welding them to longitudinal bars with quick pinches of the fingers, contact-plates in their gauntlets discharging the requisite gout of energy. Behind came the concrete-spray man, mix hissing out of his revolving spider, followed by two finishers, nervous men working with furious energy, stroking the concrete into a glossy polish. Fedor Miskitman marched back and forth, testing the reinforcement, gauging the thickness of the concrete, making frequent progress checks on the chart to the rear of the rotary cutter, where an electronic device traced the course of the tunnel, guiding it through the system of conduits, ducts, passages, pipes, and tubes for water, air, gas, steam, transportation, freight, and communication which knit the City into an Organized unit.

The night shift ended at four o'clock in the morning. Miskitman made careful entries in his log; the concrete-spray man blew out his nozzles; the reinforcement workers removed their gauntlets, power packs, and insulating garments. Luke Grogatch straightened, rubbed his sore back, and stood glowering at the shovel. He felt Miskitman's ox-calm scrutiny. If he threw the shovel to the side of the tunnel as usual and marched off about his business, he would be guilty of disorganized conduct. The penalty, as Luke knew well, was declassification. Luke stared at the shovel, fuming with humiliation. Conform or be declassified. Submit—or become a Junior Executive.

Luke heaved a deep sigh. The shovel was clean enough; one or two swipes with a rag would remove the dust. But there was the ride by crowded man-belt to the warehouse, the queue at the window, the check-in, the added distance to his dormitory. Tomorrow the process must be repeated. Why the necessity for this added effort? Luke knew well enough. An obscure functionary somewhere along the chain of bureaus and commissions had been at a loss for a means to display his diligence. What better method than concern for valuable City property? Consequently the absurd directive, filtering down to Fedor Miskitman and ultimately to Luke Grogatch, the victim. What joy to meet this obscure functionary face to face, to tweak his sniveling nose, to kick his craven rump along the corridors of his own office. . . .

Fedor Miskitman's voice disturbed his reverie. "Clean your shovel. It is the end of the shift."

Luke made token resistance. "The shovel is clean," he growled. "This is the most absurd antic I've ever been coerced into. If only I—"

Fedor Miskitman, in a voice as calm and unhurried as a deep river, said, "If you do not like the policy, you should put a petition in the suggestion box. That is the privilege of all. Until the policy is changed you must conform. That is the way we live. That is Organization, and we are Organized men."

"Let me see that directive," Luke barked. "I'll get it changed. I'll cram it down somebody's throat. I'll—"

"You must wait until it is logged. Then you may have it; it is useless to me."

"I'll wait," said Luke between clenched teeth.

With method and deliberation Fedor Miskitman made a final check of the job, inspecting machinery, the teeth of the cutter head, the nozzles of the spider, the discharge belt. He went to his little desk at the rear of the rotary drill, noted progress, signed expense account vouchers, finally registered the policy directive on minifilm. Then with a ponderous sweep of his arm he tendered the yellow sheet to Luke. "What will you do with it?"

"I'll find who formed this idiotic policy. I'll tell him what I think of it and what I think of him, to boot."

Miskitman shook his head in disapproval. "That is not the way such things should be done."

"How would you do it?" asked Luke with a wolfish grin.

Miskitman considered, pursing his lips, jerking his bristling eyebrows. At last with great simplicity of manner he said, "I would not do it."

Luke threw up his hands and set off down the tunnel. Miskitman's voice boomed against his back. "You must take the shovel!"

Luke halted. Slowly he faced about, glared back at the hulking figure of the foreman. Obey the policy directive or be declassified. With slow steps, with hanging head and averted eyes, he retraced his path. Snatching the shovel, he stalked back down the tunnel. His bony shoulder blades were exposed and sensitive; Fedor Miskitman's mild blue gaze, following him, seemed to scrape the nerves of his back.

Ahead the tunnel extended, a glossy pale sinus, dwindling back along the distance they had bored. Through some odd trick of refraction alternate bright and dark rings circled the tube, confusing the eye, creating a hypnotic semblance of two-dimensionality. Luke shuffled drearily into this illusory bull's-eye, dazed with shame and helplessness, the shovel a load of despair. Had he come to this—Luke Grogatch, previously so arrogant in his cynicism and barely concealed Nonconformity? Must he cringe at last, submit slavishly to witless regulations? . . . If only he were a few places farther up the list! Drearily he pictured the fine incredulous shock with which he would have greeted the policy directive, the sardonic nonchalance with which he would have let the shovel fall from his limp hands. . . . Too late, too late! Now he must toe the mark, must carry his shovel dutifully to the warehouse. In a spasm of rage he flung the blameless implement clattering down the tunnel ahead of him. Nothing he could do! Nowhere to turn! No way to strike back! Organization: smooth and relentless; Organization: massive and inert, tolerant of the submissive, serenely cruel to the unbeliever . . . Luke came to his shovel and, whispering an obscenity, snatched it up and half-ran down the pallid tunnel.

He climbed through a manhole and emerged upon the deck of the 1123rd Avenue Hub, where he was instantly absorbed in the crowds trampling between the man-belts, which radiated like spokes, and the various escalators. Clasping the shovel to his chest, Luke struggled aboard the Fontego man-belt and rushed south, in a direction opposite to that of his dormitory. He rode ten minutes to Astoria Hub, dropped a dozen levels on the Grimesby College Escalator, and crossed a gloomy dank area smelling of old rock to a local feeder-belt which carried him to the District 8892 Sewer Maintenance Warehouse.

Luke found the warehouse brightly lit, the center of considerable activity, with several hundred men coming and going. Those coming, like Luke, carried tools; those going went empty-handed.

Luke joined the line which had formed in front of the tool storeroom. Fifty or sixty men preceded him, a drab centipede of arms, shoulders, heads, legs, the tools projecting to either side. The centipede moved slowly, the men exchanging badinage and quips.

Observing their patience, Luke's normal irascibility asserted itself. Look at them, he thought, standing like sheep, jumping to attention at the rustle of an unfolding directive. Did they inquire about the reason for the order? Did they question the necessity for their inconvenience? No! The louts stood chuckling and chatting, accepting the directive as one of life's incalculable vicissitudes, something elemental and arbitrary, like the changing of the seasons. . . . And he, Luke Grogatch, was he better or worse? The question burned in Luke's throat like the aftertaste of vomit.

Still, better or worse, where was his choice? Conform or declassify. A poor choice. There was always the recourse of the suggestion box, as Fedor Miskitman, perhaps in bland jest, had pointed out. Luke growled in disgust. Weeks later he might receive a printed form with one statement of a multiple-choice list checked off by some clerical flunky or junior executive: "The situation described by your petition is already under study by responsible officials. Thank you for your interest." Or, "The situation described by your petition is temporary and may shortly be altered. Thank you for your interest." Or, "The situation described by your petition is the product of established policy and is not subject to change. Thank you for your interest."

A novel thought occurred to Luke: he might exert himself and reclassify *up* the list. . . . As soon as the idea arrived he dismissed it. In the first place he was close to middle age; too many young men were pushing up past him. Even if he could goad himself into the competition. . . .

The line moved slowly forward. Behind Luke a plump little man sagged under the weight of a Velstro inchskip. A forelock of light brown floss dangled over his moony face; his mouth was puckered into a rosebud of concentration; his eyes were absurdly serious. He wore a rather dapper pink-and-brown coverall with orange ankle-boots and a blue beret with the three orange pompoms affected by the Velstro technicians.

Between shabby, sour-mouthed Luke and this short moony man in the dandy's overalls existed so basic a difference that an immediate mutual dislike was inevitable.

The short man's prominent hazel eyes rested on Luke's shovel, traveled thoughtfully over Luke's dirt-stained trousers and jacket. He turned his eyes to the side.

"Come a long way?" Luke asked maliciously.

"Not far," said the moon-faced man.

"Worked overtime, eh?" Luke winked. "A bit of quiet beavering, nothing like it—or so I'm told."

"We finished the job," said the plump man with dignity. "Beavering doesn't enter into it. Why spend half tomorrow's shift on five minutes' work we could do tonight?"

"I know a reason," said Luke wisely. "To do your fellow man a good one in the eye."

The moon-faced man twisted his mouth in a quick uncertain smile, then decided that the remark was not humorous. "That's not my way of working," he said stiffly.

"That thing must be heavy," said Luke, noting how the plump little arms struggled and readjusted to the irregular contours of the tool.

"Yes," came the reply. "It is heavy."

"An hour and a half," intoned Luke. "That's how long it's taking me to park this shovel. Just because somebody up the list has a nightmare. And we poor hoodlums at the bottom suffer."

"I'm not at the bottom of the list. I'm a Technical Tool Operator."

"No difference," said Luke. "The hour and a half is the same. Just for somebody's silly notion."

"It's not really so silly," said the moon-faced man. "I fancy there is a good reason for the policy."

Luke shook the shovel by its handle. "And so I have to carry this back and forth along the man-belt three hours a day?"

The little man pursed his lips. "The author of the directive undoubtedly knows his business very well. Otherwise he'd not hold his classification."

"Just who is this unsung hero?" sneered Luke. "I'd like to meet him. I'd like to learn why he wants me to waste three hours a day."

The short man now regarded Luke as he might an insect in his victual ration. "You talk like a Nonconformist. Excuse me if I seem offensive."

"Why apologize for something you can't help?" asked Luke and turned his back.

He flung his shovel to the clerk behind the wicket and received a check. Elaborately Luke turned to the moon-faced man and tucked the check into the breast pocket of the pink and brown coveralls. "You keep this; you'll be using that shovel before I will."

He stalked proudly out of the warehouse. A grand gesture, but—he hesitated before stepping on the man-belt—was it sensible? The technical tool operator in the pink-and-brown coveralls came out of the warehouse behind him, giving him a queer glance, and hurried away.

Luke looked back into the warehouse. If he returned now he could set things right, and tomorrow there'd be no trouble. If he stormed off to his dormitory, it meant another declassificaton. Luke Grogatch, Junior Executive. Luke reached into his jumper and took out the policy directive he had acquired from Fedor Miskitman: a bit of yellow paper, printed with a few lines of type, a trivial thing in itself—but it symbolized the Organization: massive force in irresistible operation. Nervously Luke plucked at the paper and looked back into the warehouse. The tool operator had called him a Nonconformist; Luke's mouth squirmed in a brief weary grimace. It wasn't true. Luke was not a Nonconformist; Luke was nothing in particular. And he needed his bed, his nutrition ticket, his meager expense account. Luke groaned quietly—almost a whisper. The end of the road. He had gone as far as he could

go; had he ever thought he could defeat the Organization?
Maybe he was wrong and everyone else was right. Possible,
thought Luke without conviction. Miskitman seemed content
enough; the technical tool operator seemed not only content
but complacent. Luke leaned against the warehouse wall,
eyes burning and moist with self-pity. Nonconformist. Misfit.
What was he going to do?

He curled his lip spitefully, stepped forward onto the man-
belt. Devil take them all! They could declassify him; he'd
become a Junior Executive and laugh!

In subdued spirits Luke rode back to the Grimesby Hub.
Here, about to board the escalator, he stopped short, blinking
and rubbing his long sallow chin, considering still another
aspect to the matter. It seemed to offer the chance of—but no.
Hardly likely . . . and yet, why not? Once again he examined
the directive. Lavester Limon, Manager of the District Office
of Procurement, presumably had issued the policy; Lavester
Limon could rescind it. If Luke could so persuade Limon, his
troubles, while not dissipated, at least would be lessened. He
could report shovel-less to his job; he could return sardonic
grin for bland hidden grin with Fedor Miskitman. He might
even go to the trouble of locating the moon-faced little technical tool operator with the inchskip. . . .

Luke sighed. Why continue this futile daydream? First
Lavester Limon must be induced to rescind the directive—
and what were the odds of this? . . . Perhaps not astronomi-
cal, after all, mused Luke as he rode the man-belt back to his
dormitory. The directive clearly was impractical. It worked
an inconvenience on many people, while accomplishing very
little. If Lavester Limon could be persuaded of this, if he could
be shown that his own prestige and reputation were suffering, he might agree to recall the ridiculous directive.

Luke arrived at his dormitory shortly after seven. He went
immediately to the communication booth, called the District
8892 Office of Procurement. Lavester Limon, he was told,
would be arriving at eight-thirty.

Luke made a careful toilet, and after due consideration
invested four Special Coupons in a fresh set of fibers: a tight
black jacket and blue trousers of somewhat martial cut, of

considerably better quality than his usual costume. Survey-ing himself in the washroom mirror, Luke felt that he cut not so poor a figure.

He took his morning quota of nutrition at a nearby Type RP Victualing Service, then ascending to the Sublevel 14 and rode the man-belt to District 8892 Bureau of Sewer Construc-tion and Maintenance.

A pert office girl, dark hair pulled forward over her face in the modish "robber baron" style, conducted Luke into Lavester Limon's office. At the door she glanced demurely backward, and Luke was glad that he had invested in new clothes. Responding to the stimulus, he threw back his shoulders and marched confidently into Lavester Limon's office.

Lavester Limon, sitting at his desk, bumped briefly to his feet in courteous acknowledgment—an amiable-seeming man of middle stature, golden-brown hair brushed carefully across a freckled and suntanned bald spot; golden-brown eyes, round and easy; a golden-brown lounge jacket and trousers of fine golden-brown corduroy. He waved his arm to a chair. "Won't you sit down, Mr. Grogatch?"

In the presence of so much cordiality Luke relaxed his truculence, and even felt a burgeoning of hope. Limon seemed a decent sort; perhaps the directive was, after all, an admin-istrative error.

Limon raised his golden-brown eyebrows inquiringly.

Luke wasted no time on preliminaries. He brought forth the directive. "My business concerns this, Mr. Limon: a policy which you seem to have formulated."

Limon took the directive, read, nodded. "Yes, that's my policy. Something wrong?"

Luke felt surprise and a pang of premonition: surely so reasonable a man must instantly perceive the folly of the directive!

"It's simply not a workable policy," said Luke earnestly. "In fact, Mr. Limon, it's completely unreasonable!"

Lavester Limon seemed not at all offended. "Well, well! And why do you say that? Incidentally, Mr. Grogatch, you're . . . ." Again the golden-brown eyebrows arched inquiringly.

"I'm a flunky, Class D, on a tunnel gang," said Luke.

"Today it took me an hour and a half to check my shovel. Tomorrow, there'll be another hour and a half checking the shovel out. All on my own time. I don't think that's reasonable."

Lavester Limon reread the directive, pursed his lips, nodded his head once or twice. He spoke into his desk phone. "Miss Rab, I'd like to see"—he consulted the directive's reference number—"Item seven-five-four-two, File G ninety-eight." To Luke he said in rather an absent voice: "Sometimes these things become a trifle complicated."

"But can you change the policy?" Luke burst out. "Do you agree that it's unreasonable?"

Limon cocked his head to the side, made a doubtful grimace. "We'll see what's on the reference. If my memory serves me . . ." His voice faded away.

Twenty seconds passed. Limon tapped his fingers on his desk. A soft chime sounded. Limon touched a button and his desk-screen exhibited the item he had requested: another policy directive similar in form to the first.

PUBLIC WORKS DEPARTMENT. PUBLIC UTILITIES DIVISION
AGENCY OF SANITARY WORKS. DISTRICT 8892
SEWAGE DISPOSAL SECTION

Director's Office

Policy Directive:	2888 Series BQ008
Order Code:	GZP—AAR—REF
Reference:	OP9—123
Date Code:	BR—EQ—LLT
Authorized:	JR D-SDS
Checked:	AC
Counterchecked:	CX McD

From: Judiath Ripp, Director
Through:
To: Lavester Limon, Manager, Office of Procurement
Attention:

    Subject: Economies of operation
   Instant of Application: Immediate
   Duration of Relevance: Permanent

Substance: Your monthly quota of supplies for disbursement
            Type A, B, D, F, H is hereby reduced 2.2%.
            It is suggested that you advise affected person-
            nel of this reduction, and take steps to insure
            most stringent economies. It has been noticed
            that department use of supplies Type D in
            particular is in excess of calculated norm.

            Suggestion: Greater care by individual users of
            tools, including warehouse storage at night.

"Type D supplies," said Lavester Limon wryly, "are hand-
tools. Old Ripp wants stringent economies. I merely pass
along the word. That's the story behind six-five-one-one." He
returned the directive in question to Luke and leaned back in
his seat. "I can see how you're exercised, but"——he raised
his hands in a careless, almost flippant gesture—"that's the
way the Organization works."

Luke sat rigid with disappointment. "Then you won't revoke the directive?"

"My dear fellow! How can I?"

Luke made an attempt at reckless nonchalance. "Well,
there's always room for me among the junior executives. I
told them where to put their shovel."

"Mmmf. Rash. Sorry I can't help." Limon surveyed Luke
curiously, and his lips curved in a faint grin. "Why don't you
tackle old Ripp?"

Luke squinted sideways in suspicion. "What good will that
do?"

"You never know," said Limon breezily. "Suppose light-
ning strikes—suppose he rescinds his directive? I can't agi-
tate with him myself; I'd get in trouble—but there's no reason
why you can't." He turned Luke a quick knowing smile, and
Luke understood that Lavester Limon's amiability, while
genuine, served as a useful camouflage for self-interest and
artful playing of the angles.

Luke rose abruptly to his feet. He played cat's-paw for no one, and he opened his mouth to tell Lavester Limon as much. In that instant a recollection crossed his mind: the scene in the warehouse, where he had contemptuously tossed the check for his shovel to the technical tool operator. Always Luke had been prone to the grand gesture, the reckless commitment which left him no scope for retreat. When would he learn self-control? In a subdued voice Luke asked, "Who is this Ripp again?"

"Judiath Ripp, Director of the Sewage Disposal Section. You may have difficulty getting in to see him; he's a trouble-some old brute. Wait, I'll find if he's at his office."

He made inquiries into his desk phone. Information re-turned to the effect that Judiath Ripp had just arrived at the Section office on Sublevel 3, under Bramblebury Park.

Limon gave Luke tactical advice. "He's choleric—something of a barker. Here's the secret: pay no attention to him. He respects firmness. Pound the table. Roar back at him. If you pussyfoot he'll sling you out. Give him tit for tat' and he'll listen."

Luke looked hard at Lavester Limon, well aware that the twinkle in the golden-brown eyes was malicious glee. He said, "I'd like a copy of that directive, so he'll know what I'm talking about."

Limon sobered instantly. Luke could read his mind: *Will Ripp hold it against me if I send up this crackpot? It's worth the chance.* "Sure," said Limon. "Pick it up from the girl."

Luke ascended to Sublevel 3 and walked through the pleasant trilevel arcade below Bramblebury Park. He passed the tall, glass-walled fishtank open to the sky and illumi-nated by sunlight, boarded the local man-belt, and after a ride of two or three minutes alighted in front of the District 8892 Agency of Sanitary Works.

The Sewage Disposal Section occupied a rather pretentious suite off a small courtyard garden. Luke walked along a passage tiled with blue, gray, and green mosaic and entered a white room furnished in pale gray and pink. A long mural of cleverly twisted gold, black, and white tubing decorated one wall; another was swathed in heavy green leaves growing-from a chest-high planter. At a desk sat the receptionist, a plump pouty blond girl with a simulated bone through her nose and a shark's-tooth necklace dangling around her neck. She wore her hair tied up over her head like a sheaf of wheat, and an amusing black-and-brown primitive symbol decorated her forehead.

Luke explained that he wished a few words with Mr. Judiath Ripp, Director of the Section.

Perhaps from uneasiness, Luke spoke brusquely. The girl, blinking in surprise, examined him curiously. After a moment's hesitation she shook her head doubtfully. "Won't someone else do? Mr. Ripp's day is tightly scheduled. What did you want to see him about?"

Luke, attempting a persuasive smile, achieved instead a leer of sinister significance. The girl was frankly startled.

"Perhaps you'll tell Mr. Ripp I'm here," said Luke. "One of his policy directives—well, there have been irregularities, or rather a misapplication—"

"Irregularities?" The girl seemed to hear only the single word. She gazed at Luke with new eyes, observing the crisp new black-and-blue garments with their quasi-military cut. Some sort of inspector? "I'll call Mr. Ripp," she said nervously. "Your name, sir, and status?"

"Luke Grogatch. My status—" Luke smiled once more, and the girl averted her eyes. "It's not important."

"I'll call Mr. Ripp, sir. One moment, if you please." She swung around, murmured anxiously into her screen, looked at Luke, and spoke again. A thin voice rasped a reply. The girl swung back around and nodded at Luke. "Mr. Ripp can spare a few minutes. The first door, please."

Luke walked with stiff shoulders into a tall, wood-paneled room, one wall of which displayed green-glowing tanks of darting red and yellow fish. At the desk sat Judiath Ripp, a tall, heavy man, himself resembling a large fish. His head was narrow, pale as mackerel, and rested backward-tilting on his shoulders. He had no perceptible chin; the neck ran up to his carplike mouth. Pale eyes stared at Luke over small round nostrils; a low brush of hair thrust up from the rear of his head like dry grass over a sand dune. Luke remembered Lavester Limon's verbal depiction of Ripp: "choleric." Hardly appropriate. Had Limon a grudge against Ripp? Was he using Luke as an instrument of mischievous revenge? Suspecting as much, Luke felt uncomfortable and awkward.

Judiath Ripp surveyed him with cold unblinking eyes. "What can I do for you, Mr. Grogatch? My secretary tells me you are an investigator of some sort."

Luke considered the situation, his narrow black eyes fixed on Ripp's face. He told the exact truth. "For several weeks I have been working in the capacity of a Class D Flunky on a tunnel gang."

"What the devil do you investigate on a tunnel gang?" Ripp asked in chilly amusement.

Luke made a slight gesture, one signifying much or nothing, as the other might choose to take it. "Last night the foreman of this gang received a policy directive issued by Lavester Limon of the Office of Procurement. For sheer imbecility this policy caps any of my experience."

"If it's Limon's doing, I can well believe it," said Ripp between his teeth.

"I sought him out in his office. He refused to accept the responsibility and referred me to you."

Ripp sat a trifle straighter in his chair. "What policy is this?"

Luke passed the two directives across the desk. Ripp read slowly, then reluctantly returned the directives. "I fail to see exactly—" He paused. "I should say, these directives merely reflect instructions received by me which I have implemented. Where is the difficulty?"

"Let me cite my personal experience," said Luke. "This morning—as I say, in my temporary capacity as a flunky—I carried a shovel from tunnel head to warehouse and checked it. The operation required an hour and a half. If I were working steadily on a job of this sort, I'd be quite demoralized."

Ripp appeared untroubled. "I can only refer you to my superiors." He spoke aside into his desk phone. "Please transmit File OR nine, Item one-two-three." He turned back to Luke. "I can't take responsibility, either for the directive or for revoking it. May I ask what sort of investigation takes you down into the tunnels? And to whom you report?"

At a loss for words at once evasive and convincing, Luke conveyed an attitude of contemptuous silence.

Judiath Ripp contracted the skin around his blank round eyes in a frown. "As I consider this matter I become increasingly puzzled. Why is this subject a matter for investigation? Just who—"

From a slot appeared the directive Ripp had requested. He glanced at it, then tossed it to Luke. "You'll see that this relieves me totally of responsibility," he said curtly.

The directive was the standard form:

PUBLIC WORKS DEPARTMENT, PUBLIC UTILITIES DIVISION

Office of

The Commissioner of Public Utilities

Policy Directive: 449 Series UA-14-G2
Order Code: GZP—AAR—REF
Reference: TQ9—1422
Date Code: BP—EQ—LLT
Authorized: PU-PUD-Org.
Checked: G. Evan
Counterchecked: Hernon Klanech

From: Parris deVicker, Commissioner of Public Utilities
Through: All District Agencies of Sanitary Works
To: All Department Heads
Attention:

Subject: The urgent need for sharp and immediate economies in the use of equipment and consumption of supplies.

Instance of Application: Immediate
Duration of Relevance: Permanent

Substance: All department heads are instructed to initiate, effect, and enforce rigid economies in the employment of supplies and equipment, especially those items comprised of or manufactured from alloy metals or requiring the functional consumption of same, in those areas in which official authority is exercised. A decrement of 2% will be considered minimal. Status augmentation will in some measure be affected by economies achieved.

Directive reviewed and transmitted: Lee Jon Smith, District Agent of Sanitary Works 8892

Luke rose to his feet, concerned now only to depart from the office as quickly as possible. He indicated the directive. "This is a copy?"

"Yes."

"I'll take it, if I may." He included it with the previous two.

Judiath Ripp watched with a faint but definite suspicion. "I fail to understand whom you represent."

"Sometimes the less one knows the better," said Luke.

The suspicion faded from Judiath Ripp's piscine face. Only a person secure in his status could afford to use language of this sort to a member of the low High Echelon. He nodded slightly. "Is that all you require?"

"No," said Luke, "but it's all I can get here."

He turned toward the door, feeling the rake of Ripp's eyes on his back.

Ripp's voice cut at him suddenly and sharply. "Just a moment."

Luke slowly turned.

"Who are you? Let me see your credentials."

Luke laughed coarsely. "I don't have any."

Judiath Ripp rose to his feet, stood towering with knuckles pressed on the desk. Suddenly Luke saw that, after all, Judiath Ripp *was* choleric. His face, mackerel-pale, became suffused with salmon pink. "Identify yourself," he said throatily, "before I call the watchman."

"Certainly," said Luke. "I have nothing to hide. I am Luke Grogatch. I work as Class D Flunky on Tunnel Gang Number Three, out of the Bureau of Sewer Construction and Maintenance."

"What are you doing here, misrepresenting yourself, wasting my time?"

"Where did I misrepresent myself?" demanded Luke in a contentious voice. "I came here to find out why I had to carry my shovel to the warehouse this morning. It cost me an hour and a half. It doesn't make sense. You've been ordered to economize two per cent, so I spend three hours a day carrying a shovel back and forth."

Judiath Ripp stared at Luke for a few seconds, then abruptly sat down. "You're a Class D Flunky?"

"That's right."

"Hmm. You've been to the Office of Procurement. The manager sent you here?"

"No. He gave me a copy of his directive, just as you did."

The salmon-pink flush had died from Ripp's flat cheeks. The carplike mouth twitched in infinitesimal amusement. "No harm in that, certainly. What do you hope to achieve?"

"I don't want to carry that blasted shovel back and forth. I'd like you to issue orders to that effect."

Judiath Ripp spread his pale mouth in a cold drooping smile. "Bring me a policy directive to that effect from Parris deVicker and I'll be glad to oblige you. Now—"

"Will you make an appointment for me?"

"An appointment?" Ripp was puzzled. "With whom?"

"With the Commissioner of Public Utilities."

"Pffah!" Ripp waved his hand in cold dismissal. "Get out."

Luke stood in the blue mosaic entry seething with hate for Ripp, Limon, Miskitman, and every intervening functionary. If he were only chairman of the board for a brief two hours (went the oft-repeated daydream), how they'd quickstep! In his mind's eye he saw Judiath Ripp shoveling wads of wet waste with a leaden shovel while a rotary driller, twice as noisy and twice as violent, blew back gales of hot dust and rock chips across his neck. Lavester Limon would be forced to change the smoking teeth of the drill with a small and rusty monkey wrench, while Fedor Miskitman, before and after the shift, carried shovel, monkey wrench, and all the worn teeth to and from the warehouse.

Luke stood moping in the passage for five minutes, then escalated to the surface, which at this point, by virtue of Bramblebury Park, could clearly be distinguishable as the surface and not just another level among coequal levels. He walked slowly along the gravel paths, ignoring the open sky for the immediacy of his problems. He faced a dead end. There was no further scope of action. Judiath Ripp had mockingly suggested that he consult the Commissioner of Public Utilities. Even if by some improbable circumstance he secured an appointment with the Commissioner, what good would ensue? Why should the Commissioner revoke a policy directive of such evident importance? Unless he could be persuaded—by some instrumentality Luke was unable to define or even imagine—to issue a special directive exempting Luke from the provision of the policy. . . . Luke chuckled hollowly, a noise which alarmed the pigeons strutting along the walk. Now what? Back to the dormitory. His dormitory privileges included twelve hours' use of his cot per day, and he was not extracting full value from his expense account unless he made use of it. But Luke had no desire for sleep. As he glanced up at the perspective of the towers surrounding the park he felt a melancholy exhilaration. The sky, the wonderful clear open sky, blue and brilliant! Luke shivered, for the sun here was hidden by the Morgenthau Moonspike, and the air was brisk.

Luke crossed the park, thinking to sit where a band of hazy sunlight slashed down between the towers. The benches were crowded with blinking old men and women, but Luke presently found a seat. He sat looking up into the sky, enjoying the mild natural sun warmth. How seldom did he see the sun! In his youth he had frequently set forth on long cross-city hikes, rambling high along the skyways, with space to right and left, the clouds near enough for intimate inspection, the sunlight sparkling and stinging his skin. Gradually the hikes had spread apart, coming at even longer intervals, and now he could hardly remember when last he'd tramped the wind-lanes. What dreams he had had in those early days, what exuberant visions! Obstacles seemed trivial; he had seen himself clawing up the list, winning a good expense account, the choicest of perquisites, unnumbered Special Coupons! He had planned to have a private air-car, unrestricted nutrition, an apartment far above the surface, high and remote.... Dreams. Luke had been victimized by his tongue, his quick temper, his obstinacy. At heart, he was no Nonconformist—no, cried Luke, never! Luke had been born of tycoon stock, and through influence, a word here, a hint there, had been launched into the Organization on a high status. But circumstances and Luke's chronic truculence had driven him into opposition with established ways, and down the Status List he had gone: through professional scholarships, technical trainee appointments, craft apprenticeships, all the varieties of semiskills and machine operation.Now he was Luke Grogatch, flunky, unskilled, Class D, facing the final declassification. But still too vain to carry a shovel. No: Luke corrected himself. His vanity was not at stake. Vanity he had discarded long ago, along with his youthful dreams. All he had left was pride, his right to use the word "I" in connection with himself. If he submitted to Policy Directive 6511 he would relinquish this right; he would be absorbed into the masses of the Organization as a spatter of foam falls back and is absorbed into the ocean.... Luke jerked nervously to his feet. He wasted time sitting here. Judiath Ripp, with conger-like malice, had suggested a directive from the Commissioner of Public Utilities. Very well, Luke would obtain that directive and fling it down under Ripp's pale round nostrils.

How?

Luke rubbed his chin dubiously. He walked to a communication booth and checked the directory. As he had surmised, the Commission of Public Utilities was housed in the Organization Central Tower, in Silverado, District 3666, ninety miles to the north.

Luke stood in the watery sunlight, hoping for inspiration. The aged idlers, huddling on the benches like winterbound

sparrows, watched him incuriously. Once again Luke was
obscurely pleased with his purchase of new clothes. A fine
figure he cut, he assured himself.

How, wondered Luke. How to gain an appointment with
the Commissioner? How to persuade him to change his views?

No inkling of a solution presented itself.

He looked at his watch: it was still only midmorning.
Ample time to visit Organization Central and return in time
to report for duty. . . . Luke grimaced wanly. Was his reso-
lution so feeble, then? Was he, after all, to slink back into the
tunnel tonight carrying the hated shovel? Luke shook his
head slowly. He did not know.

At the Bramblebury Interchange Luke boarded an express
highline northbound for Silverado Station. With a hiss and a
whine, the shining metal worm darted forward, sliding up to
the 13th Level, flashing north at great speed in and out of the
sunlight, through tunnels, across chasms between towers,
with far below the nervous seethe of the City. Four times the
express sighed to a halt: at IBM University, at Braemar, at
Great Northern Junction, and finally, thirty minutes out of
Bramblebury, at Silverado Central Luke disembarked; the
express slid away through the towers, lithe as an eel through
waterweed.

Luke entered the tenth-level foyer of the Central Tower, a
vast cave of marble and bronze. Throngs of men and women
thrust past him: grim, striding tycoons, stamped with the
look of destiny, High Echelon personnel, their assistants, the
assistants to their assistants, functionaries on down the list,
all dutifully wearing high-status garments, the lesser folk
hoping to be mistaken for their superiors. All hurried, tense-
faced and abrupt, partly from habit, partly because only a
person of low status had no need to hurry. Luke thrust and
elbowed with the best of them, and made his way to the
central kiosk, where he consulted a directory.

Parris deVicker, Commissioner of Public Utilities, had his
office on the 59th Level. Luke passed him by and located the
Secretary of Public Affairs, Mr. Sewell Sepp, on the 81st
Level. No more underlings, thought Luke. This time I'm

going to the top. If anyone can resolve this matter, it's Sewell Sepp.

He put himself aboard the lift and emerged into the lobby of the Department of Public Affairs—a splendid place, glittering with disciplined color and ornament after that mock-antique décor known as Second Institutional. The walls were of polished milk glass inset with medallions of shifting kaleidoscopic flashes. The floor was diapered in blue and white sparklestone. A dozen bronze statues dominated the room, massive figures symbolizing the basic public services: communication, transport, education, water, energy, and sanitation.Luke skirted the pedestals and crossed to the reception counter, where ten young women in handsome brown-and-black uniforms stood with military precision, each to her six feet of counter top. Luke selected one of these girls, who curved her lips in an automatic empty smile.

"Yes, sir?"

"I want to see Mr. Sepp," said Luke brazenly.

The girl's smile remained frozen while she looked at him with startled eyes. "Mr. who?"

"Sewell Sepp, the Secretary of Public Affairs."

The girl asked gently, "Do you have an appointment, sir?"

"No."

"It's impossible, sir."

Luke nodded sourly. "Then I'll see Commissioner Parris deVicker."

"Do you have an appointment to see Mr. deVicker?"

"No, I'm afraid not."

The girl shook her head with a trace of amusement. "Sir, you can't just walk in on these people. They're extremely busy. Everyone must have an appointment."

"Oh, come now," said Luke. "Surely it's conceivable that—"

"Definitely not, sir."

"Then," said Luke, "I'll make an appointment. I'd like to see Mr. Sepp some time today, if possible."

The girl lost interest in Luke. She resumed her manner of impersonal courtesy. "I'll call the office of Mr. Sepp's appointment secretary."

She spoke into a mesh, then turned back to Luke. "No

appointments are open this month, sir. Will you speak to someone else? Some under-official?"

"No," said Luke. He gripped the edge of the counter for a moment, started to turn away, then asked, "Who authorizes these appointments?"

"The secretary's first aide, who screens the list of applications."

"I'll speak to the first aide, then."

The girl sighed. "You need an appointment, sir."

"I need an appointment to make an appointment?"

"Yes, sir."

"Do I need an appointment to make an appointment for an appointment?"

"No, sir. Just walk right in."

"Where?"

"Suite Forty-two, inside the rotunda, sir."

Luke passed through twelve-foot crystal doors and walked down a short hall. Scurrying patterns of color followed him like shadows along both the walls, grotesque cubistic shapes parodying the motion of his body: a whimsey which surprised Luke and which might have pleased him under less critical circumstances.

He passed through another pair of crystal portals into the rotunda. Six levels above, a domed ceiling depicted scenes of legend in stained glass. Behind a ring of leather couches doors gave into surrounding offices; one of these doors, directly across from the entrance, bore the words:

OFFICES OF THE SECRETARY
DEPARTMENT OF PUBLIC AFFAIRS

On the couches, half a hundred men and women waited with varying degrees of patience. The careful disdain with which they surveyed each other suggested that their status was high; the frequency with which they consulted their watches conveyed the impression that they were momentarily on the point of departure.

A mellow voice sounded over a loudspeaker: "Mr. Arthur Coff, please, to the Office of the Secretary." A plump gentleman threw down the periodical he had fretfully been examining and jumped to his feet. He crossed to the bronze-and-black glass door and passed through.

Luke watched him enviously, then turned aside through an arch marked *Suite 42*. An usher in a brown-and-black uniform stepped forward: Luke stated his business and was conducted into a small cubicle.

A young man behind a metal desk peered intently at him. "Sit down, please." He motioned to a chair. "Your name?"

"Luke Grogatch."

"Ah, Mr. Grogatch. May I inquire your business?"

"I have something to say to the Secretary of Public Affairs."

"Regarding what subject?"

"A personal matter."

"I'm sorry, Mr. Grogatch. The Secretary is more than busy. He's swamped with important Organization business. But if you'll explain the situation to me, I'll recommend you to an appropriate member of the staff."

"That won't help," said Luke. "I want to consult the Secretary in relation to a recently issued policy directive."

"Issued by the Secretary?"

"Yes."

"You wish to object to this directive?"

Luke grudgingly admitted as much.

"There are appropriate channels for this process," said the aide decisively. "If you will fill out this form—not here, but in the rotunda—drop it into the suggestion box to the right of the door as you go out—"

In sudden fury Luke wadded up the form and flung it down on the desk. "Surely he has five minutes free—"

"I'm afraid not, Mr. Grogatch," the aide said in a voice of ice. "If you will look through the rotunda you will see a number of very important people who have waited, some of them for months, for five minutes with the Secretary. If you wish to fill out an application, stating your business in detail, I will see that it receives due consideration."

Luke stalked out of the cubicle. The aide watched him go with a bleak smile of dislike. The man obviously had Nonconformist tendencies, he thought . . . probably should be watched.

Luke stood in the rotunda, muttering, "What now? What now? What now?" in a half-mesmerized undertone. He stared around the rotunda, at the pompous High Echelon folk, arrogantly consulting their watches and tapping their feet. "Mr. Jepper Prinn!" called the mellow voice over the loudspeaker. "The Office of the Secretary, if you please." Luke watched Jepper Prinn walk to the bronze-and-black glass portal.

Luke slumped into a chair, scratched his long nose, looked cautiously around the rotunda. Nearby sat a big, bull-necked man with a red face, protruding lips, a shock of rank blond hair—a tycoon, judging from his air of absolute authority.

Luke rose and went to a desk placed for the convenience of those waiting. He took several sheets of paper with the Tower letterhead and unobtrusively circled the rotunda to the entrance into Suite 42. The bull-necked tycoon paid him no heed.

Luke girded himself, closing his collar, adjusting the set of his jacket. He took a deep breath, then, when the florid man glanced in his direction, came forward officiously. He looked briskly around the circle of couches, consulting his papers; then catching the eye of the tycoon, frowned, squinted, walked forward.

"Your name, sir?" asked Luke in an official voice.

"I'm Hardin Arthur," rasped the tycoon. "Why?"

Luke nodded, consulted his paper. "The time of your appointment?"

"Eleven-ten. What of it?"

"The Secretary would like to know if you can conveniently lunch with him at one-thirty?"

Arthur considered. "I suppose it's possible," he grumbled. "I'll have to rearrange some other business. . . . An inconvenience—but I can do it, yes."

"Excellent," said Luke. "At lunch the Secretary feels that he can discuss your business more informally and at greater length than at eleven-ten, when he can only allow you seven minutes."

"Seven minutes!" rumbled Arthur indignantly. "I can hardly spread my plans out in seven minutes."

"Yes sir," said Luke. "The Secretary realizes this, and suggests that you lunch with him."

Arthur petulantly hauled himself to his feet. "Very well. Lunch at one-thirty, correct?"

"Correct, sir. If you will walk directly into the Secretary's office at that time."

Arthur departed the rotunda, and Luke settled into the seat Arthur had vacated.

Time passed very slowly. At ten minutes after eleven the mellow voice called out, "Mr. Hardin Arthur, please. To the Office of the Secretary."

Luke rose to his feet, stalked with great dignity across the rotunda, and went through the bronze and black glass door.

Behind a long black desk sat the Secretary, a rather undistinguished man with gray hair and snapping gray eyes. He raised his eyebrows as Luke came forward: Luke evidently did not fit his preconception of Hardin Arthur.

The Secretary spoke. "Sit down, Mr. Arthur. I may as well tell you bluntly and frankly that we think your scheme is impractical. By 'we' I mean myself and the Board of Policy Evaluation—who of course have referred to the Files. First, the costs are excessive. Second, there's no guarantee that you can phase your program into that of our other tycoons. Third, the Board of Policy Evaluation tells me that Files doubts whether we'll need that much new capacity."

"Ah," Luke nodded wisely. "I see. Well, no matter. It's not important."

"Not important?" The Secretary sat up in his chair, stared at Luke in wonder. "I'm surprised to hear you say so."

Luke made an airy gesture. "Forget it. Life's too short to worry about these things. Actually there's another matter I want to discuss with you."

"Ah?"

"It may seem trivial, but the implications are large. A former employee called the matter to my attention. He's now a flunky on one of the sewer maintenance tunnel gangs, an excellent chap. Here's the situation. Some idiotic jack-in-office has issued a directive which forces this man to carry a shovel back and forth to the warehouse every day, before and after work. I've taken the trouble to follow up the matter and the chain leads here." He displayed his three policy directives.

Frowningly the Secretary glanced through them. "These

all seem perfectly regular. What do you want me to do?"

"Issue a directive clarifying the policy. After all, we can't have these poor devils working three hours overtime for tomfoolishness."

"Tomfoolishness?" The Secretary was displeased. "Hardly that, Mr. Arthur. The economy directive came to me from the Board of Directors, from the Chairman himself, and if—"

"Don't mistake me," said Luke hastily. "I've no quarrel with economy; I merely want the policy applied sensibly. Checking a shovel into the warehouse—where's the economy in that?"

"Multiply that shovel by a million, Mr. Arthur," said the Secretary coldly.

"Very well, multiply it," argued Luke. "We have a million shovels. How many of these million shovels are conserved by this order? Two or three a year?"

The Secretary shrugged. "Obviously in a general directive of this sort, inequalities occur. So far as I'm concerned, I issued the directive because I was instructed to do so. If you want it changed, you'll have to consult the Chairman of the Board."

"Very well. Can you arrange an appointment for me?"

"Let's settle the matter even sooner," said the Secretary. "Right now. We'll talk to him across the screen, although, as you say, it seems a trivial matter. . . ."

"Demoralization of the working force isn't trivial, Secretary Sepp."

The Secretary shrugged, touched a button, spoke into a mesh. "The Chairman of the Board, if he's not occupied."

The screen glowed. The Chairman of the Board of Directors looked out at them. He sat in a lounge chair on the deck of his penthouse at the pinnacle of the tower. In one hand he held a glass of pale effervescent liquid; beyond him opened sunlight and blue air and a wide glimpse of the miraculous City.

"Good morning, Sepp," said the Chairman cordially, and nodded toward Luke. "Good morning to you, sir."

"Chairman, Mr. Arthur here is protesting the economy directive you sent down a few days ago. He claims that strict application is causing hardship among the labor force: demoralization, actually. Something to do with shovels."

The Chairman considered. "Economy directive? I hardly recall the exact case."

Secretary Sepp described the directive, citing code and reference numbers, explaining the provisions, and the Chairman nodded in recollection. "Yes, the metal shortage thing. Afraid I can't help you, Sepp, or you, Mr. Arthur. Evaluation sent it up. Apparently we're running short of minerals; what else can we do? Cinch in the old belts, eh? Hard on all of us. What's this about shovels?"

"It's the whole matter," cried Luke in sudden shrillness, evoking startled glances from Secretary and Chairman. "Carrying a shovel back and forth to the warehouse—three hours a day! It's not economy, it's a disorganized farce!"

"Come now, Mr. Arthur," the Chairman chided humorously. "So long as you're not carrying the shovel yourself, why the excitement? It works the very devil with one's digestion. Until Policy Evaluation changes it collective mind—as it often does—then we've got to string along. Can't go counter to Policy Evaluation, you know. They're the people with the facts and figures."

"Neither here nor there," mumbled Luke. "Carrying a shovel three hours—"

"Perhaps a bit of bother for the men concerned," said the Chairman with a hint of impatience, "but they've got to see the thing from the long view. Sepp, perhaps you'll lunch with me? A marvelous day, lazy weather."

"Thank you, Mr. Chairman. I'll be pleased indeed."

"Excellent. At one or one-thirty, whenever it's convenient for you."

The screen went blank. Secretary Sepp rose to his feet. "There it is, Mr. Arthur. I can't do any more."

"Very well, Mr. Secretary," said Luke in a hollow voice.

"Sorry I can't be of more help in that other matter, but as I say—"

"It's inconsequential."

Luke turned, left the elegant office, passed through the bronze-and-black glass doors into the rotunda. Through the arch into Suite 42 he saw a large, bull-necked man, tomato-red in the face, hunched forward across a counter. Luke stepped forward smartly, leaving the rotunda just as the authentic Mr. Arthur and the aide came forth, deep in agitated conversation.

Luke stopped by the information desk. "Where is the Policy Evaluation Board?"

"Twenty-ninth Level, sir, this building."

In Policy Evaluation on the 29th Level Luke talked with a silk-mustached young man, courtly and elegant, with the status classification *Plan Coordinator.* "Certainly!" exclaimed the young man in response to Luke's question. "Authoritative information is the basis of authoritative organization. Material from Files is collated and digested in the Bureau of Abstracts, and sent up to us. We shape it and present it to the Board of Directors in the form of a daily précis."

Luke expressed interest in the Bureau of Abstracts, and the young man quickly became bored. "Grubbers among the statistics, barely able to compose an intelligible sentence. If it weren't for us . . ." His eyebrows, silken as his mustache, hinted of the disasters which in the absence of Policy Evaluation would overtake the Organization. "They work in a suite down on the Sixth Level."

Luke descended to the Bureau of Abstracts, and found no difficulty gaining admission to the general office. In contrast to the rather nebulous intellectualism of Policy Evaluation, the Bureau of Abstracts seemed workaday and matter-of-fact. A middle-aged woman, cheerfully fat, inquired Luke's business, and when Luke professed himself a journalist, conducted him about the premises. They went from the main lobby, walled in antique cream-colored plaster with gold scrollwork, past the small fusty cubicles, where clerks sat at projection-desks scanning ribbons of words. Extracting idea-sequences, emending, excising, condensing, cross-referring, finally producing the abstract to be submitted to Policy Evaluation. Luke's fat and cheerful guide brewed them a pot of tea; she asked questions which Luke answered in general terms, straining his voice and pursing his mouth in the effort to seem agreeable and hearty. He himself asked questions.

"I'm interested in a set of statistics on the scarcity of

metals, or ores, or something similar, which recently went up to Policy Evaluation. Would you know anything about this?"

"Heavens, no!" the woman responded. "There's just too much material coming in—the business of the entire Organization."

"Where does this material come from? Who sends it to you?"

The woman made a humorous little grimace of distaste. "From Files, down on Sublevel Twelve. I can't tell you much, because we don't associate with the personnel. They're low status: clerks and the like. Sheer automatons."

Luke expressed an interest in the source of the Bureau of Abstracts' information. The woman shrugged, as if to say, everyone to his own taste. "I'll call down to the Chief File Clerk; I know him, very slightly."

The Chief File Clerk, Mr. Sidd Boatridge, was self-important and brusque, as if aware of the low esteem in which he was held by the Bureau of Abstracts. He dismissed Luke's questions with a stony face of indifference. "I really have no idea, sir. We file, index, and cross-index material into the Information Bank, but we concern ourselves very little with outgoing data. My duties in fact are mainly administrative. I'll call in one of the under-clerks; he can tell you more than I can."

The under-clerk who answered Boatridge's summons was a short, turnip-faced man with matted red hair. "Take Mr. Grogatch into the outer office," said the Chief File Clerk testily. "He wants to ask you a few questions."

In the outer office, out of the Chief File Clerk's hearing, the under-clerk became rather surly and pompous, as if he had divined the level of Luke's status. He referred to himself as a "line-tender" rather than as a file clerk, the latter apparently being a classification of lesser prestige. His "line-tending" consisted of sitting beside a panel which glowed and blinked with a thousand orange and green lights. "The orange lights indicate information going down into the Bank," said the file clerk. "The green lights show where somebody up-level is drawing information out—generally at the Bureau of Abstracts."

Luke observed the orange and green flickers for a moment. "What information is being transmitted now?"

"Couldn't say," the file clerk grunted. "It's all coded. Down in the old office we had a monitoring machine and never used it. Too much else to do."

Luke considered. The file clerk showed signs of restiveness. Luke's mind worked hurriedly. He asked. "So—as I understand it—you file information, but have nothing further to do with it?"

"We file it and code it. Whoever wants information puts a program into the works and the information goes out to him. We never see it, unless we went and looked in the old monitoring machine."

"Which is still down at your old office?"

The file clerk nodded. "They call it the staging chamber now. Nothing there but input and output pipes, the monitor, and the custodian."

"Where is the staging chamber?"

"Way down the levels, behind the Bank. Too low for me to work. I got more ambition." For emphasis he spat on the floor.

"A custodian is there, you say?"

"An old Junior Executive named Dodkin. He's been there a hundred years."

Luke dropped thirty levels aboard an express lift, then rode the down escalator another six levels to Sublevel 46. He emerged on a dingy landing with a low-perquisite nutrition hall to one side, a lift-attendants' dormitory to the other. The air carried the familiar reek of the deep underground, a compound of dank concrete, phenol, mercaptans, and a discreet but pervasive human smell. Luke realized with bitter amusement that he had returned to familiar territory.

Following instructions, grudgingly detailed by the under-file clerk, Luke stepped aboard a chattering man-belt labeled *902—Tanks*. Presently he came to a brightly lit landing marked by a black-and-yellow sign: *Information Tanks. Technical Station*. Inside the door a number of mechanics sat on stools, dangling their legs, lounging, chaffering.

Luke changed to a side-belt, even more dilapidated, almost

in a state of disrepair. At the second junction—this one unmarked—he left the man-belt and turned down a narrow passage toward a far yellow bulb. The passage was silent, almost sinister in its dissociation from the life of the City.

Below the single yellow bulb a dented metal door was daubed with a sign:

INFORMATION TANKS—STAGING CHAMBER
NO ADMITTANCE

Luke tested the door and found it locked. He rapped and waited.

Silence shrouded the passage, broken only by a faint sound from the distant man-belt.

Luke rapped again, and now from within came a shuffle of movement. The door slid back and a pale placid eye looked forth. A rather weak voice inquired, "Yes, sir?"

Luke attempted a manner of easy authority. "You're Dodkin the custodian?"

"Yes, sir, I'm Dodkin."

"Open up, please, I'd like to come in."

The pale eye blinked mild wonder. "This is only the staging room, sir. There's nothing here to see. The storage complexes are around to the front; if you'll go back to the junction—"

Luke broke into the flow of words. "I've just come down from the Files; it's you I want to see."

The pale eye blinked once more; the door slid open. Luke entered the long, narrow, concrete-floored staging room. Conduits dropped from the ceiling by the thousands, bent, twisted, and looped, and entered the wall, each conduit labeled with a dangling metal tag. At one end of the room was a grimy cot where Dodkin apparently slept; at the other end was a long black desk: the monitoring machine? Dodkin himself was small and stooped, but moved nimbly in spite of his evident age. His white hair was stained but well brushed; his gaze, weak and watery, was without guile, and fixed on Luke with an astronomer's detachment. He opened his mouth, and words quavered forth in spate, with Luke vainly seeking to interrupt.

"Not often do visitors come from above. Is something wrong?"

"No, nothing wrong."

"They should tell me if aught isn't correct, or perhaps there's been new policies of which I haven't been notified."

"Nothing like that, Mr. Dodkin. I'm just a visitor—"

"I don't move out as much as I used to, but last week I—"

Luke pretended to listen while Dodkin maundered on in obbligato to Luke's bitter thoughts. The continuity of directives leading from Fedor Miskitman to Lavester Limon to Judiath Ripp, bypassing Parris deVicker to Sewell Sepp and the Chairman of the Board, then returning down the classifications, down the levels, through the Policy Evaluation Board, the Bureau of Abstracts, the File Clerk's Office—the continuity had finally ended; the thread he had traced with such forlorn hope seemed about to lose itself. Well, Luke told himself, he had accepted Miskitman's challenge; he had failed, and now was faced with his original choice. Submit, carry the wretched shovel back and forth to the warehouse, or defy the order, throw down his shovel, assert himself as a free-willed man, and be declassified, to become a Junior Executive like old Dodkin—who, sucking and wheezing, still rambled on in compulsive loquacity.

". . . Something incorrect, I'd never know, because who ever tells me? From year end to year end I'm quiet down here, and there's no one to relieve me, and I only get to the up-side rarely, once a fortnight or so, but then once you've seen the sky, does it ever change? And the sun, the marvel of it, but once you've seen a marvel—"

Luke drew a deep breath. "I'm investigating an item of information which reached the File Clerk's Office. I wonder if you can help me."

Dodkin blinked his pale eyes. "What item is this, sir? Naturally I'll be glad to help in any way, even though—"

"The item dealt with economy in the use of metals and metal tools."

Dodkin nodded. "I remember the item perfectly."

It was Luke's turn to stare. "You *remember* this item?"

"Certainly. It was, if I may say so, one of my little interpolations. A personal observation which I included among the other material."

"Would you be kind enough to explain?"

Dodkin would be only too pleased to explain. "Last week I had occasion to visit an old friend over by Claxton Abbey, a fine Conformist, well adapted and cooperative, even if, alas, like myself, a Junior Executive. Of course, I mean no disrespect to good Davy Evans, like myself about ready for the pension—though little enough they allow nowadays—"

"The interpolation?"

"Yes, indeed. On my way home along the man-belt—on Sublevel Thirty-two, as I recall—I saw a workman of some sort—perhaps an electrical technician—toss several tools into a crevice on his way off-shift. I thought, now there's a slovenly act—disgraceful! Suppose the man forgot where he had hidden his tools? They'd be lost! Our reserves of raw metallic ore are very low—that's common knowledge—and every year the ocean water becomes weaker and more dilute. That man had no regard for the future of Organization. We should cherish our natural resources, do you not agree, sir?"

"I agree, naturally. But—"

"In any event, I returned here and added a memorandum to that effect into the material which goes up to the Assistant File Clerk. I thought that perhaps he'd be impressed and say a word to someone with influence—perhaps the Head File Clerk. In any event, there's the tale of my interpolation. Naturally I attempted to give it weight by citing the inevitable diminution of our natural resources."

"I see," said Luke. "And do you frequently include interpolations into the day's information?"

"Occasionally," said Dodkin, "and sometimes, I'm glad to say, people more important than I share my views. Only three weeks ago I was delayed several minutes on my way between Claxton Abbey and Kittsville on Sublevel Thirty. I made a note of it, and last week I noticed that construction has commenced on a new eight-lane man-belt between the two points, a really magnificent and modern undertaking. A month ago I noticed a shameless group of girls daubed like savages with cosmetic. What a waste, I told myself; what vanity and folly! I hinted as much in a little message to the Under-File Clerk. I seem to be just one of the many with these views, for two days later a general order discouraging these petty vanities was issued by the Secretary of Education."

"Interesting," Luke muttered. "Interesting indeed. How do you include these—interpolations—into the information?"

Dodkin hobbled nimbly to the monitoring machine. "The output from the tanks comes through here. I print a bit on the typewriter and tuck it in where the Under-Clerk will see it."

"Admirable," sighed Luke. "A man with your intelligence should have ranked higher in the Status List."

Dodkin shook his placid old head. "I don't have the ambition nor the ability. I'm fit for just this simple job, and that only barely. I'd take my pension tomorrow, only the Chief File Clerk asked me to stay on a bit until he could find a man to take my place. No one seems to like the quiet down here."

"Perhaps you'll have your pension sooner than you think," said Luke.

Luke strolled along the glossy tube, ringed with alternate pale and dark refractions like a bull's-eye. Ahead was motion, the glint of metal, the mutter of voices. The entire crew of Tunnel Gang Number 3 stood idle and restless.

Fedor Miskitman waved his arm with uncharacteristic vehemence. "Grogatch! At your post! You've held up the entire crew!" His heavy face was suffused with pink. "Four minutes already we're behind schedule."

Luke strolled closer.

"Hurry!" bellowed Miskitman. "What do you think this is, a blasted promenade?"

If anything Luke slackened his pace. Fedor Miskitman lowered his big head, staring balefully. Luke halted in front of him.

"Where's your shovel?" Fedor Miskitman asked.

"I don't know," said Luke. "I'm here on the job. It's up to you to provide tools."

Fedor Miskitman stared unbelievingly. "Didn't you take it to the warehouse?"

"Yes," said Luke. "I took it there. If you want it go get it."

Fedor Miskitman opened his mouth. He roared, "Get off the job!"

"Just as you like," said Luke. "You're the foreman."

"Don't come back!" bellowed Miskitman. "I'll report you before the day is out. You won't gain status from me, I tell you that!"

"Status?" Luke laughed. "Go ahead. Cut me down to Junior Executive. Do you think I care? No. And I'll tell you why. There's going to be a change or two made. When things seem different to you, think of me."

Luke Grogatch, Junior Executive, said good-by to the retiring custodian of the staging chamber. "Don't thank me, not at all," said Luke. "I'm here by my own doing. In fact—well, never mind all that. Go up-side, sit in the sun, enjoy the air."

Finally Dodkin, in mingled joy and sorrow, hobbled for the last time down the musty passageway to the chattering man-belt.

Luke was alone in the staging chamber. Around him hummed the near-inaudible rush of information. From behind the wall came the sense of a million relays clicking, twitching, meshing; of cylinders and trace-tubes and memory-lakes whirring with activity. At the monitoring machine the output streamed forth on a reel of yellow tape. Nearby rested the typewriter.

Luke seated himself. His first interpolation: what should it be? Freedom for the Nonconformists? Tunnel gang foremen to carry tools for the entire crew? A higher expense account for junior executives?

Luke rose to his feet and scratched his chin. Power . . . to be subtly applied. How should he use it? To secure rich perquisites for himself? Yes, of course, this he would accomplish, by devious means. And then—what? Luke thought of the billions of men and women living and working in the Organization. He looked at the typewriter. He could shape their lives, change their thoughts, disorganize the Organization. Was this wise? Or right? Or even amusing?

Luke sighed. In his mind's eye he saw himself standing on a high terrace overlooking the city. Luke Grogatch, Chairman of the Board. Not impossible, quite feasible. A little at a time, the correct interpolations ... Luke Grogatch, Chairman of the Board. Yes. this for a starter. But it was necessary to move cautiously, with great delicacy.

Luke seated himself at the typewriter and began to pick out his first interpolation.

THE FUTURE OF LIBERTY

by Jerry Pournelle

> Stated most simply, if mankind is to live in the state of
> material well-being that technology can make possible,
> then, given the finite size and resources of the planet, there
> are just too many of us already.   —Philip Handler,
> President, National Academy of Sciences, July 1975

The Limits to Growth, a report to the influential Club of
Rome, first appeared in 1972 and may have been the most
influential book of that decade. Certainly an entire generation of college students read it, and for many it changed their
lives.

The Limits to Growth was based in large part on a book
that few of the *Limits* adherents had ever seen: *World
Dynamics*, an erudite tome prepared by Professor Jay Forrester
of the Massachusetts Institute of Technology. Forrester's
book gave detailed accounts of a very large computer simula-
tion of the world: Its population, resources, food, health
services, birth and death rates were all entered into an
enormously complex program which proceeded to project all
these values into the future.

And lo, Forrester's computer foretold doom. No matter
what he did, no matter what assumptions were changed,
civilization was coming to an end—possibly as soon as the
year 2050. Moreover, technology couldn't save us; indeed, if
we increased investment in technology, we merely hastened
the end through increased pollution and depletion of our
natural-resource base. Our best strategy was Zero-growth:
stabilize the population by any means possible, cease con-
structing new industries, learn to live with a declining standard of living; expect less, make do, we have left the era of
growth and entered the era of limits.

But that wouldn't save us either: With the most drastic
program of birth control and zero industrial growth, most of
the world was doomed to perpetual poverty, while Western
civilization would itself decay; by the year 2400 or so there's
nothing left of technological civilization, and no way to
rebuild it.

This message was received in different ways by different people. The intent of the Club of Rome (wealthy industrialists all; *they* won't experience poverty no matter what) was that we should learn to accept limits. Governor Jerry Brown of California became the symbol of the "make do with less" movement. The environmental and conservationist movements became explicitly anti-technology—and generally remain so to this day. However, there was a different reaction by others: "Eat, drink, and be merry, for the computers prove there can't be a tomorrow." The "me generation" was born twin to the "era of limits."

Now it is clear that for freedom to survive, civilization must also. It is all very well to speak romantically of noble savages, but in fact most *real* freedoms are the product of industrial civilization. True, civilization can take away with the left hand what it gives with the right. The transportation system that allows fast travel to wherever you wish can also bring the police where you do not want them—or sightseers onto "your" stretch of the John Muir trail. The fact remains that penicillin, electric lights, oil and gas pipelines, railroads, high-speed dental drills, novocaine, Xerox, the telephone, transistors, and suchlike have given more people more *real* choices—which is to say real, not theoretical, liberties—than any other development in history. Sanity requires us to find ways to humanize industrial society—but not to abolish it or let it go away. We need technology.

This insight was not lost on politicians of the 1970s. They sought to preserve industrial society through the most explosive growth of regulation in human history. The result has not been universally appreciated; carried far enough it could, one fears, lead to the state Tocqueville warned of:

> I think, then, that the species of oppression by which democratic nations are menaced is unlike anything that ever before existed in the world; our contemporaries will find no prototype of it in their memories. I seek in vain for an expression that will accurately convey the whole of the idea I have formed of it; the old words *despotism* and *tyranny* are inap-

propriate; the thing itself is new, and since I cannot name it, I must attempt to define it.

I seek to trace the novel features under which despotism may appear in the world. The first thing that strikes the observation is an innumerable multitude of men, all equal and all alike incessantly endeavoring to procure the petty and paltry pleasures with which they glut their lives. Each of them, living apart, is as a stranger to the fate of all the rest; his children and his private friends constitute to him the whole of mankind. As for the rest of his fellow citizens, he is close to them, but he does not see them; he touches them, but he does not feel them; he exists only in himself and for himself alone, and if his kindred still remain to him, he may be said at any rate to have lost his country.

Above this race of men stands an immense and tutelary power, which takes upon itself alone to secure their gratifications and to watch over their fate. That power is absolute, minute, regular, provident, and mild. It would be like the authority of a parent if, like that authority, its object were to prepare men for manhood; but it seeks, on the contrary, to keep them in perpetual childhood; it is well content that the people should rejoice, provided that they think of nothing but rejoicing. For their happiness such a government willingly labors, but it chooses to be the sole agent and the only arbiter of their necessities, facilitates their pleasures, manages their principal concerns, directs their energy, regulates the descent of property, and subdivides their inheritances; what remains, but to spare them all the care of thinking and all the trouble of living?

Thus it every day renders the exercise of the free agency of man less useful and less frequent; it circumvents the will within a narrower range and gradually robs a man of all the uses of himself. The principle of equality has prepared man for all these

things; it has predisposed them to endure them, and
often to look on them as benefits.

We may not yet have constructed that *democratic despotism* Tocqueville warned of; but surely we have come closer to
it than we like.

Yet, say those whose models foretell doom, what is the
point of the discussion? Whatever we do, we shall not preserve the present. Slave or free hardly matters: our descendants will inevitably look on this time as a Golden Age, and
our wishes in the matter are of little consequence. We must
have Zero-growth, not merely of population but also of industry, and we must have it now while there is yet time.

Or, say those who believe the models but reject the advice,
perhaps it would be better simply to eat the seed corn. Why
make sacrifices? There is no point in saving, investing for the
future; it is not that we wish our descendants ill, we merely
know—for Forrester's models have told us—that the future
will be grim no matter what we do. Better, then, that we at
least are, if not precisely happy, at least satiated. . . .

And thus liberty has no future: to achieve Zero-growth will
require stringent regulations, multiplication of government
power, the society of the story "Raid"; while failure to impose
the limits will lead inevitably to collapse and death. So say
the computers. . . .

But why must we trust computer models constructed by
economists? In the real world, economists have yet to make
successful predictions for a single nation for a decade ahead;
why must we believe them when they forecast for the world
over centuries?

In fact, of course, the models are plain wrong.

Interestingly, technology has made it easier to show this.
When Dr. Forrester produced his *World Dynamics*, there
were in this world few computers capable of running his
programs; certainly there were none widely available. Now,
though, as technology marches forward, nearly anyone can
examine the Forrester models, run them, change them, play
about with them. I have recently taught Ezekial, my friend

who happens to be a Cromemco Z-2 computer, to run the
World Dynamics models; and I have found that the model,
unaltered, does indeed predict doom.

It is also a *very* limited model. The World Dynamics program generally begins in the year 1900. This is sensible,
because it requires the model to "predict" the years from
1900 to the present, allowing us to examine how well its
results fit the real world. If they don't fit at all, then we have
to change the input assumptions.

On the other hand, some of the inputs don't stay the same;
even the primary variable of birth rate changes, affected by
new technology such as the Pill. (In 1900 there really wasn't
any effective birth-control device.)

Thus the model has "switches": means for drastic changes
in some of the input assumptions, the change to take effect at
some designated year. You can, with these switches, change
birth rates and agricultural returns and capital investment—

But you can't change the natural-resource base. That is
fixed for all time.

Forrester's models say—not explicitly where you can see it,
but deep inside the structure of the program, where it is not
at all obvious—that all the natural resources there will ever
be were known in 1900, and have been slowly diminishing
since. We can slow the rate at which we use natural resources,
but we can never cease using them entirely—and we will
never have more than we have now.

But that is nonsense.

On July 20, 1969, we heard: "Tranquillity Base here. The
Eagle has landed."

And the world cannot be the same now.

On that day, the resource base changed forever. Formerly
we were limited to "Only One Earth." Now, we can, if we like,
have access to nine planets, fifty moons, a million asteroids, a
billion comets, and a thermonuclear generator we call the
sun. Out there in space there are nearly limitless resources—
so many resources that even Forrester's models cannot kill us
for thousands of years.

Progress is possible. We need only a strategy; a strategy of
progress to produce—and distribute—wealth.

With wealth comes freedom and liberty. It is all very well to speak of the freedom of the prisoner and the slave; to sing of the nobiliy of a man who may be poor, yet he is free; but most of us would feel a great deal more free if we had a great deal more wealth. Certainly that is true of the Third World, of those who literally eat bread by the sweat of their faces, and often can find none, sweat as they will. How is one free if one's children starve as you watch?

But that need not happen, nor need we impoverish the West to save the Third World. There is wealth enough for all. When the great rockets thundered upward from Canaveral, they sang—if only we knew it—of a time of real freedom, of liberty and wealth for all; and though we have retreated from our destiny, it is not yet too late.

We of this generation have found the means of grace and the hope of glory; we can, if we have the will, secure the blessings of liberty to ourselves and our posterity—aye and to everyone's posterity. We can reach the stars.

ACKNOWLEDGMENTS

Research for the essays "The Future of Freedom" and "Freedom in the Wake of Hegel and Marx" was supported in part by a grant from the Vaughn Foundation and Tyler Junior College of Tyler, Texas. Research for the work as a whole was supported in part by grants from the Vaughn Foundation and the L-5 Society. Opinions expressed in these works are those of the authors and are not necessarily approved by the research sponsors.

The kind assistance of Ms. Sherry MacNeal, my former research associate, is gratefully acknowledged.

This book would not have been possible without the able assistance of its associate editor, John F. Carr, who does the onerous work of reading submissions, writing rejection letters, negotiating rewrites with nervous authors, and doing the myriad other tasks that make anthology editing such a chore; so that putting this book together has, for me, been largely enjoyment.

Jerry Pournelle
Hollywood, 1980

CLASSIC BESTSELLERS
from FAWCETT BOOKS

☐ MAGGIE: A GIRL OF THE STREETS by Stephen Crane	30854	$2.25
☐ SATAN IN GORAY by Isaac Bashevis Singer	24326	$2.50
☐ THE RISE AND FALL OF THE THIRD REICH by William Shirer	23442	$3.95
☐ THE WIND by Dorothy Scarborough	04579	$2.25
☐ ALL QUIET ON THE WESTERN FRONT by Erich Maria Remarque	23808	$2.50
☐ TO KILL A MOCKINGBIRD by Harper Lee	08376	$2.50
☐ NORTHWEST PASSAGE by Kenneth Roberts	24095	$2.95
☐ THEM by Joyce Carol Oates	23944	$2.95
☐ THE FLOUNDER by Gunter Grass	24180	$2.95
☐ THE CHOSEN by Chaim Potok	24200	$2.95
☐ THE SOURCE by James A. Michener	23859	$3.50

Buy them at your local bookstore or use this handy coupon for ordering.

COLUMBIA BOOK SERVICE
32275 Mally Road, P.O. Box FB, Madison Heights, MI 48071

Please send me the books I have checked above. Orders for less than 5 books must include 75¢ for the first book and 25¢ for each additional book to cover postage and handling. Orders for 5 books or more postage is FREE. Send check or money order only.

Cost $_____	Name _____	
Sales tax*_____	Address _____	
Postage _____	City _____	
Total $_____	State _____	Zip _____

*The government requires us to collect sales tax in all states except AK, DE, MT, NH and OR.

This offer expires 1 March 82